Patterned Aimlessness

 Patterned Aimlessness

Iris Murdoch's Novels of
the 1970s and 1980s

Barbara Stevens Heusel

The University of Georgia Press
Athens and London

© 1995 by the University of Georgia Press
Athens, Georgia 30602
All rights reserved
Designed by Walton Harris
Set in 10/14 Electra by Tseng Information Systems, Inc.
Printed and bound by Thomson-Shore, Inc.
The paper in this book meets the guidelines for permanence and
durability of the Committee on Production Guidelines for Book
Longevity of the Council on Library Resources.

Printed in the United States of America
99 98 97 96 95 C 5 4 3 2 1

Library of Congress Cataloging in Publication Data
Heusel, Barbara Stevens.
Patterned aimlessness : Iris Murdoch's novels of the 1970's and 1980's /
Barbara Stevens Heusel.
p.   cm.
Includes bibliographical references and index.
ISBN 0-8203-1707-1 (alk. paper)
1. Murdoch, Iris—Criticism and interpretation.   2. Philosophy in
literature.   3. Fiction—Technique.   4. Literary form.   I. Title.
PR6063.U7Z844   1995
823'.914—dc20   94-28260

British Library Cataloging in Publication Data available

In memory of Jay and Ruth Stevens,
who each exemplified "a just and loving gaze"

Contents

Preface ix

Acknowledgments xi

List of Abbreviations xiii

ONE *Metaphysics as a Guide to Morals* and Iris Murdoch's Ongoing Dialogues with Other Philosophers 1

TWO Iris Murdoch's Wittgensteinian Voice 23

THREE Iris Murdoch's Wittgensteinian Voice: *A Word Child, Nuns and Soldiers,* and *The Sea, The Sea* 43

FOUR Radical Otherness: *Sartre, Romantic Rationalist; Sovereignty of Good;* and *The Fire and the Sun* 82

FIVE Iris Murdoch's Novelistic Discourses: *An Accidental Man* 100

SIX Polyphonic Novels: *The Philosopher's Pupil* and *The Black Prince* 118

SEVEN Women's Discourse: *Nuns and Soldiers* and *The Message to the Planet* 140

EIGHT Characters Patterning Their Pilgrimages 156

NINE Philosophical and Psychological Patterns Underlying the World of Iris Murdoch's Novels 207

Conclusion 257

Notes 265

Bibliography 291

Index 301

 Preface

Teaching the novels of Dame Iris Murdoch for more than ten years has convinced me that even during a "fast read" most non-Anglophiles identify immediately with Murdoch's characters and situations. Such readers recognize at the same time that they are envisioning only the tip of the submerged iceberg. Acting out a philosophical truth Murdoch argues for in *Metaphysics as a Guide to Morals* (1992), they intuit that there is more "somewhere else" (508). The readers who choose to follow the process beyond the fast read to subsequent stages may want to investigate ways in which Murdoch's ideas about art and philosophy function in her philosophy as well as in her novels. Paying attention to numerous perspectives is a process Murdoch employs at all levels of investigation; she calls it "imaginative cognitive activity."

Murdoch uses this cogent sentence in *Metaphysics as a Guide to Morals* to explain the value and complexity of art; it also proposes why she does not write philosophy exclusively: "Art exhibits, what is less clear elsewhere, the mystery of the synthesis of different levels of cognition, how complexly integrated these levels are, and how therein the 'brute particular' is transcended and retained (known)" (339). Murdoch suggests the many "different levels of cognition" she has used to examine numerous perspectives and to work through the long process of creation. This book sets out to explore the mystery of Murdoch's philosophical, linguistic, pictorial, dramatic, and psychological syntheses, and the stages by which she has reached her narrative stance.

Murdoch studies has reached a stage at which it can now benefit from the leavening of new perspectives. Thanks to several recent investigations, John Fletcher's statement in *Dictionary of Literary Biography*—that academic critics on the whole have not taken the texts of Iris Murdoch seriously—no longer applies. I see this book as contributing to the discourse generated since the 1970s by philosophy and literary theory and helping to apply such considerations to the writings of this major author. In addition, non-British readers, whether inside or outside the college classroom, will appreciate watching the process of Murdoch's developing as a philosopher and novelist. I have therefore grounded this study of the novels of the 1970s and 1980s in Murdoch's multiplicity of voices, and I let her speak for herself. This technique places in context the wildly paradoxical patterns and anxiety-ridden content that disorient and sometimes frustrate the reader. The conventional methods that have allowed Murdoch to find her individual rhythm—repetition of jarring allusions, surprising syntax, and parallels and ironic and parodic juxtapositions—contribute to what I call her patterned aimlessness. Murdoch's statement in *The Sovereignty of Good* suggested the term to me: "Form in art is properly the simulation of the self-contained aimlessness of the universe" (86). In referring to the "aimlessness of the universe," Murdoch's expression names the macrocosm; mine, the microcosm of her carefully crafted art.[1]

Subsequent studies of Murdoch's creativity would do well to place her in fresh contexts, particularly the Anglo-Irish literary tradition. Such a perspective might help to alleviate the anxiety of readers who feel uneasy whenever Murdoch's characters, or their author, dabble in magic. Abandoning the rules of the scientific age, Murdoch reflects her place in a long line of writers, like Yeats and Joyce, who refuse to limit themselves to the staid realism of the English tradition. In exploring Murdoch's creative magic, I have worked to avoid the temptation to describe master narratives that explain the complexities and contradictions that make Murdoch's fiction so challenging and so much fun. Hamlet's reminder to his classmate, which Dame Iris quotes in *A Message to the Planet*, also applies to such Murdochian complexities: "There are more things in heaven and earth Horatio, than are dreamt of in your philosophy" (quoted in *The Message to the Planet* 337).

Rather than lumping all her novels into one master narrative, I have chosen here to focus on the later novels, especially those of the 1970s and 1980s. My argument is that Murdoch redefines, in this postmodern era, the boundaries of the novel of formal realism in order to address moral issues that are still unresolved in this final decade of the twentieth century.

Acknowledgments

For more than ten years the texts of Iris Murdoch and her many voices within those texts have captivated me. I express my gratitude to all those who have contributed to the success of this project. The Research and Publication Fund at Wake Forest University first supported me with a grant to study Iris Murdoch's holograph notebooks at the University of Iowa Libraries. Later grants from the National Endowment for the Humanities and from the Faculty Research Committee and the Culture of Quality program at Northwest Missouri State University made it possible for me to incorporate important materials from the notebooks into this study. For their support, I thank these organizations as well as my colleagues at Northwest, particularly James Saucerman and Glenn Morrow, and also Robert McCown and his staff at the University of Iowa Special Collections. I thank Iris Murdoch and the University of Iowa Libraries, Special Collections, for granting me permission to quote from the holograph notebooks. Also, I thank Iris Murdoch for permission to quote from her interview with me and from several of her letters to me.

Iris Murdoch's interest and generosity in answering questions have been more than a scholar is entitled to expect from an artist. Participating in the international Iris Murdoch Society has proven a stimulating way to pursue many of the issues that I address here. Scholars who have been generous in their support include Daniel Schwarz, James Edwards, and Peter Conradi, each of whom I thank for reading sections of earlier versions of this text.

My daughters, Heidi, Lisa, and Gretchen, have been generous in their emotional support of my scholarship as well as my teaching. Most of all, I thank Dennis Moore for believing in me and for helping me as I sought words to express my ideas about Iris Murdoch.

Earlier versions of portions of this manuscript previously appeared in the following publications: the *University of Windsor Review*, *Twentieth Century Literature*, the *University of Dayton Review*, and *Studies in the Humanities*.

 Abbreviations

IRIS MURDOCH'S NOVELS:
AM   *An Accidental Man*
B   *The Bell*
BP   *The Black Prince*
HC   *Henry and Cato*
MP   *The Message to the Planet*
NG   *The Nice and the Good*
NS   *Nuns and Soliders*
PP   *The Philosopher's Pupil*
SPLM   *The Sacred and Profane Love Machine*
SS   *The Sea, The Sea*
TA   *The Time of the Angels*
U   *The Unicorn*
WC   *A Word Child*

IRIS MURDOCH'S PHILOSOPHY:
AD   "Against Dryness"
FS   *The Fire and the Sun*
ME   "Metaphysics and Ethics"
MGM   *Metaphysics as a Guide to Morals*
NP   "Nostalgia for the Particular"
SBR   "The Sublime and the Beautiful Revisited"
SG   *The Sovereignty of Good*
SRR   *Sartre, Romantic Rationalist*

MIKHAIL BAKHTIN'S TEXTS:
DI   *The Dialogic Imagination: Four Essays*
PDP   *Problems of Dostoevsky's Poetics*

LUDWIG WITTGENSTEIN'S TEXTS:
PI   *Philosophical Investigations*
CV   *Culture and Value*
T   *Tractatus Logico-Philosophicus*

JULIA KRISTEVA'S TEXT:
WDN   "Word, Dialogue, and Novel"

Patterned Aimlessness

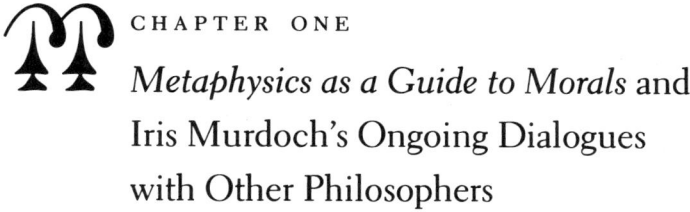

CHAPTER ONE

Metaphysics as a Guide to Morals and Iris Murdoch's Ongoing Dialogues with Other Philosophers

Iris Murdoch's desire to think about the lives of human beings and their relationship to morality has drawn her simultaneously to writing philosophy and fiction. Her novels "are *not connected* with philosophy," she insists (Letter to the author, April 24, 1993).[1] Art and philosophy use imagery in different ways to describe the world;[2] for Murdoch, philosophy is a rational activity, while fiction draws on unconscious as well as rational activity. Neither discourse can capture all of life's mystery. Her novels contribute images of minds thinking—reflecting inner as well as outer experience; her philosophy contributes metaphysical pictures or systems that may be used as guides to the Good. Her distinguishing philosophy from literature does not, however, signify that she walls one off from the other. She is continually empowered by each discourse, and in turn each empowers the other. An understanding of Murdoch's moral concerns and her stance in relation to other philosophers enlightens any reading of her novels.

Murdoch seems to think her job as a philosopher is not only to create her own philosophy but also to scrutinize others' philosophies: examining how they work, applying to them the questions that have been asked for centuries, and coming up with her own analysis of what a given philosophy contributes to the larger system of ideas. Calling herself a "Wittgensteinian neo-Platonist" (Chevalier, *Rencontres* 90), she is a thinker who has the special knack of seeing within an idea a whole spectrum of positions and of holding all the positions in her mind as she weighs their strengths and weaknesses. This is the way she proceeds in *Metaphysics as a Guide to Morals* (1992), her major philosophical text. Here she studies conceptual change: looking at the old Western truths in light of new ideas about truth, juxtaposing Cartesian concepts and those of quantum physics, or Platonic idealism and structuralism—the broad term she uses to include not only Saussurean systems but also the poststructuralism and deconstruction that have swept Western academia.[3] According to Murdoch, Jacques Derrida, who has said that "Heidegger is the last metaphysician," is himself a metaphysician and his structuralism (deconstruction) "look[s] like another metaphysic" (MGM 197). She argues that structuralist theory in general and Derridean practice in particular, "by its removal of the 'old' idea of truth and truth-seeking as moral value," inhibits philosophical study of conceptual change: "If all meaning is deferred our ordinary distinctions, for instance between what is clearly true and what is dubious and what is false, are removed and we begin to lose confidence . . . in what is made to seem the simple, old-fashioned, ordinary concept of truth" (MGM 194).[4] Like any metaphysician, Derrida is incapable of opting for *not* creating systems, Murdoch points out, and is therefore also incapable of ending metaphysics.

Murdoch's vision is large and comprehensive; she wants to save not absolute truth, not Platonic forms (they are only indicators), but the relationship between what is outside the body and what is inside the mind, no matter how arbitrary that relationship is. She has the ability to tolerate more incongruities than the philosophers who find that her work is unorthodox. Murdoch has always preferred moral philosophy to analytic or linguistic philosophy. Since her days at Oxford and Cambridge, she has been leery of jumping onto any philosophical bandwagon. Immersed during her school days at Oxford in the atmosphere of the analytical philosophy of Bertrand Russell, A. J. Ayer, Gilbert Ryle, and Ludwig Wittgenstein, she preferred the moral philosophy of G. E. Moore and Plato. The closest she has come to joining the dominant or popular philosophical crowd was during her twenties when she discovered existentialism. But her first published work, *Sartre, Romantic Rationalist* (1953), demonstrates her clear-sighted criticism of existentialism (see chapter 4). Since 1977 she has been publicly contemplating Derrida's deconstruction, which she flatly labels "plausible amoralist determinism" (MGM 198). Yet Murdoch is able to empathize with Derrida and others who are comfortable with forms of determinism: "it satisfies a deep human wish: to *give up*, to get rid of freedom, responsibility, remorse, all sorts of personal individual unease, and surrender to fate and the relief of 'it could not be otherwise' " (MGM 190). She finds that structuralism, including deconstruction, threatens empirical views of truth and value.[5]

While the determinist may be inhibiting the study of philosophical change, however, the moral collapse in contemporary society is an immediate and more concrete problem. Murdoch has argued moral philosophy with a dogged attentiveness much of her life, and she insists that the ideal of a transcendent good, which Derrida obfuscates, is "essential to both morality and religion" (MGM 511). She envisions humans struggling to apprehend a perfection that they can only vaguely understand. *Metaphysics as a Guide to Morals* is her reiteration that Plato's proof of the necessity of Good is "a background to moral philosophy, . . . a bridge between morals and religion, and . . . [is] relevant to our new disturbed understanding of religious truth." She insists, furthermore, that the world needs a theology that "can continue without God" and without the supernatural (MGM 511) and a metaphysics that can, as the title of her book reminds readers, point to morals.

Murdoch defines traditional metaphysics as "a search for hidden *a priori* determining forms, constituting an ultimate reality" (MGM 6), in other words, a transcendent or deduced system that strives "to reach the basis of things and show us what . . . *must* be there" (MGM 259). She therefore shares with the structuralists a yearning for structures. "Philosophers are artists," she writes, "and metaphysical ideas are aesthetic; they are intended to clarify and connect, and they certainly satisfy deep emotional needs" (MGM 37). The metaphysical process connects "different considerations and pictures so that they give each other mutual support" (MGM 511). With each change of worldview comes a change of images. Younger generations of metaphysicians consider issues from a new worldview and determine to break the old pictures, their goal being to demythologize the illusions or errors made by earlier metaphysicians. Some philosophical moves, like the early Wittgenstein's separation of fact and value, demythologize and yet manage to remove errors without destroying mystery or the cultural horizon. Murdoch has persistently employed the "terms of ordinary language and its 'naive' truth values" (MGM 199) to argue that mystery is as important as duty and reason. She summarizes the process, going so far as to say that "demythologisation is not a single road, nor need it imply or *mean* a disappearance of myths and icons, or some profound 'rectification' of ordinary language. The modern scene includes (I hope) an enlargement of our concept of religion through our greater tolerance and knowledge of other religions" (MGM 454). Rituals, by sparking the imagination, provide sources of energy. Some metaphysicians, however, attempt to obliterate the cultural horizon or, overwhelmed by their hubris, imagine that they do. Such egoism takes them too far. In fact, the major development one notices in Murdoch's philosophical stance since *Sovereignty of Good* (1967) is her struggle with this new brand of demythologizing that denies the overarching cultural background of truth.

This chapter explores Murdoch's many-layered vision by showing the way she has employed four decades of dialogue with her fellow philosophers to hammer out a practicable moral philosophy that celebrates the Good. In *Metaphysics as a Guide to Morals*, Murdoch stands like a rock of classical Greek moderation amid the waves of contemporary theoretical interpretation. She warns of the difficulty of finding a balance between "faithfulness to the text" and "inventiveness."[6] In regard to literary theory, Murdoch seems to want to find a mean between the formalist who argues that a complete understanding of the text is possible and the deconstructionist who argues that there is no one answer because meaning is always deferred and finding meaning is an ongoing process. For her, theorizing can often become an end and may unfortunately become "another way of losing the original" (MGM 510). With this problem always in the foreground, her larger philosophical argument has as its central issues the relation of value and fact, of consciousness and thought, and of art and philosophy to morality. Her philosophy dramatizes a broad range of voices who speak to these issues.

Being also a storyteller, Murdoch makes it easy for the reader to watch the unfolding of her philosophical process and to take part in her digressions and qualifications. For her, the history of philosophy reveals a series of metaphysical systems hypothesized by a series of philosophers, many demythologizing the immediately preceding system. Being herself more an iconoclastic pilgrim than a demythologizer, she portrays in *Metaphysics as a Guide to Morals* a sequence of dramas, in each of which one philosopher demythologizes another. Although she does not depict the sequence in explicitly Freudian terms, the pattern is familiar: each generation must overthrow the preceding one,[7] substituting its own construct D for the construct C, which in its day superseded construct B, and so on. Such a drama recalls Harold Bloom's "anxiety of influence," each genius arguing that he had found the center of things, Heidegger's "*Dasein*" replacing Schopenhauer's "will" replacing Kant's "thing-in-itself" replacing Locke's Substance. Murdoch can only be an outsider in these scenes, having no father per se to overthrow. She did, however, identify with Elizabeth Anscombe and Phillippa Foot, who served as valuable role models.[8] To put the sequence of male philosophers in perspective, Murdoch ingeniously adopts what she elsewhere calls "a mythological or dramatic mode of presentation"; in "Broken Totality," an unpublished chapter of *Sartre, Romantic Rationalist*, she uses the expression to describe seeing the world made up of dramatic personalities and scenes (133).[9] When Murdoch stages such philosophical conflicts, readers' excitement is more visceral if they recognize this strategy. Adopting a Renaissance perception of life as a drama and human beings as dramatis personae, Murdoch peoples her texts with major characters (Plato, Wittgenstein, Kant, and Sartre) and minor ones (Anselm, Descartes, Schopenhauer, and Derrida). Weaving her own philosophy out of particular concepts promulgated by the major characters, she demonstrates her logical agreements and disagreements with all of them. While she never posits a continuum reaching from good to evil, it is clear that she would place Plato at the former extreme and Nietzsche and Derrida at the latter.

A major new emphasis in Murdoch's ongoing discussion of epistemology is "the idea of a self-contained unity or limited whole . . . [as] a fundamental instinctive concept." She argues in the opening sentences of the first chapter of *Metaphysics as a Guide to Morals*, "We see parts of things, we intuit whole things. We seem to know a great deal on the basis of very little." Furthermore, her jumping in in medias res focuses on the drama of human perception, the point where inner and outer experience meet, assuming her reader's knowledge of the mechanics of perception and cognition. In simply saying "We see parts," she assumes the reader is an observer who knows how the human eye works together with the brain to grasp a whole picture when only parts can be seen. Her immediate challenging of contemporary discussions of "the self" raises the stakes: "Oblivious of philosophical problems and paucity of evidence we grasp ourselves as unities, continuous bodies and continuous minds" (MGM 1). In this discussion of self-contained unity, she makes gestures toward arguments concerning the Lacanian "self" and the Derridean *aporia*,[10] apparently assuming that the reader knows that infants enter the Mirror Stage between six and eight months of age and begin to learn that they are discrete entities. Of course, she does not say that humans have unity or that time and space have continuity, but often her references to the ontological givens of Western culture are unclear, perhaps ambivalent. For example, she heartily disagrees with Martin Buber's reading of Plato: "Philosophy is grounded on the presupposition that one sees the absolute in universals" (quoted in MGM 461). For Murdoch, Buber's statement is an example of a common misunderstanding of

5

Plato's doctrine: "all is patently not one, our human world is not determined by a hidden unity or universal harmony, we are strained and stretched out (like the *Anima Mundi* in the *Timaeus*), we live with intuitions of what we also realise are very distant. . . . Plato spoke only of (perhaps) glimpsing the Form of the Good" (MGM 462).[11] Even Socrates did not achieve it. Even so, Murdoch's saying that human beings "assume the continuity of 'time and space' " implies that society will consider abnormal anyone who never absorbs these concepts. To achieve the fast-paced opening of *Metaphysics as a Guide to Morals*, she sacrifices the specificity that might result from defining as broad a term as *instinctive*. She forces her reader to question whether such expressions as *instinctive* and *common sense* have precise meanings, inside or outside philosophical discourse.[12]

Murdoch had good reason to organize the first two chapters of *Metaphysics as a Guide to Morals* in a way that calls attention to the diminished valuation of morality by modern and postmodern culture. Opening with value, as she sees it manifested in Plato's philosophy and in art, creates the opportunity to dramatize a crucial problem: Kant's and the early Wittgenstein's separation of fact and value. Their segregating "value in order to keep it pure and untainted" resulted in "a marginalisation of 'the ethical' " (MGM 25). Marginalizing value calls into question the cherished unities such as the self and the art object and concepts such as history and truth: as Nietzsche, Heidegger, and Derrida have suggested, the Greek horizon of our culture is, in Nietzsche's phrase, being "sponged away" (MGM 2).

In the struggle over the demise of value, Murdoch occupies a position of moderation.[13] She is not blind to the jumbled, rudderless condition of the contemporary world, one manifestation of which is the global reemergence of fundamentalism, and another the ubiquitous exploitation of powerless and poor people. Nor does she find Derrida's picture of humans drowning in language to be an empirical reality, let alone a beneficial insight. She describes as elitist his suggestion that only authors and philosophers have any control over the ocean of language in which all people are submerged. Her position on language is more complex. Agreeing with Saussure's descriptive theory of language because it includes the qualitative "*as if* it were a vast ocean of linkages and possibilities over which we cannot see very far" (MGM 274), Murdoch disagrees with any metaphysician's need to freeze a living organism like language.

Decades ago Murdoch jettisoned the ideas of Descartes and the concept of a personal deity. She insists that "God does not and cannot exist. But what led us to conceive of him does exist and is *constantly* experienced and pictured" (MGM 508). She will not, however, dismiss as valueless the intuitive unities people create for themselves. One might think she would see these as illusions. Cynics who are rendering innocuous the traditional icons, rituals, and ceremonies of the Greek, Judeo-Christian heritage ignore the evidence that human beings are moral and that this condition is inherent. Murdoch acknowledges the same moral failure in society as the cynic who "might say of our age that it is the end of the era of 'the virtuous individual,'" but she also recognizes "the remarkable continued return to an idea of goodness as unique and absolute" (MGM 427). For Murdoch, philosophers are certainly free to think extreme positions in the abstract—doing so is part of the philosophical give-and-take—but it is an abuse of power when philosophers impose such abstract positions on people who have to live with them at a concrete level. For philosophers like Nietzsche to prophesy, or decree, that God is dead is thus to act amorally. His prophecy creates an escapist fiction—"moral-less, value-less societies of the future"—making more difficult the ordinary lives of ordinary people (MGM 473).[14] Saint Paul's dictum, Be careful that your sin does not make some other person fall, seems appropriate here. Grounding her argument in a simple reality, Murdoch raises the issue of whether the ordinary parent teaches the ordinary child the Nietzschean notion that God is dead or that goodness is dead. She questions whether parents can find values in the husks of the old rituals to nurture their children's latent goodness. Moreover, she reminds the reader that most children ultimately learn to judge whether a smile is "mocking" or "tender" and learn moral concepts through vocabulary like "generous," "gentle," "reckless," "envious," "honest" (MGM 385). She emphasizes Wittgenstein's statement in *Culture and Value* that certain experiences of upbringing could lead a person to believe in God (MGM 415).[15] Wittgenstein also argues that the duty of teachers of young children is to train them in the "world picture" of the culture to give them a foundation for learning.

In *Metaphysics as a Guide to Morals*, as in Murdoch's earlier philosophical writings, Plato is central to the discussion of the pictorial nature of the philosophical process and of language. As she has always contended, morality depends on cognition and language, the imagery of vision: "Our world, source of our deep imagery and thought-modes, is a visual world. . . . We know when we are being satisfied with superficial, illusory, lying pictures which distort and conceal reality" (MGM 462). Here Murdoch distinguishes between deep "dominant metaphors in metaphysics," which humans easily recognize, and other pictures that easily fool them. Activities such as "'change of aspect' and 'seeing as' are ubiquitous [human] activities" (MGM 279), according to Murdoch and Wittgenstein. There is, however, a negative aspect to these image-making and image-apprehending potentialities of the mind, which exacerbate the already prevalent fantasizing and make humans victims of illusion. Plato theorizes many levels of illusion, particularly *eikasia*, "the lowest condition in the Cave" (MGM 317).[16] Murdoch finds that Platonism, the ground for Western cultural ideas, continues to be a vital guide; she continues to consider the metaphysics of vision (knowledge, attention) as less egoistic than the metaphysics of movement (will), as I will discuss later in regard to Kant and Wittgenstein. Because Christianity absorbed Platonism, both metaphysics are part of secularized Christian culture. For her, paradoxically, although humans have an instinctive idea of self-contained unity (MGM 1), no hidden unity determines the world (MGM 462). She writes in a letter: "There is no clear set up unity. (We set up our only unities.)" (Letter to the author, April 24, 1993).

A poet as well as a philosopher, Plato generated apt images long since buried in the collective unconscious or simply in the cultural ideology. His parable of the spiritual quest from appearance to reality employs the images of the cave and of the sun, the Form of Good which is the supreme unifying power. Murdoch employs not only in her philosophy but also in her novels the images surrounding the pilgrimage and Plato's Forms—"models, archetypes: universals, general concepts as distinct from particular entities, and, in their ethical role, moral ideals active in our lives, radiant icons, images of virtue" (MGM 10). The pilgrimage is inspired by "the disturbing magnetism of *truth*, involving *ipso facto* a purification of energy and desire in the light of a vision of what is *good*" (MGM 14). Such a position of "moral spiritual *desire*" obviates the issues of determinism and discontinuity (MGM 24). The advantages of the Platonist myth are its simplicity and its lack of dependence on the continuation of religious belief, but, she asserts, "religion can exist without this western concept of a personal God" (MGM 432). She considers Platonism a valid alternative to a religion dominated by suffering and masochism. Meeting the other through love and perceiving the other without fantasy create a change of consciousness.

By emphasizing otherness and inner speech, Plato's texts offer a rationale for sowing the seed of love. Although Murdoch expressly places Plato first in *Metaphysics as a Guide to Morals* in order to focus on conceptions of unity, especially art, she does foreground love and inner change by explaining the transformation of "base egoistic energy and vision (low Eros) into high spiritual energy and vision (high Eros)" (MGM 24). To demonstrate the part the other plays in the process, Murdoch quotes in *The Fire and the Sun* (1977) a dialogue from *Sophist*. Her use of this quotation argues that the other sets up not a binary system but a larger spectrum: "not-being does seem to be rather interwoven with being (240c), and the stranger explains that not-being is not the opposite of being, but that part of being which is different or other (257–58). When we deny that something is X, we are not denying that it *is* but asserting that it is other" (FS 29). The discourse of love requires disciplining oneself to do "the work of attention" in discovering and seeing the other, and not just one other but many. The metaphor of vision can help explain how one goes about altering the consciousness by changing vocabulary and eventually composing a new self. "Goodness," Murdoch writes, "is connected with the attempt to see the unself, to see and to respond to the real world in the light of a virtuous consciousness" (SG 93). Plato says, according to Murdoch, "truth and knowledge live, and plausibility and falsehood too" in inner speech (FS 30). Incorporating Plato's concept of energy to explain moral change, a notion Freud takes from Plato, helps Murdoch to dramatize a "slow shift of attachments wherein *looking* (concentrating, attending, attentive discipline) is a source of divine (purified) energy" (MGM 25). Gathering all the value in the Idea of the Good, Plato sees it working in humans as love or Eros (MGM 50).

The philosophers with whom Murdoch identifies best are those who possess a religious sensibility, including the major characters important to her philosophical drama: Plato, Kant, and Wittgenstein, philosophers who combine conceptions from Plato and empiricism.[17] In a letter to me, she responded to a question about the perceived distance between Platonism and empiricism: "I see no problem about Plato and 'empiricism.' . . . Plato's Ideas are not distant abstractions but concern the perception of what is real (as contrasted with our usual conditions of casual egoistic illusion)" (Letter to the author, January 12,

1983). Just as humans can perceive objects and sounds, they can perceive evidence of good in the world. For Plato, knowledge comes from sense experience as long as it is informed by the knowledge of the Idea or participates in the Idea. Believing knowledge comes from sense experience, Plato and Murdoch, like Kant and Wittgenstein, share a belief in transcendence (e.g., Wittgenstein writes of metaphysics as "seen against the background of the eternal" [MGM 422]). Wittgenstein makes these distinctions clear to metaphysicians in his first published work. "*Tractatus* Wittgenstein," as Murdoch calls the early Wittgenstein, "like Kant, has two 'subjects,' one which is locked on to the world of fact, and one which is totally independent of the world" (MGM 27).[18] Wittgenstein carries further the task of separating these two; Murdoch worries that this "division of language itself between fact and value not only isolates and diminishes value, it may damage the concept of truth" (MGM 455). She faults early Wittgenstein and Kant for their well-meaning but problematic separating of fact from value. By doing so they unwittingly participated in laying the groundwork for the contemporary condition of Western philosophy. Her criticism doubtless explains her preference throughout *Metaphysics as a Guide to Morals* for the "*Tractatus* Wittgenstein." She appears to funnel much of her reading of *Philosophical Investigations* through her Oxbridge–G. E. Moore–Elizabeth Anscombe view of Wittgenstein.

Murdoch would have certainly preferred a more Platonic path for Kant and Wittgenstein. Nevertheless, she expresses great respect for both men and is quite positive about her agreements with them. She does not appear to have changed her mind significantly over the years about either's contributions to philosophy. In *Metaphysics as a Guide to Morals* she devotes more energy and space to Wittgenstein's ideas than to Kant's, perhaps because Wittgenstein stops just short of where she treads. She does not keep silent, as Wittgenstein, in a letter to Friedrich Waismann, said he wanted to do: "to put an end to all the claptrap about *ethics*—whether intuitive knowledge exists, whether values exist, whether the good is definable" (quoted in MGM 29). *Metaphysics as a Guide to Morals* discusses Wittgenstein's refusal in the *Tractatus* to analyze "what is higher in order to keep it (its own kind of magic) safe, to emphasise its separateness, its inevitably *mystical* character, its silence, its absolute lack of connection with science, that is with the empirical world" (422). Such refusal Murdoch finds frustrating.

Ultimately Wittgenstein's investigation made him uncertain about using any language to talk about religious sensibility and ethical vision. He begins to analyze the tension between fact and value in "A Lecture on Ethics" (1929), a text not found in the index of *Metaphysics as a Guide to Morals*. For him, the act of discussing ethics is nonsensical: "our words will only express facts," considering that "the essence of the Good has nothing to do with facts and therefore cannot be explained by any proposition" ("Lecture" 7, 15). He humbly admits sharing a characteristic with humans in general: needing to challenge one's own factual, scientific language in order to attempt to communicate absolute judgments, trying "to go beyond the world and that is to say beyond the significant language":

> My whole tendency and I believe the tendency of all men who ever tried to write or talk Ethics or Religion was to run against the boundaries of language. This running against the walls of our cage is perfectly, absolutely hopeless. Ethics as far as it springs from the desire to say something about the ultimate meaning of life, the absolute good, the absolute value, can be no science. What it says does not add to our knowledge in any sense. But it is a document of a tendency in the human mind which I personally cannot help respecting deeply and I would not for my life ridicule it. ("Lecture" 11–12)

Later, in the *Tractatus*, he explains his view about the sense of life: "the sense of the world must lie outside the world. . . . [I]n it no value exists" (6.41).[19] In *Metaphysics as a Guide to Morals*, Murdoch compares Kant's "phenomenal world . . . devoid of value, self-contained and absolute" with the factual world of the *Tractatus* (222).

She further argues that Wittgenstein, unable to talk about transcendental reality, left it out of the *Tractatus*. Not being able to find a perspective from which to view ethics, he points to a value somewhere else, already there outside his world: "Ethics is transcendental" (6.421). Murdoch describes Wittgenstein's decision about examining ethics in this way: "We *enact* morality, it looks after itself"; Wittgenstein's solution is "to say nothing except what can be said, i.e. propositions of natural science—i.e. something that has nothing to do with philosophy" (MGM 30). Since he cannot change the way the world is, his relation to it must be that of an "attitude of mind" (MGM 54). Murdoch says he conveys in *Tractatus* "a strong impression of his own moral style"; she agrees with him that humans "rightly accept many things as mysteries" (MGM

282). She does not, however, agree that "'talk about' moral decisions, whether 'rational,' or 'philosophical,' or 'ordinary,' . . . [is] itself suspect and likely to be other than it seems" (MGM 315). She insists that, as a moral philosopher, she has no choice but to raise the issue of value and to talk about inner thought.

Murdoch cites two letters to demonstrate that Wittgenstein's often reiterated refusal to talk about morality and ethics and his cordoning off of whatever is transcendental argue that, for him, the transcendental exists. Speaking of the *Tractatus* in a letter to Ludwig Ficker, Wittgenstein says, "The book's point is an ethical one. . . . I believe that where many others today are just gassing I have managed in my book to put everything firmly in place by being silent about it" (quoted in MGM 28–29). Wittgenstein's irony is also evident in a letter to Waismann: "Anything we might say is *a priori* bound to be mere nonsense. Nevertheless we run up against the limits of language. . . . This running up against the limits of language is *ethics*" (quoted in MGM 29). For Wittgenstein, what is beyond is ethics. Murdoch also points out that at least three of Wittgenstein's texts reveal his religious sensibility. *Culture and Value* discusses "religion and even God," arguing that "suffering 'deepens' our lives and drives us toward some sense of an absolute" (MGM 415–16). *Notebooks 1914–1916* focuses on ethics, and the last section of the *Tractatus* proposes a "religious view" (MGM 415). Wittgenstein, like Kant, wanted to save a "safe space for (some form of) religious faith" (MGM 50). Murdoch also wants to save a space.

Because of Wittgenstein's ethical vision, Murdoch finds more in him to proclaim than to contest. Wittgenstein allows for the mysterious, and therefore allows for intuition, even if he will not talk about either. His celebration of mystery demonstrates his respect for the other, the alien. In accepting that humans have experiences of thought that are "initially beyond and hidden," Murdoch wants Wittgenstein to agree that "at the border-lines of thought and language we can often 'see' what we cannot say" (MGM 283). He, however, will only say this much: There are "cases where someone has the sense of what he wants to say much more clearly in his mind than he can express in words" (CV 79). He says even less about language's relationship to inner thought in *Philosophical Investigations*. Both philosophers nevertheless situate their thinking at the borders where reason and imagination, the obvious and the mysterious, meet. Even though Murdoch cannot have Wittgenstein as an ally in the argument about the way experience is recorded, she is empowered by his oeuvre: his method of questioning concepts and his logical arguments have influenced not only her rationale for ethical action but also her empirical worldview, her definition of language, and her attitude toward the thought process. In the same 1983 letter to me that I quoted above, she acknowledges the breadth of his effect on her thinking: "I have been affected (I hope) by his slow and meticulous methods of working. Also, I agree with many of the fundamental ideas and methods in *Philosophical Investigations*, and with the solutions therein of various problems about meaning and thought, old Cartesian problems and those posed by British empiricism" (Letter to the author, January 12, 1983).[20] Wittgenstein's willingness to question the very foundations of philosophy fascinates Murdoch and seems to have contributed to her ability to open her own imagination to the chaos of contingency. A surprising number of his conceptions—especially his "illusion-free perspective on reality,"[21] which reveals his debt to Plato's parable of the cave (259)—meet her need for a cultural ideal grounded in her Greek, Judeo-Christian heritage.

Murdoch has incorporated many of his concepts into her own philosophy and has freed herself from traditional restraints in the same way he had done. The difference between Murdoch's explicit moral philosophy and the early Wittgenstein's ineffable moral sensibility is a difference in style—the Austrian genius brooding over his perceptions and the British social critic attempting to stem a tide. In her 1971 collection of philosophical essays, *The Sovereignty of Good*, Murdoch takes an empirical stance similar to Wittgenstein's:

> I assume that human beings are naturally selfish and that human life has no external point or telos. . . . I can see no evidence to suggest that human life is not something self-contained. There are probably many patterns and purposes within life, but there is no general and as it were externally guaranteed pattern or purpose of the kind for which philosophers and theologians used to search. We are what we seem to be, transient mortal creatures subject to necessity and chance. (SG 78)

Here Murdoch agrees with Wittgenstein that life is self-contained and that no general pattern, such as Derridean language theory, determines the world.

But even with this view, Murdoch's reaction to life is an ethic of love, a philosophy of unselfing, ascesis. For her, an "active moral agent" focuses "a just and loving gaze . . . upon [an] individual reality" (SG 34). Using the discourse of love requires disciplining oneself to do "the work of attention";[22] if one thinks in loving words, one can move toward becoming moral, the imperative to love preparing the mind to create a groundwork of values that allow the will to rest. Murdoch's finding such a precedent for a moral response to this condition "of contingent states of affairs" is analogous to Wittgenstein's return to the same traditional background in *Philosophical Investigations* (published posthumously in 1953). Having accepted the empirical view of the universe but dissatisfied with the empiricist's picture of humans and their potential, both philosophers opt for the Greek, Judeo-Christian view of humans as creatures with religious sensibility. In their respective philosophies they do discover an answer to the dilemma of whether to be moral in an immoral world. Each proposes that if humans would search for "an illusion-free perspective on reality" and accept contingency, they could put their energy into attending to and being awed by the complexity and mystery of life.[23] Such sensibility can lay the groundwork for good. While jettisoning the traditional linguistic concepts of the *Tractatus*, Wittgenstein retains his underlying moral sensibility in *Philosophical Investigations*. Ethics, he insists, must grow out of a humble realization that human beings cannot find the conceptual models to describe the whole of reality, or "the truth." That sensibility clearly forces Wittgenstein to see the world as a miracle, not a battleground for egoistic self-assertion.

Emphasizing her ethic of love, Murdoch, like Wittgenstein, refuses to accept the ethic of principle that has obsessed Kant and his successors. One problem Murdoch finds with the Kantian moral imperative—"survey all the facts, then use your reason" (MGM 26)—is that moral discrimination is almost always inherent in the defining, selecting, and evaluating of facts. Murdoch seems incredulous that anyone would think there are "sets of neutral facts": "In deciding what the initial data are we are working with *values*. Value goes right down to the bottom of the cognitive situation" (MGM 384). For Murdoch, "To be conscious is to be a value-bearer or value-donor" (MGM 256). Whereas Kant based his morality on reason, not imagination, Murdoch's morality requires imagination.

The greater problem with the Kantian view is that it conceives of a moral sensibility that depends on technique and centers on ego: "'How shall I act?' seems to most of us the paradigmatic ethical question," writes James C. Edwards, "and it seems only to admit answers formulated in terms of general and substantial first principles; 'Act only on that maxim which you can at the same time will to become universal law' or 'Act always so as to produce the greatest good for the greatest number'" (*Ethics Without Philosophy* 238). Based on this perception, the moral life demands knowledge of what the greatest good is. Since morality is then necessarily a riddle and a long, arduous struggle, one must search for right principles of action. Such principles are hidden and must be discovered, tested, and decided on; and, of course, such determinations depend heavily on pseudoscientific analysis. The will is in charge of this problem of technique, which deals with people in a conspicuously paternalistic fashion—as objects that need to be treated morally.

Insisting that her readers keep in mind Wittgenstein's unorthodox use of the concept *will*, Murdoch demonstrates that what the early Wittgenstein called the will was actually "not a particular thrust or emotive drive among others, but a total change of being in relation to everything" (MGM 53–54). Murdoch feels it necessary to make the following distinction: for Wittgenstein, "change of being, *metanoia*, is not brought about by straining and 'will-power,' but by a long deep process of unselfing" (MGM 54). It is a change of "attitude of mind." This metaphysical idea of will employed by Schopenhauer, early Nietzsche, and young Wittgenstein is "a liberating force capable of removing the illusions and miseries of mundane egoism" (MGM 54). Using Simone Weil's phrase, Murdoch contends that this unorthodox use of the concept *will* is better "set aside" as "a recipe for moral improvement." Even though Wittgenstein does not suggest how one follows the path to good, Murdoch calls him a "brave young man," one who reflects in *Notebooks 1914–1916* "a strong impression of his own moral style" (54): "The life of knowledge is the life that is happy in spite of the misery of the world [because it] can renounce the amenities of the world" (81).

In contrast to the Kantian view, Murdoch and Wittgenstein conceive of a moral sensibility that centers on miracle and mystery, activating love rather than egoism. Schopenhauer and Wittgenstein see Kant's concept of duty "as a narrow mandatory account of the moral life" (MGM 448); for Kant, "truthfulness is an unconditional duty" (MGM 383). Instead, Schopenhauer and Wittgenstein opt for moral sensibility as opposed to "'duty' . . . a mere arbitrary listing of divinely commanded particular tasks" (MGM 295). It is "inadequate," Murdoch writes, "to define morality solely in terms of duty, and without reference to quality of consciousness" (MGM 383). Moral attraction to Christ or to the Form of the Good is innate; Kant disapproves of such an intuitive attraction (MGM 24). For Murdoch, constant attention to changing one's consciousness is primary: the growth being "a slow shift of attachments wherein *looking* (concentrating, attending, attentive discipline) is a source of divine (purified) energy" (MGM 25). This kind of sensibility distrusts the Kantian principle, which can lead one to idolize duty and make duty the center of the moral life, the ostensible reason for Jesus' confronting the Pharisees.

Love, as Murdoch defines it—getting beyond the self—is an occasion for an immediate, instinctual response. Murdoch in her fiction rather than her philosophy, and Wittgenstein in his philosophical writings, show transactions they see in the world but refuse to interpret; a tempting analogy involves the early Jews who were too awed by their God to name him. Moral autonomy, rarely achieved and never permanent, seems to come, according to Murdoch, from successfully learning to discover good and to pay attention in all its permutations. Murdoch says in "The Idea of Perfection" that "the argument for looking outward at Christ and not inward at Reason is that self is such a dazzling object that if one looks there one may see nothing else. . . . Where virtue is concerned we often apprehend more than we clearly understand and *grow by looking*" (31). Although Wittgenstein does not employ the word *love*, he does insist on the same selfless "attention to the individual realities" that Murdoch demands.

Murdoch and Wittgenstein each find that the state of a person's mind determines his or her religious sensibility. For example, in "Sovereignty of Good," in reference to reveries, Murdoch writes that religion "regards states of mind as the genetic background of action: pureness of heart, meekness of spirit. . . . Our states of consciousness differ in quality, our fantasies and reveries are not trivial and unimportant, they are profoundly connected with our energies and our ability to choose and act. And if quality of consciousness matters, then anything which alters consciousness in the direction of unselfishness, objectivity and realism is to be connected with virtue" (SG 83–84). Astonishment at the existence of the world dominates Wittgenstein's state of mind, as is evident in the *Tractatus*: "It is not *how* things are in the world that is mystical, but *that* it exists" (proposition 6.44); and in "A Lecture on Ethics" (1929): "Now in this situation I am, if I want to fix my mind on what I mean by absolute or ethical value. And there, in my case it always happens that the idea of one particular experience presents itself to me which therefore is, in a sense, my experience *par excellence*. . . . I believe the best way of describing it is to say that when I have it *I wonder at the existence of the world*" (8). The earlier

Notebooks 1914–1916 reveal his discovery that the sense of life is wondrous: "Ethics does not treat of the world. Ethics must be a condition of the world" (77). Murdoch empathizes with Wittgenstein's argument in the *Tractatus* for attending to "the world in a detached manner from the outside, as if it were a work of art" (MGM 31). Her understanding of his position in *Philosophical Investigations* is not as clear. She calls prophetic Wittgenstein's now famous proposition 6.44, while at the same time disagreeing with his view that there is no place for an idea of moral facts, or a moral vocabulary. What argues most eloquently for the moral sensibility of both Murdoch and Wittgenstein is the humility each manifests in the presence of life's awesome mystery. Murdoch and Wittgenstein both see that the blatantly obvious symptom of the diseased human understanding is bewitchment, extremism, or following "a total creed" (SBR 255).[24] Neither espouses the kind of "total creed" that Kant or Sartre did; Wittgenstein's thinking was open to many voices, as Murdoch's continues to be.

Kant has long served as the whetstone to her growth as a philosopher. For decades she has been grounding her arguments in his. In 1953, in the draft of an unpublished chapter of *Sartre, Romantic Rationalist*, Murdoch voiced a traditional position: Kant "set the scene upon which the dramas of philosophy are still enacted" by instituting two crucial notions: the transcendental solution—the world's structure "is determined for us by elements which are held in common between subject and object"—and the idea that "the mind is *free* to impose law upon itself in accordance with the absolute demands of reason" (125–26). In 1992 she said that Kant, whose thoughts about God began the modern age, is among "the greatest systematic 'demythologisers' of Christianity" (MGM 444) and that he opened space for agnosticism, encouraging the eventual movement toward seeing God as duty or as superscientist (MGM 440). She uses Kant in her argument to support her reliance on the traditional givens, such as "intuitive certainty" (MGM 439), crediting him with recognizing reason as a universal faculty that helps each person judge right and wrong: "What is absolute and unconditional is what each man clearly and distinctly knows in his own soul" (MGM 439). The categorical imperative is Kant's ontological proof. Moral good is an absolute that one can discover empirically: "As for God, must we just say that it is *as if* he were there, there is a *space* left for faith?" (MGM 439). As I discuss later, Murdoch endorses this "as if" strategy.

Murdoch's eclecticism makes room for Kant's contention that each person has knowledge of good and for her own reaction to the effect Kant's extremism has had on modernism, especially literary modernism. Kant has, in her opinion, influenced the state of mind or quality of consciousness manifested during the first half of the twentieth century. For many years, criticism of Murdoch's novels has been stuck on a distinction Murdoch made in a 1959 essay about the dichotomy between two branches of liberalism: scientific liberalism (e.g., linguistic empiricism) and existentialism. For her, neither branch pays enough attention to the complexity of human beings, their interaction, and their inner life. Her many disagreements with Kant, which she explains in this essay, "The Sublime and the Beautiful Revisited," grow out of his "equation that virtue is freedom is reason. Virtue [for him] is not a knowledge of anything," Murdoch reasons; "it is rather an ability to impose rational order" (SBR 248). Kant's total creed includes the ultimately romantic view of the personality, which leads to both the "strength and the . . . weakness of the Liberal theory of personality." Murdoch uses the term *liberal* in the "traditional historical sense" as "the philosophy of John Stuart Mill is a Liberal philosophy" (SBR 248). Calling both existentialism and linguistic empiricism neo-Kantian, she argues that they have these motives and doctrines in common: they "are against traditional metaphysics, attack substantial theories of the mind, have a touch of puritanism, construe virtue in terms of will rather than knowledge, emphasize choice, [and] are markedly Liberal in their political bias" (SBR 253). Throughout her career, Murdoch has wished to "purge" the liberal theory of its romanticism: its emphasis on the moment of choice for the solitary moral agent (SBR 248).[25] For Murdoch, Kant's romanticism and his moral imperative come from the same condition: desiring to "turn away from the chaos of empirical inwardness to the clarity of overt actions" (SBR 254). For her, such a turning away is an escapist illusion. Her desire is to capture the "thingyness," the particular and the eccentric in human personality, not to accede to the monistic will. She celebrates these qualities in Sartre's texts even while criticizing his romanticism.[26]

The alteration of consciousness and its moral quality have been central to Murdoch's philosophy and her novels. For her, a decline in literature is tied to a decline in morality. The issue she raises in *Metaphysics as a Guide to Morals* is a continuation of her intention in "The Sublime and the Beautiful Revisited," in which she addresses "changes in the portrayal of characters in novels as symptoms of some more general change of consciousness" (SBR

247). Such a change involves paradigm shifts in Western discourses: physics, history, philosophy of science, and linguistics. Murdoch's philosophical outlook here tilts her argument toward the "anti-religious," "non-moral" thrust of the late structuralist metaphysics (MGM 200). The worldviews of linguistic empiricism ("the tradition of Moore and Wittgenstein") and existentialism ("the work of Sartre") correspond to bourgeois convention and neurotic rebellion, respectively. Rather than describing these poles as ends of a continuum, Murdoch finds them to be the two alternatives from which novelists choose in fleshing out these two prevalent worldviews. Her diagnosis is that ills inherent in the philosophies are also inherent in the modern decline of literature (SBR 253). Her examination of Sartre and his philosophy shows that she diverges from his concepts at the point where his characters become less rounded than characters have traditionally been in the texts of such authors as Tolstoy and George Eliot. Sartre, himself a complex and rounded human being, produces "Totalitarian Man," a romantic character who whines and then surrenders to neurosis or to "*Angst*, which is *Achtung* minus confidence in universal reason" (SBR 254). For her, the opposite extreme provides no better representation of real people: "Ordinary Language Man," in life or in novels, surrenders to convention, his choices being subject to the rules of society. These two opposing philosophies are enemies of understanding, and the devaluing of humanity that they promulgate suggests to Murdoch that exploration of human beings is no longer valuable. Because the philosophical and literary establishment has what Wittgenstein would have described as diseased human understanding, literature has found it difficult to create robust characters—real personalities with real consciousnesses.

Moreover, Murdoch accuses modern writers of being unwilling to record chaos and contingency and of desiring "significance completely contained in itself," not writing of "what is feared": "history, real beings, and real change" (SBR 260). The modern novel is either "a tight metaphysical object" that is self-contained or the other extreme, "a loose journalistic epic" (SBR 264). Yearning to escape such a binary trap, Murdoch wants to treat the two opposites as ends of a continuum between which she and other novelists can construct fiction based in contingency. Her emphasis in her moral philosophy and in her novels on human consciousness strongly suggests that she finds unhealthy the contemporary dearth of Lears and Hamlets. Life is made of muddle, and good art records the contingencies. What modern novelists fail to recognize, she says, is that "virtue is not essentially or immediately concerned with choosing between actions or rules or reason, nor with stripping the personality for a leap [but] with apprehending that other people exist" (SBR 269–70). This argument's very clarity—that human consciousness is a moral value to be recorded—has proved a trap for some critics.

Throughout her philosophical writings, Murdoch has seemed annoyed with philosophers who, because they cannot figure out how mental processes work, give up and assume that there is nothing to analyze or discuss publicly. She explores in *Metaphysics as a Guide to Morals* the broad differences among philosophers, who at one extreme assume the idea of the "contents of consciousness" as if consciousness were a container, while those at the opposite extreme, like phenomenalists Russell and Ayer, "have postulated 'sense data' which may or may not be said to be strictly introspectible" (MGM 219–20), what Murdoch calls a behaviorist stance. Somewhere toward the middle of the spectrum, Hume and Berkeley assume "atomic mental contents, impressions, ideas" (MGM 219). Kant would not accept that scientific knowledge came from Hume's association of ideas or that conceptions of time and space "presupposed these conceptions" (MGM 221). Kant argued that the "understood, experienced world was a product of conjoined forms of organisation (*a priori* and empirical concepts)" (MGM 221–22).

Murdoch is being traditional in grounding her argument in Kant's analysis of the rational mind as moral. Putting cognition at the center of his philosophy, Kant demonstrates the mind organizing experiences. In the draft of the unpublished chapter of *Sartre, Romantic Rationalist*, Murdoch alludes to Kant's texts to ask whether science represents mental events in legitimate or valid ways. According to Murdoch, Kant sees the mind not only "as constituting a real objective world for itself, but as seeking at the same time to comprehend this world as a complete rational intelligible system. (The mind is like a static grid through which reality pours; it is also like a dynamic movement toward a more complete and intelligible ordering of everything that is.)" (125). Decades after referring, in that unpublished chapter, to the mind as "a static grid" and in *Under the Net* to Wittgenstein's "fine square network," a symbol of theorizing without getting under the net to reality, Murdoch refers to language as a network: "Language is transcendental, a final network which we cannot creep under" (MGM 234). Murdoch keeps circling back in her philosophical essays to the need for philosophical research on "inner mental happenings" (NP 243).

She bewails the modern philosophers' (especially linguistic analysts') disregard of such a need, insisting that Ayer and Ryle cannot enlighten the definition of *thinking* by simply dividing and subdividing mental phenomena. What is more important to her than pseudoscientific analysis is the fact that an artist such as Rainer Maria Rilke can deal in words that reveal the "rich and pregnant" particulars (MGM 258). Calling for concerted attention, Murdoch reiterates the need to go beyond logic and grapple with "the cloudy and shifting domain of the concepts which men live by" (MGM 122).

Recalling that the concept of the individual has presupposed the idea of consciousness since Homer, Murdoch pursues her study of the mind's "'moment-to-moment flow and the procedure . . . of the inner monologue or inner life'" (MGM 259). Questioning how much increased awareness has exacerbated the contemporary predicament, she contemplates the ways thought runs through the mind: thoughts flow by and are mostly lost to memory. To illustrate her explanation of William James's term *stream of consciousness*, she cites Molly Bloom, a character in Joyce's *Ulysses* (MGM 258). Her motive here is to ask whether "every moment [is] morally significant," suggesting that all "our 'presents' are very various in quality" (MGM 257). Teachers of writing know that students can record their own streams of consciousness while overhearing them flow, an example of an empirical commonsense proof for Plato's point that "truth and knowledge live, and plausibility and falsehood too," in inner speech (FS 30). Every writer will no doubt fail, however, to keep up with the ubiquitous movement that Hegel calls the *ragbag*. Murdoch has been attempting to pin down this issue of "the moving substance of our mind" at least since she brought up the question in regard to Moore in her 1952 essay, "Nostalgia for the Particular."

Four decades later, when ontological uncertainty is a powerful threat to humankind, Murdoch continues to call for examination of "self-existence [that] continues unknown in the dark": "This concerns what it is to be human, the enigma at the centre" (MGM 258). Perhaps for her, the human is a limited whole, the transcendental part being the center of darkness or the unconscious—the centered self being merely an outworn cultural illusion. Murdoch suggests that the study of the enigma of the self could end in doubt, in "relativism, cynicism, doubts about morals, doubts about *order*" (MGM 258). She sees herself as a philosopher who is willing to look into the deep dark of the cave, the void,[27] and still control her human anxiety, an attitude similar to

Rilke's when he describes Cézanne as looking objectively at reality with the focused "attention of a dog" (MGM 246). Just as Rilke suggests that it is good to *say* art instead of judging it, Murdoch finds it desirable to *say* all of reality without judging it. In the regression of certainty and absolute reference points, the battles that she records in her philosophical writing—because they are about the human condition—continue to be played out in her novels.

CHAPTER TWO
Iris Murdoch's Wittgensteinian Voice

Murdoch's dialogue with Derrida in *Metaphysics as a Guide to Morals*, her 1992 book of philosophy, may seem even more forceful than her continuing dialogue with Wittgenstein. The surprising dynamism surely emerges from arguing with an extremely vocal, living opponent. Murdoch admits that Derrida is a worthy adversary, but he is "a *literary man*" (MGM 289); Wittgenstein is a philosopher. Wittgenstein's iconoclastic example has helped Murdoch to move beyond the Cartesian worries of "how mind reaches the world" (MGM 27) to address post-Wittgensteinian philosophy. Her experience as a student of philosophy has freed her to choose not to be conventional or logical or consistent in her novels. It is to her credit that her novels disturb critics like Harold Bloom, who writes: "Consistency of stance is one of Murdoch's problems" (*Iris Murdoch* 1).[1] What Bloom does not say is that inconsistency, like contingency and paradox, is a phenomenon Murdoch especially wants to capture in her novels. She refuses to console readers by fulfilling their expectations; she undermines realistic representation and teaches readers to unlearn their perceptions. Murdoch simply sees art from a different angle. Her rainbow of perspectives, which I describe in chapter 1, suggests the extent to which her conceptions about language, logic, ethics, and morality are Wittgensteinian, not Derridean.[2] This chapter demonstrates that the quality of Murdoch's contact with Wittgenstein's revolutionary texts and with the Oxbridge scene renders irrelevant such criticism as Bloom's, which has more to do with readers' conventional expectations than with Murdoch. Her ability to provoke Bloom suggests her vigorous, albeit complex, approach to thinking and writing. Yet, as much as she disagrees with Derrida's view that language is a deterministic sea, readers like Bloom do interpret her novels as dramatizing just such a deterministic world. What sets Murdoch apart from other novelists, as well as from her fellow Oxbridgians, is not her continuing to work with the various grand narratives of legitimation, but rather her comedic dramatization, in novel after novel, of the struggles among such grand narratives.

Moreover, this chapter explores the trend in her novels of the 1970s and 1980s toward exploring the lives and thoughts of teachers, pupils, philosophers, and mystics. Throughout this study I emphasize Murdoch's preoccupation with Wittgenstein, a connection which Murdoch criticism has not ignored but has not yet adequately addressed, either. In fact, one of Murdoch's best proofs that she is an antiphilosophical novelist is her interest in Wittgenstein, himself an anti-philosophical philosopher; her dialogue with him is partly responsible for her postmodern narrative strategies. Further exploring Murdoch's fascination with Wittgenstein and his texts can help to fill a gap in Murdoch criticism, which has so far scrutinized other influences. For example, Peter Conradi and Elizabeth Dipple have analyzed Murdoch's fictional use of Plato's ideas, Conradi has emphasized the connection with the romanticism of Jean-Paul Sartre, and Antonia Byatt has written a brilliantly argued explanation of Murdoch's interest in and use of Simone Weil. Murdoch's novels are to some extent a response to Wittgenstein, who had no other vehicle than philosophy, and a response more generally to his philosophy, which, she says, "has been *forcing upon us* a certain picture of experience as a kind of illusion, thereby discrediting the density and real existence of inner thinking" (MGM 279). Murdoch not only argues empirically that philosophers can discuss inner thought but also shows in her fiction hundreds of consciousnesses in the process of thinking. Murdoch's voice has been empowered by her dialectical response to Wittgenstein's voice.

Murdoch's sensibility was defined long ago by a series of circumstances that included her exposure to Wittgenstein, a man who has changed the way of perceiving the world. Of all the philosophers in Murdoch's consciousness, Wittgenstein is the one who turns up most regularly as a name and a model, and it is his ideas she most ironically and joyously juggles. Her work with refugees from World War II, added to her earlier conditioning, contributed to Murdoch's empathy for her fellow human beings—an empathy similar to Wittgenstein's sound human understanding, or ethical vision.[3] Murdoch attributes to Wittgenstein more than a superficial change in her ideas; he instigated a change from within. Wittgenstein says the style is the person, and in a letter to me dated January 12, 1983, Murdoch says that Wittgenstein "has influenced my philosophical style." Studying her notebooks demonstrates that his "slow and meticulous methods of working" and his epigrammatic Socratic irony have also influenced her writing habits in general[4] and that what she calls "many of the fundamental ideas and methods in *Philosophical Investigations* and the solutions therein about meaning and thought" have worked their way into her thought, becoming part of her worldview and her writing habits. In addition, Wittgenstein's contribution—his conceptions of language as game (PI. 1:23) and of the "sound human understanding" (an illusion-free perspective on reality) (*Remarks* 157)—is basic to Murdoch's narrative strategies and not merely a skeleton key to her writing, as some might argue. If Murdoch has been significantly influenced by Wittgenstein—who said traditional philosophy should not be practiced—then one sign of his influence is her refusal to make simplistic philosophical solutions central to her novels. Both Murdoch and Wittgenstein argue for humility in the presence of life's mystery; each conceives of a moral sensibility that is neither egoistic nor technological, as opposed to the Kantian view that man must know the truth and exercise the will.[5] Her interest in his early theory has no doubt freed her imagination to consider mystic flight a realistic possibility, and her dialectical relationship to his later theory, which she plays out in *Metaphysics as a Guide to Morals*, has given her the freedom to see beyond the "scientific," or analytical, model of philosophy. When Murdoch sees what cannot be said, she finds a stylistic solution such as juxtaposition, paradox, or contingency.

Murdoch's move in the 1980s toward examining eccentric philosopher figures, in her twentieth through twenty-fourth novels, is a direct offshoot of her longtime fascination with Wittgenstein, his circle, and his philosophy.[6] By matriculating at Oxford at the end of the 1930s, Murdoch happened to arrive in the midst of a revolutionary atmosphere in which students were encouraged to become protégés of the charismatic philosophers and mathematicians who espoused logical positivism. Her reading of the *Tractatus* at that time and eventually becoming part of a circle who passed on Wittgenstein's current views in *The Blue and Brown Books* confirms Ayer's recollection that Oxford undergraduates studied contemporary controversial linguistic works (*Part of My Life* 115–20). Ayer, an important participant in promoting Wittgenstein as a superior and revolutionary thinker before and after Wittgenstein had moved away from the position he held in the *Tractatus*, was at the center of the Oxford revolution. His autobiography, *Part of My Life* (1977), demonstrates the entrenchment of the Oxford philosophy in the half decade or so before Murdoch matriculated in 1938. Gilbert Ryle had introduced Ayer to the *Tractatus* in 1931, Ayer's final year as an undergraduate. At the end of that school year, Ayer read a paper on the *Tractatus* for the Jowett Society, the first public discussion at Oxford of Wittgenstein's work. When Ryle introduced Ayer to Wittgenstein in 1932, Ayer felt he had been taken on "as a protégé" (*Part of My Life* 120). After returning from graduate work at the University of Vienna, Ayer began in 1933 to lecture at Oxford on Bertrand Russell, Ludwig Wittgenstein, and Rudolf Carnap. In 1936 he published his own controversial work, *Language, Truth, and Logic*.[7]

The entrenched ideology underlying this revolution that Murdoch experienced as an undergraduate was the reading of Classical Moderations and Greats. Ved Mehta, a journalist, interviewed a friend he simply called John, an Oxford philosopher who talked "too frankly and unprofessionally to wish to be identified" (*Fly and the Fly-Bottle* 15). Mehta's discussion with John, whom Murdoch says she has forgotten, helps establish the kind of experience Murdoch would presumably have had but does not discuss. John says that the Oxford undergraduates of his day (circa 1950) had a great deal of freedom in Greats to follow their own interests, even being encouraged to study recent works written by their teachers.[8] The reason John cites for students' reading contemporary philosophers—"because the philosophers at Oxford are concerned only with their own puzzles"—suggests why students like Murdoch absorbed so much contemporary Oxford and Cambridge philosophy: contemporary philosophers "are not very much occupied with problems that interested earlier philosophers, even as little as forty years ago" (*Fly and the Fly-Bottle* 16). Mehta's naming of the works that were part of John's curriculum corroborates Oxford's valuing of particular texts from the time Murdoch attended, 1938–42, through the 1950s.[9]

Murdoch explained to Mehta that she went to Cambridge after World War II to study French philosophy and later returned to Oxford "to look at English philosophy afresh": "I was in London during the war . . . and afterward went to Brussels to do refugee work. In Belgium, there was a tremendous ferment going on; everyone was rushing about reading Kierkegaard and Jean-Paul Sartre. I knew something about them from my undergraduate days, but then I read them deeply" (Mehta, *Fly and the Fly-Bottle* 54). Because she came into contact with fervent Wittgensteinian disciples during her year at Cambridge in 1947,[10] her interest in moral philosophy—specifically existentialism—began to merge with her interest in linguistic philosophy. Her study of both existentialism and Wittgenstein's metamorphosing philosophy gave her the freedom to go beyond Aristotelian and Cartesian limits. Her philosophical eclecticism is evident in her early novels, in which she employs ideas from Sartre and

Wittgenstein. In her first novel, *Under the Net* (1954), the existential protagonist writes a book about a hero who recognizes a Wittgensteinian reality: The philosopher, if he or she is to find answers, must apprehend particular details by getting under the net of theorizing.[11]

Unfortunately, Wittgenstein decided to retire in December 1947, just as Murdoch arrived at Cambridge, and she heard none of his lectures. She was, however, drawn into the Wittgensteinian revolutionary excitement by John Wisdom, Wittgenstein's most distinguished pupil, and Elizabeth Anscombe, a pupil and translator of Wittgenstein (Mehta, *Fly and the Fly-Bottle* 55). She explains in a letter that she had read the *Tractatus* at Oxford and "imbibed a lot of Wittgenstein's later ideas [before they had been published posthumously in 1953 in *Philosophical Investigations*] from people who had studied with him in Cambridge; these ideas were 'in the air,' and I was taught by various people, including D. H. MacKinnon.... I was however taught, in extensive conversations then and later, by several of his closest disciples" (Letter to the author, January 12, 1983). Having met Wittgenstein twice after her year at Cambridge, she gives Mehta a novelist's picture of him:

> He was very good-looking.... Rather small, and with a very, very intelligent, shortish face, and piercing eyes—a sharpish, intent, alert face and those very piercing eyes. He had a trampish sort of appearance. And he had two empty rooms, with no books, and just a couple of deck chairs and, of course, his camp bed. Both he and the setting were very unnerving. His extraordinary directness of approach and the absence of any sort of paraphernalia were the things that unnerved people. I mean, with most people, you meet them in a framework, and there are certain conventions about how you talk to them, and so on. There isn't a naked confrontation of personalities. But Wittgenstein always imposed this confrontation on all his relationships. I met him only twice and I didn't know him well, and perhaps that's why I always thought of him, as a person, with awe and alarm. (Mehta, *Fly and the Fly-Bottle* 55)

Murdoch's repetition of "piercing eyes" suggests her fascination with this genius.

For numerous reasons, the anxiety of influence perhaps being one, Murdoch has been fascinated with genius in general and with Wittgenstein in particular. At the most superficial level, she was young and impressionable when she first met him, and he was young and handsome. Murdoch was overjoyed to have a long, private conference with him (apparently seeing him to some extent as a kindred spirit), and she has said to me that he was fascinating. His devoted students became her teachers. Like them, she considered him an elusive, godlike person, understanding that he was both a mystic and a revolutionary. Murdoch's veritable preoccupation, first with what might be called the more general aspects of Wittgenstein's charisma, and later with his ideas, has produced numerous references and parallels in her novels. Wittgensteinian philosophy is thoroughly self-conscious about bewitchment by language constructions that individuals accept as literal and binding.

How is it that Murdoch seems never to have wavered from her conviction that teachers, mentors, are supreme? What qualities have allowed her to work so congenially with traditional patriarchal figures as teachers and colleagues? Murdoch's career has required her to wade through the philosophical world of sexist metaphor and role-playing, yet her patience is saintly. Before the 1980s she published novels that mined a stratum [12] of characters that critics called egoistic male enchanters. Beginning in the mid-1980s, she has moved deeper into her imagination, where she has found more eccentric, larger-than-life philosopher figures. Murdoch's fictional Marcus Vallar (MP) and Rozanov (PP), lost in their own philosophical puzzles, attest to Murdoch's knowledge of male egoism and narcissism; none of the charismatics she examines is a hero like, for example, Nelson Mandela.

It is no wonder that Murdoch's fiction frees voices in her imagination that have congregated around teacher-pupil-mentor experiences. She has observed a succession of teacher-student relationships (mostly male) during her life as a student and a teacher and as the wife of John Bayley, Oxford don and literary critic. Examples include historical teacher-student, mentor-mentee relationships: Socrates–Plato, Bertrand Russell–Wittgenstein, Wittgenstein–Alice Ambrose, John Bayley–Peter Conradi; fictional ones include John Robert Rozanov–George McCaffrey and Marcus Vallar–Alfred Ludens. Murdoch is candid in describing the ways individuals might feel about the power teachers have over students. *The Book and the Brotherhood*, for example, not only examines a series of relationships between a teacher and several of his students but also arranges a group of students around a charismatic leader and explores the differing effects on men and women. A more focused example that she volunteered is her use of the dramatic death of Professor Moritz Schlick, who in the early 1920s influenced the Cambridge School of Analysis. His death suggested to Murdoch the ambiguous death of John Robert Rozanov in *The Philosopher's Pupil*. Schlick, who became the leader of the Viennese positivists when he came in 1922 to occupy a chair of philosophy at Vienna University (Ayer, *Part of My Life* 128), had formed the group after being stimulated by the ideas of his friend Wittgenstein, whose *Tractatus Logico-Philosophicus* had appeared in 1921. Murdoch's appropriation of Schlick's experience and her particular attitude toward mentors shows that her view of a university lecturer is not always reverential. She said in an interview with me that

> one of the original ideas in the creation of [*The Philosopher's Pupil*] was the fate of Schlick, who is mentioned in it, a philosopher of the Vienna School, who was murdered by one of his pupils. The notion that you kill your teacher is deep in various situations in education [laughing], just as you may kill your analyst. And the illusion that George [a major character] is under is one I have seen in many cases. It can be funny, it can be almost tragic: the pupil *thinks* that the teacher is deeply interested in him, has gone on thinking about him, is delighted to see him again, will eagerly read any stuff he has written—when this is not the case. (Heusel, "Dialogue" 9)

One sees her good-humored, patient acceptance of what is—a world where students find reasons to murder mentors and good must struggle with evil. She ranges the characters in her comedies, in some of the same ways that Dante does in the *Divine Comedy*, making some seem saintly and some seem as if they belong in the Inferno. Wittgenstein had one mentor who never became a part of the connecting circles of teachers and students at either Oxford or Cambridge: Nikolai Bakhtin, Mikhail's brother.[13] Through him, Wittgenstein imported ideas from the Soviet Union into the predominantly English scene. Nikolai Bakhtin's conversations with Wittgenstein were one factor that influenced the shift from the logical positivism of the *Tractatus* to the more broadly speculative concerns of *Philosophical Investigations*.[14] In his essay "Wittgenstein's Friends" Terry Eagleton uses the friendship to argue that "Wittgenstein is indirectly related to the mainstream of Marxist aesthetics" (76). Eagleton's essay compares and contrasts Bakhtin's and Wittgenstein's attitudes toward language. Wittgenstein, like the Bakhtin brothers, was interested in the concrete uses of language, and not in essence. He focused on ordinary language, by which he meant the language human beings use every day, as opposed to the "extraordinary" languages of mathematical logicians and natural scientists.[15]

Murdoch's questions about the function of teachers and their value suggests her reason for examining them. Her regard for her early teachers unexpectedly surfaced in an interview with me as I asked for her definition of *good people*: "'invisible' people can be very good. I think of schoolteachers, for instance. I went to a highminded school with lofty ethical standards. I think some of the teachers there did exemplify a kind of goodness. They weren't pursuing wealth or fame or power: they were really unselfish people" (Heusel, "Dialogue" 6).[16] Then, in response to a question about masochism and power, she elaborated: "Yes, often that is an aspect of—not of being good, because nobody is totally good—but being the same as some of the people I mentioned earlier like teachers who lack identity. They're not self-assertive" (Heusel, "Dialogue" 12). Such mentor figures, then, take on increasing fascination for Murdoch in her novels of the 1970s and 1980s. Of course, there are teachers and students from the very beginning, as in *Under the Net* and the full-scale exploration of "a highminded school with lofty ethical standards" in *The Sandcastle*.

In the four novels Murdoch published after *Nuns and Soldiers* (1980), the charismatic male thinker who has a message for the world dominates; of the four, Jesse Baltram is the least effective but perhaps the funniest.[17] Such thinkers have perhaps caused readers to assume that Murdoch is advancing some philosophical polemic. Murdoch hardly needs to be a philosopher, however, to find the traditional romantic myth of the genius who falls into madness worthy of serious and playful comedic and tragicomedic interest without ever touching on the philosophic. In addition, the issue of egomania can be funny, and romantic groupies even funnier. Readers see that the characters who trail after the charismatic heroes are romantics who, needing illusions in order to thrive, perpetuate the myth of the hero. Murdoch, having herself gotten caught up in a group of Wittgensteinian followers in her postadolescent days, may well be exploring some nexus of her past and laughing at the Oxbridge atmosphere.

Murdoch draws no particular dividing line between egoistic male enchanters, important from the beginning in *Under the Net* (1954) and *Flight from the Enchanter* (1956), and male gurus, important in *The Message to the Planet* (1989); often, as in *Under the Net*, they overlap. But in her later novels she shows increasingly a trend toward undermining the larger-than-life male thinkers. Beginning with Bledyard in *The Sandcastle* (1957),[18] one can imagine a growing list of various kinds of thinkers: James Arrowby, a Buddhist, in *The Sea, The Sea* (1978); Guy Openshaw, a scholar, in *Nuns and Soldiers* (1980); John Robert Rozanov, a philosopher, in *The Philosopher's Pupil* (1983); and David Crimond, a Marxist writer, in *The Book and the Brotherhood* (1987). Some of these men are mystics; some, Platonists.

Murdoch reflects the influence of Wittgenstein in her tendency to puzzle and play, using her writing to "puzzle out" her ideas like a cat worries a string, a simile she mentions in a *Washington Post* interview (Conroy, "Lasting Powers" F6). Her relatively subtle use of mystery, mysticism, and the paranormal in those novels put reviewers in the position of intuiting a new direction in her fiction, a direction that caused them to speak out in consternation and confusion, occasionally blurring such subjects as mystery and the paranormal.[19] She has always played with the paranormal, but in earlier novels she seemed merely to be having fun. For example, there is the mystery, in *The Black Prince*, of Bradley Pearson's editor: is he Apollo? And then, in *The Sea, The Sea*, the reader experiences strange magic—poltergeists and death by mental powers. Although the latter novel won the Booker Prize, reviewers did not immediately welcome it. Anne Cavidge's vision of Christ in *Nuns and Soldiers* has also made critics squeamish, and in *The Message to the Planet*, Marcus Vallar appears to raise Patrick Fenman from the dead. Perhaps it is simply a joke that the latter novel begins with a question about meaning, as *Nuns and Soldiers* began with the word *Wittgenstein*:

"Of course we have to do with two madmen now, not with one."
"You mean Marcus is mad too?"
"No, he means Patrick is mad too."
"What do you mean?" (MP 1)

Murdoch is obviously exploring not only questions of meaning but also innumerable methods for discovering meaning.

She absorbed several cues from Wittgenstein, particularly through his interest in Buddhism, that the paranormal and mysticism can be legitimate subjects. Murdoch understands what Bertrand Russell apparently did not, at least at the time of Wittgenstein's death. Russell said that "his one-time student (and teacher) was 'more or less of a mystic.' "[20] Nieli disagrees with Russell: "a statement which, if intended to mean a person who has known at least one high level religious experience, was no doubt correct. Russell was misleading, however, when to this he added: 'which shows itself here and there in the *Tractatus.*' For, far from being, as both Russell and Carnap thought, an unintegrated work, a treatise on logic with mystic themes sprinkled 'here and there' (or perhaps only in the last few pages), the *Tractatus* is in its entirety, so conceived from the very first lines, an explication and interpretation of an experience of mystic flights" (quoted in *Wittgenstein* 69). Furthermore, Wittgenstein says about the mystic experience that it is "absolutely safe": it is a "state of mind in which one is inclined to say 'I am safe, nothing can injure me what ever happens'" ("Wittgenstein's Lecture on Ethics" 8). Murdoch's interest in such mystic experience, which for her characters is not always safe, suggests Wittgenstein's influence. Perhaps even her interests in Buddhism and meditation have some basis in her familiarity with Schopenhauer and his influence on Wittgenstein.

Murdoch's storytelling methods can juggle innumerable perspectives on the realities of human behavior, actively weaving in and out of treacherous labyrinths, much as some Demiurge or magician might. Mystic flight is a dangerous subject for any twentieth-century writer, as is bizarre humor. Murdoch appears to share Nieli's assessment of Wittgenstein as an ascetic who "was not alone among European thinkers to seek a way out of the malaise of modern times through an understanding of human culture as *Spiel*" (*Wittgenstein* 254). In her novels, but not her philosophy, Murdoch appears to be exquisitely, even erotically, open to such play, a factor some critics miss, perhaps assuming Murdoch writes fiction as she writes philosophy. As a thinker fascinated with Wittgenstein, Murdoch sets herself apart from the philosophers who merely write "scholastic exercises thoroughly lacking . . . either humor or play" (Nieli, *Wittgenstein* 257). Murdoch's play with the serious and the humorous continues the tradition celebrated in the writings not only of Wittgenstein but also of Dostoevsky. The latter served as a freeing influence. One of Murdoch's most poignantly negative statements appears in a holograph notebook in the University of Iowa Special Collections: "Life is like Dostoevsky," she says: "you forget the funny bits." "Humour is not a mood," Wittgenstein says in *Culture and Value*, "but a way of looking at the world" (78).[21] For example, Wittgenstein might make a distinction that God and Plato are "worthy of being taken with full seriousness, . . . [but] human affairs partake of a lesser level of importance and reality" (Nieli, *Wittgenstein* 255). Precisely such a distinction between levels of seriousness is evident throughout Murdoch's fiction.

Her more blatant refusal in *The Message to the Planet* to bury in jokes her investigation of the paranormal can be disconcerting, an effect that is deliberate on her part. But some readers may be too timid to follow Murdoch into regions unknown. Reactions to this novel—reviewers' joking that Murdoch might have gone over the edge this time—show that critics have not been paying attention to her explorations. Readers in general do not seem to be interested in Marcus Vallar as a figure who incarnates many of Wittgenstein's characteristics. Vallar and Wittgenstein have a stereotypical trait in common from their Jewish heritage: guilt; some of the characters interpret the guilt to be madness, genius, beauty, austerity, ritual, or mysticism.[22] Both men enjoyed teacher-student relationships, conversations, and ideas, and both are identified with notations, notebooks, and suicide. In Murdoch's stories, teachers write or their students record the teacher's ideas in notebooks (corresponding to Wittgenstein's dictation of the blue and brown books), and sometimes students record their own ideas in notebooks.[23] In *The Message to the Planet* she creates in Alfred Ludens a connection between the historian's need for texts and the philosopher's need to preserve for posterity the lecture notes from his teacher.

Another echo of the Wittgensteinian legend in *The Message to the Planet* is the climactic discovery of the boxes of notebooks and notes written by Marcus, the mystical philosopher, and found after he commits suicide. The paradigm for such posthumous circulation of a master's notes points to Wittgenstein: the writing that he left behind gave others the opportunity to publish after his death and indeed spurred a scholarly industry. The first paragraph of the Editors' Preface in *Ludwig Wittgenstein: Zettel* illustrates this phenomenon: "We publish here a collection of fragments made by Wittgenstein himself and left by him in a box-file. They were for the most part cut from extensive typescripts of his, other copies of which still exist. Some few were cut from typescripts which we have not been able to trace and which it is likely that he destroyed but for the bits that he put in the box. Others again were in manuscript, apparently written to add to the remarks on a particular matter preserved in the box" (iv). That Elizabeth Dipple does not account for the Wittgensteinian legend in her study *Iris Murdoch: Work for the Spirit* has to do with the level of her interest but also perhaps with her focus on Puritanism. Lack of any deep interest in Wittgenstein suggests why Dipple does not account for Murdoch's movement in her novels in the direction of the charismatic male thinker. Dipple does argue that Murdoch uses much philosophical detail from three major sources—Wittgenstein, Plato, and Kant—and that Murdoch is interested in human aspiration toward the real, the true Platonic Good (*Work* 28). Dipple also comments on "the catalog of quasi-mysticism" in *The Philosopher's Pupil* and says that "added to this list is Murdoch's own mystical adherence to the efficacy of the eloquent religious Word" (*Unresolvable Plot* 201). Yet, finding that the references to Wittgenstein or to Wittgensteinian patterns is superficial, she calls for a moratorium on tracing Murdoch's Wittgensteinian allusions. Dipple is right in observing that "the temptations towards narrow Wittgensteinian interpretation are enormous" (*Work* 313), but she dismisses the Wittgensteinian influence, seeing it as one more indication of a misunderstanding to be eradicated. Granted, Murdoch has fought against being labeled a philosophical novelist, but her novels continue, nevertheless, to insist that readers be reminded of and pay attention to Wittgenstein when they read.

Dipple addresses an important issue in her disagreement with Bloom, who says that Murdoch's "novels insist that religious consciousness, in our postreligious era, must begin with the conviction that only death centers life" (*Iris Murdoch* 6–7). In discussing *The Good Apprentice*, Dipple writes that the character Stuart Cuno carries the burden of argument for saving the "subtle and complex language" on which ethical thought depends. Dipple says, furthermore, that "the fear that a cultural and spiritual Logos might be removed from the world lies behind much of Murdoch's fiction, and here she applies it specifically to the dehumanized threat of computer intelligence" (*Unresolvable Plot* 202). *Metaphysics as a Guide to Morals*, as well as statements by Murdoch that Stuart is the good apprentice character, demonstrate that Dipple has a better understanding of Murdoch's moral concerns than Bloom has.

A Word Child reveals Murdoch's explicit interest in Logos and in Wittgenstein; the obsessed protagonist has no choice but to withdraw from the tower of babble. Some of the issues Hilary Burde reacts to and maneuvers around no doubt grew out of Murdoch's own complicated attitudes throughout her life about language and its function. She thinks, like Wittgenstein, that learning languages moves individuals outside their narrow perspectives.

She is distressed, however, that individuals are forced to learn languages as opposed to learning them for the purpose of communication and for studying texts in the original. Murdoch expresses that anger in response to a question in an interview: "Do you speak Gaelic?" "No. I think it would be a waste of time. I think it's unfortunate that people are forced to learn it, as in Wales. It's good to keep an old language alive, but that should be a voluntary matter. Precious school time should be given to languages such as French, German, Russian, Latin, Greek" (Heusel, "Dialogue" 2). Murdoch's primary value here is communication within the community, and she apparently defines the community as extending beyond nationalistic boundaries. I see the key as her word *voluntary*, which makes her stance dialogic, not monologic. Murdoch writes in *Metaphysics as a Guide to Morals*, "We may hold dialogues or 'dialogues' with other people, with works of art, with animals, with symbolic figures, with parts of our own soul" (421).[24] Such a stance refutes any unilateral, solipsistic attitude toward language. To accommodate this expansive view of language, Murdoch has always allowed herself increasingly large expanses: the average length of her novels nearly doubled from the early 1970s to the late 1980s.

Wittgenstein has influenced Murdoch's tendency to puzzle and play, and as a teacher or prophet calling thinkers away from mistakes in philosophy, he has emphasized close analysis of perception and cognition and paradoxically undermined the traditional scientific model of philosophy and of science.[25] Murdoch's view of ordinary language comes from the same sources as Wittgenstein's. She agrees with his understanding of language as it relates to what it means to be a human being and to have and use knowledge. About his methods she says, he "assumes that language refers to the world, and (in the *Investigations*) that unsystematic philosophical things can be said about how this happens" (MGM 235). She, as well as Wittgenstein, sees language as the work that the human brain performs; she knows, as he did, that syntax and grammar work as a frame to determine what a person is able to think.

Murdoch also espouses the conviction that human beings are victims of illusion. This Platonic-Wittgensteinian belief undergirds all the ideas and patterns she sets forth in her philosophical and fictional texts. Her novels of the 1970s and 1980s manifest Wittgenstein's revolutionary ideas about language, in addition to openness to mysticism and a profound interest in ethics. These novels explore at least four of Wittgenstein's revolutionary contentions about human beings' habits of communications: (1) Because human beings fear reality, they tend to create language games, such as philosophy, religion, or even logic, not only to survive but to attempt to explain the inexplicable and to escape into consoling fancy. (2) Because they are bewitched by their own grammatical system, their language games often create nonsense. (3) Human beings have the alternative of countering these tendencies by looking at reality through perspectives other than logic, viewing reality most clearly when objects are compared. (4) Eschewing fantasy frees them from the bewitchment of grammatical pictures.

Of course, as a philosopher Murdoch values metaphysics, arguing its usefulness in the title of her 1992 book. She is less extreme than Wittgenstein in not regarding metaphysics as magic or philosophy as nonsense. As a novelist, however, she has the freedom to depict characters who represent Wittgensteinian hypotheses. Because she is dialogically addressing numerous perspectives in the novels, she can wholeheartedly embrace these four positions among others. Her fiction often parallels the situations Wittgenstein describes among philosophers. Although illusion pervades the lives of all her characters, few of them struggle with their illusions; most act blindly, never recognizing that they are deluded.

The second revolutionary contention that Murdoch has incorporated into her novels is Wittgenstein's definition of language as game. Wittgenstein responds in *Philosophical Investigations* to his earlier illusion that one can pin down truth by picturing reality in elementary propositions. He had explained in the *Tractatus* that elementary propositions have an isomorphic correlation with the facts they represent: a word matches the object it names. It would be possible, therefore, to determine the meaning of any proposition by looking at the object or data to which the proposition refers. The metaphor he employs in the *Tractatus* for language is language as a picture, based on the principle that what a logical proposition offers is a picture of the logical structure of a fact:

We picture facts to ourselves. (T 2.1)

A picture presents a situation in logical space, the existence and nonexistence of states of affairs. (T 2.11)

A proposition is a truth-function of elementary propositions. . . . (T 5)

The totality of propositions is language. (T 4.001)

In *Philosophical Investigations*, however, Wittgenstein contradicts this traditional view of language as picture and argues instead that language transactions are equivalent to moves in a game that the human animal performs in order to fulfill its needs and purposes. In defining the term *language game* in *Philosophical Investigations*, Wittgenstein places examples side by side and then refers self-deprecatingly to his own earlier position:

> Here the term "language-*game*" is meant to bring into prominence the fact that the *speaking* of language is part of an activity, or of a form of life.
> Review the multiplicity of language-games in the following examples, and in others:
>
> Giving orders, and obeying them
> Describing the appearance of an object, or giving its measurements
> Constructing an object from a description (a drawing)
> Reporting an event
> Speculating about an event
> Forming and testing a hypothesis
> Presenting the results of an experiment in tables and diagrams
> Making up a story; and reading it
> Play-acting
> Singing catches
> Guessing riddles
> Making a joke; telling it
> Solving a problem in practical arithmetic
> Translating from one language into another
> Asking, thanking, cursing, greeting, praying.
>
> It is interesting to compare the multiplicity of the tools in language and of the ways they are used, the multiplicity of kinds of word and sentence, with what logicians have said about the structure of language. (Including the author of the *Tractatus Logico-Philosophicus*.) (PI. 1:23)

Here Wittgenstein compares language to games in order to break the hold of the Western philosophical notion—his own earlier position—that language can be a picture of something metaphysical beyond itself. For him language is instead a toolbox, each word a tool that a person may use for some jobs but not for others. Each game has its own rules and its own context. For example, in *A Word Child*, Hilary Burde's "play-acting" is no more appropriate in "reporting an event" than "singing catches" would be. Wittgenstein asserts that whereas the "scientific" philosopher has been bewitched into thinking that language transactions can function as heuristic devices or as final standards of sense, such transactions function merely as forms of animal behavior, as pieces of public reality; the meaning of an utterance is only the use it has.

Murdoch's interest in the major Western cultural illusion that individuals can comprehend or explain truth by employing the scientific mode of philosophy grows out of Wittgenstein's revolutionary subversion of philosophy. In revising the early language theory he had devised in the *Tractatus* (1921), Wittgenstein discarded the illusion that the traditional Western model of philosophy can supply human beings with all the information they need for understanding reality and for determining their behavior. Wittgenstein observed that the scientific philosopher looks only through the lens of logic, missing great areas of reality. For Wittgenstein, man's bewitchment by "scientific" reasoning and by the grammatical system of his "scientific" language is a condition that requires therapy.

A third revolutionary contention of Wittgenstein is his notion of perspicuous presentation. Employing the Latin *perspicere*, "to see through or into," Wittgenstein convincingly suggests that viewing data from many angles allows one to conjure up more potential pictures, to see more of reality:

> A main source of our failure to understand is that we do not *command a clear view* of the use of our words. Our grammar is lacking in this sort of perspicuity. A perspicuous presentation produces just the understanding which consists in "seeing connexions." Hence the importance of finding and inventing *intermediate cases*.
>
> The concept of perspicuous presentation is of fundamental significance for us. It earmarks the form of account we give, the way we look at things. (PI. 1:122)

He concludes that the philosopher's job is to note the relationship among language transactions: "The language-games are rather set up as *objects of comparison* which are meant to throw light on the facts of our language by way not only of similarities, but also of dissimilarities" (PI. 1:130). Because the goal of his new method of philosophy is not to discover new facts, he is free to look at the obvious facts human beings have been missing: "'trivial' things—'things we know already'" ("Wittgenstein's Lectures" 284). Language games being transactions that show, not say, their meaning, he chooses simply to transcribe, not analyze them. As I show in chapter 5, Murdoch has appropriated this style as a narrative strategy.

Wittgenstein understands that people accept the grammatical images implicit in the language games they have been taught; learning such language games involves excluding other potential images. Even if people are not open to growing and changing their "perception-sensibility," they may change their perception when they experience a perspicuous presentation of the grammar surrounding language games via Wittgenstein's method. This Wittgensteinian emphasis on a broad context came from aesthetics (Edwards, *Ethics Without Philosophy* 143). Wittgenstein recognized that the aesthetician convinces an individual to improve his understanding by showing "intermediate cases" of good art (PI. 1:122), cases that come between a work the individual originally valued and the one he or she finally finds superior.

In her fiction, Murdoch implements not only the issue of illusion but a style patterned after the aesthetic instead of the scientific model—recording comparisons, not explaining cause and effect, one reason the reader has so many questions after reading a Murdoch novel. Wittgenstein argues that the aesthetician, unlike the philosopher, has always known that mystery can be shown only, not explained, and that the best one can do is " 'to draw [another's] attention to a thing,' to 'place things side by side' " ("Wittgenstein's Lectures" 278). The following statements from *Philosophical Investigations* suggest why his conclusions are not cast in the form of the traditional philosophical argument but follow the aesthetic model:

> The language-games are rather set up as *objects of comparison* which are meant to throw light on the facts of our language by way not only of similarities, but also of dissimilarities. (1:130)

> Our mistake is to look for an explanation where we ought to look at what happens as a "proto-phenomenon." That is, where we ought to have said: *this language-game is played*.
> The question is not one of explaining a language-game by means of our experiences, but of noting a language-game. (1:654–55)

This process is similar to the instruction found in Murdoch's novels. Murdoch prefers to *show* the particular muddle of life, not to discuss or explain it.

A fourth Wittgensteinian contention Murdoch dramatizes in her novels is that human beings, because of cultural influences (most pointedly grammatical pictures or the rules of their grammar), tend to interpret pictures literally. As a result, they pigeonhole data into categories that neatly fit their expectations, thereby missing other obvious data. By forcing data in any given sentence to conform to the grammatical pictures in their thought patterns, people often miss potential meaning. The only way to extricate oneself from this limitation is to study other language systems and other cultures. Realizing one's narrow perspective, one would then be less likely to confuse data and facts. Wittgenstein's discussion in section 122 of *Philosophical Investigations* is a recapitulation of his criticism of James G. Frazer's forcing anthropological data into preconceived patterns. By doing so, Frazer destroyed what Murdoch says Wittgenstein found "deep in the magical (and the mystical)" (MGM 423).

Wittgenstein discusses the way pictures, or grammatical models, "fix the sense *unambiguously*" (PI. 1:426), the way language determines human perception. The mind has grammatical pictures of the forms in which people think and speak. Once established pictures have conjured up an image of a soul, for example, or of the mind thinking, changing that picture requires a great deal of work. The pictures help human beings to form sentences spontaneously, without forethought: when speakers are bewitched by certain pictures, they have no need to expand their horizons and imagine all the other ways there might be to think the same thought. Wittgenstein's goal is to encourage human beings to expand their grammatical expectations instead of settling for the consolation of scientific definitions. Human beings' blinding narrow-mindedness can be overcome by a lucid look at the words and constructions they use.

Wittgenstein says that grammar encourages speakers to equate certain kinds of statements and questions that in reality cannot be equated. For example, the idea "I saw nobody" can be conveyed with different conceptual models: if Alice uses *nobody* as a pronoun and the King interprets *Nobody* as a noun, nonsense reigns. Nonsense occurs between speakers when they use shorthand constructions,[26] such as failing to place a term in a genus and give it exact differentia. To the extent that grammar is pervasive, Wittgenstein's statement—that "one thinks that one is tracing the outline of the thing's nature over and over again, and one is merely tracing around the frame through which we look at it" (PI. 1:114)—describes a paradigm for a ubiquitous phenomenon: human beings continue to call up and become bewitched by the syntactical constructions that they have absorbed along with vocabulary. These constructions, or frames, help define ideology.

Murdoch, like Wittgenstein, records language transactions that she chooses not to analyze, understanding that the author's silence makes space for the reader's creative process. In order to have the reader analyze the grammar of her characters' language, she presents long, untagged stichomythic dialogues with few clues as to which character is speaking which lines. These language games, sometimes choruses of nonsense similar to those in French absurdist drama, simulate the experience of overhearing cocktail party conversations. When there are three or more speakers and counting lines does not help, the reader must examine the characters' syntax or style or must search for clues in the context. In Notebook 5 of *An Accidental Man*, Murdoch's marginal notes amount to dialogues with herself about structuring stichomythic dialogues, including as many as twelve different voices, and choruses of epistolarity. She consistently lists who sends letters to whom. For example, on an otherwise virtually blank verso, there are twelve notes beginning: "Clara to Dorina. Matt to Austin. A. to Dorina. D. to A. Karen to Seb[astian], Seb to Karen." (See chapter 5 for my discussion of discourse in *An Accidental Man*.)

Murdoch arranges large patterns with chapters of stichomythic dialogues and letter sequences, but generally the chapters shift back and forth between comments by a first- or third-person narrator and dialogues between two or more characters. In inventing language games for particular kinds of characters, Murdoch seems to have more fun with the word children; the range of their language games is more spectacular, bordering on play as Derrida describes it. For example, she engages in play similar to Lewis Carroll's when, in *A Word Child*, the office staff is employing stichomythic banter to tease Hilary Burde about his girlfriend and his sister's unwanted fiancé, Arthur Fisch. They play with the rejoinder "That's no lady, that's my—[wife]" (WC 31). Eventually the chorus of voices manipulates the line into "That's no lady, that's my Fisch." "That's no lady, that's my Burde!" (WC 32). Murdoch's joke provides an example of the way our grammar can easily provide a structure for nonsense. In *Nuns and Soldiers*, too, her language games range from sense to nonsense. Having lines from Wittgenstein and Schopenhauer vie there for notice, for example, creates nonsense, as does the novel's double-voicedness.

Applying Wittgenstein's revolutionary contentions about language games, bewitchment, perspicuous presentation, and grammatical pictures in chapter 3, I appropriate Wittgenstein's philosophical style and Murdoch's narrative style to show the reader "intermediate cases" of human behavior. This Wittgensteinian approach—recording comparisons and juxtaposing details rather than spelling out the relationship, be it cause and effect, problem and solution, or discovery and proof—is a quality of Murdoch's novels that often discourages readers. But looking beyond causal relations or other logical patterns in Murdoch's novels and asking how her comparison of language games functions is rewarding. Doing so can move readers from looking only for logical patterns and symbols toward seeing what Wittgenstein questions as "fine shades of behaviour—Why are they *important?* They have important consequences" (PI. 2:11.204). These intermediate cases can change a sympathetic reader's perception, his or her way of looking at the characters and the relationships. Murdoch's aim in her novels is like Wittgenstein's in his philosophy to the extent that it is to reconstruct the reader's habits. This aim requires a silent, slow process. As Wittgenstein argued so radically that aesthetics is giving reasons for focusing on one object rather than on some other, Murdoch shows how one value functions in a particular social situation under certain contingencies and then how it functions differently in another. Each new Murdoch novel reveals that she is becoming progressively more at ease in using the writing process to address the issues she finds crucial. Murdoch's characters demonstrate the ways people use language; she uses the aesthetic method in her novels to lay out ranges of social and antisocial behavior.

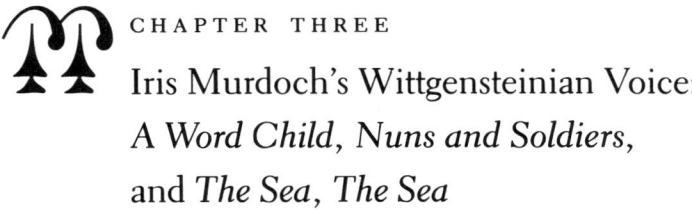

CHAPTER THREE

Iris Murdoch's Wittgensteinian Voice: A *Word Child, Nuns and Soldiers,* and *The Sea, The Sea*

Ludwig Wittgenstein's influence is particularly evident in A *Word Child* (1975), *The Sea, The Sea* (1978), *Nuns and Soldiers* (1980), and *The Message to the Planet* (1989). Each explores the ways human beings use language to impede communication rather than to communicate reality. Like human beings, the characters create and employ language games partly out of fear: the games help them to escape both the knowledge that life has no overall pattern and the responsibility of real intimacy with others. Readers sometimes fail to notice the need for equating the necessary with Murdoch's patterns and the contingent with the characters' reactions: their language games reveal how they control their behavior within Murdoch's larger patterns of cyclical fate. They evoke order as a defense against the fear of chaos. In her five 1980s novels, she constructs a stratum of thinkers who have a Faustian willingness to investigate linguistic possibilities beyond sense and nonsense. Hilary Burde, like these thinkers, crassly uses language to romanticize experience and to rationalize culpability. Such language games are evident in most of the characters' thought patterns as well as in their linguistic transactions. The characters' contentment with a myopic perspective leads to absurd consequences for them and for everyone in their respective spheres. The reader must decide whether Murdoch inadvertently or intentionally shows characters drowning under a Derridean sea of language. If she intends to simulate what she does not believe, she is juggling voices; if what seems like determinism to Bloom and others is inadvertent, then the novels cannot be philosophical and deterministic at the same time. Whether the result is deliberate or inadvertent, it is not philosophical.

Both A *Word Child* and *Nuns and Soldiers* directly refer to Wittgenstein and his language theory. The numerous references are not merely clever wordplay but part of the scaffolding of Murdoch's fictional world. Hilary, the protagonist of the first novel, fails to communicate even though he is superficially fascinated with words; a patriarch in the second novel, although compared to the god of poets, also fails to communicate—perhaps—because he has so many more perspectives than anyone around him. In *A Word Child* and *The Sea, The Sea*, Murdoch tells a story about a protagonist who is telling a story. Hilary in *A Word Child* recounts the story orally as it happens, and Charles Arrowby in *The Sea, The Sea* writes a novel. Each denies the responsibility of choosing the cyclical, determined pattern he is tracking, and Charles contradicts the evidence he records. Neither is free enough to admit his blindness and accept guilt, and neither investigates the complexity of his motives.

In *A Word Child*, Murdoch dynamically introduces her excavation into a new stratum of both subject matter and character types. Of course, these word children do resemble earlier word children, like those in *Under the Net*, in important ways. From 1975 until 1990 the word children became progressively more antisocial and mystical; moreover, between 1973 and 1978 Murdoch created three word children who each narrate a first-person novel. Although she has never wandered far from this subject, she had never made it absolutely central before 1975. Comparing the first novel in which Murdoch presents a word child and *The Message to the Planet* (1989) helps to define the direction in which she has moved. Characters in both books go beyond the limits of others' grammar and move into areas that are traditionally referred to as nonsensical. Other characters assume that Guy Openshaw and Marcus Vallar are bewitched, in a traditional sense, by concepts of something beyond or outside this earth. Their not being earthbound causes others to see them as perhaps mad.

Against a Wittgensteinian background, Murdoch's title *A Word Child* tempts, even dares, the reader to assume that the protagonist is an enlightened language user in the way that Wittgenstein might describe one. One reader, for example, proposes that "Jake Donaghue [the protagonist of *Under the Net*] has grown up into Hilary Burde, or the Ludwig Wittgenstein of the *Tractatus* has undergone the revelations that bring him to the *Philosophical Investigations*" (Aiken, "Accidental World" 33). Of course, such an explanation is overly simple. Any assumption that Hilary understands the purpose of language in the Wittgensteinian sense misses the ethical implications of Wittgenstein's later theory.[1] Furthermore, if the potential danger of words is as palpable for the reader as it is for Murdoch and Wittgenstein, the reader would suspect irony in such a title. In Hilary, Murdoch is satirizing the belief she shares with Wittgenstein that studying languages is "one of the few ways a human being can get outside of himself, his solipsism, his culture,"[2] negotiating a relation to the other. Studying other language systems does not render Hilary capable of a perspicuous perspective. He, like other characters, often processes data by simply classifying people, events, ideas, art, and love relationships into narrow categories.

Murdoch also demonstrates that language games have their own rules, their own contexts; that, in order to throw light, the philosopher must assemble all the perspectives he can; and that the aesthetic method reflects more truth than the scientific method. Echoing Wittgenstein when she writes about the critic in *The Sovereignty of Good*, Murdoch describes the approach she takes as an artist, an approach that coincides with Wittgenstein's aesthetic method: "We can only understand others if we can to some extent share their contexts. (Often we cannot.) Uses of words by persons grouped round a common object is [sic] a central and vital human activity. The art critic can help us if we are in the presence of the same object and if we know something about his scheme of concepts. Both contexts are relevant to our ability to move towards 'seeing more,' towards 'seeing what he sees'" (SG 32). The ideal, then, for both Murdoch and Wittgenstein is devoted attention to all of reality. In "The Idea of Perfection," Murdoch insists that one can gain the "Good" through love, through the direction of "a just and loving gaze . . . upon an individual reality" (SG 34). One can achieve love only by viewing the love object from many perspectives, learning his or her vocabulary, grammar, and context.

Murdoch's method of inventing "intermediate cases" of language transactions in her novels so that the reader cannot avoid comparing them can sometimes be distressing, but it does instruct the reader and provides an opportunity to help write the text. Supplying the reader with notations rather than explanations, Murdoch incorporates in the process complexity, inexplicableness, and pathos. Her goal is to open up new perspectives, not to impose an arbitrary order on the microcosm she creates.

A Word Child is Murdoch's first explicit analysis of the ways human beings use language for purposes other than communication. To reduce the violent impulses he perpetually feels, Hilary patterns his life on the rational game of learning languages. This strategy saves him from becoming a juvenile delinquent but not from becoming a killer. Learning languages has helped him make his way in the world and avoid suicide, which Wittgenstein called the elementary sin. Hilary's life is an example of "a neurotic form of existence . . . set forth as a defense against the greater threat of psychotic disintegration and chaos." Hilary uses language not only to survive, however, but to wall himself off from others. One of his colleagues is correct when he suggests that Hilary is like a dog who has learned a trick in order to elicit admiration from people.

In this novel of the early 1970s, Murdoch has not yet begun to focus on the philosopher, a person Wittgenstein finds bewitched by his language. Hilary is a student of language, bewitched by his grammar until chaos comes again in his recurring cycle of disaster. He has not always used language to impose continuity on his life: he became a word child when Mr. Osmand, his teacher-mentor, passed on his own pattern of language study in order to give the potentially delinquent adolescent some stability. Hilary speaks gratefully of his mentor: "I learnt from Mr. Osmand how to write the best language in the world accurately and clearly and, ultimately, with a hard careful elegance" (WC 21). Learning languages helped him dilute his own pain: "I discovered words and words were my salvation. I was not, except in some very broken-down sense of that ambiguous term, a love child. I was a word child" (WC 21). The word is made flesh in Hilary's life. He tells the reader expressly that words gave order to his life in the beginning as daily scheduling gives his life order in the present: "My 'days' gave me identity, a sort of ecto-skeleton" (WC 28). He explains that language helped him learn to cope with existence: "I relied upon routine, had done so perhaps ever since I realized that grammatical rules were to be my salvation; and since I despaired of salvation" (WC 27).

He worked obsessively on "irregular verbs and gerundives and sequence of tenses" not for the prize he won, not because he loved the language (although he says he loves languages, he does not understand the implications of language in a Wittgensteinian sense), but because he wanted to survive: "I was working not only for myself but for Crystal [his sister]" (WC 23). But his routine failed to stave off "the grimy misery of . . . childhood" (WC 24). His black conception of life, himself, and humanity at large forces him to discover a rational pattern that consoles him. Mr. Osmand, being the first person besides Crystal "to pay attention" to Hilary, is able to introduce him to this survival technique—the game of words. Through this game he gains a "respect for accuracy" and for truth—he thinks. Wittgenstein would argue that Hilary has found one narrow lens only, for although Hilary has absorbed the grammar, he rejects communication: "Art meant little to me. . . . I loved words, but I was not a word-user, rather a word-watcher, in the way that some people are bird-watchers. I loved languages but I knew by now that I would never speak the languages that I read. . . . Art must invent new beauty, not play with what had already been made. . . . Only I was not inventive" (WC 28). The character is complex enough, however, to reveal a Wittgensteinian insight when he says: "I early saw that the nature of words and their relationship to reality made metaphysical systems impossible" (WC 28).

Murdoch shows that Hilary's salvation by language is only temporary and is based on a conviction that Murdoch shares with Wittgenstein: that studying languages is one of the few ways a person can get outside himself, his solipsism, his culture. But Murdoch uses Hilary's salvation ironically, for he gains no alternate perspective of reality. He refuses to leave London in order to communicate with people from other cultures, and therefore can never reap the harvest of what other languages can teach him.

The study of languages becomes a narrow, mechanical obsession that gives his life a concrete basis, gives him status among his peers, and blinds him to the needs others are trying to communicate to him. At the Impiatts' dinner party, where his only hope for recognition is through showing off his ability to memorize languages, Hilary unwittingly reveals the psychological motivation for his obsession: "Nothing humbles human pride more than inability to understand a language. It's a perfect image of spiritual limitation. The cleverest man looks a fool if he can't speak a language properly" (WC 98). Being afraid of human relationships, Hilary is not prepared to converse in all the languages he knows—foreign languages or interpersonal languages. Laura Impiatt sums up his problem when she says: "Hilary, you don't value yourself enough. There's so much of you and you make so little of it. It's as if you'd lost all your courage, just absolutely lost your nerve" (WC 131). The language games he uses merely as an internal coping mechanism include inflating self-worth, diminishing others, rejecting intimacy, starting arguments, speaking coarse language, and lying.

Hilary does not see languages as games that radiate different meanings in different contexts; his conception is more Tractarian. A passage from the *Tractatus* that A. S. Byatt applies to her study of *Under the Net* is basic to one of Murdoch's intentions not only in *A Word Child* but in the other novels I discuss in this chapter. Speaking of Newtonian mechanics, Wittgenstein makes the following statement about the human need to see the universe as unified and the danger inherent in imposing a one-grid pattern on the complexity of life:

> Let us imagine a white surface with irregular black spots. We now say: Whatever kind of picture these make I can always get as near as I like to its description, if I cover the surface with a sufficiently fine square network and now say of every square that it is white or black. In this way I shall have brought the description of the surface to a unified form. This form is arbitrary, because I could have applied with equal success a net with a triagonal or hexagonal mesh. It can happen that the description would have been simpler with the aid of a triangular mesh; that is to say we might have described the surface more accurately with a triangular, and coarser, than with the finer square mesh, or vice versa, and so on. (quoted in Byatt, *Degrees of Freedom* 16)

While he is still very young, Hilary, instead of being free enough to look at reality through many lenses or perspectives, each supplying a small piece of reality, lays over his life a "fine square network" of grammar. He finds in the translation of languages the scientific logic, or grammar, that reassures him that one can find order in the rules of grammar. He is not interested in communication but in survival. Wittgenstein's statement, "Laws, like the law of causation . . . treat of the network [Newtonian physics] and not of what the network describes" (quoted in Byatt, *Degrees of Freedom* 16), if applied to Hilary, suggests that the latter is a man who fixates on the laws of grammar and never understands the implications of the language the grammar describes.

The title of Murdoch's first novel shows that for her, as much as for Wittgenstein, it is important that human beings work their way under the net. This grid that philosophy throws over reality, if not over the truth (whatever truth is), is layered within a text-within-a-text, as she suggests in *Under the Net*.[3] When one attempts to make sense of things, to find more of reality, one must crawl under the net or grid and look at particulars. But again, these particulars are embedded within layers of interpretation of what is real. Murdoch proposes in an article for the Aristotelian Society that the human plight is to "search for 'a particular and immediate kind of experience . . . which should be independent of our ordinary modes of understanding'" (quoted in Byatt, *Degrees of Freedom* 15n). Byatt explains that *Under the Net* radiates different meanings in different contexts: "It is Hugo, or Hugo in the figure of Annandine, as he is presented by Jake in Jake's book, *The Silencer*, who uses the image of the net in a philosophical sense, as a symbol for theorizing, or forming concepts about a situation" (*Degrees of Freedom* 15).[4] Murdoch's pun in the character's name, on the term *anodyne*, prepared readers for the analysis of pain in many of her other novels, including the twenty-fourth. The integral connection between Murdoch's first novel and *The Message to the Planet* is her exploration of the pain required to get under the net and communicate. This pain, which may be the message from great thinkers on this planet to other planets, manifests itself in varying levels of talk and silence, the necessary Logos. *The Message to the Planet* seems a culmination of the examination of pain she pointedly refers to when she mentions Derrida's *pharmakeus*, or drug for pain.

In the 1980s, the focus in Murdoch's novels moved from a series of organizers, or theorizers, who supposedly make sense, to a series of supposed madmen who make supposed nonsense. Does the title *The Message to the Planet* point as specifically as the 1954 title, *Under the Net*, to an answer that lies squarely in front of the reader's face? One perspective on Murdoch's possible message to the planet is Gildas's at a particular moment at the end of the novel: "Everything is accidental. That's the message" (MP 562). The reference to accidentalness sends the reader back to *An Accidental Man* (see chapter 5), a direction Murdoch continues and then expands in a confrontation between Gildas and Ludens. Annandine's reference to flight in *Under the Net* (Byatt, *Degrees of Freedom* 15) resonates a desperate speech by Ludens, the Oxford historian who is simultaneously the recorder and silencer of Marcus Vallar: "I think I shall run away. Marzillian [Marcus's psychiatrist] said something about flight, fugue, it's a technical term, it's something desperate people do, when they run away and hide and don't tell their friends and live secretly in lonely hotels" (MP 562). In sounding as if he is talking himself into running away, Ludens focuses on his mentor, Marcus, seeming to blur the labels *master* and *monster*: "I'll walk on the beach and pick up stones and meet friendly dogs and no one will know me, and I'll gradually come together again and I'll think it all and endure it all and survive. But Oh my dear monster, my friend and my master, my dear dear wounded monster, my poor dead monster" (MP 562). Ludens seems to be taking an escape route identical to the one taken by the egoistic Charles Arrowby. Ludens's focus on water, stones, and dogs calls to mind not only *The Sea, The Sea* and its prototype, *The Tempest*, but also *An Accidental Man*, *Nuns and Soldiers*, and *The Philosopher's Pupil*.

Furthermore, the ending includes Ludens's reference to the Hebrew Logos, a reference that, although it comes before the devastating view that everything is accidental, still mitigates the pessimism:

> "You know what Midrash means? Commentaries on scripture, interpretation of stories, weaving and connecting up of sayings and stories, a kind of continuous making of history."
> "I know that—I'm surprised you do."
> "Daniel Most spoke about it, he said someone said that the stories people told each other in the camps were like that. I think he thought that Marcus might be worked over and woven in and assimilated in that way." (MP 560)

Ludens's weaving Marcus into the Midrash parallels the way that Murdoch has woven Wittgenstein into her texts.

Being a philosopher interested in particulars and not in theorizing, Murdoch does all she can to cast her characters uninhibited into the cauldron of her imagination, where they must find the skills to survive. In populating her cavelike world and juxtaposing intermediate cases as Wittgenstein does, she recognizes that simultaneous continua compete in fictional worlds as well as in the nonfictional world. The characters work in their own respective strata at their own pace, struggling toward the light of reality. Murdoch juxtaposes characters not only with other word children but with versions of themselves in different positions along their various paths toward the sun. The protagonists and major characters in these novels begin as vehicles for Murdoch's plans, but the freedom she gives them and their own intensity lead them into chaotic vortexes. Perhaps one of her comments about Dostoevsky gives a clue to her consciousness of such matters: "Something about those wild scenes in Dostoevsky fed my imagination very deeply . . . the absurd situation, the breakdown of order, the unexpected" (Heusel, "Dialogue" 8). Ludens's reference to "something about flight, fugue, it's a technical term" ties together many passages in Murdoch's novels and philosophical texts, passages in which Murdoch equates theorizing and flight and equates flight and running away from communication.

In *A Word Child*, Hilary employs language as flight, as a way to diminish everyone except Anne and Kitty, the two women he romanticizes. The following dialogues show that Hilary remains tangled in the net of grammar. So that he can be sure of protecting himself, Hilary builds a wall between himself and the Impiatts. Demonstrating the language games of the roué, he speaks to Laura and then to the reader: "'I've been admiring your luscious stockings, I can't take my eyes off your ankles.' I talked this sort of vulgar nonsense to Laura. I always acted the goat with the Impiatts, they seemed to expect it. Sometimes there was not a pin to choose between me and Reggie Farbottom, the office comic" (WC 7). The barriers Hilary builds with his language and his routines are, however, obvious to his friends. Freddie sees that Hilary imposes strict rules of grammar on his relationships, treating others as objects, and comments explicitly on Hilary's inability to deal directly with reality: "He likes to live in other people's worlds and have none of his own" (WC 8). His friends recognize the incongruity of Hilary's knowing so many languages but never traveling in order to use them: "He never leaves the perimeter of the royal parks" (WC 10). Stichomythic dialogues at a subsequent dinner party demonstrate that Laura is truly interested in Hilary's psychological condition but that Freddie recognizes the social danger inherent in Hilary's language games:

> "What language are you going to learn next, Hilary?"
> "Sanskrit. I've met a wonderful Indian girl who'll teach me."
> "I'm jealous! I can't think of why you would want to learn a dead language."
> "He knows all the living ones," said Freddie.
> "No, I don't. I don't know Chinese or Japanese or any Indian or African or Polynesian language. My Turkish is shadowy. My Finnish is poor—"
> "Hilary loves showing off."
> "I always thought the Tower of Babel such a sinister myth," said Freddie. . . .
> "What about Esperanto?" said Laura. "Hilary, do you know Esperanto?"
> "Of course."
> "Do you think it—?". . . .
> "I can't think how the words of all those languages don't get all mixed up in your head," said Laura. "They would in mine."
> "Word pie." (WC 97–98)

Here Murdoch allows Hilary to reveal ingenuously that his mind does not process all these languages for communication; the words of the languages pile up as a useless jumble, disconnected from their purpose. Laura analyzes Hilary's language games correctly when she replies to his "I chatter artlessly in your presence" with "you do nothing artlessly. You use words as a hiding place. You're always *hiding*. But what from?" (WC 51).

Clifford Larr is an even sharper critic of Hilary's linguistic behavior. Since Larr knows more about Hilary's past than Hilary's other friends, he can evaluate Hilary more correctly. When the two argue about whether Arthur Fisch is an appropriate husband for Crystal, Larr ends the conversation with, "You are the sort of lower class product who never grows out of his grammar school. Always the little prize boy who was top in the exam. Always envious, always anxious. You exist by excelling, by knowing just that little more than the others and understanding nothing" (WC 79). Hilary's acquaintances recognize his neurotic need to raise himself up and his illusions of grandeur.

Hilary manifests this mode of behavior with Tommy, his lover and probably the most stable influence on his life. Because she insists on working toward an intimate relationship with him and also wants to marry him, he starts arguments with her that help him escape intimacy. His general attitude toward her is critical; he makes no effort to see her realistically. For him, Tommy is "a failed dancer, failed minor actress, failed deputy stage-manager, failed assistant scene-painter, failed unpaid typist, failed extra and Green Room dogsbody" (WC 34). He has enjoyed sparring with her since the beginning of their relationship, apparently finding her less threatening than most females, because he suggests that the language game, or argumentation, can keep them at a perpetual distance: "We did indeed understand each other and this was rare and now that we had given up on the sex act I still enjoyed the word act with her, simply the unusual experiences of communicating" (WC 43). He openly admits that he "could never develop a language of tenderness" (WC 35).

Murdoch plays a game with language when she introduces the reader to Hilary's language games with Tommy. A Friday evening chapter, which takes place at Tommy's flat, opens with an untagged dialogue:

"You've got a cold."
"I haven't."
"You have. You've got a cold and you're concealing it."
"What makes you think I've got a cold?"
"It's obvious. Your cheek is hot. Your nose is red. Your lip is inflamed.

A Word Child, *Nuns and Soldiers*, and *The Sea, The Sea*

You keep surreptitiously dabbing with that filthy handkerchief."
"It isn't filthy!"
"Don't wave it at me. You know the rule about colds. I never see people with colds."
"You and your stupid rules!"
"You've got a streaming cold. I'm going home."
"Go then, go!" (WC 37)

Until the reader recalls that Friday is Tommy's night, there is no clue as to the identity of either speaker. Even when one realizes that it must be Tommy and Hilary arguing, there is still no way to know which one has the cold. When one speaker mentions the word *dabbing*, which might connote stereotyped feminine behavior, the reader suspects that the person being addressed is a woman. That clue, with the other speaker's announcement, "I'm going home," and the chapter title all confirm which speaker is Hilary and whom he is visiting. The reader's uninformed perspective simulates overhearing a conversation in medias res.

Using language to reduce the other characters to absurdity, Hilary tells the reader that his beloved sister Crystal, a short, dumpy woman with thick, fuzzy orange hair, often appears to be stupid. He pictures Arthur, Crystal's fiancé, as a driveling simp with a "lunatic beaming smile" (WC 95) and as a "wet" who is "not notably vertebrate" (WC 61). He even reduces to his own level Ludwig Wittgenstein, a philosopher whose name Hilary's friends would recognize, by superficially comparing the philosopher's eating habits to his own: "I sympathize with Wittgenstein who said he didn't mind what he ate as long as it was always the same" (WC 9). Of course, Hilary prefers foraging his friends' food to simply eating baked beans at home. In reference to his scrounging off poor Arthur, he fancies yet another parallel to Wittgenstein: "On Tuesdays chez Arthur supper was always the same winter and summer. (Wittgenstein would have liked that.) It consisted of tinned tongue with instant mashed potatoes and peas, followed by biscuits and cheese and bananas" (WC 86). His rationalizing is clearly superficial: Wittgenstein, unlike Hilary, actually was an ascetic. Murdoch has characters in *A Word Child* and *Nuns and Soldiers* elevate one game in particular to a sport: Wittgenstein bashing.

The reader who ignores these references to Wittgenstein misses Murdoch's biting criticism of Hilary's character and his use of language to fantasize. Overlooking Murdoch's verbal, dramatic, and situational irony may lead the reader to assume that Hilary, being a word child and knowing so many languages, enjoys multiple perspectives on reality. Instead of being enlightened by all his linguistic knowledge, Hilary is merely bewitched by language. In this respect he is the opposite of Guy Openshaw, a character Murdoch uses in *Nuns and Soldiers*, another of her novels that contains Wittgenstein's name, to explore language from multiple perspectives. In these two texts she subtly criticizes extremes of language use: being caught in the net of theory encourages one to escape reality; viewing data from many perspectives gives one an opportunity to see reality.

Whereas Murdoch uses Hilary to examine the linguist ensnared in the net of theory (specifically, Wittgenstein's picture theory in the *Tractatus*), she uses Guy to demonstrate the potentially bizarre freedom one gains by moving beyond linguistic theory (here, Wittgenstein's language as game in *Philosophical Investigations*). Guy is the opposite of Hilary: instead of grasping languages as a buoy, this dying man, a reader of Wittgenstein, continues his earlier analysis of language while his mind weaves in and out, ranging through indeterminate levels of consciousness to unconsciousness. The pattern of his last words, which seem a jumble to his listeners (perhaps proving a Wittgensteinian point: that they are too close to life to recognize the obvious), is Murdoch's method of showing that Guy has managed to move beyond the grammar of his language to mystery and that she has come closer than ever before to creating a philosopher figure.

Guy evokes a more recent patriarchal figure who has literally spent his life trying to move beyond the grammar. In Marcus Vallar, the mysterious philosopher of *The Message to the Planet*, Murdoch fleshes out a character who is the opposite of the "professor with a measuring-rod up his sleeve" that Virginia Woolf describes in *A Room of One's Own* (106). Aware of the British professorial tradition, Murdoch applies her own measuring rods to the stratum of larger-than-life thinkers. If she is using the teacher-philosopher relationship to test the limits of language as it molds the lives of individuals, she obviously sees death as the necessary limit to this human investigation. Her teachers, who have family resemblances to Wittgenstein, step into the chaos and search for the Logos before they are swept up by death. Both Guy and Marcus seem to be using language to pierce the veil of mystery. Their excursions are rooted in He-

A Word Child, Nuns and Soldiers, and *The Sea, The Sea*

brew tradition, and their values are consistent with religious and philosophical Weltanschauung.

Nuns and Soldiers and *The Message to the Planet* contain dialogues somewhat similar to Socratic dialogues, except that Murdoch allows two opposing discourses to "disrupt the assimilation of differences sought by monologic discourse" (Herrmann, *Dialogic and Difference* 15). Each dialogue involves a pair of scholars, one of them Jewish in each case, and Murdoch furnishes ambiguous evidence suggesting that any or all of them may have stepped over the edge of sanity. Dipple thinks that the reader of such playful dialogues as those in *Nuns and Soldiers* should squelch any desire to be a "puzzle-solver" (*Work* 313); Murdoch, however, says that "measuring and counting are 'felicitous aids' (602d) by which reason leads the soul from appearance to reality. Paradoxes of sense experience inspire us to philosophy" (FS 44). Juxtaposing two elaborate theories about Guy's speeches—one by Dipple, which she candidly describes in *Iris Murdoch: Work for the Spirit*, and one that I developed in 1980—will demonstrate the postmodern ambivalence of Guy's words.[5] Murdoch is apparently striving in *Nuns and Soldiers* for an effect similar to the indeterminancy of *An Accidental Man*. Allowing for alternative readings of *Nuns and Soldiers*, Murdoch invites her reader to participate in the creation of the text; the dialogical effect of the various readings evokes the mystery of hallucination, illness, and death.

The references to Wittgenstein in *Nuns and Soldiers* are much more multileveled than Dipple suggests. She describes her own puzzle solving:

> I culled the images of the net and picture from the *Tractatus Logico-Philosophicus*, as well as the ideas of tribal language, family resemblance, the chess game and forms of life from *Philosophical Investigations*. In this novel where a painter does net pictures, where the social setting comprises an extended Jewish family who share the same tribal "language" and whose moral similarity constitutes easy communication in a shared *Sprachspiel*, where [Guy's wife] Gertrude and the Count cannot play chess because of a failure of communication, the set-up looks dangerously tempting, even though Guy dies fairly early in the novel and thereafter no mention of Wittgenstein is made. (*Work* 313)

As thorough as her inventory is of these plot elements, Dipple misses concepts like *play* and *dance*.

Dipple's interpretation that Guy "debunks the 'dance of bloodless categories' in his former idol Wittgenstein's thought" (*Work* 306) is suspect. This sentence seems a purposeful variation of a phrase by the Platonist F. H. Bradley that Murdoch quotes in *The Fire and the Sun:* the "ghostly ballet of bloodless categories" (81). Since Murdoch has her characters apply it to Wittgenstein, however, the phrase demonstrates that Guy is thinking specifically of the *Tractatus,* not generally about Wittgenstein's philosophy—which is the dialogue between the visionary *Tractatus* and, according to Murdoch, the quasi-behavioristic *Philosophical Investigations.* Guy's pulling together of references to "bloodless categories," idealism, and Schopenhauer demonstrates that he is not debunking Wittgenstein per se but rather the early Wittgenstein; Guy addresses issues from which Wittgenstein distanced himself when he wrote *Philosophical Investigations.* Disagreeing with Kant, Schopenhauer believed that "'the solution to the riddle of the world must come from an understanding of the world itself'" (quoted in Nieli, *Wittgenstein* 104). But Wittgenstein, a onetime devotee of Schopenhauer, believed that "'the solution to the riddle of life in space and time lies outside of space and time'; '[t]he meaning of the world must lie outside the world.' And the difference between the two formulations shows clearly the difference between the experience which is most central to *The World as Will and Representation* [Schopenhauer] and the more radical experience that forms the radiating core of the *Tractatus,* the difference, that is, between *apatheia* [which Nieli calls 'ocean-like calmness of the spirit'] and *ekstasis* [which he calls 'mystic-ecstatic state']" (quoted in *Wittgenstein* 105).

Murdoch is quite serious about exploring the possibility of individuals' moving outside the constraints of time and space. Nieli analyzes Wittgenstein's attitude toward Schopenhauer's work, clearing up some of the mystery: "The 'world' Wittgenstein was delineating in the *Tractatus* was just the world one stands outside of (*ek-stasis*) in the mystic flight, the logical system of the *Tractatus* being a precise delineation of the profane world which is left behind in the transcendental encounter with the Sacred. One might call proposition 6.432—'God does not reveal himself *in* the world'—the *Tractatus* in miniature" (*Wittgenstein* 98). Another crucial sentence in Guy's dialogue—"That one knows anything at all . . . is not guaranteed . . . by the game" (NS 5)—reminds Murdoch's reader that Wittgenstein's legacy has been summed up at times as the belief that language games represent function rather than knowledge. In proposing that Gertrude "hated religion and anything 'mystical'" and that Gertrude "saw Guy's irrationality as something terrifying and almost disgusting, a kind of mental incontinence" (NS 16), the narrator diminishes Gertrude's capacity.

If she were as worried about being labeled a philosophical novelist as Dipple implies, Murdoch could have stopped giving Wittgensteinian attributes to her characters years ago. Something deeper, more imaginative and uncontrolled, is taking place. As Murdoch has indicated in an interview, she leaves the character development to her imagination: "For me a novel begins in a great cauldron of ideas and images, impulses and feelings" (Heusel, "Dialogue" 9). "I don't write anything," she says, "until I have invented the whole thing. Until it is all there, I would not write the first sentence. . . . But I think the period of reflection—when one has nothing, except notes, of course, to remind one— is very important; it's a kind of deep free reflection which may be more difficult later on. . . . [I]f you get hold of a good character, he will invent himself" ("Dialogue" 4). I take the phrase "will invent himself" literally. To the extent that she allows her characters to do so, Murdoch relinquishes control of any Wittgensteinian characteristics, so that such characteristics come from the depth of her imagination.

Murdoch began the 1980s with a novel that shows the mysteries of life instead of saying them. Her characters in *Nuns and Soldiers* use puzzling language games—which Murdoch develops through specialized narrative strategies—in a playful, postmodern, and indeterminate way. Wittgenstein's aesthetic method is an especially valuable approach to considering the constellation of language games at the opening of the novel. Murdoch invites the reader to place side by side several alternate readings of those language games in order to experience the process of writing, reading, and interpreting simultaneously. The reader can participate in the writer's and the critic's explorations, demonstrating that one person's language game is always the grist for someone else's critical mill. This process both illustrates Wittgenstein's view that a series of notations representing a series of perspectives will help perceptive beings see how a language game like Guy's functions and reinforces the truism that, as individuals mature day by day and change perspectives, they often change their minds. In the process of applying Wittgenstein's aesthetic model, I will explore alternatives rather than attempting to prove a theory— or to force examples into any preconceived categories.

Veering off slightly from the usual kind of word child she has been creating—a linguist manqué in *A Word Child* or a writer in *The Black Prince* and *The Sea, The Sea*—Murdoch creates a philosopher-dilettante whose hallucinations show her interest in the way the brain functions when people grow old or become ill. She takes a postmodern turn in giving the reader three or four protagonists and in proposing indeterminate outcomes and ambivalent evidence. This technique is not new, as I will show in my discussion of *An Accidental Man* in chapter 5, but in *Nuns and Soldiers* she combines it with a positive touch.

In an open, novelistic world, Murdoch constructs a new niche, or stratum, for characters who are charismatics or mystics. How appropriate that she launch it with the word *Wittgenstein*, the first word of *Nuns and Soldiers*. Lightheartedly playing her most elliptical game with the reader yet, Murdoch opens *Nuns and Soldiers* with a dying patriarch who chants seemingly incomprehensible prophecy. Perhaps, because the play in this novel is free and indeterminate, what Guy says is less important than that he is a new kind of character for Murdoch. The novel's first five pages, an apparently incoherent conversation, announce that the issue of language as communication underlies her more obvious issues: the mystery of love, suffering, and death. Less obvious is whether anyone is in control of these issues. Guy, an Anglicanized Jew, now agnostic, conveys his love and wisdom in his last three conversations but does not communicate his final revelation to the other characters. The reader is on her own.

Not feeling it necessary to produce authenticity, autonomy, or unity, Murdoch sets up in these first few pages a network of reverberating fragments of language that allows the novel to structure itself through accretion around the puzzlement of the other characters, suggesting a socially constructed self located within networks of discourse. The reader must puzzle out what it is that Guy, with his convoluted terms, intends to convey to his survivors. The same sort of freedom is in evidence in her twenty-fourth novel, *The Message to the Planet*; the same question may be asked of Marcus Vallar, the (perhaps) mad professor in that book. In *Nuns and Soldiers*, Murdoch gives the reader, as well as the characters, the opportunity to search inductively for clues that might unravel Guy's puzzling prophecy. Juxtaposing the two novels raises certain questions: Why give the reader this responsibility? Why does Murdoch repeat the process ten years later when she introduces Marcus? Perhaps she wants to understand, to feel these states on which she concentrated during that decade. She did study Eastern religion and practice meditation. Perhaps she also uses feminist narrative strategies to disrupt and subvert the traditional realistic stance.

Marcus, the mystery man of the later novel, has more space and time to develop a personality and a puzzling prophecy of his own. As linguist, painter, indignant father, and charismatic leader, Marcus confuses the minds and engages the hearts of hundreds of people. His faithful servant Ludens, an Oxford history professor, plans to record for posterity all of Marcus's moves—that is, until the psychiatrist Marzillian demands silence. The reader shares Ludens's shock on discovering that a lifelong project to which he has already given too much time is to be silenced. Ludens, along with the reader, wonders: Does history demand a forum? Is the public sphere more important than the private?[6] Assuming that the solution to the riddle of life lies outside the world, Ludens, when he hears Marcus's voice on tape after Marcus has died, says to Marzillian that he wonders if Marcus had discovered "the formula, the message to the planet, the universal understanding" (MP 508). Ludens explains that at first Marcus searched for an original language, but eventually he settled for the universal language of pain. Deciding that "the meaning of [pain] lies beyond," just as Murdoch says value does, Ludens repeats the phrase "the murmur of contingency" (MP 509).

This phrase describes the same sort of mystery Murdoch was getting at in Guy's murmurings about "the upper side of the cube." A few sentences earlier, Guy questioned the whereabouts of Gerald, the astronomer of the family: "Gerald talks about the cosmos, but that's impossible, you can't talk about everything. That one knows anything at all . . . is not guaranteed . . . by the game" (NS 5) In *The Message to the Planet*, Ludens finds that Marcus talks "as if the planet, talking to itself, cries out and complains. Perhaps when distant people on other planets pick up some wave-length of ours all they hear is a continuous scream. Anyway, what Marcus was uttering certainly sounded like a human language, something which made sense. Perhaps he had passed some barrier—he was talking in a sort of dreamy reflective tone, not like someone frightened or hysterical" (MP 509). One implication is that Marcus had communicated with creatures from another planet.

It would be instructive to keep Marzillian's response to Ludens in mind while surveying possible solutions to the strange language spoken a decade earlier by Guy: "I doubt if what we have just heard . . . will enable us to look beyond that barrier, if indeed such a barrier exists. You spoke of a continuous scream. Saint Paul spoke of the whole of creation groaning and travailing in pain" (MP 509). These mystics, expressly Marcus and his student Ludens, have a goal: perhaps they are looking for their Jewish heritage. Murdoch's humor—Marzillian's having only vestiges of language with which to talk about such phenomena, the cores having been destroyed by modern science—emphasizes the human dilemma: "As I have said to you before, our knowledge of the soul, if I may use that unclinical but essential word, encounters certain seemingly impassable limits, set there perhaps by the gods, if I may refer to them, in order to preserve their privacy, and beyond which it may be not only futile but lethal to attempt to pass—and though it is our duty to seek for knowledge, it is also incumbent on us to realise when it is denied us, and not to prefer a fake solution to no solution at all" (MP 509). Murdoch explores the strange and wonderful eccentricities of human beings by having these two characters recognize that fundamental questions remain unanswered and that Marcus continues to remain a mystery.

What becomes clear in Murdoch's later novel, she has already established in the earlier one—that the phrases the men radiate have different meanings in different contexts. Perhaps readers of *Nuns and Soldiers* are asking the wrong questions if they press for the meaning of the swan and the cube. Wittgenstein has taught readers to rephrase the questions and to ask how the language functions rather than trying to decipher what it symbolizes. Murdoch's stories function to bring the group of characters together; within the story, her people struggle to communicate, using language as a tool. What Guy says is important because the reader has implicitly agreed to play this game by the rules. The process of asking certain questions is central, then, to reading *Nuns and Soldiers*: How many of Murdoch's scholars, teachers, and/or philosophers have messages for the planet? How many have messages for other planets? How many communicate their messages? Do the messages function as prophecies? Hypothesizing answers seems, in this post-Wittgensteinian age, more valuable than the kind of mere symbol hunting Murdoch sees as wasteful if not destructive.

In *The Message to the Planet*, the message functions as the sacred Hebraic word for God. In one ear the reader hears silence, and in the other, the reader hears alternative guesses. Marcus talks in a language no linguist can recognize; Ludens reveals that Marcus had wanted to discover the universal language.

The tone here is much different from the one Murdoch uses when she sardonically mentions Hilary Burde's illusions about finding a universal language. *A Word Child* is a dark and sophisticated novel, and *The Message to the Planet* has not yet won high marks for being either dark or sophisticated, but in each novel Murdoch examines and illustrates the Wittgensteinian phrase, "The only useful philosophy is death."

The dying words of Marcus and those of Guy generate radically different effects within their respective novels.[7] As kind and intelligent as Guy is, he has little effect on the other characters after his death; Marcus, as strange and enigmatic as he is, does have a lasting effect. In each novel the community continues to speculate on the meaning of otherworldly comments. In the earlier text, the Count is the wretched follower who will be left behind, as Ludens is when Marcus dies. Marcus dies thinking of the Holocaust; Guy, in sleep or thinking of "'the ring' and 'logical space' and 'the upper side of the cube' and 'the white swan' . . . [and] Heidegger and Wittgenstein" (NS 99).

Into Guy's seemingly incoherent language transactions, Murdoch weaves a mysterious pattern that his wife describes as "spells or charms." Guy's first conversation is with his most intimate male friend, Peter (the Count). The Count and Gertrude, in awe of Guy's condition, try to decipher Guy's use of three expressions: "the white swan," "the ring," and "the upper side of the cube." Gertrude speaks first in this decidedly stichomythic dialogue:

"Did you have the white swan?"
"No."
"Or 'She sold the ring'?"
"Yes."
"What's that?"
"I don't know—"
"Who—what ring—oh God. The upper side of the cube?"
"Yes."
"What is this cube?"
"I don't know," said the Count. "It could be something in presocratics."
"Have you looked?"
"Yes. I'll look again."
"Or about painting?"
"Could be." (NS 16)

This conversation sets up a treasure trove of historical and cultural associations and an abundantly rich intertextuality. The characters think, at the end of the novel, that they have found the meaning of the references to the ring and the upper side of the cube, but even if the reader accepts the characters' answers, he or she is still left to explain the relation of the white swan to the other terms. If one were tempted to study Murdoch's perspective on mythology in order to find a key to understanding Guy's otherwise cryptic references, such an analysis of these language fragments might point obliquely to Tim.

What follows is a series of potential interpretations. Anne, Gertrude's most intimate friend, provides the first tempting clue to Murdoch's puzzle when she realizes that Guy's allusion to the ring—"she sold the ring, she should have kept the ring" (NS 477)—is to Shakespeare. In *The Merchant of Venice*, Jessica gives up her birthright for love, escaping her patriarch with a casket of gold and jewels. Shylock later discovers that she has exchanged the ring that Shylock's wife gave him for a monkey. Gertrude supplies the information that Guy, a Jew, identified with Shylock, feeling "that one day he would have to drop everything and run" (NS 477). The reader begins to suspect that Guy's words are part of a love game. The Shakespeare play is about unexpected marriages as well as about mystery: Jessica has eloped with her father's money and without his consent. Guy knew that Gertrude herself would be free to dispose of her wedding ring after his death. Since Murdoch reiterates several times that Guy thinks of both Gertrude and Tim, her subsequent young husband, as children, the reader has reason to suspect that Guy fears Gertrude will exchange her wedding ring, her beautiful married life, for a monkey—Tim. If nothing else is clear, Guy does focus on Jewish birthright. Because they look through only one lens, logic, these other characters miss Guy's meaning. Perhaps equally clearly, the other characters misinterpret language games.

Murdoch is most enigmatic about the third piece of the puzzle: the characters never figure out what Guy means when he says, "Hey, hey, the white swan" (NS 70). One might assume that the comment simply signals a hallucination and is therefore meaningless in the Murdochian scheme—or is a trick to mislead the reader. But does Murdoch mislead her readers? She often sets up mysterious patterns that appear to lead nowhere. The White Swan is a popular name for pubs in Britain, and the novel's references to the white swan as a pub makes the reader think of Tim, the major pub-crawler in the novel.

In a talk with Anne, Gertrude recalls having occasionally heard Guy mention the white swan in connection with a pub (NS 104).

Traditionally the mythological swan is a symbol of love and lust, and the reader knows that Tim had been interested in the subject of Leda and the swan before Guy died. When Tim receives his commission from Gertrude to go to France to paint, he leaves her his painting *Leda and the Swan*, a painting Guy may well have seen in his unofficial role as Tim's patron. Later, when Tim and Gertrude become reconciled in their marriage, Tim begins drawing "on graph paper, a series of compositions of Leda and the swan. The battling struggling bodies, Leda's thighs, her breasts, her head bent forward or thrown wildly back, the swan's slim curving neck, his beating wings and powerful feet, these forms in prolific developing patterns emerged out of a background which he began more and more to think of as determined, and he worked at them in a kind of furious obedience" (NS 475–76). This rush of images suggests that Murdoch sometimes experiences writing in this dynamic way.

Tim obviously feels he is being driven by some source beyond himself to work out through swan imagery the sensuality he has experienced with Gertrude. Murdoch's echo of the fragments of W. B. Yeats's "Leda and the Swan"—"beating wings," "thighs," and "breast"—suggests the mythical power of the god Eros and the prophetic power of the poet. Such allusiveness suggests that Tim's otherwise inexplicable new inspiration might have come from Eros by way of his mentor Guy or by way of Gertrude.

As he dies, Guy is obviously concentrating on ways he can free Gertrude from mourning. Knowing that she is still young and healthy, he celebrates her potentially fruitful life after his death, so much that he laments the present state of their relationship. During his conversation with the Count, he bewails the power of death and the gifts it takes with it: "Sex goes, you know. A dying man with sexual desire—that would be obscene—" (NS 3). He demonstrates that he has now chosen to read poetry that has themes analogous to his situation as parting and, finally, separated lover. Because he knows that the men in Gertrude's social circle will vie for her hand when he is gone, he sees himself in the position of Odysseus returned from his wanderings and eventually in the position of the knight in "The Twa Corbies." Guy begins to draw these parallels when he tells the Count that he needs no other reading material than the *Odyssey*, explaining it will "see me out" (NS 4). The Count carries the analogy further. He suddenly realizes after his conversation with Guy that the dying man, by calling himself Odysseus, was referring to "setting sail upon his last journey and [that] he would not return again to his house and his home. And Penelope. . . . Penelope and the suitors! The siege of Penelope by the suitors; but no master ever to return now to claim his true wife. She was to be the prey of lesser men" (NS 43).

Later, as Guy encourages Gertrude to admit that no one exists after death, he recites to her the Scottish ballad, hoping to make her see the pragmatism of taking another mate: "In that future when I won't exist any more. There won't be any me any more and long grief will be stupid. People mourn because they think it does some good, it's a kind of tribute. But there's no recipient. 'Many a one for him makes moan, but none shall know where he is gone! . . . His lady's ta'en another mate'" (NS 96). In encouraging Gertrude to marry again and be happy, he reminds her that the Count loves her and proposes that the Count would be a natural successor as husband. But Guy is farsighted enough to leave the door open for an unexpected suitor who might catch her fancy: "Heaven knows what will happen to you next year. It may be something entirely unexpected [next year is a week away]. But I so much . . . want you to be . . . safe . . . and happy . . . when I'm not around" (NS 97). Only Guy, then, a man who has moved beyond the concerns of the ordinary world, can eschew rational and conventional stereotypes. As soothsayer, he attempts to free Gertrude to communicate her sensuality, even to a man who is much younger than herself and who is economically outside her flock of appropriate suitors. The extremes in Gertrude's experiences allow her to move from a marital relationship with an Apollonian father figure to a marital relationship with a younger, decidedly Dionysian man. The swan references are quite hedonistic, emphasizing drinking and mysteriously sensuous eroticism.

Underlying the novel's overt allusions, a substructure of more subtle classical and Renaissance allusions creates a network of equivocal and mythical crosscurrents. Some Murdoch does not define precisely, such as the connection between the picture of Leda and the Wittgensteinian network pictures on which Tim works next. Murdoch draws another parallel of which Guy may be unaware: his position is that of a dying Apollo metamorphosing into a swan, hence the refrain, "Hey, hey, the white swan." As a metaphor for Guy himself, the swan echoes Horace's "Ode II, XX," in which the poet metamorphoses into a swan as he is dying. By associating himself with Apollo's bird, Horace identifies with the god of music, poetry, art, and prophecy. Furthermore, by identifying with Apollo he identifies with Apollo's messenger, the Delphic oracle, who chants a cryptic prophecy. If Murdoch is proposing, then, that the enigmatic words of Guy are the prophecy of a dying poet, that prophecy provides a piece the reader needs to put Murdoch's puzzle together.

Murdoch employs bizarre imagery to reinforce the idea that the chanting priest is indeed metamorphosing. In his conversation with Anne, Guy has begun to change physically: "Anne took hold of the thin papery hand, feather-light in her strong grasp" (NS 70). Literally the emaciated hand is lightweight, but at a figurative level Guy simulates the feathered swan, mute until he is dying.[8] Suspended between life and death, he prophesies both mystical and obvious things to come: Gertrude will marry Tim; Guy himself will move into the upper side of the cube; individuals will find that death is simply the termination of life.

Guy, patriarch, scholar, and author, paradoxically has not been silent in the past, and at his death he may as well have remained mute because his potential listeners are too caught up in life to hear his prophecy. He, like the oracle at Delphi or like Wittgenstein, pours forth truths and refuses to explain, since truth must be shown, not said. His line "Hey, Hey, the white swan" is comparable to a refrain from a ballad intended to be his swan song. By alluding to the swan, Murdoch metaphorically relates the creativity of Guy and Tim: the swan references combine the aggressiveness of Zeus dramatized in "Leda and the Swan" with the prophetic power of Apollo. The mythological swan, however, has a certain ambivalence, like Murdoch's playfulness. Because it evokes not only the aggressiveness of Zeus but the beauty of Venus, Murdoch can use it to tie Gertrude, the third member of the triangle, into the motif. In addition to being beautiful and erotic, she is twice a bride. Murdoch may also have had in mind the *Prothalamion*, in which Edmund Spenser imagines the two brides, Lady Elizabeth and Lady Katherine Somerset, changing into swans.

Once the language games played by characters, author, and reader become evident, there should be no question about why Murdoch opens *Nuns and Soldiers* with the name of a philosopher who says that the only useful philosophy is death. Her strategic placement of Wittgenstein's name raises a question that prepares the reader for the mysterious insight of a character much influenced by the philosopher's language theories. If, as the other characters assume, Guy begins his conversation with the name *Wittgenstein* in order to demote the philosopher to amateur status, a question arises: Why would Guy want to discredit a man he had formerly admired? Perhaps the Count was correct in thinking that Guy "needed to feel that Wittgenstein too would not survive" (NS 1). The irony Murdoch creates by having Guy demean the philosopher and at the same time encase his devaluation in Wittgensteinian conceptions is double-edged. Guy pigeonholes Wittgenstein's outlook as a "naive and touching belief in the power of pure thought" (NS 1). He must be referring to the *Tractatus* when he adds, "Linguistic idealism [is a] dance of bloodless categories" (NS 2). But the reader can see from Murdoch's interest in Guy's mysterious terms that she is intending more. Since Guy later expresses his belief that all men should be judged, and because Murdoch compares Guy to Apollo the poet-prophet, the reader can assume that Guy's demotion of Wittgenstein does not simply result from irritability or hallucination.

Questions of demotion aside, the reader can assume that Guy may be singing a prophetic truth, since Murdoch considers accepting the reality of death the locus around which the rest of a good life moves. Similarly, for Wittgenstein, once the obvious fact of death dominates man's attention, the rational grids he has applied to reality fast become nonsense. As he is dying, he says to the Count:

"How much I wish I could—"
"Could—?"
"See it—"
"See?"
"See it . . . the whole . . . of logical space . . . the upper side . . . of the cube." (NS 5–6)

The experience of dying is releasing Guy from the language game of logic. Murdoch hints that Guy, at moments, crosses the barrier between life and death. Since Wittgenstein never recorded having had such an experience, Guy concludes that he is one up on the philosopher, for he has become the soothsayer.

On the other hand, perhaps Murdoch is questioning Guy's sanity. Other word children worry about sanity, and other characters are often concerned about the sanity of a loved one. Murdoch's readers must not ignore Wittgenstein's fear of insanity. Nieli suggests that Wittgenstein, fearing his own inwardness and solipsism, focused on public discourse and public activities: "His

A Word Child, Nuns and Soldiers, and The Sea, The Sea

defense of common-sense and ordinary language was at least partially motivated by a desire to direct the mind away from its own depth and inwardness, which was sensed as potentially dangerous. . . . This obsessive pre-occupation with the external, one might say, is the price of psychic stability; a neurotic form of existence is set forth as a defense against the greater threat of psychotic disintegration and chaos" (*Wittgenstein* 219–20).

In addition to the concepts of death and sanity, particular philosophical analysis may be relevant here as well. Wittgenstein's use of cube illustrations would perhaps be known only to the Count, with whom Guy has been having philosophical conversations. Guy could be referring to Wittgenstein's exploration of perception and cognition and a specific cube illustration, such as the final one in *Philosophical Investigations* (2:193). Before discussing the different aspects that a cube illustration might take on, Wittgenstein refers to the now-familiar duck-rabbit drawing from *Fact and Fable in Psychology*. Exploring the question "Could there be human beings lacking in the capacity to see something *as something* . . . ?" Wittgenstein decides to call such a lack "aspect-blindness" (PI. 2:213). In discussing the important connection "between the concepts of 'seeing an aspect' and 'experiencing the meaning of a word'" (PI. 2:214), he employs an illustration of a cube. He asks, "Ought [the aspect-blind man] to be able to see the schematic cube as a cube? . . . But for him it would not jump from one aspect to the other." To illustrate this point, he demonstrates that in a picture of a cube, "appearing in several places in a book, . . . something different is in question every time: here a glass cube, there an inverted open box, there a wire frame of that shape, there three boards forming a solid angle. Each time the text supplies the interpretation of the illustration" (PI. 2:193). He says he "must distinguish between the 'continuous seeing' of an aspect and the 'dawning' of an aspect" (PI. 2:194). Toward the end of this discussion he asks, about the process of changing aspects, "Was it *seeing* or was it thought?" (PI. 2:204). If Guy looked at one of these illustrations, he could not see the upper side of the cube because the upper side is not illustrated. Murdoch, being interested in the dawning of an aspect and in aspect-blindness, might well be examining the questions of whether Guy is any more or less aspect-blind than the novel's other characters. Similarly, the reader of *The Message to the Planet* might ask whether Marcus is more or less aspect-blind than that novel's other characters. By raising such questions, Murdoch creates dialogism.

Much of the rest of the conversation between Guy and the Count also echoes Wittgenstein's ideas in *Philosophical Investigations*. But Guy's remarks are ambiguous and may be taken several ways. Like Wittgenstein, Guy discredits the delusions of philosophers, uses the term *language game* (NS 3), accepts the incomprehensibility of the universe, and sees death as an obvious fact. Before he comes to these positions, however, he makes fun of language games in his phrase "language games, funeral games" and dismisses Wittgenstein's prophetic sense, since he thought man would never travel to the moon. But ultimately Guy realizes that death, when it comes, dominates man's attention and gives him a new perspective. Guy's statement, "Death drives away what rules everywhere else, the aesthetic" (NS 3), is his negative response to Schopenhauer's optimism, which he ridicules: "To see the world without desire is to see its beauty. The beautiful makes happy" (NS 2). Guy eventually accepts such a Buddhist-like attitude: when it comes, he is at ease with death, and he recognizes his connection to Schopenhauer and Wittgenstein.

Before reaching this stage, Guy lists the ways he can think of to depreciate Wittgenstein's contribution. From a scientific perspective he judges harshly the philosopher's inability to imagine that science could conquer space and get to the moon (NS 4). Guy is clearly focusing on space and man's effort to comprehend it. There may be another mysterious space that man cannot know—unless he is leaving terrestrial limits. Murdoch purposely juxtaposes at this point two beliefs: Guy's humble Wittgensteinian understanding that human beings can know only a small part of reality, and the scientist's faith in his ability to know all through logic alone. In proposing that many of the mysteries of life can be shown only, not said, Guy points to his own muteness as prophet while also echoing propositions 5–6.522 of the *Tractatus*: "There are . . . things that cannot be put into words. They make themselves manifest. They are what is mystical."

Before he is comfortable with the mystery of the world, Guy uses a seemingly incoherent phrase, "language games, funeral games" (NS 3), juxtaposing the logic game that Wittgenstein says philosophers play (and that Guy says Schopenhauer, Mauthner, and Karl Kraus play) and the game Guy is now playing: the game of dying. Murdoch makes economical use of Guy's phrase, tying together the marriage theme and the language theme by echoing Hamlet's comment to Horatio about Gertrude's sudden lustful marriage to a man less noble than the elder Hamlet: "Thrift, thrift, Horatio! the funeral bak'd meats / Did coldly furnish forth the marriage table" (I.ii.179–80). Murdoch demonstrates here that Guy is thinking simultaneously of death, lust, and the inability to communicate through language. Such intertextuality raises the question whether Guy is as conscious as Murdoch that Gertrude's name echoes that of Hamlet's mother.

In this first conversation, Guy reflects not only Wittgenstein's theories but his view of human life: a meaningless universe peopled by illusion-creating individuals. The reader infers Guy's attitude from a series of negative statements, some puzzling, some clearly Wittgensteinian: "She shouldn't have sold the ring" (NS 5); "Everything's gone wrong since Aristotle, we can see why now. Liberty died with Cicero" (NS 5); "I used to believe my thoughts would wander in infinite spaces, but that was a dream" (NS 5); and the Count's paraphrase of Guy's comment that "death is supposed to show us truth, but is its own place of illusion" (NS 1). Guy's statements in his last two conversations are also negative. He tells Anne that Christianity is "a lie. There are final conclusions, one is shortly to be reached in this house" (NS 66). He addresses Gertrude in a similar way: "In that future . . . I won't exist any more" (NS 96). Guy speaks for Murdoch when he says that his philosophical study has convinced him that death is the end and that all is vanity, since for her, as for Plato—and Wittgenstein—"[philosophy] is the study of death" (SG 68).

Murdoch's ironic language games put in play this mysterious character who uses Wittgenstein's contentions to discredit Wittgenstein. Because Guy has constructed his philosophy on the inevitability of death, he is free to voice elliptical insights that may go beyond ordinary human understanding. He not only prophesies then that Gertrude will marry Tim but predicts that death is the end, that his thoughts will not "wander in infinite spaces" (NS 5). Perhaps the Count is right: Guy "needed to feel that Wittgenstein too would not survive" (NS 1). Most conspicuously in *The Sea, The Sea*, whose protagonist is a novelist-narrator, Murdoch argues that a reader must be wary of any artist's language. Always juggling the perspectives of Plato and Freud on an artist's reasons for creating, comparing them with her own, she allows her first-person protagonist enough rope to hang himself. She has said in her philosophy that because language is imprecise, abstract, and ambiguous, all language users tend to lie unwittingly. In *The Fire and the Sun* she paraphrases Plato: "Human beings are natural liars, and sophists and artists are the worst" (42). Murdoch admits that "language transcends its user, meanings are ambiguous, words are clarified through discrimination" (MGM 193–94). The language user who attempts to transform subjective inner data into novelistic form most often finds numerous opportunities for distortion. The transaction is a three-step process: words written for the public are twice removed from the experience itself. First, after having an experience, the language user imagines abstract images and/or says abstract words to him- or herself. Then, in order to convey these conceptions to someone else, the language user casts them in words whose meaning the public will agree on. But anyone hearing the words has a different history and, therefore, a different perspective on or context for those words. Since words are not actual names of the objects they represent, misinterpretation frequently occurs.

The Sea, The Sea is arguably a novel about the way that writing novels is a form of wish fulfillment. This novel's emphasis is not on Charles Arrowby's thoughts and perceptions but rather on the language games he uses to describe them. Murdoch creates a character whose mind is a cave, and she gives the reader clear indications that her own language games and narrative strategies are to be distinguished from her protagonist's. Her own function is to set this story in the broader context of Plato's cave myth and Shakespeare's *Tempest* and to juxtapose the necessary and the contingent, the real and the deceptive. The novel demonstrates the way a mind works when it insists on rationalizing rather than on simply processing materials—the space between perception and cognition. Insofar as all human beings are victims of illusions, Charles is typical. Often the protagonist's visual equipment records the real but his mind substitutes imagery he would prefer to see, and furthermore, when he writes down the material he distorts reality again. His interior monologue shows how thoroughly he is bewitched by his own narrow perspective on life. With his giant ego and small character, his selfishness and his sexism, this Prospero manqué is bright enough to recognize that his language, his motives, and his life are all in question. This rich intertexuality frees Murdoch to introduce voices that Charles remembers from the public arena and many voices he hears coming from deep within his own mind.

Within Murdoch's exploration of the kind of deceptive language that artists, being like everyone else, employ to fool themselves and their readers about their intentions, Charles spends most of the novel deciding where to focus his mind's eye and deciding how to organize his book. Charles does not have writer's block but myopia—a condition Wittgenstein might think of as viewing reality through one lens only. Apparently, as Charles grew from childhood to adulthood without ever maturing, his imagination used all its energy to defend his existence. Because his imagination has had to work overtime at this exclusively personal level, worrying about and defending Charles, he is oblivious to most phenomena outside his body. To get Charles's attention, Murdoch must create bizarre occurrences in the novel, the noise of poltergeists and the appearances of monsters.

Murdoch gives Charles considerable control over his ramblings, in his imagination and along the seaside; his interminable wandering must be annoying even to Murdoch. As a first-person narrator, Charles is responsible for recording reality in what he first considers his memoirs, and he wants to do so in his book within Murdoch's book, but he has trouble finding any reality to record. His mind furnishes old pictures of people in his past, or old versions of them keep popping up to mask the real people in his present life. Unlike Hilary, the great fantasizer Charles, because of his need to write down his experience, reveals many more voices or aspects of his character in his fantasies, his barely hidden wishes. Murdoch makes her job doubly difficult by letting such a narrator escape her control, but she seems to relish her struggle: keeping Charles working at his book and keeping him out of serious trouble—that is, committing murder or being murdered.

She prepares the reader immediately to recognize Charles's tendency to use language to distort the reality of the natural phenomena he investigates. His language games block out reality, keeping it safely hidden below the surface. This distortion helps explain her focusing on water imagery and the seaside setting. Charles transcribes his memoirs, or penseés, against a background of simple, sensuous descriptions of weather and scenery, but ironically, he fails to see the dangers in the reality surrounding him. His style as he opens his book is reminiscent of Matthew Arnold's "Dover Beach"; Arnold and Murdoch both recognize the scene's inherent complexity, but Charles seemingly does not; he merely records the surface beauty of the sea. Murdoch's placement of this first paragraph of the novel, which follows the heading "Prehistory," calls attention to Charles's hints that, below what he calls the "surface skin of colour," lies unrecognized disaster. Charles's writing is a good example of dialogism; the voices continue to compete, with none becoming dominant:

> The sea which lies before me as I write glows rather than sparkles in the bland May sunshine. With the tide turning, it leans quietly against the land, almost unflecked by ripples or by foam. Near to the horizon it is a luxurious purple, spotted with irregular lines of emerald green. At the horizon it is indigo. Near to the shore, where my view is framed by rising heaps of humpy yellow rock, there is a band of lighter green, icy and pure, less radiant, opaque however, not transparent. We are in the north, and the bright sunshine cannot penetrate the sea. . . . [The sky's] blue gains towards the zenith and vibrates there. But the sky looks cold, even the sun looks cold. (SS 1)

In the second paragraph, his comments on a contingency that disturbs nature introduce a sudden change in style and tone, again reminiscent of Arnold's poem: "I had written the above, destined to be the opening paragraph of my memoirs, when something happened which was so extraordinary and so horrible that I cannot bring myself to describe it even now after an interval of time" (SS 1). Charles's creation of suspense elicits a dynamic response from the reader.

It takes four pages of talk about egoism and discipline, autobiography and cookbooks for Charles to record the rest of the coastline he sees from his "sea-facing window" (SS 2). By this time the reader is quite annoyed. Charles musters his most bureaucratic newspeak: "The above observations have been written on a sequence of different days" (SS 4). A feature of the coastline that he misses on his initial look portends danger:

> Here and there the water has worn the rocks into holes, which I would not dignify with the name of caves, but which, from the swimmer's-eye-view, present a striking and slightly sinister appearance. At one point, near to my house, the sea has actually composed an arched bridge of rock under which it roars into a deep open steep-sided enclosure beyond. It affords me a curious pleasure to stand upon this bridge and watch the violent forces which the churning waves, advancing or retreating, generate within the confined space of the rocky hole. (SS 5)

Employing *sinister*, *violent*, and *churning*, Murdoch subtly creates the discrepancy that prepares the reader to recognize the cave as a metaphor for Charles's mind and the wildness of the sea as a metaphor for his unconscious. Murdoch sets his busy inner life in a quiet village where the inhabitants insist that it is foolhardy to swim and where Charles metaphorically drowns and Titus, his would-be lover's son, literally drowns. The placid imagery represents Charles's overblown illusions about his ability to escape his stance as director of the theater and change himself into a disciplined, humble, moral human being. His running away is reminiscent of Wittgenstein's various attempts to change his occupation and do something he thought more useful than philosophy: "Now I shall abjure magic and become a hermit: put myself in a situation where I can honestly say that I have nothing else to do but to learn to be good" (SS 2), as if learning such a lesson will be easy. Charles's eyes see, but his consciousness does not register the complexity and danger of the sea before him or of the life before him.

Charles has had opportunities to discover the dangerous realities of existence. After spending all his adult years in playacting, he knows intellectually that "the theatre is certainly a place for learning about the brevity of human glory: oh all those wonderful glittering absolutely vanished pantomimes!" (SS 1–2). Charles is also realistic in recording the purple, indigo, blue, silver, and emerald green of the sea. But Murdoch suggests in Charles's opening paragraph that he is incapable of penetrating the "surface skin" of this beauty and perceiving the mystery and complexity at the depths of human reality. Her language in this passage suggests not only that Charles has a tunnel-like perspective but that, because of middle age, his eyes do not focus quickly from figure to ground and he needs reading glasses: "Near to the shore, . . . my view *is framed by* rising heaps of humpy yellow rock" (SS 1; emphasis added). Murdoch has him describe atmospheric conditions in a way that suggests his own state of mind; he is so confused that no insights could penetrate the chaos, any more than "the bright sunshine [could] penetrate the sea" (SS 1). The reader sees how distraught Charles is when immediately, in the second paragraph, he digresses from the plan of his memoir. By recording even his stream-of-consciousness interruptions, he at first teases the reader into believing that he is a writer who wants to get down to the whole truth, including these hidden psychological digressions. Charles's mind is so obtuse, however, that the reader soon understands how unlikely he is to pursue truth seriously, let alone successfully.

His juxtaposing a calm view of the sea and the mysterious references to a disturbing hallucination plants the idea that he could be a man close to the brink of madness. Charles has seen, rising out of the sea, a sea monster that is apparently the embodiment of his worst enemy, the vast egoism he will be unable to drown simply by willing it to happen. Murdoch's strategies for maneuvering Charles's complex inner processes suggest she is anticipating his final moral change.[9] Charles does realize eventually that what his cousin James says is true: human beings become monsters for themselves and each other. Charles's re-creation of his monstrous vision and one of his interpretations of that vision provide an emphasis, unconsciously male, on the rising of a phallic, red, snakelike creature:

> Just before I saw my huge monster I had been closely inspecting, in the rock pool, a little monster, the red bristling worm, whose five or six inches of wriggling body appeared big in the confined space of the pool. Was it possible that through some purely optical mechanism, some unusual trick of the retina, I had "thrown" the image of the worm out onto the surface of the sea? This was an interesting idea but totally implausible, since the red worm bore no resemblance to the bluish-blackish monster, except in so far as both of them had wreathed into coils. Besides, I had never heard of any such retinal "cinematography." (SS 20–21)

Murdoch allows for numerous readings by suggesting all the possibilities of phallocentric epistemology: optics, optical illusion, myopia, cinema, and Wittgensteinian aspect-blindness. Even as he uses fairly dynamic, almost violent language, Charles attempts to convert this forceful scene, this confrontation between a Prospero and a Caliban, into a cerebral topic for reflection. But if sight, in the post-Lockean schema, is the most useful faculty of human beings, then Charles is in trouble because of his myopia. The Freudian contradictions in his language are again apparent when he says, virtually in the same breath, that he came to the sea to "repent of egoism" and that he feels "it is time to *think* about myself at last. . . . I have in fact very little sense of identity" (SS 3). He thinks he is ready to reject his role as a power-crazed Machiavellian sorcerer (SS 183), but doing so will require eschewing his monstrous jealousy, from which he has derived his psychic energy throughout his life. Because he was made to feel that his family was inferior to that of his cousin James, and because, consequently, he has always felt inferior to James, he cannot remember being free to see himself as a whole person.

A Word Child, Nuns and Soldiers, and *The Sea, The Sea*

At first the reader sympathizes with Charles's desire to escape to the sea and rethink his past, delving into the progress of his life from childhood to the present. But the reader soon notices that Murdoch is using the diary technique to demonstrate that writing is only potentially a form of revelation. Charles is using language as a tool that has the potential for helping him discover the reality about himself; his planned quest could make him whole. He lacks, however, the will to get out from under his lifelong illusions and to look at himself as honestly as he believes he is about to do. Life's surprises intrude on his plans.

Charles attempts to order his writing experience by dividing his book into three parts. Whereas Charles announces in the "Prehistory" that his purpose is to write about his affair with Clement, an older woman who helped him become powerful in the theater, the reader hears very little about Clement because Charles begins to realize as he writes that he must work out what occurred in his relationships with his mother and father, with Aunt Estelle and Uncle Abel, and ultimately with James. This analysis of his childhood leads to his need to finish the adolescent relationship he once had with his first love, Hartley. The reader continues to sympathize with Charles as long as he is questing for answers that will solve his problem of identity. The reader begins to distrust Charles's words, however, when he abandons his original rational path in the "History" and frenetically attempts to relive his ancient love affair. The reader does understand, of course, that Charles is predestined to act in a childish manner because, instead of having resolved his past long ago, he has escaped into playacting and directing others' lives.

In inventing intermediate cases of language transactions for Charles, Murdoch gives him a great deal of freedom for interminable digressions. In showing his growth toward maturity, she ranges each set of language games—those for speaking to himself, to the reader, to Hartley—to display the progress Charles makes. Murdoch employs imagery from Plato's myth of the cave to show the stages beyond which Charles, having left the theater, must now go to leave behind his habitual realm of illusion. Murdoch interweaves Platonic stages of moral change and stagecraft metaphors. For example, when Charles feels his world disintegrating because Hartley reveals that she is still married, Murdoch couches even his psychological insights in theatrical metaphors: "A whole world of possibilities gradually folded themselves up, like some trick of stagecraft, quietly collapsing, folding, merging, becoming very small and vanishing" (SS 115). Near the end of the "Prehistory," Charles struggles with the realization that, if his book is to be honest, he must recount those shafts of light, or enlightenment, that keep coming to the surface of his mind. The struggle he records as the writer's dilemma is not only concrete but poignant:

> Since I started writing this "book" or whatever it is I have felt as if I were walking about in a dark cavern where there are various "lights," made perhaps by shafts or apertures which reach the outside world. (What a gloomy image of my mind, but I do not mean it in a gloomy sense.) There is among those lights one great light towards which I have been half consciously wending my way. It may be a great "mouth" opening to the daylight, or it may be a hole through which *fires emerge* from the *centre of the earth*. And am I still unsure which it is, and must I now approach in order to find out? This image has come to me so suddenly, I am not sure of what to make out of it. (SS 77; emphasis added)

His next sentence reveals that the "one great light" is his memory of Hartley.

In *Metaphysics as a Guide to Morals*, Murdoch does a thorough job of describing inner chaos and language that comes from mysterious places. Whatever its source for Charles, his descriptions clearly evoke Plato for the reader. In *The Fire and the Sun*, Murdoch explains Plato's ideas about the states of awareness the pilgrim experiences, stages

> whereby the higher reality is studied first in the form of shadows or images. These levels of awareness have . . . objects with different degrees of reality; and to these awarenesses, each with its characteristic mode of desire, correspond different parts of the soul. The lowest part of the soul is egotistic, irrational, and deluded, the central part is aggressive and ambitious, the highest part is rational and good and knows truth which lies beyond all images and hypotheses. (5)

Charles convinces himself that he sincerely believes that he can grow morally, even announcing prematurely on the third page: "There has been a moral change." He recognizes that possibilities for looking out into the real world are presenting themselves to him: the "great 'mouth' opening to the daylight" may swallow him up, "or it may be a hole through which fires emerge from the centre of the earth." These images refer to the memory of his experience with Hartley, with whom he decides, in his next paragraph, he must immediately risk dealing. The reader celebrates here Charles's willingness to court disaster by writing about Hartley, his "alpha and omega" (SS 77). Unfortunately, Charles does not understand, as Murdoch does, that evil is passing on pain to others.

Because a magnificent power is set loose in the universe and because the sea monster is denied his victim, Hartley's son, the innocent Titus, must be sacrificed to the sea. Charles, in contemplating his guilt for the death of Titus, remembers James's implication that individuals become monsters for each other: "My vanity had killed Titus just as James's vanity had killed the sherpa. In each case our weakness had destroyed the thing we love. And now I remembered something else which James had said. White magic is black magic. A less than perfect meddling in the spiritual world can breed monsters for other people, and demons used for good can hang around and make mischief afterwards" (SS 471–72). But the reader realizes later that if Charles really were ready to advance to a new stage as a moral being, he would have reacted differently than he does when he encounters Hartley by chance in the last sentence of "Prehistory." If he had internalized Plato's and Murdoch's advice, he would have been satisfied to cast on Hartley a concentrated, loving regard. He would have studied her external form for what it now is and attempted to chart her mature thinking process and her unique vocabulary. Instead, although he records her form in exactly the same way as he records the form of the sea, he refuses to see that his perspective of both is narrow and superficial.

His distance from Hartley matches the pattern most of his relationships assume: he has learned neither to accept what he sees nor to listen to what other people say. He tends to move into the realm of artifice rather than listening, to think of his acquaintances as characters in a novel; instead of acknowledging the integrity of others, his mind patterns internal dialogues for them. Moreover, he manifests this dishonest behavior in his relationship with Hartley from the day he rediscovers her in the seaside village.

The novel juxtaposes a series of Charles's revelations about the real Hartley and the rationalizations he imposes to preserve his illusions. In his descriptions of his conversations with her, his language games trace the movement of his mind, back and forth between present reality and his illusions in the past. Within the first few hours after he sees her, he reveals a dichotomy in his thinking that continues throughout the book. In the last sentence of his "Prehistory," Murdoch names the paradigm she is illustrating. Charles exclaims as he looks at Hartley, "cowering back against the rock [as Rosina nearly runs her down].... The woman did not resemble Hartley. *She was Hartley*" (SS 110). Murdoch's narrative strategy resembles the perception she frequently calls "a switch of gestalt." Not until the next day does Charles realize that Hartley has aged in the real world just as he has: "She was over sixty, Hartley was over sixty. I had never put it to myself that Hartley too was growing old" (SS 112). His incantation of the statement suggests the difficulty he is having in absorbing this ugly-old-woman image of her. All his adult life he has imagined her as perpetually deerlike—thin and lithe, a runner and rope jumper.

When he is forced to adjust to reality and to realize that she is no longer young and comely, he finds other methods of consolation. Allowing the magnetism of love to divert his reason, he prays for his favorite fantasy: "Let me find Hartley and let her be alone and let her love me and be made happy by me forever.... I went on praying and then in a strange way it was as if I had fallen asleep" (SS 113). No doubt Murdoch has Charles refer to prayer and sleep to inform the reader that instead of holding the obvious firmly in his consciousness, he uses these escapes to help him drift off into wishing, a behavior perhaps similar to writing novels.

Murdoch's sentence structure in the following passage charts the patterns Charles uses when he explains his behavior. The sentence simply and strongly captures reality—"I saw"—and then proposes that the image Charles had been nurturing for years may "perhaps" be destroyed, or may perhaps "hover" interminably in the parallax effect of a kaleidoscope: "I saw: a stout elderly woman in a shapeless brown tent-like dress, holding a shopping bag and working her way, very slowly as if in a dream, along the street, past the Black Lion in the direction of the shop. This figure, which I had so vaguely, idly, noticed before was now utterly changed in my eyes. The whole world has its background. And between me and it there hovered, perhaps for the last time, the vision of a slim long-legged girl with gleaming thighs" (SS 113). If an individual wants enough to see something, the imagination can supply it. Rather than actually being aspect-blind, Charles habitually deludes himself, creating shifts or aspects that are not there.

At their first meeting, Charles is disoriented by his realistic version of Hartley and by her reaction to him. He admits his psychological need to search frenetically "for ways to blend the present with the far past":

> Hartley's face, which now seemed absolutely white, expressed such an appalling terror that I would have felt terrified myself had I not been engaged in some urgent almost mechanical search for "similarities," for ways to blend the present with the far past. Yes, that was Hartley's face, though it was haggard and curiously soft and dry. A sheaf of very fine sensitive wrinkles at the corner of the eye led upwards to the brow and down towards the chin, framing the face like a wreath. There were magisterial horizontal lines upon the forehead and long darkish hairs above the mouth. She was wearing a moist red lipstick and face powder which had caked here and there. . . . But the shape of her face and head and the look of her eyes conveyed something untouched straight from the past into the present. (SS 114)

Charles's eyes and his words record that she is not a pretty sight. But he also records that he is distracted from the reality by an inner need to find resemblances to the youthful image he has cherished for so many years. Since he cannot survive if the fantasy image is obliterated, his imagination searches for methods of preserving it.

One such method is imposing on the consciousness of another either his own feelings and thoughts or those he would prefer the other to have; another method is creating a story about her. In addition, as a playwright-director/word child, he creates others' internal monologues instead of searching to discover what the other is actually experiencing. Only later can he tell the reader ingenuously: "It occurred to me later that I never for a second doubted that her emotion was as strong as my own; although this could well have been otherwise" (SS 115). He recognizes their failure to communicate here: "Speech of any sort seemed the problem, as if we spoke different languages and must teach each other to talk" (SS 115). But ironically he fails to make a concerted effort to discover her vocabulary or her context even when she becomes candid later. He never gives her a chance to tell him who she is.

A characteristic internal monologue juxtaposes two sides of Charles's character: the weakness of his lack of independence and the strength of the fabulation in which he rejects reality. At the time he forces himself on Hartley at her home, he continues to reveal that he has not yet accepted her outward appearance or her state of mind: "I got the shock again of her changed appearance, since [in] my intense and cherishing thought she had become young again" (SS 123).

In his imaginary script, Charles would have Hartley confess that her life has been destroyed because she has not married him. When she says she has had a happy marriage, he moves to a defensive position: he cannot afford to believe that she has experienced a complete life without him. In 1978 some critics did not distinguish between the soap opera they thought Murdoch was writing and the one Charles is writing. Although his mind works in the following passage at confronting reality, his egotistic self drives him to find a fantastic method for survival:

> Something black seemed to threaten me from a little way above my head. She had been happy all these years, yes, why not, and yet I could not believe it, could not bear it. She had existed all these years and our lives were gone. I breathed quickly through my mouth and the darkness went away. I thought, I must be *ingenious*, and the word "ingenious" seemed like a help to me. I must be ingenious and see to it that I do not suffer too much. I must look for some happiness, simply for some comfort, here, ingeniously. (SS 117–18)

Throughout the novel Charles refuses to believe in Hartley's happiness because he must finally win her in order to find his own integrity. Instead of investigating her satisfaction with life, he invents reasons, or language games, to explain why she is lying to him. Rather than accepting her claims and leaving her to continue her life, he plans his "programme for survival": "There was no doubt that I must now somehow contrive to devote the rest of my life to Hartley" (SS 121). With "vistas of madness" opening up before him (SS 118), he demonstrates that he focuses instead within himself: "How was I going to *manage* myself for the rest of my life . . . ?" (SS 119). Of course, his thoroughly selfish plans precipitate pain and, ultimately, disaster for him and for all those around him. The same is true of Bradley Pearson in *The Black Prince*. For both of these characters who are novelists, romantic escapism is, at least initially, basic to novel writing.

As objects of comparison, sometimes Murdoch's characters are similar, being from the same stratum, and sometimes they act as mirrors for other characters. Their language games often work as mirrors also, reverberating now communication, now lack of communication, but always polyphony—the other always looking from a different position. Consistent with her control over the larger issues, Murdoch orchestrates the movement of the novelistic world. She gives her characters the freedom, however, to stray from her paths, to ramble and use their language games for comfort, pretense, and lust.

Murdoch's examination of a mystic and his work with the paranormal in *The Message to the Planet* concludes with a reference to psychotic behavior. Ludens muses further on the word the psychiatrist used: "something about flight, fugue, it's a technical term, it's something desperate people do, when they run away and hide" (MP 562). A standard American dictionary defines *fugue* as "a pathological amnesiac condition during which the patient is apparently conscious of his actions but on return to normal has no recollection of them" and as "a polyphonic musical style or form in which a theme or themes stated sequentially and in imitation are developed contrapuntally." Ludens's reference not only ties together theorizing and flight and equates flight and running away from communication, but, by Murdoch's multivalent usage, gives the reader an obvious indication of her interest in polyphony. The murmur, the message, is obviously important to her. In *Metaphysics as a Guide to Morals*, she uses the term again to celebrate consciousness or "a continuous *sense of orientation*": moral individuals "may entertain a metaphor of a continuous tone, or murmur, or conversation, or perhaps a symphonic binding together of different vibrations" (260).

CHAPTER FOUR

Radical Otherness: *Sartre, Romantic Rationalist; Sovereignty of Good;* and *The Fire and the Sun*

Three philosophical texts that Murdoch wrote before *Metaphysics as a Guide to Morals* use philosophical discourse and literary criticism to interrogate novelistic discourses in general and specifically the novel's need for "the principle of radical otherness" (de Man, *Resistance to Theory* 109). An examination of these texts—*Sartre, Romantic Rationalist* (1953), *The Sovereignty of Good* (1970), and *The Fire and the Sun: Why Plato Banished the Artists* (1977)—written at the same time that Murdoch produced the bulk of her novels, helps demonstrate how radical that otherness is. It has no doubt occurred to readers to ask why these philosophical texts address novel writing. This chapter addresses these issues, including the blending of one discourse into another.

Murdoch's living in two worlds, as Ved Mehta proposes, forces her readers to address the relationship between the discourse of philosophy and that of literature. Murdoch insists that in her writing she can separate the two; what a waste of her time that since the 1950s she has had to defend the need to separate them. Need they be separated? Her interest in the future of morality in the twenty-first century and its importance to humanity has nourished both her novels and her philosophy. Furthermore, this interest situates Murdoch in the contemporary language debates. Her early philosophical essays, written in the 1950s and 1960s, move from exploration of human consciousness, to an emphasis on moral philosophy, to applying such issues to literature. Decades ago, Murdoch was addressing the ancient quarrel between philosophy and art. Her writing characteristically struggles with making sense of the modern cultural process that creates a gigantic distance between the various phenomena of life and representations of them. Before examining her metaphorical use of the cave myth in her novels, her readers, like Murdoch herself, must consider the potential distortions to which both philosophy and art are prone. Perhaps the intersecting discourses become checks on each other.

Murdoch's statements about philosophy in "Metaphysics and Ethics" (1957), for example, show that one of her goals was to investigate potential philosophical voices and their moral concepts: philosophy is studying "the writings of philosophers of the past impartially, and compar[ing] and contrast[ing] them with ourselves. We have not considered the great *variety* of the concepts that make up a morality" (120). Her philosophical texts, as well as her novels from *Under the Net* (1954) to *The Message to the Planet* (1989), have given her the opportunity and the potential vehicles for such consideration. Some critics question whether the novel is the appropriate place to address concepts of ethics and morality; perhaps they find Murdoch's novels philosophical because her characters who experience internal dramas have specific philosophical stances.[1] Still, one does not label Shakespeare a philosophical dramatist for using such a strategy.

Murdoch does not find it a problem that her desire to write about the morality of human beings has drawn her simultaneously to moral philosophy and to novel writing: she manages to maneuver between the Scylla of philosophy and the Charybdis of art, finding the same writing strategy—often the analogical method—equally useful for both. An analogical approach to moral philosophy is useful, perhaps, because creating such philosophy "may involve the making of models and pictures of what different kinds of men are like" (ME 121). This strategy sounds not only strikingly like the process of writing novels but also like Wittgenstein's strategy of comparing "intermediate cases" (PI. 1:122), like an aesthetician who shows examples of good art to a viewer until the viewer begins to value these new works of art (see chapter 2). Even though Murdoch is not discussing novel writing in the following passage, written in 1957, it is clear that her desire and ability to make models and pictures inevitably enrich her fiction as well as her philosophy. The responsibility, if not the fear and trembling, she anticipates in writing any text is obvious: "Man is a creature who makes pictures of himself and then comes to resemble the picture" (ME 122). Such an analysis emphasizes both the narrative and the pictorial quality of her mind. The novel has proved an appropriate vehicle for her interest in morality, perhaps a reason why critics have compared her with George Eliot.

Critics' complaints that Murdoch is a philosophical novelist reflect a semantic problem, one that every writer faces. Perhaps these critics have not considered a post-Wittgensteinian view of the way philosophy works: the same as all other language. The postmodern perspective, for which Wittgenstein paved the way, includes eliminating hierarchy and finding only an arbitrary, at most semantic, difference between philosophy and art. Furthermore, postmodernism contends that all language, including philosophy, produces a surplus of meaning and that it is difficult to distinguish philosophy from art; in fact, as Clifford Geertz points out, all disciplines and all genres have become "blurred" ("Blurred Genres" 516). It may be true that novelists do not argue their philosophies or formulate propositions in their fiction, but texts nevertheless demonstrate the way signification works.[2] Murdoch is not too far from this position when she explains that Plato's separation of the artist and the philosopher was blurred; even though he was himself an artist, Plato distrusted artists and exiled them from his Republic.

She is acutely aware of "'an old quarrel' between philosophy and poetry," a pattern she analyzes in *The Fire and the Sun*. Making a characteristically humble effort to explain why Plato "sneers" at artists, she reveals, at the beginning of this text, her careful evaluation of a movement from art to philosophy. She opens with Plato's statement in the *Republic* about the philosophers being the latecomers, the poets having "existed, as prophets and sages, long before the emergence of philosophers" (quoted in FS 1). She recognizes that it was poets, Homer and Hesiod among them, who taught the Greeks about the gods. She agrees with Plato that the artist's work is seductive play: art is dangerous because it meddles and it changes the heart. The Greeks in general were not reverential about art, but Plato valued the artist's ability to create something that even the creator might not necessarily understand. Plato was impressed with the "divine or holy madness from which we may receive great blessings" (FS 2). If life is a pilgrimage from appearance to reality within a Heraclitean world of becoming, then the artist has the same struggle to achieve being as everyone else. The first forms to which Plato introduces his listeners and readers are moral ones: "The light of the Good makes knowledge possible and also life" (quoted in FS 3).

Murdoch understands that a novel, being a response to life, does not arbitrarily set itself off from its author's philosophy. A novel is simply a different kind of response: "The novel itself, of course, the whole world of the novel, is the expression of a world outlook. And one can't avoid doing this. Any novelist produces a moral world and there's a kind of world outlook which can be deduced from each of the novels. And of course I have my own philosophy in a very general sense, a kind of moral psychology one might call it rather than philosophy" (quoted in Conradi, *Saint* 1). Whereas other critics focus on this "kind of moral psychology," I concentrate here on more concrete ways of talking about what it is that Murdoch calls her "world outlook." In this chapter I examine texts that are evidence of Murdoch's moral psychology. My analysis of Murdoch's worldview in chapter 9 focuses on her novelistic patterns.

Addressing one of the dangers that Murdoch recognizes in the life of the artist, Conradi writes, "'Art' itself is an analogue of the process by which we create in life a self-serving world view in which other people figure merely as subsidiary characters" (*Saint* 15). He cautions that worldviews tend to be androcentric and exploitative. Murdoch skirts this danger by using her characters to embody Enlightenment values that are androcentric but then ultimately critiquing those values. It is true that the behavior of her characters denies autonomy and a self-legislating self, but she does not live this view. Through her rejection of the patriarchal and the monologic and her celebration of the marginal and the dialogic, she resists the temptation to impose her private fantasies on the text. Murdoch struggles, then, like everyone else, to stifle both the human tendency to distort reality and subsequent re-presentation of that distortion.

Coming of age in the midst of Oxbridge during a language revolution, Murdoch has incorporated in her philosophy the relationship of artists and novelists to certain worldviews and to certain kinds of art. In her first full-length published text, she demonstrates her awareness of conflicting discourses and analyzes her responses by carrying the ferment about language at all levels into both her philosophical and novelistic worlds.[3] Three philosophical texts—*Sartre, Romantic Rationalist*, *The Sovereignty of Good*, and *The Fire and the Sun: Why Plato Banished the Artists*—give readers a clear conception of what Murdoch values in the novel. Moreover, these texts combine the genres of philosophy, essay, literary criticism, intellectual history, and, some might say in the case of *The Fire and the Sun*, literature. Why has Murdoch not had to defend herself against intertexuality here as she has had to in her novels? An equally important issue is that Murdoch, having been on the cutting edge of the language revolution in the 1940s and 1950s,[4] rejected modernist goals. For her, negotiating with the other is crucial to novel writing. Unless individuals are "mutual objects of attention," they will not use a common vocabulary (SG 33). If discourse is language in use, then loving is a specialized language in use. Murdoch's discourse of love, the focus of her philosophy, has penetrated her novelistic discourse.

Sartre, Romantic Rationalist is a vast storehouse of Murdoch's opinions about the novel, realism, and character and about other writers and their relationship to language. Employing a philosophical discourse here, Murdoch stakes out her position on the language crisis of the twentieth century, describing the shift that causes problems for writers: "Language was no longer thought of as naming things . . . ; it was seen as a way of delimiting, interpreting, and predicting sense experience" (SRR 28). In establishing herself as a sophisticated intellectual historian of this revolution, she defines her relationship to Sartre's work, while also defining her philosophy of language for the reader.[5] In establishing her view of the language crisis, she reveals her familiarity in the late 1940s with the seeds of contemporary French critical theories.

Perhaps Murdoch's past helps account for her commitment to otherness. Reaching maturity during a world crisis and then beginning her independence by attempting to relieve the horror of World War II marked Murdoch as a deeply moral person. A character in *The Message to the Planet* says that the Holocaust reminds people of their positioning in the world. Having been changed by the reality of the war, she came to see the pre–World War II modernists as romantic and unrealistic. At that time she refused to fall into the trap that she associates with James Joyce, Marcel Proust, and Virginia Woolf: focusing on the author's own play with language at the expense of the outside world, where one encounters real events and real people. She uses Joyce and Woolf, as well as Sartre, to illustrate the kind of discourse she thinks novels require: the discourse of the other, or dialogical discourse, which Mikhail Bakhtin describes as dynamic utterance in which at least two voices are superimposed and create a "bond" (PDP 189).

When Murdoch superimposes philosophical discourse and literary criticism in *Sartre, Romantic Rationalist*, the reader can often distinguish different stances. For example, when she argues that the shift from the traditional perception of language causes problems for writers, she speaks in a gentle voice, sympathizing with the High Modernists' dilemma, the need to work within a desiccated language: "To lose the discursive 'thingy' nature of one's vision and yet to feel the necessity of utterance is to experience a breakdown of language" (SRR 27). She finds their solution to be an obsession with particularity. They use means as ends: "We can no longer take language for granted as a medium of communication. Its transparency has gone. We are like people who for a long time looked out of a window without noticing the glass—and then one day began to notice this too" (SRR 26). For her 1953 taste, the modernists are too distracted by the glass; in *Metaphysics as a Guide to Morals*, she has moved beyond this view, praising Proust. Using philosophical discourse in *Sartre, Romantic Rationalist*, she develops at great length her perspective on the crisis of language, a crisis that novelists must understand. In the following passage she recounts the illusions of the Victorian era that she soundly rejects:

> The smaller, expanding world of the nineteenth century, where the disruptive forces were not only dispossessed and weak but incoherent, disunited, and speechless, could think itself a single world wherein rational communication on every topic was a possibility. This assumption can no longer be made. The breakdown of the notion of meaning in certain spheres, which might appear to be an achievement of the linguistic philosophers working in isolation, or as the handmaids of science, may also be seen as the consequence of a tragic discovery: the discovery that rational men can have different "natures" and see the world with a radical difference. So perhaps it was the loss of an actual common background, after all, which occasioned the linguistic sophistication, and not the latter which exposed the former as an illusion. (SRR 29–30)

In order to question literature's attempt to achieve a metaphysical task, Murdoch shifts into the discourse of literary criticism:

> The novel, traditionally, is a story, and the telling of a story seems to demand a discursive referential use of language to describe one event after another. The novelist seemed to be, by profession, more deeply rooted in the ordinary world where things were things and words were still their names. Yet, in time, a deep change came about both in the structural technique of the novel and in its page-to-page use of language. The novelist, too, seemed now to turn to literature as to a metaphysical task whereon the sense of the universe was at stake. Compare the attitude of Proust to his work with that of Tolstoy or even Conrad. The writings of the two latter show forth, are nourished by, their answers to life's ques-

tions; Proust's work *is* his answer to life's questions. The human task has become a literary task, and literature a total enterprise, wherein what is attempted might be called reconciliation by appropriation. (SRR 30)

If no one is the enemy because what went before was illusion, then, according to Murdoch, the writer who takes the novel and uses it as a metaphysical life raft is simply verifying the old truisms voiced by Plato and Freud: artists are neurotic children and incorrigible liars. Unwilling to place herself in either category, child or liar, Murdoch insists on another place that is beyond pretentious narcissism.[6] For novelists to assume blindly that they might save the universe by saving themselves in art, Murdoch realizes, is anthropocentric if not hubristic. When she said Sartre "has the style of the age" (SRR 7), she was referring to solipsism.

Murdoch suggests that logical positivism drove artists of the romantic ilk into stream-of-consciousness novel writing. Mapping out the change in the self-consciousness of philosophers about language between the Victorian era and the 1950s, she emphasizes the peak years of logical positivism and the resulting obsessions regarding verification: "Language was suddenly construed on the model of the scientific definition: the meaning of a sentence being exactly determined by an explanation of the particular sensible observation which would decide its truth. . . . Metaphysical objects were eliminated and physical objects disintegrated into the appearances, or sense, which justified statements about them" (SRR 28).

The conclusion of her historical analysis suggests some of the phases of Wittgenstein's philosophical quest: "Gradually the philosopher came to see language not as a structural mirror, or even as a categorical frame, of experience of the sensible world, but as one human activity among others. Language and the world no longer stood apart; language now fell into focus as a part of the world, and with this came a readiness to study, on their own merits, the complex ways in which ethical, political, and religious propositions operated" (SRR 29).[7] Everything became the province of science, providing many more illusions to dispel. This upheaval wrought by logical positivism led Murdoch to begin *The Sovereignty of Good* ten years later with the flat statement that "the position in question, in current moral philosophy, is one which seems to me unsatisfactory" (1).[8]

Murdoch refers to this now familiar dichotomy—nominalism versus insistence on verification—to introduce philosophical misconceptions about moral philosophy: "Boldly, the language was divided between descriptive (empirical) uses, and emotive uses; and the propositions in question were then said to have 'emotive meaning,' to be expressions of feeling without external reference. Even the meaning of poetry became a subject for psychological measurement rather than logical investigation" (SRR 28–29). She laments the loss of confidence in the communicative powers of language that the move toward science brought about. Since communication depends on speakers' experiencing "a common world, to whose reliable features the uses of words can be related by firm conventions . . . [the word] 'Good' was no longer thought to name an objective quality, nor 'democracy' an identifiable form of government" (SRR 29). When Murdoch raises the question "Does the world change first and pull language after it, or does a new awareness of language suddenly make us see the world differently?" (SRR 28), she echoes a Wittgensteinian and postmodern question about seeing oneself. My saying to Murdoch that her strategies are sometimes postmodern evoked in her the response that such a term is American. *Postmodernist* describes Murdoch at least insofar as her desire to escape the bounds of one way of looking matches the postmodern impulse to get outside the mind to see the mind thinking.[9] Murdoch's texts insist that in order to look outside oneself to see the self looking, one must first see the self in the other. She shows, then, that Sartre, as well as Wittgenstein, contributed to the language revolution.[10] The ways Murdoch was exposed to the beginnings of postmodernism are no mystery—the beginnings are in modernism and Victorianism.

Murdoch accepts experimentation as crucial: when worldviews change, literature must change to reflect the reality of the world. Nevertheless, she refuses to stop creating unique and palpable human characters; no matter what has changed in the world, people still have a range of positive and negative characteristics. The death of the character need not follow the death of God; for Murdoch, the life of the character is the purpose of the novel form.

It is not experimentation that Murdoch abhors in modernism, or its means, but solipsism, an end. Her goal has consistently been one she shares with Plato, Wittgenstein, and Freud: to reveal humans obsessed with illusions and struggling toward reality, each moving at a different pace. What distresses her are the vestiges of the nineteenth-century ideological convention that the true artist must be indifferent, must be a solipsist. In her view, the problems for the

High Modernists are this solipsism that interferes with communication and the sickness of the language. Murdoch says that the crisis in the way humans see language is inevitable. For her as a Platonist, it is one of the contingencies along the path toward good. "Fragmentation may sometimes appear as the pure joy of a new discovery, a more exact observation," she writes. "It was with no sense of loss that Monet declared that the principal person in a picture was the light. . . . [The] writer . . . suffer[ed] a more distressing upheaval" (SRR 26). If fragmentation uncovers an illusion and leads toward knowledge, Murdoch accepts it with equanimity.

Sartre, Romantic Rationalist clears away a great deal of misunderstanding about Murdoch's theory of the novel and her theory of language, just as the more recent *Metaphysics as a Guide to Morals* has done. Criticisms that Murdoch is antimodern, anti-Joyce, and anti-Woolf, and the implications that her novels are Victorian or New Victorian, seem ludicrous beside her conclusion that the passing of the Victorian world has changed humankind's view of reality and language. What Murdoch rejects and what she celebrates in *Sartre* tell the reader much about her values in 1953. Murdoch has sympathy but not praise for the novelist who, like Sartre, is under the illusion that one views the ordinary world from the inside only. If context governs text, the writer should be aware of the large, outside view of him- or herself writing the novel or performing the stratifying impulse. Of course, she valued Sartre early in her career because he wanted "to find a middle way (a third force) between the ossification of language and its descent into the senseless" (SRR 36).

Part of the body of this text lays out Murdoch's quarrel with three major writers and their romantic, subjective use of language. She seems distressed that Joyce, Woolf, and especially Proust have not faced up to the fact that all human activity, not just recollection, involves language and that living is more than a literary task in a cork-lined room; High Modernists focus on "the senseless fragmentation of our experience or on the fabricated nature of its apparent sense" (SRR 17). In an interview published in the *Washington Post* in 1990, Murdoch says that Proust is a favorite of hers and adds, expressing pleasure, that she "know[s Proust's] novels by heart" (Conroy, "Lasting Powers" F6). Living more securely in the world of social give-and-take and being perhaps more practical, Murdoch never fell into the old fin-de-siècle trap of art for art's sake. In *Metaphysics as a Guide to Morals* Murdoch no longer sides with Georg

Lukács and takes his view of the High Modernists. Between 1953 and 1992, Murdoch moved from Lukács's view of modernism to Theodor Adorno's view.

Considering herself a novelist who replicates the dynamic and event-filled chaos of the world, she finds the modernist's world static. She reveals her own interests when she says of Woolf: "One is after all at liberty to stand back and simply record the particulars as they swirl by, making out of them what wistful personal beauty one can. 'Life is a luminous halo, a semi-transparent envelope surrounding us from the beginning of consciousness to the end'" (SRR 31–32). Murdoch, however, has chosen to create chaotic novels. She has wanted her characters not only to "play cricket, cook cakes, make simple decisions, remember their childhood, and go to the circus . . . [but also to] commit sins, fall in love, say prayers . . . [and] join the Communist Party" (SRR 35); she does not want them to stand and be swept away by a barrage of images. Murdoch characteristically considers the welfare of the reader: "If a character is presented with an excess of lucidity and transparency," she says, "a sense of futility may overcome the reader" (SRR 39).

Murdoch thinks that too much authorial self-analysis fragments "the firm configuration," the construct that convention calls the character. Even more destructive can be "an 'impure' analysis. . . . Good glass is invisible, inferior glass can be seen as well as seen through. . . . If, however, the author cuts up the inner landscape too finely . . . we may cease to be interested in estimating the good faith of the narrator, and may simply turn to enjoying the subtlety and finesse of the author as this displays itself in the various moments of the analysis" (SRR 38). She cites Woolf as an example of an author whose style overshadows characterization: "The person is presented as a series of more or less discrete experiences, connected by tone and colour rather than by a thread of consistent struggle or purpose—and both person and author seem content" (SRR 38). Whereas Murdoch finds Woolf solipsistic, she finds Sartre both solipsistic and monological. He follows a more philosophical path than Woolf does: "In *La Nausée* Roquentin experiences a disintegrated world, but, unlike the heroine of that other lyric upon the absurdity of everything, *Mrs. Dalloway*, he does so with acute distress; he feels it *ought not* to be so" (SRR 38). Murdoch's problem with the modernists, including Sartre, is that in their solipsism they skim over the basic realities that humans are social beings and that there is something outside themselves. She regrets that Sartre "has a dream of human companionship, but never the experience. He touches others at the fingertips" (SRR 25), a touch from a distance, like that between God and Adam in Michelangelo's fresco. Murdoch reveals her frustration at continuing to find "the same note of emptiness and weariness" in Sartre's solipsistic discourse. She seems bothered that Brunet in "*Les Chemins* [is] a rather stick-like character, though one who is clearly liked and respected by his author" (SRR 21). But finding "the flicker of a real 'I-Thou'" relationship between Brunet and Schneider,[11] Murdoch implies that Sartre could portray deeper characterization rather than "a momentary intensity verging on the sentimental," so unlike "that brilliant study of being-for-others" in *Middlemarch* (SRR 41).

Still, Murdoch questions whether Sartre "really succeed[s] in creating people who are neither 'pale nor pathological'" (SRR 39). Suggesting the kind of Dostoevskian social interaction she admires even in internal monologue, Murdoch finds a good model of what she values in *Daniel Deronda*, referring admiringly to the description of Gwendolen Harleth's decision to marry Grandcourt: "The anguish and the 'bad faith' of the heroine are presented in a mixture of external detail and introspective description: the urgent 'picture book' recollections, the warm sense of the possible escape, the 'yes' which she speaks as if in a court of justice" (SRR 39–40). Admiring George Eliot's execution of the stages of Gwendolen's movement toward maturity, Murdoch finds it difficult to understand why Woolf or Sartre fail to devote time to the "efforts of human beings to understand each other" (SRR 41). Her analysis of the problems in Sartre's novels is even more thorough.

Murdoch discloses her exasperation at Sartre's having recognized the literary possibility of creating otherness and yet not having worked to honor its existence. She does not fail to understand the psychological state of doubt in which Roquentin finds himself in *La Nausée*. Clothing the feeling in Platonic language and seeming to be familiar with such a feeling, perhaps experiencing doubt during the postwar period, she sympathizes: "The metaphysical doubt which seizes Roquentin is an old and familiar one. It is the doubt out of which the problem of particularity and the problem of induction arise. The doubter sees the world of everyday reality as a fallen and bedraggled place—fallen out of the realm of being into the realm of existence. The circle does not exist; but neither does what is named by 'black' or 'table' or 'cold.' The relation of these words to their context of application is shifting and arbitrary. What *does* exist is brute and nameless, it escapes from the scheme of relations in which we imagine it to be rigidly enclosed, it escapes from language and science, it is more than and other than our descriptions of it" (SRR 13). Roquentin's "brooding over the doubt is the neurotic distress about language" (SRR 13). Roquentin's solipsism, romantic and destructive—and, Murdoch would say, like Sartre's—is a sickness.

Moreover, Murdoch knows that Sartre wants to give his characters freedom; that is also her goal. Quoting a passage from *L'Etre et le Néant*, she seems surprised that Sartre does not follow his own advice: "Character has no distinct existence except as an object of knowledge to other people. Consciousness does not know its own character—except in so far as it may consider itself reflexively from the point of view of another. . . . This is why pure introspective description of oneself does not reveal a character: Proust's hero 'has' no character which can be grasped directly" (quoted in SRR 37). Murdoch says in response to Sartre that this ideal depiction of character "need not point to more than a technical problem for the novelist: the problem of how to work in a variety of outside views of each person, so that we may obtain an 'objective' picture" (SRR 37).

Murdoch recognizes that Sartre fails to evaluate what he sets up. Here she might be mistaken for a contemporary French feminist:

> "The reflective consciousness is the moral consciousness," Sartre said, because it is the revealer of incompleteness and so of the vision of "value," the whole whose shadow defines a lack. Yet the reflective consciousness of Sartre's fictional characters is empty and their reflexion merely denuding. Sartre's individual is neither the socially integrated hero of Marxism nor the full-blooded romantic hero who believes in the reality and importance of his personal struggle. For Sartre the "I" is always unreal. The real individual is Ivich, opaque, sinister, unintelligible and irreducibly other; seen always from outside. Real personal communication is the communication Ivich has with Boris. (SRR 52)

This passage gives an excellent summary of Murdoch's understanding of the other, "the whole whose shadow defines a lack," and her vision of the spatial quality of her novelistic world. In responding to Sartre's ideas about the relationship of the characters' discourse to society, Murdoch turns to Lukács, a Hegelian Marxist, to make an additional criticism of the perspective of modernists, especially their use of the internal monologue, which he thinks should be kept "on a short leash" (SRR 37). Murdoch agrees with Lukács that representation of reality is not accomplished by recording flux or photographic images and that character is outside oneself and can only be reflected in the other. Just as she abhors the modernists' use of specificity for its own sake, she abhors in Sartre generalizations for their own sake. She quotes Lukács to prepare for her examination of Sartre's characters, masks for ideas, who almost never look outside themselves: "'The psychologists' punctilious probing into the human soul and their transformation of human beings into a chaotic flow of ideas destroy no less surely every possibility of a literary presentation of the completely human personality,' no less surely, that is, than does a crude 'objectivist' naturalism" (SRR 37).[12] Sartre's emphasis, when he discusses character in relation to consciousness, focuses more on reflection and emptiness than Dostoevsky or Murdoch would. In Murdoch's view, Sartre creates monological characters as instruments with which to argue his ideas.

Like Sartre, Murdoch chooses to be specific, not subtle, about morality. She identifies with Sartre's recognition of serious political and social problems in the real world and his attempts to move toward the light, toward the good: "Sartre has recommended moral concern as a recipe for good writing. We shall wish to see how the vertical aspiration to truth (which I have no doubt Sartre would consider Virginia Woolf to lack) affects his portrayal of his own people, and in what exactly that aspiration consists" (SRR 39). Murdoch cannot identify with Sartre's compulsions: the extremes to which he goes in overemphasizing political issues, promoting existentialism, and depicting characters that are not the least full-bodied. His use of political rhetoric in a novel to persuade the reader to act undercuts the energy that would traditionally go into creating vital characters. In addition, Murdoch is put off by the abstract knowledge Sartre writes into a novel: "When one is concerned to persuade and communicate one is, as Sartre himself has put it, too much inside language to see it as a structure of the external world" (SRR 8). Without an interest in character development, ordinary or intellectual, Sartre's author-controlled discourse is inevitably monological, a tendency with which Murdoch quarrels.

Being temperamentally a different kind of writer and prone to alterity, Murdoch works well as a mirror to help others see who Sartre is. More to the point, he is a mirror who helps define who she was in 1953. Her background in philosophy gave her the confidence to argue that character is of major importance to the novel—human beings the stuff of human life—and to dare to challenge

Sartre, a major philosopher at the time. In dramatizing her consciousness as it not only observed but perceived another, she authored her own values.

Two more of Murdoch's philosophical texts help the reader understand her conception of otherness as it pertains to novel writing. In 1977 Murdoch mirrored for the world another important philosopher with whom she began her negotiation of the other. In reflecting Plato, she did not, as Virginia Woolf said women do, make him ten feet taller. Her discussions of Plato help explain why she is not averse to the blurring of philosophy and literature. Her understanding of the other has benefited from Plato's discussions of an ancient, primitive relationship to the other. Her experience with the history of this concept drives her interpretation of Plato's philosophy in *The Fire and the Sun: Why Plato Banished the Artists*. Although this text is not a discussion of novel writing, it demonstrates Murdoch's alterity, putting her theory into practice. Her situatedness in the text is quite different from Sartre's situation in *Les Chemins*. In presenting her challenge to the major philosophical discourse of Western culture, she gives Plato seventy-six pages and takes only thirteen for herself. One might argue that she lets Plato participate as a character in the philosophical discussion. As an expert at negotiating the other, Murdoch is working in a tradition she knows well, the tradition of Plato's "Dialogue of the Dead," in which individuals can argue with thinkers of the past. She also humbles herself to allow Plato's voice to speak. This method is similar to that in her novels, in which the characters are free to work out their trials in the metaphorical cave, making their own responses in their own discourse (see chapters 6, 7, and 8). Murdoch is self-conscious in this text, knowing that the artist is most prone to lies. She is appropriately worried about writing words down, an attitude similar to that of Bradley Pearson in *The Black Prince*.[13]

In addressing major issues about language, Murdoch draws on Plato's description, in the *Sophist*, of the other and the value to him of talk over writing.[14] Murdoch's comments evoke her own controversy with Jacques Derrida:[15] "The dialogue explains that if we are to see how false judgements are significant we must avoid the old Eleatic confrontations of absolute being with absolute not-being. . . . Theaetetus is led to agree that not-being does seem to be rather interwoven with being (240c), and the stranger explains that not-being is not the opposite of being, but that part of being which is different or other (257–58). When we deny that something is X, we are not denying that it *is*, but asserting that it is other" (FS 29). Here Plato's emphasis on difference and otherness sets up a dichotomy, just as Plato sets up a dichotomy of the soul in *Republic* (439). Later, however, he prefers a "tripartite division of the soul" in which the parts need to be in harmony. For this model, Freud is indebted to Plato. Each philosopher realized, according to Murdoch, that "an unmediated fight does not present a realistic picture of human personality" (FS 37). Murdoch understands that alterity and psychoanalysts' search for the truth are closely allied, as are psychoanalytic and novelistic discourses. Recognizing the great benefits Freud derived from being a serious student of Plato and of literature, Murdoch explores the interaction between the ideas of the two master discourses. She shows that in staging a dialogue between patient and analyst, Freud was reenacting the confrontation that Greek drama had represented between the self and its other, between protagonist and antagonist.

Like Plato, Freud's analyst expects talk to be more truthful than writing. A speaker can change his or her mind instantaneously, giving the listener a moment-by-moment replay of new thoughts. Listeners have simultaneous access to all the verbal and nonverbal signs of the speaker, whereas reading filters out verbal gestures, intonation patterns, parody, and irony. Murdoch agrees with Plato's statement that "philosophy is essentially talk. *Viva voce* philosophical discussion . . . is the purest human activity and the best vehicle of truth. Plato *wrote* with misgivings, because he knew that truth must live in present consciousness and cannot live anywhere else" (FS 21). Here Murdoch addresses the problem that writers like Plato and Wittgenstein had because they disagreed with their written words soon after having written them.

Plato's emphasis, according to Murdoch, is on the positive value of the spoken word: "Only words inscribed on the soul of the hearer enable him to learn truth and goodness; such spoken truths are a man's legitimate sons. Writing spoils the direct relationship to truth in the present. Since truth (relation to the timeless) exists for incarnate beings only in immediate consciousness, in live dialectic, writing is precisely a way of absenting oneself from truth and reality" (FS 22). Similarly, she had warned in *Sartre, Romantic Rationalist* that "writing can easily become a kind of lying, something frivolously pursued for its own sake, in fact an art form. True understanding comes suddenly to trained thinkers after sustained and persistent discussion; and there is little danger of a man forgetting the truth once he has grasped it since it lies within a small compass" (SRR 22–23).

In *The Sovereignty of Good*, Murdoch develops metaphorically Plato's view of alterity, or moving beyond the self, by staging a drama within the mind of a character, M. In a now-famous passage Murdoch creates this mother-in-law who seeks to convince herself that she loves her daughter-in-law, D. Neutralizing her original hostility and accepting D as she is, M finds her other in D. If in this process M teaches herself the truth about D, that D can be lovable, there is no chance whatsoever that M will forget this truth. A test of whether she has learned that the daughter-in-law is lovable is whether she forgets to feel love (SG 17). With this episode Murdoch ensures that instead of misinterpreting her moral imperative, her conception of the process of human love, the reader will see the discourse of love in action. She demonstrates that moving toward perfecting one's own potential to be good requires a major displacement of the ideologies of childhood. M's hypothetical struggle appears to be between class ideology and newly acquired moral ideology—its logic of categorization, its vocabulary. In attempting to talk one's consciousness into loving another, she suggests a discourse that is detached from subjectivity. M is learning that human spiritual energy, when directed toward the other, can produce good. By expressing good, M is overthrowing the social hierarchy impressed on her in childhood and the gulf between the either/or definition of vulgar versus graceful, to some extent a gulf that reflects and helps differentiate socioeconomic conditions. The work and the attention to the vocabulary of loving are an endless task. M progresses from seeing her daughter-in-law inaccurately to seeing her accurately, justly, and lovingly—but, of course, if self were to intervene, M might readily revert to egoism.

Murdoch's discourse of love, the focus of her philosophy, has penetrated her novelistic discourse. Being quite precise about the use of words, whether in love or in creation, she says: "I would like on the whole to use the word 'attention' as a good word and use some more general term like 'looking' as the neutral word. Of course psychic energy flows, and more readily flows, into building up convincingly coherent but false pictures of the world, complete with systematic vocabulary. . . . Attention is the effort to counteract such states of illusion" (SG 37).[16] *The Sovereignty of Good* is crucial to a reader's understanding of Murdoch's discourse of love, which is based on attention to whatever is outside the characters.

This discussion of language in *The Sovereignty of Good* focuses on the possibility of changing one's language in order to change one's experience. Murdoch's open call for defenders of moral philosophy has resulted in its rebirth in certain areas such as women's literature. When the book appeared, moral philosophy was "daunted and confused, and in many quarters discredited and regarded as unnecessary. . . . [Murdoch speaks of it as if it were fossilized and] ought to be defended and kept in existence as a pure activity, or fertile area, analogous in importance to unapplied mathematics or pure 'useless' historical research" (SG 76). Here she challenges philosophers to find a new vocabulary to discuss morality. To address the lack of such a vocabulary, she creates a discourse of love. By doing so, she also initiates a new philosophical discourse that combines philosophy and psychology. The following challenge has had an appreciable impact on scholars in the last twenty years: "Moral philosophy needs a new[,] . . . more realistic, less romantic, terminology if it is to rescue thought about human destiny from a scientifically minded empiricism which is not equipped to deal with the real problems" (SG 71). Women in the fields of moral philosophy and psychology have looked to *The Sovereignty of Good* and to Murdoch for guidance and inspiration—a dynamic response to Murdoch's unpretentious plea. Numerous scholars have answered the challenge, albeit with a direct purpose. For example, Carol Gilligan and Nona Plessner Lyons, answering Murdoch's call "for psychology and philosophy to join in creating a 'new working philosophical psychology'" (quoted in *Mapping the Moral Domain* 43), are doing just that. Much of the theorizing has blossomed from the work of women, like Carol Gilligan, looking for alternatives to the conventional ways to explain female desire. Nancy Chodorow's *The Reproduction of Mothering: Psychoanalysis and the Sociology of Gender* prepared the ground for such a harvest with its argument that women have "more flexible or permeable ego boundaries," and thus are perhaps better able to tolerate ambiguity (169).[17]

Since for Murdoch all human action and thought has to do with morality, novel writing has to record human action, moral or immoral. Before one sets to work to achieve the discourse of love, one must learn the process of unselfing (ascesis). Perhaps Murdoch is suggesting, in her search for moral definitions, that love is an altering of consciousness and that the discourse of love is an interior discipline, like altering one's body temperature with a mantra. Or perhaps Murdoch is suggesting that when humans love, they allow one voice or language in the mind to step down and another voice to take over. "Goodness," Murdoch writes, "is connected with the attempt to see the 'unself,' to see and respond to the real world in the light of a virtuous consciousness" (SG 93).[18]

She insists that such respondings—as in an unexpected, loving response to the beauty of a bird—can change a person from a brooding, anxious, resentful creature to a ecstatic celebrant: "The surprise is a product of the fact that, as Plato pointed out, beauty is the only spiritual thing which we love by instinct" (SG 85). Unselfing is a negotiation in which one voice in the mind hands over power to another voice, letting the bird or the artwork receive attention.

This deepening process of building up values that depends on words and attention sounds very much like what Murdoch explains the writing process to be. If discourse is language in use, then loving is a specialized language in use. Murdoch's philosophical discourse often appears to blend into her novelistic discourse, especially when loving is at issue. Such blending is inevitable because all Murdoch's discourse manifests the principle of alterity, or going beyond the self.

CHAPTER FIVE
Iris Murdoch's Novelistic Discourses: *An Accidental Man*

Each of Murdoch's novels is a social phenomenon that celebrates language in use, and taken together her fiction is a critique of monologism. The particular discourses Murdoch chose to include in the novels of the 1970s and 1980s and the utterances of her most memorable characters demand readings that take into account the social context of discourses and the ways they intersect. Insisting that language cannot be separated from the human struggle and that any utterance can have contested interpretations, she creates narrative strategies to explore not only verbal content but also the contingent flux of the nonverbal part of utterance, the gestures and the anticipation. Mikhail Bakhtin is the most accessible source of such social language theory; his habit of personifying and dramatizing these theoretical concepts has made his model not only appealing and accessible but also exact. Moreover, because so much of his conception of language and the way it works corresponds to concepts that Wittgenstein and Murdoch also discuss, I am appropriating his concepts, terms, and definitions in order to be precise about Murdoch's unusual narrative strategies, strategies for capturing the quirkiness of life. Her strategies highlight the competing elements between the author's language and the protagonist's, the protagonist's and that of the other characters, and the language of the text and other texts.[1] "Languages are continually stratifying," Bakhtin writes, "under pressure of the centrifugal force, whose project everywhere is to challenge fixed definitions. Represented characters in a novel exist in order to find, reject, redefine a stratum of their own; formal authors exist to coordinate these stratifying impulses" (DI 433).[2] The linguistic goals of novels respond to social conditions, and authors release stratifying impulses with which they attempt to subvert socioeconomic hierarchies of power within their novels.[3] Among late twentieth-century novelists, Murdoch is unusual in humbling herself, becoming incarnate in the world of her characters, a habit characteristic of Dostoevsky, whom Bakhtin praised for that ability.[4] Murdoch, like Dostoevsky, also acts as the choragos, an architect-choreographer who provides imaginative strata in which particular characters can act out and define their rituals. As the choragos, she leads her characters occasionally in soothing, beautiful language, but most often in wild, staccato clashes.

Murdoch also gives her characters freedom to discover new strata; for example, George, the pupil in *The Philosopher's Pupil*, challenges the fixed definition of the pupil-teacher relationship, finding for himself a new layer, the stratum of the rogue. In *The Philosopher's Pupil*, whether there are only two philosophers or a whole a group of youths, each stratum has at least one language.[5] These different discourses come from a variety of groups in society, including social, economic, and educational groups, but also professional and age- and gender-specific groups. This juxtaposition of elements within society occurs, no doubt, as a result of what Louis Althusser proposes: that all human beings (and therefore all characters) are subjects of ideology.

Murdoch's novels of the 1970s and 1980s reveal a tendency not only to assimilate new genres but to free her discourse from authoritative practices. One of her major goals throughout her career has been to explore discourse; the following statement from *The Sovereignty of Good* captures her general attitude toward heteroglossia: "Word-utterances are historical occasions. . . . Words said to particular individuals at particular times may occasion wisdom. Words, moreover, have both spatio-temporal and conceptual contexts. We learn through attending to contexts, vocabulary develops through close attention to objects, and we can only understand others if we can to some extent share their contexts. (Often we cannot.) Uses of words by persons grouped round a common object is [sic] a central and vital human activity" (SG 32). For Bakhtin, too, the conditions surrounding any written or spoken utterance and the goals of the speaker determine the kind of utterance:

> At any given time, in any given place, there will be a set of conditions—social, historical, meteorological, physiological—that will insure that a word uttered in that place and at that time will have a meaning different than it would have under any other conditions; all utterances are heteroglot in that they are functions of a matrix of forces practically impossible to recoup, and therefore impossible to resolve. . . . Heteroglossia is as close a conceptualization as is possible of that locus where centripetal and centrifugal forces collide; as such, it is that which a systematic linguistics must always suppress. (DI 428)

The narrative strategies Murdoch employs to get beyond the monologic to capture the heteroglot, or what she would simply call language, render irrelevant her lack of familiarity with Bakhtin's theories. Her novels experiment dynamically with choruses of letters and dialogue, journalism, prefaces, postscripts, and confessions in order to capture chaos, open-endedness, unreliability, and undecidability, demonstrating that each utterance, oral and written, has goals and responds to social conditions. In her moral insistence on negotiation with the other, Murdoch explores in her novels a multiplicity of consciousnesses as they grow toward new consciousness. Bakhtin sees "authorship [as] the problem of one consciousness perceiving another consciousness" (Emerson, "The Tolstoy Connection" 70). Furthermore, Murdoch is optimistic that the phenomenon of heteroglossia cannot be controlled by political authorities. She is concerned with such effects when in *Metaphysics as a Guide to Morals* she writes: "Techniques of political oppression in modern civilisation may tend (as pictured in Orwell's 1984) to weaken and simplify and starve ordinary speech, depriving it of concepts. However time . . . will (we hope) continue at intervals to restore the divine power of language (as it has begun to do in eastern Europe since 1989)" (459). The majority of the sentences in her novels demonstrate that words condition the other words with which they collide. For example, the words and their juxtapositions in Murdoch's opening sentence in *A Word Child* condition each other: "I say, an absolutely stunning coloured girl was here looking for you" (1). Dropping out *coloured* makes the sentence change tone, direction, implication; without the connotations of colonialism, the smell of the sentence changes.

Murdoch most often draws on one set of distinct voices, one stratum, that carries the burden of her exploration of heteroglossia: thinkers—teachers, pupils, writers.[6] Thinkers must find language that is not immediately ephemeral, discourses that will retain their perception of truth. Philosophers often find it difficult to cast their understanding of the basics of human communication in the simplest and most enduring language. Wittgenstein, however, spends pages and pages on discussions of pain, and Murdoch's *Message to the Planet* explores the possibility that truth is inherent in suffering. The novel's voices of student and guru struggle toward a truth. The moral thrust of the dialectic, as it embodies that struggle, undermines potential argument after potential argument.[7]

The following dialogue in *The Message to the Planet* critiques Wittgenstein's statement that "to imagine a language means to imagine a form of life" (PI 1:19). A significant portion of this novel's plot is Alfred Ludens's quest for Marcus Vallar. The student's quest centers on finding the text that will enlighten and the man who will enlighten the text. Ludens pleads to know what Marcus, who has many of Wittgenstein's characteristics, has been thinking. The way one speaker intuits the next move of the other is uncanny:

> "Oh well," said Marcus, capturing his left hand again, "I *suppose* it's *about* what makes human consciousness possible, or rather it's about what human consciousness *is*, which is to say what, and how, the world is, how *anything* is. You see what I mean when I say it's nothing new, it's been endlessly talked *around*. How language makes the world, how thought makes being. But it just may be that *now*, when we've got rid of so many *wrong* ideas, *now, at last*, is the moment when we might be able to frame—an answer."
>
> "Go on, go on—what would be something *like* an answer?"
>
> "It's not anything to do with biology or psychology or any science or the old philosophies—it's something so deep that even the most delicately poised approach almost inevitably occludes it. It is a place covered by a cloud."
>
> "Language hides it?"

Murdoch makes communication work here by having each speaker anticipate the response of the other in his reply. For example, when Marcus says "covered by a cloud," Ludens anticipates: "Language hides it?" Throughout the dialogue, the reader can watch them adjusting to each other's goals:

> "It is more as if the gods hide it. In mathematics too there are such dark places. One cannot just dig it out of language as I thought once."
>
> "An experience, an action, a mode of life?"
>
> "True thinking is all of these."
>
> "But are they alternatives?"
>
> "Wait. I think the sort of answer you want is this. What is sought is a device. Something like an electrical circuit. Something present in a flash, intuitively seen to be necessary, which cannot be otherwise."

Here the teacher anticipates what the student wants:

> "Marcus, like *what?*"
> "Like Gödel's theorem or the Ontological Proof."
> "Oh. How can it be like both?"
> "*Crede ut intelligas!* You want me to tell you something and I am telling you something. When I say it's the sort of answer you *want* I mean it's the sort that might help you! Since it is a crude oversimplification it might also mislead you. I could have mentioned *cogito ergo sum*, only I detest that shallow but influential maxim, now I'm glad to say discarded."
> "Oh, is it? But the Ontological Proof is religious, it's moral, it's about how God can't not exist."
> "I said *like*. These are hints, pictures. What is sought is not one thing among others, but the foundation of things. As I said, something *necessary*, something which *must* be so. Such a search cannot but be an ordeal, indeed a metamorphosis. One must be worthy, an intense purity and refinement of thought is required, even one might say a kind of holiness."
> (MP 163)

This dialogue is, of course, a dance of ideas as well as choruses of voices. *The Message to the Planet* is open on both ends; the answers that could be messages, the mundane answers, are that contingency and suffering exist. One of Murdoch's goals is to release philosophical discourse into the atmosphere of the novel and yet to neutralize it with a theological discourse, juxtaposing the two discourses—and thereby replicating what Bakhtin celebrates as heteroglossia. The voices throughout Murdoch's fiction make the reader question whether hearing philosophical discourse in a novel makes that text philosophical.

Peter Conradi is a good source of information on Murdoch's stratifying impulses as well as on the socioeconomic range in her fiction, a range that Richard Todd seems to miss in emphasizing the narrow social and cultural scope of the characters in *An Accidental Man*, a narrowness that Todd says in turn affects language. Murdoch once said to Conradi, "One can only write well about what one thoroughly understands" (quoted in *Saint* 8); as Conradi shows, however, she animates characters from all classes. Just as Murdoch's father and Murdoch herself were civil servants, so the most populated stratum is the middle-class intelligentsia. As Conradi points out, it is not unusual for a character to be simultaneously a civil servant and an Oxford scholar: "The

British professional classes often lead such in-bred coterie lives, . . . feed[ing] off Shakespeare . . . , as well as off life" (*Saint* 7–8). Murdoch has noted, in an essay in *Partisan Review*, that "equality of opportunity produces, not a society of equals, but a society in which the class division is made more sinister by the removal of intelligent persons into the bureaucracy and the destruction of their roots and characteristics as members of the mass" (quoted in Conradi, *Saint* 8).

An Accidental Man is a wonderfully comedic rendition of the potential mayhem in the lives of the middle-class intelligentsia. This novel begins a phase of major linguistic experimentation on Murdoch's part in the 1970s. Having a thorough background in the philosophy of language and having thought deeply and critically about language, Murdoch relishes calling into question the social veracity of discourses, such as professional discourses, and the social history of those who speak the discourse. Valuing language as a moral force for change, Murdoch employs the strategies of parody and stylization to achieve a striking picture of social reality. In *The Black Prince*, for example, she uses both techniques in Francis Marloe's language. Knowing that language is a pervasive force that not only perpetually changes but also changes people, she seeks new ways to simulate dynamic human conditions, and she allows characters the freedom to explore their innumerable complexities. This resistance to the monologic helps her create full-bodied, contingent characters who change as often and display as many sides or selves as real people. As she pointedly argues in *The Sovereignty of Good*, humans can consciously change their feelings by changing their words. In her novels, characters realistically mirror the phenomenon—speaking different languages when they speak to different individuals.

Two important issues Murdoch raises appear to make Todd uncertain that *An Accidental Man* qualifies as the novel Murdoch hoped to achieve. Looked at from a different perspective, the same two points make even more convincing the argument that Murdoch's fiction is dialogical or multivoiced. When Murdoch explains her goals for this novel, it is almost as if she has read Bakhtin's discussions of centrifugal and centripetal forces. It is, she says, "a deliberate attempt to exclude the central nucleus and to have a lot of different attachments pulling the plot and the interest away into further corners," and the characters "have lives of their own and . . . are pursuing dramas of their own which are quite alien to the central story" (quoted in Todd, *Shake-*

spearean Interest 48). For Todd, Murdoch's remarks imply that she fails to invite the reader "to sense the organic unity of plot and subject which is so characteristic a feature of Shakespeare's maturer drama" (*Shakespearean Interest* 48). But, as Murdoch pointed out in *Sartre, Romantic Rationalist*, neither Shakespeare's world nor the nineteenth century exists. *An Accidental Man* is about the contingency of the 1970s, when morality is no longer at the center of philosophy; the novel and its worldview require eschewing the illusion of unity and struggling with the lack of organic unity. The particularly large canvas of characters, who are free to live their own lives except for their moments onstage, are ignorant of such abstractions as organic unity or central nucleus. Todd concludes that Shakespeare succeeds at what Murdoch does not achieve: "drawing attention away from this relationship between the parts and towards the desired otherness of character, so that what is actually apprehended appears more contingent than it in fact is" (*Shakespearean Interest* 48). Perhaps he is correct in arguing that the experiment does not produce a perfect work of art. Murdoch, whose emphasis is on process rather than on product, has numerous times revealed that she has no illusions that her novels are perfect.

Looking at Murdoch's stated goal is more productive. *An Accidental Man* is what Murdoch calls an "open" novel: the characters are intentionally and successfully set free to become whatever they wish. Murdoch has continued to write both "open" and "closed" novels, categories she first described to an interviewer in 1958: "The open novel contains a lot of characters who rush about independently, each one eccentric and self-centered; the plot to some extent situates them in a pattern but does not integrate them into a single system. The closed novel has fewer characters and tends to draw them, as it were, toward a single point" (quoted in Conradi, *Saint* 23).[8] Murdoch not only accomplishes dialogical and heterological feats in *An Accidental Man*, but she also illustrates the narrator's taking the stance of Christ instead of God and allowing the characters to live on the same level as the omniscient narrator. In other words, her creative intentions are similar to Shakespeare's: "If you get hold of a good character, he will invent himself, will invent his mode of speech and his past, make his jokes, and so on" (Heusel, "Dialogue" 4). A Murdochian pattern of aimlessness is a very carefully orchestrated process; the results look like the real accidents of life.

The content in this tragicomedy may be traditional, but the juxtaposing of multiple genres and strategies pulls the comedy off its tracks. The conventional, stable intelligentsia create the centripetal force: the majority of the characters enjoy socioeconomic stability, and a number of them either have been knighted or hope to be. But even so, as a character remarks, most are "Barkers people not Harrods people" (AM 27). The traditional plot is also stabilizing: boy wins girl, parents hinder match, manly honor intervenes, a marriage ends the story. Murdoch constructs her usual moral labyrinth, which dramatizes the horror of endless accidental occurrences causing characters to suffer—the loving characters letting it stop with themselves, but most characters allowing it to reverberate to the next person. Todd's point about "the 'peripheral' kind of fiction . . . offer[ing] an attractive solution to the problem of how to get the apprehension by one character of the suffering of another across in such a way as to show the part accident plays" (*Shakespearean Interest* 48) is helpful. Murdoch herself admitted to A. S. Byatt in a BBC interview on October 27, 1971, what she wanted to achieve: "The counterpoint . . . to the idea that one's life is a series of accidents is, of course, the notion that it is not a series of accidents because one is busy contriving often at . . . even an unconscious level that a certain kind of drama shall be enacted and re-enacted" (quoted in Todd, *Shakespearean Interest* 45). To show that life is both a series of accidents and a contriving of individual dramas, Murdoch disperses the characters beyond the local labyrinth of London into Oxford and the United States, even suggesting Vietnam. Life in this accidental world can be circular and empty, with no one, except perhaps the most marginal, actually striving for morality. Murdoch, however, is always probing, always prodding readers to define morality for themselves.[9]

To reveal the way accident works, Murdoch periodically breaks into the flow of narrative chapters. Her highlighting of prolonged choruses of disembodied voices in entire chapters of letters and of untagged stichomythic dialogues, instead of simply presenting her usual long, Socratic conversations of conventional bodied voices, is a radical departure. This strategy displays the way heteroglossia works. Each chorus, be it dialogue or letters, gives form to the concepts of simultaneity of outside perspectives and of a group of decentered personalities. Like a Greek chorus, these speakers are naive, blind, and mistaken. Being somewhat less intelligent than Greek choruses, who often apply the right evidence to the wrong individual, these people apply the wrong evidence to the wrong people.

Perhaps Shakespeare and Dostoevsky, as well as the Greek playwrights, introduced Murdoch to such strategies. Her creation of stichomythic dialogues illustrates that often language and what it signifies are songs lost in the wind. The novel not only argues against the stability of the social scene but simulates in its form the lack of resolution in life. Another way Murdoch gives the reader a dialectical experience is by mixing genres, such as fiction and drama, in unconventional ways that disorient her readers, who may momentarily miss the point of the fluid language sequences and have to reread. By confronting the reader with a network of the conventional, or centripetal, forces—forces that struggle with the disconcerting centrifugal forces and pull the novel off balance—she wheedles the reader into coming up with new connections, forcing him or her to think along writerly lines to see choruses as the artist's theatrical gestures, ways of achieving a fragmented closure.

This polyphonic novel, which propelled Murdoch toward her present phase of novel writing, weaves in other texts, most often from the Shakespearean skein preserved in her mind. She foregrounds the wild, contingent swirl of language, letting the power of context struggle with text.[10] The counterpoint she has planned, operatic in form, requires voices, and what better place to find disembodied, changing voices than in *The Tempest*,[11] whose machinations take place on a fantasy island. This drama, in which different combinations of characters keep getting lost and Ariel hunts for them, is invaluable to the construction of the novel, with its voices internal and external to the text. Murdoch has at least one good reason to be drawn to this play: Shakespeare highlights another voice named Iris, the "many-coloured messenger" who performs her song for the wedding of Miranda and Ferdinand (*Tempest* IV.i.76). By transplanting Shakespeare's opera of multivoiced dialogues into her novel, Murdoch brings about outrageous carnivalistic effects.

Murdoch pretends she is Prospero putting on a masque. Putting into play the stylized masque format or opera form, she is able to tune in not only to Shakespeare's comic voices but also to the historical voices that reverberate further back to Shakespeare's analogues. She grounds the detached voices lost at sea in Shakespeare's historical analogue: colonists bound for the New World shipwrecked in the *Sea-Adventure* off the coast of Bermuda in 1609. This strategy invites the reader to compare the experience of historical lostness to contemporary decenteredness. In addition, like Shakespeare before her, she uses a historical incident, the Vietnam War, to weave in popular culture, pitting voices from outside the text against voices inside it. Instead of actually dramatizing the wedding masque she borrows from Shakespeare, she modernizes by making the masque a postnuptial party in which all the characters present in the novel participate. The party is for the young Englishwoman Gracie and her new husband, Garth. Ludwig, the young man from across the sea, did not work out as a fiancé. Furthermore, the content of both the letters and dialogues, rather than drawing the reader's attention to the lack of a center, sends the reader and the characters off on digressions, dramatizing their repression of lostness. Events take place offstage that the reader only hears of; mysterious questions are never answered. Did Austin murder his first wife, or did she drown? Loose ends become threads leading nowhere. The world being decentered, the characters might well be a little mad and their language "a kind / of excellent dumb discourse" (*The Tempest* III.iii.38). All of Murdoch's arrangements in the notebooks at the University of Iowa Libraries make clear that the stichomythic dialogues and letters are important utterances and that they are the groundwork for some pattern. The pattern is centerlessness.

In the novel Murdoch links the rhetoric of the arts of letter writing and conversation.[12] Looking at these two types of utterances can help the reader see how Murdoch is manipulating the language through the multiplicity of voices, both male and female, and the repetition. Shakespeare and the tragicomedy form take control of the ending, giving the reader notice that Murdoch is playing with voices and that the reader must be less serious: "Now our revels are ended" six lines from the close sends the reader back into the text to look for parallels. Having constructed the novel as a swirling contingency that defies closure, Murdoch's only choice is to stop it as one might stop a merry-go-round. The story has no end, yet the novelist must stop so that the reader can have a chance to respond.

Murdoch juxtaposes the revelation of a series of mysterious events and the sequences of untagged stichomythic dialogues, destabilizing the text. Most of the novel consists of conversation: Murdoch has created nine entire chapters of letters and three chapters composed almost entirely of untagged stichomythic dialogues, in addition to one combination of the two. The important fact about a letter is that its language is pointed toward a certain person and a response is imagined (Bakhtin, PDP 205). The six-page chapter (pp. 338–43), a sequence of ten letters and one telegram, not only moves the plot of the novel forward but contains the climax of the love plot—Ludwig's decision not to marry Gracie Tisbourne. This last series of letters precedes Gracie's affair with Garth, a young Briton of her own socioeconomic group. First, the irony of juxtaposition within this group of letters is crucial in bringing about the little dénouement, or whatever closure there finally is. Ludwig, the addressee, has used a technicality—the accident of his birth in England—to escape the draft in the United States and almost certain service in Vietnam. His father, Mr. Leferrier (the addressor), and his mother finally agree here, near the end of the novel, that he has the right to stay at Oxford and get married instead of returning to the United States and having to go to Vietnam. The parents, who in earlier letters had insisted on his returning home, have begun to focus loving attention on Ludwig and are now willing "to accede cheerfully to his firm and declared wishes in this matter" (AM 338). Since the reader learns no new information between letters, it appears that Ludwig is willing, as a result of the support of that love, to give up his selfish desires, which include marrying Gracie. The reader assumes this outcome because in the next letter Ludwig tells his fiancée that he cannot marry her: "It is just that I am not in my right place in the universe" (AM 339). He is admitting that he is out of place socially as well as geographically, that he is a character who has wandered from his own stratum. This Hamlet has to spurn his Ophelia so that he may play the game of honor.

In the next letter, Murdoch allows Mrs. Tisbourne to present the social context surrounding this spurning. To focus on the upper-class expectations, Murdoch includes a letter from her to Lady Hester Odmore, implying that Gracie broke off the engagement. Mrs. Tisbourne not only lies in saying that Gracie "is quite restored and gay" (AM 340) but, having hopes that Gracie would marry the lord and lady's son, she invites the family over for dinner. Murdoch paints a backdrop demonstrating that, in Mrs. Tisbourne's competitive social stratum, mothers want their daughters to find husbands who will provide rank and elevate their prestige. In Mrs. Tisbourne's next letter, thanking Dr. Seldon for treating Gracie, who in her grief is trying to starve herself, Murdoch suggests Ophelia's conventional, slower alternative. Mrs. Tisbourne colors this letter differently: because she wants to convince the doctor of the seriousness of Gracie's condition, she says that Gracie "talks a good deal about suicide" (AM 340). She presents her plea to him openly and without guile. She also reinforces the point when he sends the sleeping pills: "Please be sure they are not the kind you can kill yourself with." At the same time the mother is writing to the doctor about starvation and suicide, Patrick Tisbourne, Gracie's younger brother, having a more practical attitude toward his sister, writes bluntly to her: "The best cure for love I'm told is falling in love again" (AM 342). After Gracie's second letter, Hester receives one from Mollie Arbuthnot, whose husband will be knighted. Mollie invites the Odmores for a weekend; her hidden polemic is to bring Sebastian, their eligible young bachelor son, together with her daughter.

The second letter Ludwig receives, a confession, introduces what Conradi calls "such in-bred coterie lives, . . . feed[ing] off Shakespeare" (*Saint* 7) and specifically off the dark sonnets. Employing "a sideward glance"[13] to test whether Ludwig is offended by homosexuality, young Andrew writes that he and Oliver "are having, in every respect, a thoroughly Grecian time (I know you are a tolerant fellow). The ancients had the root of the matter in them, don't you think? Though I suppose I shouldn't say so to a man about to marry the sweetest girl in the world! . . . What has that either to do with the sweets of marriage?" (AM 341). An unsigned letter between Gracie's brother and his schoolboy friend Ralph Odmore is a mishmash of the dark sonnets: "Be ingenious, my very dear, and keep with me our present in our future, keep our great love forever, growing, changing, overlaid, besieged, surrounded, ageing, and yet in its heart utterly uncontaminated and clear as Grail crystal" (AM 343). This letter is the most elliptical, because the significance has to be muted, but ironically the next one, from a mature man to Ludwig, suggests the same sort of liaison at Oxford. The backdrop, or context, includes other men from the same background and men's schools, this same inbred stratum, who find homosexuality preferable to heterosexuality.

In addition to echoing triangular relationships in many of Murdoch's other novels, the next letter, from Mavis to Matthew, addresses another Ophelia-like accidental drowning: "I cannot help feeling that she somehow died for us, for you and me, taking herself away, clearing herself away, so that our world should be easier and simpler" (AM 342). But Matthew has other intentions. Murdoch creates irony by positioning two letters side by side. The letter between two young male lovers is a replica of Shakespeare's to his patron: "love is time's fool" (AM 343). The placement is ironic because Matthew apparently has ideas about having a homosexual relationship with Ludwig. This juxtaposition seems to cap the crazy, neurotic quality of the whole sequence. In the final message in this novel about voyages, the young American responds to his father: "FATHER PLEASE CANCEL YOUR SAILING I AM COMING HOME LUDWIG"

(AM 343). Murdoch has not only used the letter sequence to make some major plot moves, she has let the sequence carry the climax of the plot. Ludwig, one of the major players in the love plot, discovers the great change that occurs in the lives of this group first; after the change reverberates in his life, he relays the message to his Ophelia, who responds, Ophelia-like but without Ophelia's violence.

As language transactions or utterances, these letters carry forward the plot, whereas the stichomythic dialogues help pull the plot apart. A connection between the *Waste Land* allusion and the plot is the semantic drift of this sampling of letters: away from heterosexual love to homosexual, a shift that is also an issue in *The Waste Land*.

Murdoch adds another dimension to the novel when, thirty pages later, an untagged stichomythic dialogue takes place on the occasion of Gracie and Garth's housewarming party soon after their marriage. Here the conclusion does not further the plot or reconcile conflicts or cement an issue, but cogently illustrates finalization (Bakhtin, "Speech Genre" 76). Although dialogues are most often not dialogical (e.g., see Herrmann, *Dialogic and Difference*, especially 15), this one is. The multiple allusions to *The Tempest*, *Hamlet*, and *The Waste Land* make Murdoch's prose full of other people's words. Here in its original context is Prospero's line about "revels" to which Murdoch alludes:

> Our revels now are ended. These our actors,
> As I foretold you, were all spirits and
> Are melted into air, into thin air;
> And like the baseless fabric of this vision,
> The cloud-capp'd towers, the gorgeous palaces,
> The solemn temples, the great globe itself,
> Yea, all which it inherit, shall dissolve;
> And, like this insubstantial pageant faded,
> Leave not a rack behind. We are such stuff
> As dreams are made on, and our little life
> Is rounded with a sleep.
>
> (*The Tempest* IV.i.158)

This speech concludes the wedding festivities Prospero has hosted. By alluding to it, Murdoch gives life to all kinds of reverberating voices, including Ferdinand and Miranda, Ariel and Caliban, Ophelia and Hamlet, Gertrude and Claudius, the pub women and the water nymphs, the typist and the young man carbuncular:

> "Our revels now are ended."
> "Goodnight, darling."
> "Goodnight, darling."
> "Goodnight."
> "Goodnight."
> "Goodnight." (AM 377)

In her closing, Murdoch is actually opening up the whole issue of reseeing the novel in light of these three texts. Whereas Shakespeare creates a play within the play, Murdoch is creating discourses within discourses. Before her characters, who are actually only voices, dissolve into the "baseless fabric of this vision," which is only words, two of Austin's wives have rounded their "little li[ves] . . . with a sleep"—each drowned, Ophelia-like—and the bride, Gracie, has considered suicide by way of sleeping pills. The purpose of this kind of closing is to prevent closure. In enjoying the pure jouissance of intertexuality, Murdoch wantonly catches readers in traps or boxes. (For example, we never learn whether Austin drowned his first wife.) Sometimes Murdoch leads readers into circular labyrinths of reseeing. In this characteristic she and Eliot are alike, and perhaps she and Shakespeare as well.

Having learned much from Shakespeare and Dostoevsky about intertexuality, Murdoch ingeniously manipulates many texts and contexts into the plane of her discourse without overburdening her base. Murdoch uses Shakespeare's and Eliot's discourses in the way that Bakhtin calls stylization: in choosing these other contexts that move in the direction of her purpose, she does not allow her thought to "collide with the other's thought" (PDP 193), but uses it conventionally.[14] Her stylization at the end of the novel opens up many possibilities for conjecture—that she has a mind layered with the intertexuality of Western civilization, that the issue of civilized life as opposed to the empty life dramatized in the novel is significant, that the pattern demands operatic comment similar to that in *The Tempest*.

Murdoch also parodies her materials. For example, the goal of her experimentation is not modernist in the sense of creating a perfect gem of a symbolic configuration that radiates out dozens of meanings, but postmodernist in its desire to eschew elitism in form and content. Using stylization, therefore, will do only so much for Murdoch; she must clash with her borrowed sources in order to paint a picture of contemporary reality. The major events in *The Tempest* are not accidental; they involve actions performed by a godlike man who has the learning of a magician. The beautiful young man who comes from afar is perfection, and the voices and movements are also perfect. In the world of 1970, however, no such perfection existed. *An Accidental Man* is parodic in some of the same ways as Eliot's use of *Hamlet* in *The Lovesong of J. Alfred Prufrock* and *The Waste Land*.[15] The clashes in Murdoch's texts simulate contingency, the slippage of language; in Eliot, the purpose of the clash is to create multifaceted symbolism, as he does in making the grail hero reflect Hamlet, John the Baptist, or Ludwig of Bavaria. Whereas Eliot's elitism drives him to achieve a unified perfection, Murdoch is striving to simulate contingency by creating a form to break. For many readers these strategies simply represent exaggeration; in actuality, as in *An Accidental Man*, the strategies and the untagged stichomythic dialogue are purposefully inadequate to the needs of the utterances; the inadequacy demonstrates that the middle-class intelligentsia can gossip about pretty pillows and cars and drinks but cannot fill the void of their existence, an utter vacuousness that Murdoch emphasizes by alluding to *The Waste Land*.

Eliot's purpose is to radiate many meanings, Murdoch's to allow for the possibility of no meaning beyond what the voices say—and to make the voices sound vapid. In Murdoch's critique of convention, the reader can only guess which voices belong to whom, which to men and which to women. Whereas the form is vital, the content is mundane. Voices that refer to men repeat clichés such as "like father, like son," "making millions," "coining money." The real concerns seem to be about what the young men are doing: the function is to flatter the young husband about the reviews of his book, to mention that Ralph is going to read history at Balliol, and that "Andrew is spending his sabbatical term studying Oliver," that is, engaging in a homosexual affair (AM 375). Voices that address women or refer to women show interest in decoration (dresses, rooms, cushions); other references concern matchmaking, living arrangements, marriage, pregnancies, eating, cancer, prison, drugs, a monastery. Only one vocation and one avocation are non-gender-related: a woman is buying a bookstore, and a woman is learning to play the guitar.

By intertextualizing, Eliot can achieve dozens of authentic and ironic meanings that reverberate off each other in perpetual motion. Murdoch, understanding that it is only an illusion that the author is in charge, wants also to demonstrate that no one meaning is secure—not because she is in charge as author but because the world is constantly impinging. The tightness of the enigmatic voices in Murdoch's stichomythic discourse is not to simulate Eliot's symbolic untagged discourse or to perfect his ability to create symbolic gems and constellations of ideas, but to exaggerate the silence and dumbness of ordinary language. Murdoch is a Christ-author as opposed to a god-author. Furthermore, she appears to have more sympathy for the voices she creates. Her handling of Dorina is more sympathetic than either Shakespeare's handling of Ophelia or Eliot's handling of Lil. Conventional criticism interprets Ophelia's death to be either the result of Hamlet's indecision or, more often, a reverberation of the corruption and sexism in the rotten state of Denmark; either way, the tone is more detached than Murdoch's.

In a novel where all the characters are on the periphery and none is in the middle, nothing is predictable. Murdoch's description of the closed novel is comparable to being in a concert hall in which the acoustics are well balanced and the focus is totally on the sounds of the instruments. As rich as such a symphony can be, there are a finite number of possibilities, as in the closed novel. The open novel is like an outdoor concert in that the world can impinge with infinite variety. The sounds of the birds, the rain and wind, the passing cars, and burping babies can interrupt the music. According to Murdoch, this is the way the world sounds. She makes Eliot seem like an overly fastidious, if somewhat more prolific, Bradley Pearson, the artist-narrator in *The Black Prince*.

Like Eliot, Murdoch has perfected the interruption of voices speaking untagged stichomythic dialogue. Both draw on different strata excavated by those authors who have gone before, strata already peopled with poor drowning women, unhappy lovers, and egoistic, powerful men. Often they have chosen to use the same characters from Western culture's cache of fictional types and characters, the "spirits" Shakespeare refers to above. (Murdoch carefully distinguishes this fictional world from the fantasy world in which her characters—and real people—often live.) More often than not, these characters perform different functions. Eliot not only stylizes Hamlet's indecision in *Prufrock* but also alludes parodically to Hamlet to emphasize that, whereas Hamlet finally acts, Prufrock never does. Eliot uses an array of characters, including some from opera. In *The Waste Land*, drownings can mean death or rebirth, but they always mean death in *An Accidental Man*.

It is characteristic for Murdoch, being closer to the postmodernist tradition than the modernist, to drop the wedding out of the text and into the void between chapters or offstage. The reader, instead of experiencing the wedding as is characteristic in comedy, experiences the housewarming. This final scene is both stylized and parodied. The idea of celebrating the marriage is stylization because it copies *The Tempest* and Spenser's *Prothalamion* in *The Waste Land*, but when the crowds at the party remind the reader of the gang at the pub in *The Waste Land*, the scene becomes parody. The new couple has set the big party on the birthday of the dead child who would have been seven years old. Austin, the accidental man of the title, killed the child because he was driving drunk. The party celebrates the marriage at an extremely trite level; Murdoch is criticizing, but only gently, as "Now these revels are ended" reminds us.

Murdoch has managed to work into this choral sequence an underlying misunderstanding between at least two contexts. After the reader has absorbed the whole series of references, the references to the gossip about Charlotte, Gracie's unmarried aunt, and her new lesbian relationship create polyphony. Patrick, who participates in the letter sequence, is having his own homosexual affair, has visited Charlotte, and says, "it's a hoot" (AM 376). But the guests living more conventional lives cannot readily absorb the information:

"Charlotte Ledgard is living with a weightlifter."
"I can't quite see Char reposing on a hairy bosom."
"My dear, it's a female weight-lifter." . . .
"Charlotte has gone native near Midhurst with a female acrobat." (AM 374–75)

Different voices have different perspectives: countercultural openness or conventional closedness. This musical theme and variation on heterosexual and homosexual love is reminiscent of that in *The Waste Land*. The incantation of "Hello" and "darling," at the beginning and throughout as guests arrive, is framed at the end with the "Goodnight" sequence. In that sequence, voices from all three literary works become a chorus, voices of men as well as ladies, and reverberate *The Waste Land*'s "Ta ta. Goonight, Goonight. / Good night, ladies, good night, sweet ladies" (ll. 71–72). This song immediately precedes the allusion to Spenser's "Marriage Song," which reverberates with the reminder that, while Ferdinand did not die, Hamlet did: "Goodnight sweet prince, / And flights of angels sing thee to thy rest!" (V.ii.312). Murdoch uses the choruses of voices throughout the novel to unmask hypocrisy. The chorus has no self-awareness, no self-knowledge. The final chorus's conclusion suggests a series of multivalent literary allusions, highlighting that Murdoch, like T. S. Eliot in "The Chess Game," condemns the conventional wisdom and power of the bureaucracy of 1940s Britain. This novel is a classic case of a text's being generated in relation to other texts.

CHAPTER SIX

Polyphonic Novels: *The Philosopher's Pupil* and *The Black Prince*

Another of Murdoch's polyphonic novels, even more extreme in its movement toward the carnivalesque, is *The Philosopher's Pupil*.[1] Seemingly, it is an unself-aware, unintentional revitalizing of carnivalesque discourses: journalism, philosophy, and theology compete for attention. This novel dispels any critical illusion that Murdoch is stuck in some reactionary mold. Experiments such as *An Accidental Man*, although perhaps no one's favorite novel, did bestow on Murdoch the freedom she needed for the stunning artistic leap she made in creating *The Black Prince* (1973). Before moving to that unquestioned piece of artistry, this chapter explores another experiment, more readily praised than *An Accidental Man* but less lovingly referred to than *The Black Prince*. *The Philosopher's Pupil* (1983) is an extremely successful experiment with heteroglossia.

Murdoch's writing patterns and strategies have changed over the years, becoming more and more nonconventional, even radical. As she reaches her potential as a novelist, she uses unobtrusive ways of expanding the boundaries of the novel form: postmodernist magic realism in addition to dramatic strategies and manipulation of form. Her study of Russian so that she might read Tolstoy and Dostoevsky argues for her fascination with the subversive strategies of Dostoevsky and his irreverent carnivalesque discourse (Bakhtin, PDP 101).[2] Being affected by writers like Dostoevsky and Shakespeare at both conscious and unconscious levels, she has freed herself creatively as they have, not limiting herself to one mode or genre or style, but using traditional conventions as tropes. Whatever her sources, she has apparently intuited how effectively polyphony and the carnivalesque capture contingency.[3] Such emphasis not only gives her novels energy but also fulfills her desire to deny consolation to her readers.

Murdoch's experimentation has had its negative consequences. Her spirited celebration of radical change and renewal has disoriented readers. Guilty of being sometimes philosophical and sometimes sensational, she uses the dialogic mode to test ideas, raise questions, and arouse the reader's senses with her incongruity and eccentricity.[4] Most of the faults that readers find with Murdoch's fiction can be categorized under the rubric of the novels' strong carnivalesque flavor.[5] For example, when primitivism overturns an established Christian worldview in a novel, some readers balk. Also perplexing are what appear to be inconsistencies in her published statements about art.[6] Seeming to valorize the monological, Murdoch has insisted that writing like Tolstoy is her ideal, but she has continued to write more like Dostoevsky—dialogically. Discussions of her fiction often center on the charge that it is philosophical and, therefore, not about real people. Even more common is the charge that her fiction is sensationalist and, therefore, second rate.

Questioning the seriousness of Murdoch's fiction in 1969, before she had experimented with *An Accidental Man* or *The Philosopher's Pupil*, Linda Kuehl mistakenly assumed that Murdoch might stoop to "clichés of the novelist's trade" merely to create "sensational effects." Literature about change and renewal, however, is not necessarily logical and harmonious. Kuehl complains about such narrative tricks as direct attacks on the readers ("cloak and dagger violence and shock" tactics) and insinuation ("coincidence, riddles, ironic reversal, and sexual perversion") ("Iris Murdoch" 352–53). Kate Begnal paraphrases a 1983 review of *The Philosopher's Pupil*: "A ghastly attempt to combine religious allegory, the didactic novels of ideas, and British comedy of manners . . . having all of Dostoevski's hysteria without his genius" (178). Elizabeth Dipple, on the other hand, wavers between apologizing for these phenomena and praising them. "There can be no question that certain passages and characters in Murdoch are irritating," Dipple admits, adding her own list of Murdoch's potentially sensational techniques: "curt twists of the plot," "visit[s] to future," "circularity," "endgame," "point-of-view altering postscripts," "total ambiguity," "meandering refusal of closure" (*Work* 85). Such Murdochian methods are integral to the tradition of carnival.

Murdoch refuses to confine herself to narrow definitions of genre, expanding such categories as "philosophical novelist," "realistic novelist," or even "comic novelist"; any such potential for sensationalism is clearly part of a larger pattern. Perhaps Bakhtin is right, and "carnivalization is . . . the most creative form of dialogized heteroglossia" (La Capra 315). Drawing on her training in the classics and her lifelong interest in Plato, Murdoch has revived narrative techniques that helped the Greeks and Romans portray the kind of full reality that she also sets out to create in her fiction. In dramatizing a world in which morality struggles against the powers of darkness, Murdoch juxtaposes her philosophy and arguments that test and overturn it. To free her discourse from the monological, she "grafts" voices of the carnivalesque onto her own voice.[7] Since Murdoch revels in celebrating change itself, she celebrates carnival. Murdoch employs two traditional components throughout *The Philosopher's Pupil* to embody change and renewal: a staged spectacle and a conscious use of figures or theatrical language.[8] Traditionally, carnival first stages a realistic representation and then, using language to repudiate it, provokes laughter (Kristeva, WDN 79).

Carnivalesque novels like *An Accidental Man* and *The Philosopher's Pupil* dramatize Murdoch's struggle to balance authoritarian control of patterning with the dynamic groping of realistic characters in an aimless universe. Freed to make their own patterns and not overwhelmed by the author, the characters control their spheres and thereby evoke strong feelings from the reader. In *The Philosopher's Pupil* Murdoch controls the pattern of low comedy that dominates the characters but creates a unity of effect that is hilarious. The novel fleshes out its narrator's truism: "We would all be comic characters if we were in novels" (PP 370).

In this novel the staged spectacle, one of the conventions of the carnivalesque, takes the form of a Saturnalian celebration. In his own rise and fall and rise, Tom McCaffrey, the twenty-year-old carnival king, embodies ritual death and rebirth. The primordial discrowning is that of the philosopher Rozanov, perhaps a paradoxical double of his former pupil George, who overturns the academic hierarchy. George deposits Rozanov, who has just taken an overdose of drugs, in a hot bath, but Rozanov does not rise revived; instead, he becomes the scapegoat king whose sin of pride is drowned, his death reinvigorating the community. Murdoch reverses the conventional comic relationship between the lover and the heroine's father by having old Rozanov suggest the coupling of his granddaughter with Tom. The grandfather's motive, apparently, is to help himself resist an even more scandalous temptation—incest.

Murdoch's focus on low Eros (incest, homosexuality, lesbianism, adultery) and on murder and death blasphemes the sacred taboos.[9] Promiscuity around the communal bath creates scandal, comedy's basis being in the communal square. The Bath Institute, imitating a carnival phenomenon, eliminates the "impenetrable hierarchical barriers [between people and allows them to] enter into free, familiar contact on the carnival square" (PDP 123). The narrator compares the role of the square to that of "the agora in Athens. It is the main rendezvous of the citizenry where people idle, gossip, relax, show off, hunt for partners, make assignations, make business deals, make plots" (PP 23). Because of the atmosphere, the narrator says, "more than one woman has admitted to me that she feels a sexual thrill on entering" (PP 23). Of course, the square's metamorphosis to spa helps Murdoch combine the ideas of rebirth and communion.

The novel is built on contrasts and abrupt transitions. To resist single-level discourse and to play other voices, Murdoch includes competing styles and techniques from the epic, tragic, gothic, picaresque, mythical, and romantic. For example, the comedy's first section, "An Accident," opens in medias res, jerking the reader into stichomythic dialogue, an argument between George and Stella McCaffrey. Husband abandons wife in the car, which he pushes into the river—only to find her ambiguously reborn out of the sunken car as if out of a womb. A voyeuristic priest in a gothic black hood witnesses the bizarre drama and raises an alarm. George and his younger brother Tom are picaresque characters; George's adventures begin with this attempted murder and end with his attempt to murder Rozanov, his teacher of twenty years earlier. The brothers' bizarre adventures evolve out of minds crazed by the fever running through their town: "A kind of unholy restlessness . . . attacks the town at intervals like an epidemic" (PP 19). When Rozanov arrives for a visit, the town is flooded with a frenzy it calls "Rozanovism." This turmoil is only part of a larger design that the gossips explain by citing rare portents, including reports of a flying saucer and the sudden emergence of a thirty-foot geyser from within the spa's hot spring.

The setting also offends the morality of the social community. The primordial order erupts discordantly into this modern bedroom community outside London. The backdrops that represent Ennistone suggest layers of time, particular epochs, allusions to primitive religious rites: Stonehenge, a Delos-like wasteland, Roman baths, and "cult of Venus" fountains. The mythical and literary complex juxtaposes a scandal about Shakespeare's Sonnet 153—"(see Bowcock's book, the index under 'venereal disease')" (PP 18)—and allusions to the Latona fountain built by Marsy at Versailles. The action never moves very far from dream: enchanted Latona-like foxes with cubs, and a masquerade at the Slipper House replete with blond wigs that later hang mysteriously in ginkgo trees.

Murdoch makes use of all avenues of gossipmongering: characters, narrator, letters, and newspapers. The narrator generalizes that Ennistone's young people want to modernize the Bath Institute by introducing dancing, drinking, gambling, and nude bathing. The adults are content for this center of the town's social life to remain a place "where people idle, gossip, relax, show off, hunt for partners, make assignations, make business deals, make plots" (PP 23). The narrator, who says, "It is my role in life to listen to stories" (PP 576), plots the course of the river of erratic gossip or scandal. His discordant discourse intrudes periodically to juggle the voices. The name, or nonname, Murdoch assigns to the narrator is especially appropriate in that it is precisely the algebraic notation Kristeva uses to signify "a proper name (N)" for a character in a diagram explaining "writing as trace of a dialogue with oneself (with another)" (WDN 74). N, whose voice echoes that of the stage manager in Thornton Wilder's *Our Town*, penetrates the walls between narrator and character and between character and audience, just as Wilder's does. He sounds like a stage manager when he ends "Our Town," the second section of the novel, with a listing of the ages of the dramatis personae: "At the time of the story Alex is sixty-six, George is forty-four, Brian [the third Dostoevskian brother] is forty-one, Tom is twenty, and Adam is eight" (PP 31). N, a character living and listening at the Bath Lodge, calls his town "N's town," Ennistone. His multitoned and multistyled language weaves together two spectacles—the Saturnalia at the scene of Ennistone and the Saturnalia of language. Toward the end of the novel, Murdoch juxtaposes this fecund language and the sterile language of the press to test the reduction of doubleness to monotone.

Murdoch uses the letter form for conveying "verbal agons and cursing matches" (PDP 125) between George and Rozanov. When the narrator, privy to Rozanov's thoughts, says that "the sending of a letter constitutes a magical grasp upon the future" (PP 434), the reader can assume that the philosopher, who knows best "the inadequacies of language," genuinely hopes to provoke action by writing "an intemperate letter to George" to get him off his back. The letter contains "wild phrases such as 'I would like to kill you,' and vituperation in the style of 'fake fantasy villain, mean weak impotent rat, incapable of evil but spewing out the sickening black bile of your petty spite,' and '*faux mauvais*, the execrable taste of your contemptible schoolboy pranks merely expressive of your own realisation of your mediocrity' " (PP 433). These "carnival curses" (PDP 126) do arouse the well of magic energy in the unconscious: in his recoil from the letter, George attempts to murder his mentor.

When, however, carnivalesque discourse loses this energetic ability of the diatribe to bring about radical change, it becomes moralistic. After involving the reader in violent reversals of the hierarchy—the ambivalent discrownings of Rozanov and of Tom—*The Philosopher's Pupil* submerges the reader in subartistic newspaper exposé. Such a transformation, from fruitful ritual to "single-leveled . . . naked journalism" in Ennistone's two newspapers (PDP 126), marks a great falling off. Murdoch employs repetition to show that the journalese in exposé loses its double-voiced ability to renew. She not only gives the reader one of her famous set pieces (a discrete comic scene representing carnival masquerade) but pulls together the two sides of Saturnalian spectacle, scene and language, in two comic journalistic accounts. Here she demonstrates that even when she reduces the carnivalesque to monotonous duplicity, it resists and retains its energy.

Conspicuous in the news reports are the deflations by which the press juggles innuendoes while still shielding itself from libel suits. Murdoch, progressing from deflating the Slipper House to deflating the occupants, uses repetitions of *so-called* to establish a pattern of denigration running through the two news stories. Both newspapers drift into editorializing to undermine what they consider sexual perversion. The story in the *Ennistone Gazette* appears under the sensational headline "MCCAFFREY PRACTICAL JOKE GOES TOO FAR":

> Extraordinary scenes took place on Saturday night at the *so-called* "Slipper House" . . . home [of] Miss Harriet Meynell and her maidservant. "Rehearsals" of *The Mask of Aphrodite* in the Ennistone Hall broke up in confusion when George and Tom McCaffrey led a drunken rabble to lay siege to the two damsels in their flossy seclusion. Drinking and shouting, the revellers, who included [the] parish priest . . . attempted to gain access to the house. . . . Also present were a number of young men in outrageous "drag" and their sponsor, our own Madame Diane. (PP 409; emphasis added)

The *Gazette* goes on to cast aspersions on the two adolescent women, who are innocent of all the newspaper's suggestions—but secretly guilty of being in love with the seventy-year-old Rozanov. Repeating *so-called* amplifies the innuendoes: "At last, with the connivance of the maidservant who opened the back door to him, George McCaffrey was enabled to enter the house, while his brother Tom howled with laughter outside. What happened next is not recorded! One fact has emerged. The *so-called* maid, Pearl Scotney, is no other than the sister of the aforementioned Madam D, who is the intimate friend of G. McCaffrey! . . . Picking up the pieces should constitute an interesting problem in moral philosophy" (PP 409–10; emphasis added). The anonymous reporter who makes this lame joke about maidservants and picking up the pieces is apparently not aware of Murdoch's more basic joke: Tom, howling with laughter, evokes the carnivalesque tradition of cleansing the community through laughter. If the newspaper accounts serve the same purpose for the reader, then Murdoch is illustrating the "parodistic" in Bakhtin's metalinguistics: "any reproduction of another person's word with a change of accent" (PDP 164–65), a borrowed discourse used for an opposite purpose. It is also appropriate that the other newspaper be called *The Swimmer*, the word connoting "river," a collector of garbage and gossip as well as a vehicle for rebirth. This newspaper exaggerates the hint of lesbianism suggested by deflation of the "so-called maid." N tells us that "according to *The Swimmer* the 'orgy' had been arranged by Miss 'Hattie' Meynell herself, who had turned out to be considerably less stuffy than was at first imagined. The paper also struck a note of its own, reporting that 'Our Sapphic Sisterhood of Women's Libbers were also there in force, and the *so-called* "maid" was to be seen hugging and kissing, clasped to the bosom of another long-haired Amazon'" (PP 410; emphasis added).

Here, as throughout Murdoch's novels, water imagery works radically as rebirth or as destruction—destruction by *The Swimmer* of reputations and of language.[10] The novel revels also in a second carnivalesque figure: "'inconsequent' statements (which are nonetheless 'connected' within an infinite context)" (WDN 79). Murdoch uses both water and anthropomorphic animals as vehicles for exploring the unconscious. She employs this figure to subvert, or at least bypass, the logic of causality. For her, art perceives the relationship between the aimlessness of the universe and the patterns humans impose on it. Her novels thus focus on the distinction between necessity and contingency: what *must* occur and what may or may not occur.

Reviving *Roman de Renart* (WDN 78), Murdoch evokes a mystical power rising from the unconscious by introducing foxes and references to wolves. Her method helps the reader find "accidental slit[s] into another world, weird, beautiful, dangerous, coming nearer" (PP 423), a world seen by children, grandmothers, and gypsy maids. The fox-wolf pattern, perhaps alluding to the Middle English popular satirical fable "The Fox and the Wolf," is one of Murdoch's seemingly inconsequential strands (see Murdoch's holograph sketch of Adam's dog, reproduced in figure 1). Murdoch is playing with riddles when N says that the child Adam knows to keep the foxes secret and tells us that "Alex never admitted to anyone that she saw foxes" (PP 35), and when Alex asks Ruby, the gypsy maid, not to talk about foxes. Murdoch is playing, but with Sphinx-like riddles that carry mystical weight. When Alex falls down the steps on hearing that the foxes have been killed, and this simple accident reduces the powerful matron to a weak old woman, the reader knows that the foxes embody some balance in the universe to which he or she has not been paying attention: "Alex's fall prefigured George's" (PP 572).[11] Happily, the foxes escape the exterminators, but another mystical figure, Rozanov—who embodies the old year, the winter, the old king—does not survive. His drowning makes way for marriages and spiritual growth and celebration. In *The Philosopher's Pupil*, Murdoch has used spectacle of scene and language to exteriorize, or bring to light, insights from the unconscious: insights about sexuality, birth, and death (Kristeva, WDN 78).

 In the remainder of this chapter and in chapter 7 I demonstrate Murdoch's playful experimentation with linguistic and social patterns of aimlessness that expose the human condition. She experiments not only with social stratification and the wild, contingent swirl of language but also with parody and stylization. The result, whether she intends it or not, is often carnivalesque confusion and subversion. It is my intention to look at the formal properties of these mixtures, measure their immediacy, and gauge closure and open-endedness.

More and more as her writing has matured, Murdoch has focused on thinkers such as Bradley Pearson, whose profession thrives on language, both written and oral. Murdoch's medium and message are language; therefore, her collaborating dialogically with multiple narrative voices that use different languages is both necessary and pleasurable. Her decisions about her narrator and the dialogue of voices are integral to her writing process. Her control over and

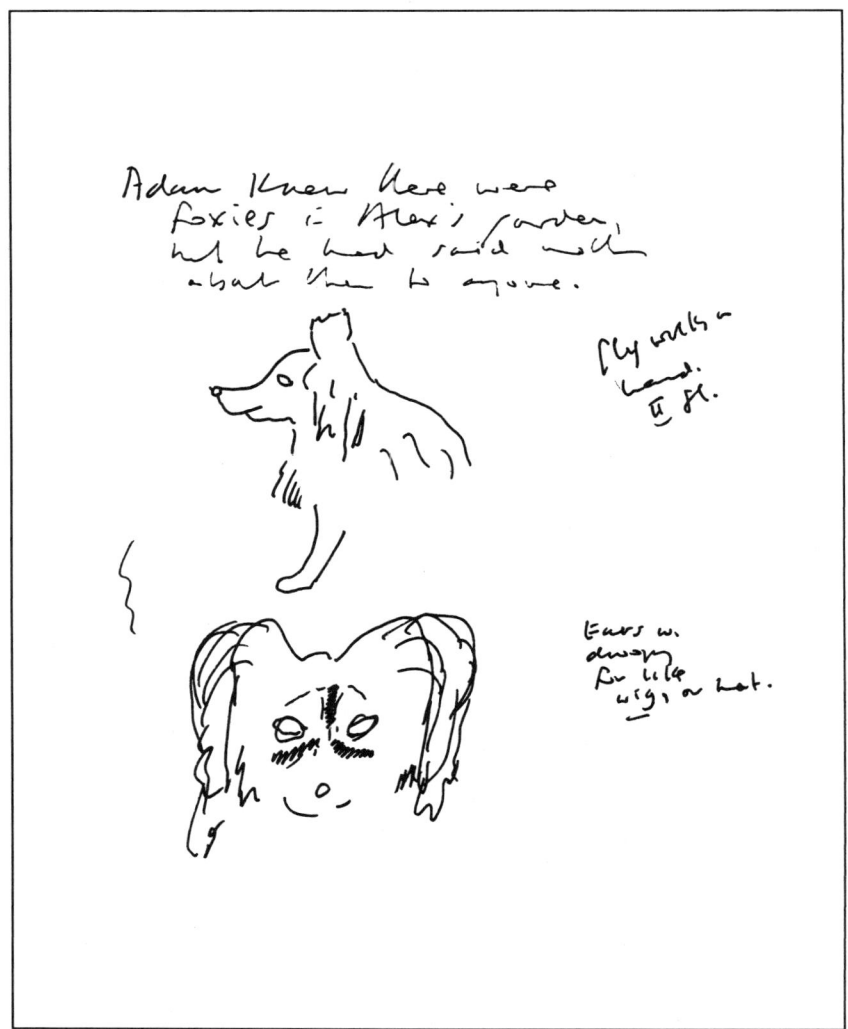

Figure 1. Holograph diagram from the manuscript of *The Philosopher's Pupil*. Reproduced with permission of Iris Murdoch; copy courtesy of Special Collections, University of Iowa Libraries.

access to her narrators and characters reflect technical decisions. She seems to have worked out her philosophy long ago. Unlike Joyce, she rejects being a god-author and instead becomes incarnate in a narrator, either first or third person, and lives in the fictional world with the characters, allowing them diverse and uninhibited voices. In 1977 she told Malcolm Bradbury that "one starts off—at least I start off—hoping every time that this [creating characters] is going to happen and that a lot of people who are not me are going to come into existence in some wonderful way. Yet often it turns out in the end that something about the structure of the work itself, the myth as it were of the work, has drawn all these people into a sort of spiral, or into a kind of form which ultimately is the form of own mind" (Bradbury, *The Novel Today* 114).

Her desire to simulate the pain of inspiration and creation in *The Black Prince* led Murdoch to structure a multivoiced, intricately framed house of cards. The novel's most recent critics agree that it is a turning point in her novel writing. The first-person narrator's multivoiced discourse, which struggles to give Bradley as writer freedom from Bradley as participant, works well for comic effect. The author, who occasionally competes with the protagonist for the floor, employs him as a mouthpiece. Bradley's confession to himself and to the world, written in direct discourse, illustrates Murdoch's successful creation of a climactic comic scene without a set piece (of which Conradi has written so enthusiastically). One of Bradley's letter sequences, near the beginning of the novel, has a quite different purpose from the climactic one in *An Accidental Man* (see chapter 5). In that earlier text Murdoch takes the risk of putting some of the crucial events of the plot into the letter sequence; here, the purpose of Bradley's sequence is to unearth all the possible conflicting voices in his personality. Francis Marloe's postscript, as an example of a hidden polemic parodically colored, takes the reader to the heart of Murdoch's analysis of masochistic fantasy—the energy that makes her world turn.

Two examples of first-person direct discourse in *The Black Prince* illustrate what Holquist and Emerson say about Bakhtin's insistence that "human coming-to-consciousness . . . is a constant struggle": on the one hand is "privileged language that approaches us from without"; on the other is "language that is the retelling of a text in one's own words" (DI 424). This centrifugal versus centripetal process, or the process of maturing, is what makes certain characters dynamic. Most critics would agree that Bradley Pearson is Murdoch's most memorable protagonist thus far. His metamorphosis from mediocre artist to good artist through his metaphorical flaying is perhaps Murdoch's most fruitful example of retelling the sacred text in one's own words. In order to exonerate himself as an artist, Bradley explains his Apollonian rebirth and confesses his ignorance and lust.[12]

Murdoch creates "in a great cauldron of ideas and images, impulses and feelings" a god who enters the text to facilitate the production of the text (Heusel, "Dialogue" 9). At first, the unsuspecting reader accepts Loxias at face value as the editor of the novel. Only in hindsight, when the reader has to contemplate that Loxias's ambivalence indicates his many ontological possibilities, does the reader begin to question: Is Loxias a character, a figment of Bradley's imagination, an inspirational voice in Bradley's head? Murdoch organizes her revelation of the process in such a way that it creates a circular effect in the novel. The process begins when Bradley on occasion directs the reader's attention backward at Loxias as something other than a real editor. By the end of the novel the reader questions the purpose of this figure, the extraterrestrial or imaginary person who is rising above the novelistic world. This rere gardant activity on the part of all participants—characters, author, and reader—is a postmodern technique.

The postscripts set the reader up for closure or consolation that never comes. Loxias is never onstage, but he does serve as a self-reflective and alienating framing device. In what sense is Loxias the father of the text? Bakhtin says about Dostoevsky's novels that "the voice of the actual 'other' in confessional dialogues is always given in an analogous setting, one pointedly external to the plot. . . . [T]hey are prepared for by the plot, but their culminating points—the peaks of the dialogues—rise above the plot in the abstract sphere of pure relationship, one person to another" (PDP 264–65). This quality of being external to the plot but also prepared for by the plot describes the relationship of Bradley and Loxias, which is beyond realism.

In this novel Murdoch must go beyond the common conventional language and the common conventional world, because these cannot describe the issues she wants to explore. Murdoch herself talks approvingly of Dostoevsky's exaggerations: "Dostoevsky has scenes which I think exhibit what you say [about the carnivalesque] and which is sublime. I mean, for instance, the long scene in *Karamazov* where Dmitry pursues Grushenka to the inn, and the riot at the fete in *The Possessed*. . . . Something about those wild scenes in Dostoevsky fed my imagination very deeply" (Heusel, "Dialogue" 8). This kind of wildness and intensity is necessary in *The Black Prince* because only radical exaggeration can convince the reader that the Greek god of poetry has become incarnate in the London world of Bradley's novel.

Both Dipple and Deborah Johnson read the following statement by Bradley as Murdoch's manifesto for art—and read it as monological:

> Yet what can one do but try to lodge one's vision somehow inside this layered stuff of ironic sensibility, which, if I were a fictitious character, would be that much deeper and denser? How prejudiced is this image of Arnold, how superficial this picture of Priscilla! Emotions cloud the view, and so far from isolating the particular, draw generality and even theory in their train. When I write of Arnold my pen shakes with resentment, love, remorse, and fear. It is as if I were building a barrier against him composed of words, hiding myself behind a mound of words. We defend ourselves by descriptions and tame the world by generalizing. (BP 58)

Moreover, Johnson finds it an opportunity for Murdoch to speak through or mimic a male author, the first of Murdoch's novels "to trace the painful tension between the author's own need for communication and her simultaneous need for self-concealment" (*Iris Murdoch* 36). Without questioning the validity of Johnson's argument, I want to emphasize the importance of Murdoch's spoofs on herself: she and Bradley use words as barriers, just as she and Arnold are both book-a-year writers.

It does seem legitimate to question whether Bradley is the author's mouthpiece in some of the novel's explorations of the nature of art. Bakhtin makes concrete the need for a distance between author and character:

> Self-consciousness, as the artistic dominant in the construction of the hero's image, is by itself sufficient to break down the monologic unity of an artistic world—but only on condition that the hero, as self-consciousness, is really represented and not merely expressed, that is, does not fuse with the author, does not become the mouth-piece for his voice; only on condition, consequently, that accents of the hero's self-consciousness are really objectified and that the work itself observes a distance between the hero and the author. (PDP 51)

Murdoch has gone out of her way to make sure that readers are very critical of Bradley and never see him as her mouthpiece.

In Bradley's funniest sequence of scenes he does not fuse with the author but rather struggles comedically against her discourse. This stage of his change of consciousness reveals the struggle among several discourses of love: the traditional, antiquated discourse of courtly love; lustful, agitated animal love; and, yes, occasionally what Murdoch would call authentic love. Murdoch parodically introduces the language of lust by way of the courtly love convention. Cast into the role of the speaker of "To His Coy Mistress," the voice spouts: "Time had already become eternity. There was a huge warm globe of conscious being within which I moved with extreme slowness, or which perhaps I was. I had only to gaze, to stretch my hands out slowly like a chameleon. It no longer mattered where I looked or what I did. Everything in the world was Julian" (BP 173). The reader has not known Bradley to be capable of this internal relaxation, this unending perspective on time and space. The reader is familiar with Bradley's hyperbole, but not such poetic hyperbole. As Bradley puts on the persona of Marvell's speaker, he apparently also contemplates that speaker's prerogatives of "tear[ing] pleasures with rough strife." Bradley illustrates Bakhtin's understanding of the way characters grow into self-awareness, for, in responding to his lustful feelings, he is freeing himself from the authoritative words of Puritanism—words that have ceased to have meaning since he fell in love. In his newly relaxed state, he takes on the voice of a god who creates and judges: "I felt that I was, at every instant, creating Julian and supporting her being with my own. At the same time I saw her too in every way as I had seen her before. I saw her simplicity, her ignorance, her childish unkindness, her unpretty anxious little face" (BP 173). The old, nervous voice of logic analyzes his behavior.

The stratagem of the plot is to ensure that all the events seem to have been building to this confession of love, this immersion in comic discourse. Bradley is able at this point to "*will* another," for the reader watches him deciding not to make Julian suffer:

> I could never never never tell my love. That this knowledge did not immediately produce a pain of which I died is a proof of the immense power, that is *ipso facto* the purity, of the love which I felt for this girl. It was enough happiness to love her. The extra piece which would be telling her about it was like a pinpoint compared with the heavenly joy of simply apprehending her. (Any further joys my beatified imagination not only

did not covet but did not even conceive.) I did not even mind when I saw her again. I had no plans to see her again. Who was I to have plans? (BP 174–75)

On this first evening, then, Bradley, a newly vitalized man, is happy simply to celebrate the gift of Julian's occasional presence. He knows that there is the danger of "the return[ing] of self," but at present he feels only "a dazzled gratitude" (BP 175). He concludes that he will love his lady from afar: "Yet I understood at once in a clear *intellectual* way that I could not ever tell Julian that I loved her. The details of this certainly (what it involved) became clearer to me later, but it stood flaming in my way at the very start. I was fifty-eight, she was twenty. I could not puzzle, burden and bedevil her young life with the faintest hint or glimpse of this huge terrible love" (BP 175). The shock of love has freed Bradley from the old sediments of his personality and thrown him into a state never heretofore activated in the presence of the reader. Changing position and perspective, he seems, in contrast with his earlier frantic attitude toward the Baffins and Frances and Christian, to exude an almost palpable aura of relaxation. This kind of selfless courage gives him the strength to be virtuous for the entire day that follows. In his newfound relaxed social openness, Bradley's discourse becomes charitable. For the first time he considers his interlocutors. He is receptive to Hartbourne's phone call, inviting him to lunch. He goes on a buying spree for Rachel and then for Julian. Knowing that there are "reconcilings" he must effect (BP 183), he attempts to gain knowledge of an individual by ordering Arnold's complete works and planning to read them "humbly and without prejudice" (BP 194). For the first time the reader sees him being kind to the most obnoxious of his acquaintances, Roger and Marigold—and to Christian, his former wife, who finds his discourse so congenial that she proposes remarriage. He manages for this one day to direct a "just and loving gaze . . . upon [several] individual real[ities]" (SG 34).

Bradley's view of the artist, before his series of ordeals, has elements of egoism, sacredness, and sentimentality, moving back and forth from romantic to classical conceptions, ranging from Apollonian to Dionysian. Murdoch handles his point of view parodically. She uses it to refract her own, which is much more like that of the sixty-year-old Bradley. The older Bradley, a Marsyas figure, has been metaphorically flayed, and this experience has given him an entirely different worldview.

For Bradley, exaggerated procrastination and anxiety often take the form of channeling time and energy into letter writing. He says that if he attends to a problem in a letter, he feels that it is solved: "To desiderate something in a letter is, I irrationally feel, tantamount to bringing it about. A letter is a barrier, a reprieve, a charm against the world, an almost infallible method of acting at a distance. (And, it must be admitted, of passing the buck.) It is a way of bidding time to stop" (BP 40–41). Murdoch reveals here her recognition that a letter is a kind of personal, private meditation,[13] and that once it is sent out into the world the missive is a missile that contains all the energy of heteroglossia: the word. Bradley is afraid of his correspondents and their words and tackles each letter as if it were addressed to an opponent. He is especially worried about being accused by Arnold and Rachel; in fact, later in the novel Rachel accuses Bradley of deliberately letting her see Arnold's cruel letter about her. She uses this excuse to justify letting Bradley take the rap for murdering her husband. To forestall any such reason, Bradley tries to create trust, but the quality of his speech is halting. His words have a cringing "sideward glance" (PDP 196), and he cringes when he says that he has no thoughts about what happened. He shields himself from Arnold, first by apologizing for being a voyeur and then by attempting to prove that he is trustworthy. He is afraid to appear to enjoy any part of Arnold and Rachel's family quarrel. He uses the metaphor of trial and witnesses and suggests in the word *intruder* that he is not an eavesdropper or voyeur.[14]

Only after Bradley has vented his innermost need to write a series of letters to Arnold, Julian, Marloe, and Christian does he remind himself that words do not always communicate their author's intention. His point echoes Murdoch's recognition that the word is magic. In each letter Bradley focuses self-consciously on his own persona, questioning how well he is representing himself. Part of the magic of the letters is that they help him to affirm himself, to will a persona—Bradley Persona. His letter to Arnold is also a supplication for help for his own problem with Christian, a plea for sympathy for a lonely man. Murdoch orchestrates Bradley's anxiety. First she shows the reader the pressure Bradley is under; Bradley's sweating after each confrontation with an opponent tells the reader that the act of letter writing produces tension. The series of letters builds to a crescendo. Intended to smooth out the near-murder that occurred between Rachel and Arnold, a problem that will reverberate to Bradley, Marloe, Julian, and Christian, his four letters achieve reactions

Polyphonic Novels

other than those he had intended. These interacting threads of tension help Murdoch to achieve a plurality of voices in Bradley's epistolarity. The two middle letters, to Julian and Marloe, are embedded between the two difficult ones, the first making him sweat, the last causing him to sweat, tremble, and pant. In Arnold's letter Bradley emphasizes himself; he uses *I* eighteen times, *me* seven, and *my* six. Even though he uses *you* fifteen times, Murdoch calls attention to his more egoistic position by putting *I* in the letter's first three sentences. The letter to Julian focuses on her. It takes a fatherly or teacherly tone that is upbeat. Marloe's letter is accusing and short, with the emphasis on *you*. The letter to Christian is formal and bureaucratic: a veneer of legalistic language only partially conceals Bradley's fear of engagement with her: "it has been brought to my attention," "This letter is to say," "I should be grateful for the continuance of our total non-communication" (BP 43). The sentence "There is nothing of a cordial or forward-looking import to be read 'between the lines'" (BP 44) seems to reflect the discourse of Christian. The latter comment betrays almost as much passionate anxiety as the fear-induced statement that is ironic for the reader: "I have forgotten you completely" (BP 44). Bradley emphasizes the potential for magic: "I reread the letter which I had written to Christian and reflected upon it. I had produced it out of some sort of immediate need for self-expression or self-defence, a magical warding-off movement, such as I have explained that I naturally indulge in as a letter writer. However a letter, as I have at times to my own cost forgotten, is not a piece of self-expression; it is also statement, suggestion, persuasion, command, and its sheer effectiveness in these respects needs to be objectively estimated" (BP 44–45). Bradley uses letter writing as a form of exorcism to change reality and as a way to fool himself into thinking he has dealt with reality. By extension, it seems safe to suspect Bradley of using the same sorts of language games throughout his novel to describe reality, thereby distorting it.

In *The Black Prince* Murdoch gives Bradley, the thinker-writer-poseur, many other distinctive characters as mirrors for his coming to consciousness. In addition to having three alter egos to reflect his behavior and character—Loxias, his Apollonian editor; Arnold Baffin, a book-a-year novelist; and Francis Marloe, his dupe—Bradley has the other dramatis personae who, acting almost like members of a jury, comment on the accused by writing postscripts to his novel. By seeing himself in them and by writing about them in his novel, Bradley has become a real artist.

Francis, Bradley's former brother-in-law, is a memorable comic figure and a complex foil to Bradley. Even though he is unable to elude Murdoch's control in the same way as characters like Franca Sheerwater in *The Message to the Planet*, whose dynamic plea moves toward feminism and against Murdoch's public image, Francis is independent enough to be especially annoying to the reader. He does have more freedom than Bradley in that he, at least, is never a spokesman for Murdoch. On the basis of the reminder Murdoch wrote to herself, saying "Absurdify Francis" as she scribbled in a heavily revised portion of the manuscript of *The Black Prince* now housed at the University of Iowa Library, it is clear he did not escape entirely from her control, did not blossom full-blown. His baroque postscript contributes many voices to the general multivoicedness of the novel. The Freudian discourse that Francis appropriates is ironically critical of him as a character in that it causes the reader to question people who use Freudian theorizing reductively. Murdoch's discourse specifically about Freud, in *The Sovereignty of Good*, is the actualizing background for her parody of his ideas in the mouth of Marloe (SG 76). By comparing the two, a reader can measure when Murdoch uses Francis's words parodically and when she doesn't. Murdoch mockingly reifies Freud's discourse in the mouth of Francis. On the other hand, whereas Murdoch praises and criticizes Freud openly in *The Sovereignty of Good*, Francis's language undermines Freud's discourse indirectly by "indirectly striking a blow" (PDP 196). Murdoch's worldview—the extent to which she agrees and disagrees with Freud—colors and helps absurdify Francis's postscript.[15]

On the whole, Murdoch's purpose in using the four postscripts by dramatis personae is to put off closure dramatically and to make clear that she is not ready to let the listener respond.[16] Even the fifth postscript, by the editor P. Loxias, does not sufficiently close the novel. Murdoch uses it to help create a reverberating, circular effect that sends the reader back to the prefaces—Loxias's and Bradley's—to see what was missed. This effect and the response it evokes are postmodern. To demonstrate the arbitrariness of human constructs and to question standards of morality, Murdoch subverts her own criteria for good. In addition, she plays with poststructuralist concepts of preface, text, and postscript. Gayatri Chakravorty Spivak discusses these concepts in her preface to Derrida's *Of Grammatology*, saying "the preface harbors a lie" (x): "The preface is a necessary gesture of homage and parricide, for the book (the father) makes a claim of authority or origin which is both true and false" (xi);

"the structure preface-text becomes open at both ends. The text has no stable identity, no stable origin, no stable end" (106). Throughout Francis's postscript in particular, multiple meanings struggle.

In saying about Bradley what is true of himself, Francis is undermining the validity of Bradley's text. Francis is a practicing homosexual whose pseudo–case study of Bradley includes his pseudo-Freudian discourse as he finds in Bradley the classic symptoms of the Oedipus complex, including hatred of women, masochism, love of a father figure (Arnold Baffin), and obsession with defecation. Likewise, Murdoch is undermining the authenticity of the entire book by having Francis question whether Loxias is a voice of Bradley rather than an authentic editor. Francis's postscript is significant in its decentering of the world of Bradley's novel and in its disruption of boundaries between discourses and between art and commodity. This postscript, the only one by a male, is the funniest and the most salable, but also the one most readily rejected by the reader because of its exaggeration. Marloe's discourse helps demonstrate centripetal versus centrifugal momentum of language, the way perspectives rearrange themselves. This postscript is an appropriate capping off for a novel that has forced the reader to question all of Bradley's utterances; as such, the entire novel becomes a celebration of heteroglossia, the protean phenomenon of language.[17]

Parodically employing bits and pieces of Freud's writing, Murdoch has great fun critiquing both the people who distort Freud for gain, artistic or economic, and Freud himself. She suggests that Francis is only one of thousands abusing Freudian discourse. Earlier in the novel, Murdoch has put Ernest Jones's Freudian reading of *Hamlet* into Bradley's mouth when he teaches the play to Julian. Here Murdoch is treating parodically a reading she considers reductive (Conradi, *Saint* 196). Murdoch's combining high Eros (Platonic) and low Eros (Freudian) in her most serious scenes suggests that she also considers Freud's readings of texts reductive. A broader intention is carnivalesque—to demonstrate the absurdity of Freudianism out of context when it is put into the mouth of a buffoon such as Marloe, demonstrating not only its comedic possibilities but its destructiveness. The languages that vie for authority here are not only Murdoch's discourse concerning her reservations about the science of Freudianism and Francis's infantile language of lust but also the languages of love (high Eros and low Eros), sexism, and homosexuality.

Francis, who sublimates his homoerotic desire for Bradley, fathers a text in which he creates a consoling fantasy. Being a nurturing, childlike man, he imagines that his duty is to be a parent to people in need, but being stuck at an infantile stage himself, he is begging to be nurtured. Since the other characters are too selfish to parent him, he is left to look after himself. The reader sees his comic potential from the first, categorizing him as a fly-in-the-ointment type who can quickly upset the equilibrium of the plot. He does just that by going off on a homosexual liaison, thus giving Bradley's distraught sister the opportunity to commit suicide.

Murdoch gleefully manipulates Francis's fantasies within his postscript, making it a piece of writing for the careful reader only. It is possible to imagine that a reader would attribute Francis's line "Most artists are homosexuals" to Murdoch, but such simplemindedness glosses over Murdoch's changing styles and parodic discourse throughout the piece. This sentence is characteristic of Francis's style and view of the world, not Murdoch's. A reader who took Francis's postscript out of context and failed to read the entire novel with care would miss the dialogic overtones, thereby creating distortion. It is possible to recognize the slapstick of a third-rate mind and perhaps even suspect the deflation, while still failing to see that there is also significant parody taking place in the text. Such a reading ironically replicates Francis's fallacy of wrenching from context. Careful readers recognize parody against the background of their ordinary language, the parody creating struggles between languages.[18]

At least three semantic intentions dominate Francis's postscript. Francis's meaning is that Bradley, whom he loves because he is lovable and good, could have been released if he had told the truth about his latent homosexuality and made a plea for sympathy. The meaning of Murdoch's words that characterize Francis is that he is a weak and selfish voyeur, a grotesque hanger-on. Murdoch and Francis agree that Bradley destroys his chances at the trial because he inappropriately takes on himself the general guilt of mankind. Francis, arguing from his infantile perspective, perverts Freudian discourse because he wants Bradley to save himself—for him, Francis. Murdoch has created a Shakespearean comic figure to lighten the protagonist Bradley's prudish, alazon-like behavior. In his shallow certainty, Francis oversimplifies as only a buffoon can. Being ingenuous, he does not understand how gauche it is to reveal his intention to make a fortune on Bradley's demise by selling pseudopsychoanalytic books and through them building a practice selling his psychological services.

He is not especially evil; he is just a dense bumbler. Murdoch's ability to hold so many meanings in place simultaneously aligns her with postmodernists.

Murdoch has styled Francis's thought processes to be busy, hectic, swirling, so that his obsessive compulsiveness convinces the reader of his half-truths. His obsessional neurosis demands that he keep up his illusions or face disaster. Francis begins his postscript by hawking his book in the language of a professional salesman of the commodity of Freudianism:

> It is my pleasure and privilege to add a critical epilogue to this unusual "autobiography." I do so gladly as homage to my old friend, still languishing in "durance vile," and I do so dutifully as a service to the cause of science. This remarkable piece of self-analysis from a talented pen deserves a thoroughly detailed commentary, for which, the publisher tells me, there is unfortunately no space in this volume. I intend however to publish in due course a lengthy book, upon which I have now been at work for some time, about the case of Bradley Pearson, and in this work the "autobiography," a prime piece of evidence in this *cause célèbre*, will of course be fully treated. What follows here is a merely a digest of a few concise points. (BP 347)

Appropriating then the authoritative word of Freud, he distorts it in order to help sublimate his own homosexuality and to give himself a springboard for advertising his services.

Immediately, in the first sentence of the second paragraph, he obfuscates his meaning, revealing by his comically circuitous syntax his lack of directness and dishonesty: "Not to skirt the obvious, Bradley Pearson presents, I need hardly to say, the classical symptoms of the Oedipus complex" (BP 347). Murdoch brilliantly twists the syntax—placing "Bradley Pearson presents" between the infinitive phrase referring to "I" and "I," causing what looks like a dangling modifier which then refers to Bradley. Since her purpose is to demonstrate that Francis, who is ostensibly talking about Bradley, is really talking about himself, making "not to skirt the obvious" refer to both men is a brilliant move. The juxtaposition in the same sentence of the "Not to skirt the obvious" and "I need hardly" continues the deferral until the end of the sentence. Similarly, by having the third sentence of this postscript begin with a reference to analysis—"This remarkable piece of self-analysis from a talented pen"—Murdoch creates another joke at the expense of Francis, who is too obtuse to notice that a reader might think for a moment that he is describing his own text as "remarkable." Francis stylizes the discourses of Bradley and of Freud. A banal generalization bombards the reader on the first page of the postscript: "Most men love their mothers and hate their fathers." Relishing Bradley's misogynistic words, Francis uses them to enhance the sensationalism of the product he wants to sell to the public. He quotes Bradley without quotation marks: "The idea of menstruation is sickening and appalling. Women smell. The female principle is what is messy, smelly and soft" (BP 347). Bradley is not particularly conscious of being misogynist, the words being details of his characterization; but the words are multiplied in intensity when Francis, a homosexual, says that Bradley "gloat[s] over women's uncleaness." Francis's chain of logic, which moves in the postscript from the crime of defecation to *gilt* to *guilt*, is worse than spurious: "Many men, often without consciousness thereof, see women as unclean." "There is no doubt that she had the misfortune to represent to him also *the shop*, that stale interior, symbolic of the rejected womb of a socially inferior mother" (BP 347). "The physical, moreover, figures the moral. Women are liars, traitors, cowards. In contrast Bradley himself appears as a self-confessed puritan, an ascetic, a tall thin man, a sort of human Post Office Tower, erect and steely. By this means, without the necessity of actual sexual prowess, our hero can see himself as 'an imaginary Don Juan.' (A touching give-away this!)" (BP 348). "That Bradley is a masochist is here a banality of criticism. (That all artists are is a further truism.)" Francis tosses around equally illogical insinuations: "Why is it a *writer* on whom Bradley fixes his love and his hate? And why is it a *writer* that he himself so obsessively dreams of being? The choice of the art is itself significant. Bradley tells us in so many words that his parents kept a *paper* shop. (Paper: papa.) The 'crime' of soiling paper (defecation) is a natural image of the revolt against the father" (BP 349). Murdoch does give Francis enough intelligence to see that Freud's work is about "the other." Being a marginal person, Francis perhaps recognizes intuitively that scapegoating is intuitive. His illogic suggests that latent homosexuality may have some hint of misogyny at its base.

Francis's repeating the misogynist words is unforgivable. Moreover, he refers to Loxias in a discourse that is, if not racist, at least a discourse of brutality: "Bradley shamelessly delights in the conception of the huge black bully (like an enormous blackamoor) who has, as he conceived it, come to discipline his life, as artist and as man. . . . The narcissism of the deviant eats up all other characters and will tolerate only one: himself, Bradley invents Mr. Loxias so as to present *himself* to the world with a flourish of alleged objectivity. He says of P. Loxias, 'I could have invented him.' In fact he did!" (BP 350). This penultimate paragraph subverts the validity of Bradley's text. The richness of the flaying has many layers. For Francis, the image of the blackamoor disciplining Bradley is prurient; because he cannot get beyond the flesh, he sees only the physical abuse. For Murdoch, Francis's view is an oversimplification or ironic equation. For Francis, it seems simply a physical reality more than a fantasy.

Murdoch manifests her style and worldview in the broader aspects of her design. Her parody is obvious in Francis's style, in particular in the alliteration and assonance of one quite funny sentence in which he momentarily waxes poetic: "Alas how readily these symbols assemble themselves in this our human life, forming great daisy chains of cause and effect from which we escape never!" (BP 347–48). The romantic notion of escape, as well as the highly postured "we escape never!" instead of "we never escape," emphasizes Francis's pretension. The style warns the reader that Francis is revealing more about himself than about Bradley.[19]

Murdoch's pointed reminder to herself in the holograph notebooks of *The Black Prince*—"Absurdify Francis"—reveals her strategy to complicate even the most seemingly inane character. In practice, this creative desire reinforces Kristeva's theory that the carnivalesque establishes a realistic representation and then uses language to provoke laughter. Within this context, Francis and Bradley are among the strong characters whom Murdoch allows to help redefine, during her creative process, their own respective strata in the novel while she as choragos orchestrates.

CHAPTER SEVEN

Women's Discourse: *Nuns and Soldiers* and *The Message to the Planet*

Occasionally critics argue that Murdoch creates variations on the same character types. Perhaps these critics are acknowledging that they find Murdoch peopling her novels with various kinds of wives or husbands or thinkers. Murdoch's giving wives as a group somewhat similar characteristics and behaviors, for example, suggests that she works like a painter making studies or, like Wittgenstein, making sketches (see Wittgenstein's statement from *Philosophical Investigations* in chapter 9). Her studies of wives evolves, no doubt, out of a different creative mixture than her studies of husbands. These differences in cultural mix resemble Bakhtin's notion of linguistic strata; for Bakhtin, particular types of characters define their own rituals and discourses, which serve as markers of type. A review of Murdoch's novels shows that marginal women characters have become less marginalized in the later novels and that the male thinkers have become marginalized.

Some important similarities exist between the women in *Nuns and Soldiers* (1980) and those in *Message to the Planet*. In the former, the characters inhabit a stratum of Murdoch's novelistic world that readers associate with the civil servant–Oxford scholar type of Briton. The novel is multivoiced and multivalent. The dialogism in the relation of character to narrator is striking in its revelations about both. Anne Cavidge, the most magnificently fleshed out of the novel's group of interesting women characters, plays out an intricate confession or self-analysis at the end of the novel as she sits in a pub called the Prince of Denmark, waiting to discover Daisy's whereabouts. At this point in the novel, Murdoch employs terms—*self-analysis* and *voice* of pride (NS 498), and metaphors like "dodging a blow" (NS 501)—to convey the struggle Anne goes through regarding her future attitude toward herself, her life, and the world in general. The seven pages begin with her anxiety and disjointedness, the one voice then breaking up into numerous voices that vie for power.

The major struggle begins between the voice that embraces change, growth, disintegration, and risk and the one that depends on integrity. The "voice of integrity" (NS 498) interrupts two-thirds of the way through and fights for Anne's wholeness, attempting to pull her back together. Anne is glad she has kept her mouth shut about her love, her need for companionship, and her impatience with the normative cultural obsession with heterosexual love, which at one point she calls a disease. She, of course, never finds integrity, but she does find that the world has its beauties.

The lashings of the first voice are couched in the language of religion: Anne, a nun who has left the order, should have directed her energy toward assisting someone else "instead of fretting about her own fate. . . . Why had she not imagined Daisy's loneliness, her possible plight, her possible despair?" (NS 494–95). This voice is perhaps responding with a sideward glance from the convent. The law of the Old Testament rings through in the vengeance implicit in her deploring of her vanity. She refers to the loss of Daisy as a professional loss of the one sheep as opposed to the ninety-nine. She "had been too absorbed in her own hopes," too cold and hostile. The narrator can even sum up the self-criticism with "her selfless, masochistic morality" (NS 495). The voice of romantic love interrupts but vacillates between feeling the pain and lashing the spirit for not having been "interested in his interest in Christ" (NS 495). This voice criticizes past times, wondering if it should have seized on rational arguments: "proper scruples, reasonable prudence, self-punishing masochism, . . . demonic pride . . . [and] censorious coldness" (NS 495–96). The gist of the seven pages is that "in order to survive a terrible loss one has to become another person" (NS 497).

The series begins with the confessing voice, which condemns Anne's past egoistic perspective. This voice is never mute until the end, and throughout it blends in with the others and continues its struggle. She criticizes herself for not thinking of the happiness of Gertrude and the Count, realizing that they need to play out a superficial game of knight and lady. She knows now that the Count could not take the full intensity of Anne's love for him—that he could survive only small doses. Here she had been interested in the opportunity of giving him her devoted attention, and she had not tried to imagine his need, which was considering how much attention Gertrude needed and how many admirers she needed to secure her happiness. Anne is peeved with herself for having ignored her age-old policy of ignoring her own interest (NS 496), a policy that bears the strong scent of masochism.

The discourse of unselfish love, a discourse that looks and listens, interrupts the confessing voice two pages later and decides that Gertrude has certain rights, and that one such right is access to the Count. Anne sounds very much like M, the mother-in-law in *The Sovereignty of Good*, when she determines to appreciate Tim, the young and irresponsible fellow with whom Gertrude has so recklessly fallen in love. Her recognition that the Count is a holy saint is hers alone: "She saw him transfigured, saw his beauty which she was sure so few could see, and her body ached for him and she mourned" (NS 497). Others seem to see him not as a whole person but as no more than a servant to Gertrude. Anne realizes that her goal in life is to make people feel less anxious.

Perhaps the voice of pain and the critical voice are the same; the voice of pain begins to gnaw at Anne's innards. This voice had missed its chance, had been too patient, was a coward: "If I had only told him then and then" (NS 495). "She should have played a bolder and more positive role, questioned the Count, not respected his secrecy and his reserve. What, in these reflections, she tried at all costs to avoid was the terrible love-yearning, the *I want him, I want him, I shall die without him* which kept returning and rising up in her heart" (NS 497) like Lear's "climbing sorrow" (II.ii.232). "To this hot desire [which Adrienne Rich labels compulsive heterosexuality], Anne opposed herself, and was cold, cold. That way indeed madness lay" (NS 497).

Anne does not ever lapse into simply feeling sorry for herself: "For the first moment Anne felt shock and distress at the image of her which had escaped somehow and was wandering abroad, bandied about over the drinking glasses. Then she relaxed and smiled. It was funny really. And by what privilege could she be exempt from so general a human fate? We are all the judges and the judged, victims of the casual malice and fantasy of others, and ready sources of fantasy and malice in our turn" (NS 503). She recognizes that now she can open herself completely to pain, including the very real pain she associates with her brother's death. In the space of several pages, to the accompaniment of the falling snow, she has emerged from the inability even to acknowledge the pain resulting from her brother's death: "And now, with a swift dart of memory, she thought she could recall how ever in the moment of hearing that Dick was dead, fallen from a cliff face in the Cairngorms, she had instinctively closed herself against pain, instinctively peered ahead into a time when she would be someone else who could be conscious of this loss without anguish" (NS 497). The time into which she had been peering ahead comes, marked by the equanimity she experiences in the novel's closing paragraphs, a time of her coming to consciousness.

One reason that Anne and Daisy have such problems at the end of the novel is that neither has friends who can be reflectors for her. Both must move to the United States to find appropriate lives to live. No pair of women in Murdoch's novels, not even Anne and Gertrude, can be compared to Franca Sheerwater and Maisie Tether in *The Message to the Planet* (1989) in their ability to mirror for each other. The hero looks at him- or herself "in all the mirrors of other people's consciousnesses[;] he [or she] knows all the possible refractions of his [or her] image in those mirrors" (Bakhtin, PDP 53). In Franca and her new friend Maisie, Murdoch demonstrates one woman becoming the mirror, and listener, for another woman. Each is on the margin of the patriarchal culture, but one, Maisie, has hopes of surviving with her self intact.

In addition to introducing an issue Murdoch has never dealt with in such depth before—women's communication with men and women—this novel gives the reader new developments in Murdoch's employment of free indirect discourse and confession, and exciting renditions of what Bakhtin names "the sideward glance" and "the loophole."[1] While Murdoch uses free indirect discourse in most of her novels, the way she manages it here—showing Franca as a "human coming-to-consciousness"—moves her in a new direction that allows her female characters more radical freedom as voices. Bakhtin says the centripetal versus centrifugal phenomenon is inherent in the process of creating free characters: it is what makes characters dynamic. Describing two types of discourse—"privileged language that approaches us from without" and "language that is the retelling of a text in one's own words"—Holquist and Emerson explain Bakhtin's position: "human coming-to-consciousness . . . is a constant struggle between these two types of discourse." The former corresponds to "an attempt to assimilate more into one's own system," and the latter to "the simultaneous freeing of one's own discourse from the authoritative word, or from previously earlier persuasive words that have ceased to mean" (DI 424–25). The maneuvers of Franca's thought process demonstrate that her mind encourages several voices to challenge each other. Franca reacts to absent speech acts of several absent speakers, such as her husband and his mistress, whose voices she has taken into herself, thereby creating a multivoiced narration. Murdoch creates a war in Franca when she gives us a character who is open to all the rules and conventions of the patriarchy and then reveals that her own feelings are creeping slowly to the surface.

Franca stands in vivid contrast to virtually all of Murdoch's other women characters, if only in terms of the freedom Murdoch gives her to go her own way. Murdoch's novels have consistently reported on the cultural and social conditions of women—including, of course, their language. In most of the novels the reader will encounter women trapped in some kind of hell without a sacred language or conventional rhetoric to help them escape. Consistently fighting fantasies and myths, Murdoch as early as *The Flight from the Enchanter* criticizes a world that crushes the marginal voice of Nina the dressmaker, an illegal immigrant. Her women in pain criticize, but not openly, and not the dominant authority; they most often criticize others within the margins. Murdoch is helping address two needs: one for more models of a woman coming to consciousness, the other for more analyses of women's choices as they grow to maturity in relation to men and the patriarchal society. Franca Sheerwater in *The Message to the Planet* has more freedom than Harriet Gavender in *The Sacred and Profane Love Machine* (1974) because Franca, being more of a mother figure, has more power over her husband. The husbands play similar games. For many years Blaise Gavender, a psychiatrist, has kept a mistress, as does Jack Sheerwater. The difference is that Jack has finally settled into having a permanent mistress, whereas Blaise had never wavered from the first one. After Harriet Gavender runs away and immediately before her violent death, she thinks:

> I will not be Blaise's slave. I will not be *their* slave. . . . If I had stayed it would have been impossible not to fall into a role of acquiesence. . . . I have found out what he is like, he would make me pity him, he would make it a matter of rescue. I am not the good person I used to think that I was. If I were forced to be their victim I could not do it with clear eyes and a humble, loving mind. I would do it with secret resentment and hatred. This kindness to him, which is just weakness really, is my only and my last resource. I shall come to it, I am coming to it, I am thinking exactly what he wants me to think, and the only escape from this is a kind of violence of which I am not capable. There is no great calm space elsewhere . . . She was caught in her own mind and condemned by her own being. (SPLM 349)

The reader is stunned by the similarity of Harriet's final two lines and a line in Franca's monologue about women's space: "It's as if my mind has suddenly broken through into a new area, a space, a vast capacity which I never dreamt I had" (MP 154).

Franca is capable also of facing up to dialogism as Paul de Man defines it: "a 'principle of radical otherness'; 'the function of dialogism is to sustain and think through the radical exteriority of heterogeneity of one voice with regard to any other, including that of the novelist *himself*'" (*Resistance to Theory* 109; emphasis added). Franca's voice has the power to veer off from Murdoch's control. In *The Message to the Planet* Murdoch achieves one of her continuing goals, a distance between author and character. In fact, Murdoch has created two women who seem to have broken free of their maker to empower their own discourse. Franca is consequently more fortunate than Harriet Gavender in that she shares her novelistic world and some of her pain with Maisie Tether and even more with the reader.

A character who has an intelligent woman friend to sustain her, a friend to whom she can speak feminine discourse, including "girl talk," was significantly new in Murdoch's fiction in 1989.[2] The intelligent women characters give this novel a lighter, more hopeful tone than some of the earlier ones that dealt with feminist issues from a male perspective, such as *The Black Prince*. Franca embodies what Elaine Showalter describes as the position of the female subject in the "wild zone." Using the model of two Oxford anthropologists, Showalter explains the zone: "Spatially it stands for an area which is literally no man's-land, a place forbidden to men" (*New Feminist Criticism* 262). Being both inside and outside the dominant ethos, Franca speaks a feminine discourse, created by marginal people. The novel defines the language of complaint, a category of feminine discourse that rebels against the patriarchal discourse without even imagining that it can bring about change. Murdoch appears to be writing her "way out of the 'cramped confines of patriarchal space'" (quoted in *New Feminist Criticism* 263).

Franca is a culturally valid example of a conservative, quiet, so-called masochistic housewife, who typically does not approve of her husband's hypocritical double standard but assumes her goal in life is to make him happy.[3] She experiences a growing self-awareness of her capabilities after her husband tells her that his new permanent mistress will now be living in their house, ensconced in their bedroom. The narrator, whom we have good reason to assume is a woman,[4] reveals Franca's struggle after Jack leaves: "She had been, throughout that amazing conversation, perfectly calm. She had looked and sounded rational, kindly, *motherly*. Had she been convincing? Yes. Had she overdone it? No. She had not said 'We'll be one happy family'" (MP 152–53). Franca's outwardly rational voice had squelched the conventional romantic language that might have suggested the last response. This question-and-answer counterpoint within the free indirect discourse is decidedly Dostoevskian, much like what Bakhtin says of Makar Devushkin in Dostoevsky's *Poor Folk*: "[The] affirmation of self sounds like a continuous hidden polemic or hidden dialogue with some other person on the theme of himself" (PDP 207). From the comprehensive background of Franca's childhood that Murdoch constructs, the reader knows that Franca has inherited the voice of traditional feminine wisdom, and therefore, supposedly, has inherited masochistic behavior from her mother, whose life has been even more hellish.

Franca replies to, contests, and makes concessions to an objectified voice of her dead mother, to her husband, and to the dark side of herself. She deals with these voices in the order of their dominance; the first voice employs a conventionally gender-related, masochistic, playacting conventional language. In the next bit, the rhythm changes when the voice of overly excited rationalization breaks in to congratulate her for burying her feelings. As the mask peels away, the language becomes progressively more poetic, more metaphorical, closer to Franca's emotions. Having kept up a good front, she cheers herself on: "Something quite extraordinary had happened, she had *achieved* something extraordinary. She was amazed at herself, at the weird awful feeling of triumph which was consuming her body, licking up over her like a flame. It was a kind of masterpiece, one of the cleverest, most complete, things she'd ever done. It was a turn of the screw of which she could never have dreamt herself capable" (MP 153). Because of the parodic reference to *The Turn of the Screw*, the reader immediately finds this unbalanced enthusiasm suspect and potentially maniacal; ultimately, Franca is shutting down a part of her mind. By following the social conventions she has been taught, she has managed to make Jack think she is not devastated by his perfidious plan. Franca, a saint in everyone else's eyes, has survived by prevaricating. She thinks she deserves her own praise for her new self-awareness, but self-awareness is just beginning.

As she eats her dinner alone, she realizes that she is "a different person: a worse person, a desperate person, but powerful and free"; furthermore, she is "*scandalised*" at herself (MP 153). Her series of questions and her murderous conclusions again suggest Dostoevskian technique as well as content:

> Or was she simply mad, suffering perhaps from some well known form of psychosis? *Free?* How could she think that when she had in fact entrammelled herself in terrible evil bonds, luxuriating even in her bondage? . . . I've never been able to think so clearly in my life before. I've never been able to think such extreme thoughts in my life before. It's as if my mind has suddenly broken through into a new area, a space, a vast capacity which I never dreamt I had. . . . I thought those dreadful fantasies I had of killing Jack were the extremity, the end. But I see now that the end is something farther, higher, more utterly frightful. Franca had indeed had those fantasies, and continued to have them, of how she would kill her husband, smashing his head with a hammer, plunging a carving knife into his side, drugging him with sleeping pills and suffocating him. (MP 154).

Apparently, as she wills herself into being as a character or personality, she realizes that all these Dickensian fantasies can be willed into being also.

Franca seems to have achieved two things: a freedom to fantasize thoughts considered evil by her culture and a great silencing of pain, evoking a condition similar to a coma. "She had bought time, a resting-place, a space. There were now many possibilities." Franca's state is reminiscent of that of Muriel in *The Time of the Angels*, "lying upon her bed in a state of coma" after her discovery that her stepsister and their father are lovers: "The intense cold seemed to dim and lower her consciousness until there was nothing except a faint flickering awareness which was scarcely aware of itself. Something lay upon her, pinning her to the bed. . . . The little daylight went soon and darkness came. Time passed. Footsteps passed. A light turned on in the corridor shone in through the half-open door of the room. But nobody came to her. Pattie did not come. Carel did not come. And Elizabeth did not ring her old familiar bell. The house fell silent" (TA 203–4).

For the reader, the most disconcerting moment of Franca's utterance is her disappointing admission that perhaps she has developed no new self-awareness; perhaps she is simply following a new version of the old acquiescence: "Could she have spoken to Jack so 'sincerely' had she not in some secret part believed what she said? Was she not indeed, not only trapping herself, but deceiving herself, being, to herself, a traitor? Dear me, thought Franca, then perhaps I might be in danger of actually becoming as saintly as I seem!" (MP 155). Franca has used a "loophole"; she has saved herself a way out.[5] She does not have to grow if she convinces herself that her maneuvers are simply methods of coming around to the same traditional behavior.

This climactic Murdochian joke is forbidding. Why does she put this pressure on the reader? To teach? Bakhtin argues that humans reserve the right Franca is reserving: "the retention for oneself of the possibility of altering the ultimate, final meaning of one's own words" (PDP 233). Here Franca reverses her course, as she does ultimately at the end of the novel. It is because Murdoch makes the reader invest so much hope in her freedom that Franca is a disturbing character. Her anticipation that she will eventually return to her early married life with Jack is palpable. What is disheartening to the reader is that she demonstrates anticipation of "the other's response and, in responding to [Jack's response, she] demonstrates" to him her dependence on him (PDP 229).[6] No matter how much Murdoch might want Franca to mature and live on her own, and no matter how much Murdoch teases the reader into believing that Franca will accomplish this goal, Franca chooses to fail. The conventional stance is easier and feels more familiar to Franca. Murdoch is not teasing for the sake of teasing; she is giving the character room to maneuver. The reader, however, might well luxuriate in feelings of betrayal when, after establishing a character who is open to the rules and conventions of the patriarchy and who at the same time experiences her own need to creep slowly to battle the conventions, Murdoch allows that character to fail.

The reader's disappointment is similar to the disappointments of real life. The method is characteristic of the way Murdoch uses reality to disorient her reader. Franca's reserving a "metaphysical or an ethical loophole" gives the space she inhabits an almost tangible intensity. Her words, retaining "the potential of another meaning . . . accompany her movements like a shadow" (PDP 233). Left alone twenty pages later, Franca returns to lying to herself. The narrator's parody of Franca's thought, echoing a children's text by Beatrix Potter, warns that Franca is fooling herself when she attempts to achieve the goals of her mother and be the perfect housewife. Isn't Murdoch acknowledging that the culture has used such stereotypes to help Franca define herself? The sentences conjoin paratactically, making her activities seem childlike and ludicrous: "Franca *liked* cleaning. She cleaned and polished and tidied and shopped and cooked and washed clothes and sewed buttons onto Jack's shirts" (MP 171). She thinks like "Mrs. Tittlemouse [who] was a most terribly tidy particular little mouse, always sweeping and dusting the soft sandy floors. . . . She swept, and scrubbed, and dusted; and she rubbed up the furniture with beeswax, and polished her little tin spoons" (Potter, *Tale of Mrs. Tittlemouse* 14, 54). The narrator's use of italics underlines the distance between the conventional terminology and the narrator's parodic attitude toward such an existence: "She even once let Alison [his permanent mistress] sew on a button and observed Alison's *gratitude*. She watched herself, she watched them all, with *amazement*. She watched. Often, in her kitchen or her boudoir, she did nothing, she simply sat absolutely still and breathed, sensing her continued existence, preserving herself, taking refuge in a timeless present" (MP 171). This character's fantasy life has to focus all its energy on sheer survival.

Although Franca thinks like a character in a child's animal fantasy, she is discovering slowly how one absorbs a situation that is contrary to society's stated norms or myths but is accepted hypocritically by society nevertheless. She has been taught to accept her bad feelings as if they were some disease she had contracted. Her syndrome is surprisingly like Gregor Samsa's state: "This state she spontaneously pictured as if she had become small, about the size of a jar of marmalade (this image appeared with a kind of authority) and had *put herself away* in a small square recess in a wall, just large enough to hold her. The wall was in an interior which was almost dark. It was silent and a little damp. In this recess Franca sat breathing quietly, taking the air in by her nostrils and expelling it by her mouth" (MP 171).[7]

The conventional religious discourse, the language of ritual taught her by her mother, soothes Franca's troubled spirit with an ironical reminder of the note of consolation that closes *The Waste Land*: "And the words 'peace, peace, peace' came to her, as if they were (but could they be?) part of an old prayer, perhaps a prayer which her mother had uttered over her before she could speak. She thought about her mother and her sudden mysterious death" (MP 171). Murdoch implies that if these words come from Franca's subconscious, as she has grown more aware she has been simultaneously returning to her forgotten life with her mother. Rather than relive the celebration of mother and child while she can, she is immediately seduced by the voice of guilt, employing words with a "sideward glance." Her "litany of remorse" includes "I have colluded with his depravity, it is all my fault. Oh the lies women believe, and will to believe and want to believe! She recalled that fatal time when she had wept because she knew she had diminished Jack, had demoted, had cracked the perfect image, had lodged in her mind that little black poisonous atom. From this it had all begun" (MP 171). Murdoch's parodic exaggeration of the "I have sinned" construction implies that Franca might go over the edge.

The voice of love, which of course ultimately wins, takes over momentarily: "At one time, even lately, she had thought that she could bear it, turning it all into pure love. She had imprisoned her anger and hate in a part of her mind, as something unworthy which could be overcome" (MP 171). The voice of reason, which considers the community's opinion of her behavior, is followed quickly by the voice of evil, what Bakhtin calls the language of the outlaw:

> I should have *screamed* [hysteria] at the start—whenever the start could now be said to be. As it is—Jack thinks I'm too quiet, dreamy, drifting away, not noticing things. Perhaps he even thinks I *don't care!* And if I were to start screaming now it would be too late. They'd be sorry for me, they'd give me whisky and aspirins and send me to a psychiatrist. The wicked mood of triumphant secret freedom which had come to her after her first *performance* of careful deliberate lying to Jack had, for the moment at any rate, left her. (MP 171)

Murdoch is rehearsing the conventional syndromes and cures that nineteenth-century medicine imposed on women. Franca's discourse changes to that of her darker side. A "depraved and diminished and shrunken" feeling shoves her back into the stance of the murderess: "I'll kill Jack and myself after. Or perhaps I won't do that. I'll just vanish and live alone in a cottage beside the sea until I go quietly mad and drown myself. And no one will even know. She saw her long hair floating like seaweed upon the waves. How, she wondered, could someone be so unhappy, so tortured by grief, and still not be mad, and still be alive" (MP 172). In ironically alluding to Ophelia, Murdoch argues that Franca's pain is primed potentially to fit into any free-floating evil construction. She even considers murdering any future progeny of Jack and Alison. This plea to get sympathy for ideologically gender-related masochism does seem simply to mirror reality. If Murdoch is indeed mirroring reality, is her character escaping from her pen and taking over?

Franca's discourse is, then, not only multivoiced but also schizophrenic. In laying this consciousness open to the reader, Murdoch comments on Franca's enduring the most horrible insult that the patriarchal system has created—the comment is that Franca survives what is known in our culture as one of the most horrendous destructions of identity, and yet she must return to Jack to survive. Where is Murdoch in all this? Here the voice is more than simply "objectified," that is, the result of typifying characterization. Here the character's voice competes with Murdoch's voice; no one would mistake Franca for a spokeswoman for Murdoch.

In *The Message to the Planet*, Murdoch gives up the monological premises of rigid points of view and finalizing definitions, changing it all into "an aspect of the hero's self-consciousness" (PDP 52). Because "the epistolary form . . . is best suited to the reflected discourse of another," she uses it periodically, along with dialogue, to get characters to react to "the other's possible reply" (PDP 205). In the case of the painter Jack Sheerwater, the reader can recognize what Bakhtin describes as "discourse that cringes with a timid and ashamed sideward glance at the other's possible response, yet contains a muffled challenge" (PDP 205). Murdoch's purpose here is to suggest that Jack's challenge is his lifelong power play, his dare to women to give in to him. The reader experiences the contrapuntal movement in Jack's two manipulative letters to his devoted, patient wife. The reader wonders whether he considers what Franca's response will be, whether he asks himself if she might rebel or if she will be a rock of stable conventionality. No matter how cruel a person he is, he must have Franca if he is to be Jack.

Jack's attempt to justify his ongoing habit of adultery and his corollary attempt to define his lack of security as love struggle in his double-voiced discourse. The distinct voices are evident in the first do-what-I-tell-you-to letter: the childish, lustful voice presents an ultimatum that ostensibly begs but actually demands—demands Franca, whom he sees as a mother, to join her husband and his permanent mistress, Alison, on a holiday. The voice is so childlike and childish that it fails to recognize its power against the other voice. Then the "imperfect husband" language that responds to society justifies the lust and cruelty by arguing that any love Jack feels is superior to conventional love and that conventional arrangements are therefore not sufficient for superior beings. Jack lives in a fantasy world where he has unending power. He uses his consort's ingrained acquiescence to consolidate his power, spreading it over larger and larger territories. Apparently, thinking of Franca in goddesslike terms lends credibility to his fantasy about his superiority: "I speak to you now like a sinner addressing God, and contending with him," he writes to Franca. *Contending* applies here because this god is in the form of a woman. He uses the stuff of the conventional Judeo-Christian myth that recuperates Eve in the Virgin Mary: "*You* are far beyond, far above. I have always looked up to you and revered you"; "my eternal love"; "you have in your keeping the greatest gift which I can receive, the *grace* which I demand" (MP 319). Bakhtin seems at one point to be describing Jack: "His affirmation of self sounds like a continuous hidden polemic or hidden dialogue with some other person on the theme of himself" (PDP 207). (Actually, this description also fits Bradley Pearson and many of Murdoch's other male characters quite well.) Jack's tone displays his uncontrolled egoism. It does not occur to Jack, born into a world of privilege, to choose sacred responsibility over listening to sycophants. Even though it is confessional, his epistolary discourse contains no coming to self-awareness.

Each letter, an entire page long, uses repetition to demonstrate his servility and fear of rejection. In the first letter he writes: "*Please, please* come soon" (MP 319). Jack seems to have two reasons for his first letter: to convince Franca to be beside him and to convince her to feel sorry for him. "I need you, we need you, I mean Alison and I and also Heather, who is an angel, you will love her. (We now have a definite plan for bringing her and Alfred together!)" (MP 319). The letter casts a sideward glance at the absent interlocutor by imagining her thoughts; knowing that she will be hurt and will very likely be hostile, Jack repeats what in some sense is the sincere desire of his childish, lustful voice. Jack's letter works magic in the sense Plato describes. Jack uses *I* twenty-nine times and puts his wife on a pedestal in the sense that he entraps her by making her a dead deity: "I *thirst*, for your presence," "I speak to you now like a sinner addressing God, and contending with him" (MP 319). Jack's tone is apologetic while it casts a sideward glance at those in society who condemn his behavior: "You have always comforted me, your kindness, your goodness, have never wavered, even when, indeed when I look back *especially when*, I was in the world's eyes a most imperfect husband" (MP 319). In Jack's clever combination of denial and cringing behavior, Murdoch manages to give the prose the ring of the Twenty-third Psalm.

In the first letter Jack addresses Franca as "dearest." In the past he had insisted that Franca, the first wife, had the highest standing and was, therefore, dearest. But in the second letter Jack can no longer stomach his pretenses and does not use the superlative degree to address his wife: "My dear, my very dear, I have to tell you the truth. Alison has presented me with an ultimatum. She cannot any more endure the situation in which [we] have placed her. She loves me and wishes to be my wife. I love her and I *cannot leave her*. She alone, of all the women whom you have so generously and so understandingly tolerated, I *cannot leave*. What she demands is, then, that I divorce you and marry her" (MP 404).

In Franca and her new friend, Maisie Tether, Murdoch shows us one woman becoming the listener for another. The reader hears this woman's discourse, a text dominated by a context—patriarchal hegemony—that inscribes the centripetal force of the conventional that the women must counter with the centrifugal force of rebellion (Bakhtin, DI 428). Maisie helps the reader see that, as a general image of married women, Franca is not an exaggerated model. Maisie sees that Jack understands Franca and knows how to change her intention to oppose his wishes by manipulating her into another perspective. Knowing how naive Franca is, Maisie crafts her criticisms in such a way that they critique hegemonic power:

> Of course he sincerely wants you back, entirely on his terms—he feels, even he, a monster like him—feels some tiny discomfort, some tiny trace of guilt at ditching you, and he wants you to remove that little stain upon the perfect happiness he keeps talking of, *his* happiness of course, *his* happy life with another woman! He wants you to forgive him, to be smiling around the place, to be *seen to consent* to his disgraceful arrangements. Can't you catch the tone of ruthlessly selfish anxiety in all this foul talk about love? He needs you, oh yes he needs you, simply to ratify the whole thing, and then when it's public and everyone can see how wonderfully it works and how civilised all three of you are, far above petty conventions and bourgeois pretences, then he'll change his tune, he'll let you slip quietly away into the background, he'll let you *diminish*, and you'll let it happen, and he knows you will! (MP 320)

As a genuine friend, Maisie attempts to be a mirror for Franca, to reflect Franca's cowardice for her. Maisie's statement about what Franca ought to admit feeling—"Jealousy is not a vice, it's a natural instinct, at least it shows you're still alive!"—releases Franca enough to be honest with herself: "Maisie had discerned it—her great secret rage would slowly be transformed into a small secret hatred, whose miserable attrition would diminish Franca, shrink her, until she became a very small animal, scarcely visible as it scuttled here and there in the house. How can I ever *think* of such a fate, Franca asked herself. Better to commit murder. Yet she knew that when, after reading the letter, she had so much wanted to telephone Jack, it had been in order to reassure him" (MP 321). Murdoch leaves clues in the text, encouraging the reader to speculate that Franca's pain as well as that of Alfred Ludens, the novel's other character who comes to consciousness, is relevant to Wittgenstein's beetle-in-the-box argument. Maisie says to Franca: "You've been living in a dark box—it's time to come out into the light" (MP 268). The psychiatrist Marzillian suggests to Ludens that most people live "the life of a beetle in a hole," and Ludens, listening to him, felt "himself shrinking, as if he were veritably turning into one of the beetles of which Marzillian had spoken" (MP 431–32).[8]

Franca's response assures the reader that Jack knew how to strike the useful chords in his wife. Murdoch's emphasis in this novel on the masochistic or loving woman who thinks always of the other person first is hardly new. Murdoch has, however, at last created in Maisie Tether a character with some of her own attributes. This is a positive movement toward a full-blown Athena-Sibyl thinker in future texts. Maisie knows Latin and Greek, could have been a college professor, loves visual art, finds that painting is a special relationship to happiness, prefers women but is not lesbian, thinks women are wiser and better. "The tiniest scrawl," this intellectual woman says,

> the merest outline or patch of colours is art—and that's true of everyone who has some talent—it may not be good but it's art—not that I approve of Picasso as a man, a perfect cad if ever there was one—and then there's Turner, all those things he called sketches, there's divinity, there's joy, just thinking of those blazing masses of colour lifts up the heart, don't you agree? Whereas if you're a writer, like a novelist, say, and you make notes for your book, *that's* not art, not in itself, the way those sketches are art—and painters can go on painting till they're old, very old—Titian painted wonderful pictures when he was over ninety—the mind doesn't *give out* as it does in other art forms, you see paint's *natural*, it's the oldest art, it's the natural art. (MP 266)

This voice is not Murdoch's exactly, but it is the most Murdochian voice the reader has heard.

Murdoch suggests that the difference between Franca's and Maisie's mothers contributes to the difference between the painful emotional dependence of Franca and the joyous independence of Maisie: "My dear mother used to paint a bit and she said it was spiritual refreshment. My mother was a saint really. She was a Bostonian too of course, she used to work with black women in the poor part of Boston—there's hell in Boston like in other cities—I'm glad I was an only child, I guess I did well having the undivided attention of those two superior beings" (MP 267). Especially here Murdoch seems to be recalling her own childhood. For example, she says in a *Washington Post* interview: "I had marvelous parents. It's rather an advantage to being an only child" (Conroy, "Lasting Powers" F1).

Murdoch's loving play with language encourages her reader to look at language and its rhetorical functions instead of looking through it. Her texts demonstrate that language is a reality that impinges on the reader daily, reflecting the contradiction and undecidability of things worldly. Murdoch's interest in discourse, then, is her interest in life itself and in art, which for her is discursive. She says in *The Fire and the Sun* that "the prescription for art is the same as for dialectic: overcome personal fantasy and egoistic anxiety and self-indulgent day-dream. Order and separate and distinguish the world justly. . . . [T]he highest art is powered by force of an individual unconscious mind, but then so is the highest philosophy" (79). In her novels Murdoch demonstrates that she launches her narrators and characters into a cavelike labyrinth and then records their utterances as they bump up against each other. In establishing and studying this process,[9] Murdoch would agree, there is no relationship if there is no language. Even though the behavior of Murdoch's characters, just like that of real human beings, is never very good, they do serve as mirrors to each other in the enlivening process of literature.

CHAPTER EIGHT
Characters Patterning Their Pilgrimages

Four novels Murdoch published from the middle 1970s to 1980—*A Word Child, The Black Prince, The Sea, The Sea,* and *Nuns and Soldiers*—feature characters in loosely parallel situations. Three of them are first-person male protagonists, and the fourth is a male artist presented by an omniscient narrator. Each character is talented and creative, and each is at a different level in the cave; Murdoch uses all four to explore artistic dilemmas. Examining the patterns these men use to control power and mythologize themselves will show that along their pilgrimages Murdoch allows her characters moments of insight achieved through cataclysmic changes in perspective and through juxtaposition of incidents. Looking at such patterns is also a way of examining Murdoch's own philosophy involving cataclysmic changes. Her fascination with sudden discoveries is so pervasive that she has allowed the creation of conflicting tensions in her portrait at the National Portrait Gallery; the artist has included *The Slaying of Marsyas* in the background.[1]

Humbly refusing to sum up the truth about life, Murdoch lays out the pieces of the characters' pilgrimages, juxtaposing the concatenations of their universe and the characters' various reactions to it. Her view of life is made up of an aimless universe whirling around "anxiety-ridden" human beings who impose patterns on the formlessness in order to stave off physical and psychological chaos. Her tragicomedies display her view of the human comedy: Murdoch in her role of author, and her characters in their independent roles, construct the "falsifying *veil*[s] which partially [conceal] the world" (SG 84), so that she might bring the reader to search for that concealed reality. Her large patterns—her interconnecting schemes of caves, networks, labyrinths, and cycles—lay the foundation for the characters' daily rat-runs of obsession.

Exposing the foibles of humanity, Murdoch allows her comic characters the paradoxical freedom to be as inexplicably inconsistent as human beings; their identities are unstable, often deferred. The exaggerated ironic reversals the characters experience demonstrate that human actions are rarely the result of rational decisions. The rationale of this stylistic method is to call attention to the characters' paradoxical freedom to behave as their inner necessity demands. Her fiction, then, like Wittgenstein's later philosophy, is exhibition, not explanation. Murdoch says that art must be made to look accidental, like life. What better way to do that than to rush the reader through a fast-paced series of events that move suddenly forward or in circles? Add paradox, inconsistency, and rapid ironic reversals to that pacing, and Murdoch's world of the novel appears.

Her cave metaphor, arguing for progress, or at least for knowledge, emphasizes *up* and *out*. Taking into account the rat-run Murdoch talks about in *The Sovereignty of Good* and her metaphor, a "novel must be a house fit for free characters to live in" (SBR 186),[2] one might visualize this house supplied with escalators of two types:[3] vertical (diagonal, actually, like the ones in department stores) and horizontal (like the moving sidewalks in airport terminals). It is difficult to find a metaphor for such a phenomenon. Her additional reference to "odd contingent ways" suggests a maze or labyrinth that argues for cyclical repetition: some characters tracking a slow movement up, some going in circles, and others doing both. Characters are free within the rat-runs; some realize they are climbing to the sun, but most do not. Picked out for special attention, the protagonists absorb their moments of enlightenment before the reader's eyes and often experience spurts of growth during their journeys. Often, however, they think they are going one way while actually going another.

Looking at these four novels in stages demonstrates the complexity of Murdoch's novelistic world. I begin with the patterns that Murdoch intentionally creates, then examine the patterns her artistic figures intentionally and sometimes unintentionally impose, and end with the patterns the characters are free to suggest.[4] Even though the reader may see the protagonists as obsessive-compulsives, men looking for love, these characters—three of them first-person narrators—often see themselves as heroic questers. Each is missing something for which he searches. Hilary Burde and Charles Arrowby search for women; Bradley Pearson and Tim Reede, for artistic accomplishment—and for women. Murdoch catches them just when they have decided to reclaim what has been lost and not yet been found. These investigations of the dark labyrinth of the psyche reveal a polyphony of small and large patterns, cycles within cycles.

Murdoch has set up these novels to experience their own aimlessness. The histories of the four characters all include circular plotting. Each man, like

M. C. Escher's ants in *Moebius II*, goes over the same ground again and again, never recognizing his entrapment. My own analogy—characters within a cavelike space traveling on giant, crisscrossing sets of escalators, one set moving up to the sun and the other down from the sun, with moving sidewalks at each level or landing the characters occupy—parallels Murdoch's habit of seeing movements in at least two dimensions: on a grand scale in a macrocosm and on a smaller scale, each individual ego a microcosm. At both levels, individual lives flow in a cyclical pattern more like that of Escher's ants than like the planets in the universe. Recording a variety of characters moving toward the sun, Murdoch monitors their behaviors, notes their symptoms, and multiplies the potential reasons for such behaviors, leaving the reader to decide the causes. When Hilary Burde rages as Oedipus does about recognizing the cycles coming around again, he is in some sense actually raging at Murdoch, his controller, even though she holds the reins loosely. She is enjoying the tension of the character pushing out against her control.

In creating the storm of Hilary and his cycles, Murdoch relies on two philosophical-psychological components that break up routine, or the daily rat-runs (SG 86) of existence. She employs gestalt to represent the perceptual shift of misseeing and seeing better, and she employs love to represent not seeing and then suddenly seeing another person. Because *A Word Child* best illustrates the Freudian mechanistic model of the mind, I will focus on a broad range of patterns involving Hilary. The other novels are valuable for demonstrating variations on those patterns, especially the writing patterns of Bradley and Charles, the abstract "network" pictures of Tim, and the Oedipal patterns of all three. Murdoch lets Charles and Tim justify superficial patterns in their work and lets Bradley justify his pattern of love. Murdoch, in fact, critiques all of the patterns of superficial love.

Superimposing the metaphor of the rat-run over the metaphors of the cave, the labyrinth, or the network reinforces the concept of cagedness—and raises questions. Do the beings caged in the labyrinth have any hope of escape, or is escape illusory? Do some characters receive only pinpoints of light? Why does one character, Bradley in *The Black Prince*, get the help of the god of light? Might Murdoch, having identified with Bradley, have allowed her psyche to pull Apollo from the depths of the unconscious, the kind of mystery that literature is about? If this is the case, are the rest of her characters simply meant to follow the thread and find their way out before the Minotaur eats them?

Murdoch's novels, their mysteries being the riddles of myth, manifest different kinds of labyrinths; the monster, the maidens, and the youths are different and yet similar. Rather than trying to please anyone else, Murdoch is simply trying to get it right. The characters follow their routine existence, and the reader follows the strings through the labyrinth.

The characters create enclosing patterns of time and metaphorical space to inscribe order: cyclical rat-runs of obsession, love triangles (Oedipal and romantic), and writing patterns. As the first mover, Murdoch creates a form that juxtaposes in quick succession, like the snapping of a high-speed camera's shutter, examples of obsession displayed side by side, which the reader has no choice but to compare. After Murdoch's original creative process has gestated for its necessary period, the obsessions of the first-person enchanters have become so pervasive that they control their owners without needing much help from Murdoch. These protagonists act out their obsessions day to day, and if they record them, they portray them in the text side by side, in parallel anecdotes.

Murdoch has described her intention as working so that the creative process allows characters to create themselves. Of the four men I examine here, Hilary is the farthest from the sun. Even though he has a talent for words, he is the least free to create. He focuses more on holding onto the wheel to which he is affixed by his heritage as orphan and his ominous experience. If he can maintain patterns that are familiar to him, he can survive. The three novels with first-person narrators show whether Murdoch does allow the characters to be in control of their actions. She controls the order in which characters are introduced—except when she hands this control over to an artist-narrator such as Bradley or Charles in *The Sea, The Sea*. She guarantees contingency in her original conception, before putting the novel on paper; the patterns Murdoch and the characters work in tandem to create make the cyclical plots open to contingency. Viewed side by side, the novels demonstrate the contiguity of characters' annual cycles. For example, both Hilary and Bradley have worked in bureaucratic government jobs. All four men experience contingency that manifests itself in at least one love affair. The only contingency that helps a character break out of a repetitive cycle is an insight along the path.

In each case, the private love interest has an overwhelming public effect on the people around the protagonist. Bradley's reverberates to the public forum through the newspaper and the halls of justice. In her 1987 essay "Art and

Eros," Murdoch's Socrates addresses the distinction between public and private: "Isn't it the nature of art to explore the relation between the public and the private? Art turns us inside out, it exhibits what is secret. What goes on inwardly in the soul is the essence of each man, it's what makes us individual people. The relation between that inwardness and public conduct *is morality*" (*Acastos* 31). In *A Word Child*, private obsessions run rampant, causing suicide and death that affect the public. Murdoch examines the public servant Hilary, a former juvenile delinquent whom society reclaims through education. Introduced to language as a way of controlling his deep-seated anger and private fantasy, Hilary learns to ease the pain of his childhood. Instead of using language to direct his energetic hyperactivity into creation, Hilary, who is not an artist like Bradley, merely recirculates it in the monotony of repetitious rat-runs. The novel attempts to turn the reader "inside out" by dramatizing the relation of Hilary's inward obsessive-compulsive energies and his public conduct as his energies erupt into the lives of the other characters.[5]

A Word Child is especially Greek in its use of ironic juxtaposition and reversal, or peripeteia.[6] This dramatic Greek word, meaning "to fall, fall into, change suddenly," has a range of uses. Its drama results from the meeting of the cyclical patterns of the fated world and the obsessive patterns of the protagonist. A major example is the reversal of Hilary's desire to make the unselfish move, followed by the accident that brings death to his love, Kitty. It is similar to Sophocles' juxtaposing the announcement that Creon will release Antigone from her prison and the messenger's announcement that she is dead (*Antigone* V.106; Exodos 17, 59). Indeed, the kind of obsessional dance taking place in Murdoch's novels is the kind that, while easy enough to label as Freudian, comes first from Sophocles. Oedipus dances among his multiple, ambivalent motives: to save the city, to save himself, to uncover the truth, to refuse to believe it. Oedipus's own impulses cause him to continue the curse that is his heritage, part of his character. Hilary's dance is similar; his conscious motivations to be free fight hopelessly against his unconscious motivations to be taken care of. He recognizes that his life cycles pattern themselves on some mysterious fate, but he never gets outside his ego to see that his fate is being himself. His life simulates the Greek circularity of necessity and contingency, as in the Oedipal curse, and his behavior results from energies long stored in his body. Hilary's virtues also become his vices, as does Oedipus's cleverness: Hilary's ability with words charms Kitty to ask a sacrifice of him. In choosing to repeat his neurotic behavior, Hilary is as blind and egoistic as Oedipus. But neither Hilary's world nor the real one is obliged to adjust to his conception of it.

One might label A *Word Child* Murdoch's critique of the mechanistic model of the unconscious. Murdoch's examination of Freudian obsessional patterns sets up the parameters within which the character is free to create and indulge in obsessions (Meltzer, "Unconscious" 145). Murdoch explores the roots of this behavior in the unconscious. Being unaware of or uninterested in such a mysterious source of energy, the characters choose routines as methods of living within the cosmically fated patterns of their own creation; these routines always have the potential of saving or suffocating. The novel's mechanistic structure is a reflection of Hilary's obsessive behavior. Apparently Murdoch, during the period of silence at the beginning of the writing process, allowed Hilary the freedom of his compulsions, which repeat dynamically of their own accord. To be able to avail herself of a character's neuroses in this way, she seems to have stirred into her cauldron what Meltzer, in discussing Freud, describes as the "hydraulic" model of the mind.[7]

Hilary is typical of Murdoch's male enchanters and archetypal in his illustration of the dynamic model of the unconscious, "more of an energy flow than a 'place'" (Meltzer, "Unconscious" 150). How appropriate that he uses language to repress the multivoiced pain from his childhood; Oedipus also uses language to repress what seems to be exuding from his unconscious mind. Oedipus weaves a safe hiding place with words—the illusion that he is the "child of Good Luck" (the "years" are his "foster-brothers"), the son of Dionysus, the year spirit—because somewhere deep inside his mind he has realized that he is the son of Laius, and the murderer (Yeats, *King Oedipus* 840). Hilary is also unable to squelch traumatic emotions. When he learns how to repress feelings with language in his early years, his mind's censor keeps the material from his consciousness. But when particular emotional breakthroughs occur and the repressed material comes flowing through like water bursting from its container, Hilary is unable to explain what is happening in his unconscious. Whatever is happening at that moment, he expects to happen again in seven years. His life is a series of cycles: first losing his mother when he is a child and then losing his first love in young adulthood and his second in middle age: "I wondered about the future. Was another cycle of misery, intensified, more dense, beginning for me? If so, it would outlast my lifetime. Did not the same crime twice committed merit more than double retribution?" (WC 382). He is painfully aware that such cycles of "crime" seem to define his existence:

> Would it help me now that I could more coolly see the ingredients of chance? Was it cynicism to hope this? . . . Or was I perhaps actually wise? . . . Certainly I could better measure now, what had been invisible to me then except as a provocation of rage, the amount of sheer accident which these things, perhaps all things, contained. Then I had raged at the accidental but had not let it in any way save me from my insistence upon being the author of everything. . . . There is a religious teaching which says that God is the author of all actions. What I wonder is its secular equivalent? (WC 382)

Hilary's soliloquy is Sophoclean both in his attribution of rage to himself and in his acceptance of responsibility. His interest in double retribution is also Dostoevskian in its emphasis on Hilary's authoring the crime and on his questioning that authoring in the text, a technique Murdoch has surely appreciated in Dostoevsky. This questioning is a major breakthrough for Hilary, who has had a few moments of insight yet has not traveled past the fire into the sun.

This condition is most cogently and tragically emphasized in the major plot pattern of the novel: falling in love, losing the love object to death, being lost in aimlessness, discovering momentary order. But Hilary authors his own disasters by failing to break out of the rhythmical structure that repeats three times. (Actually the cycle repeats itself four times. There is a variation on the theme when Hilary is approximately fourteen years old. At this point a male teacher, who does not die until later, saves him with love.) At the end of the novel, showing that he still does not understand that his condition has much to do with his egoism, Hilary questions whether he has gained any insights into the aimlessness of the universe and his inability to grow and control the consequences of his behavior. When Kitty, his present love, is dead, he fantasizes living like a bird in a cage with his sister Crystal.

The novel begins with Hilary expounding on what he calls the "amount of sheer accident" in everyday life. He tells the reader that he had had "a kind of Platonic remembrance" of the first seven years of his life as "a state of being loved" by a mother, and that when she died "a sense certainly of some lost brightness, an era of light" vanished (WC 17). This is the dream world he would like to construct with Crystal at the end of the novel. Even though he realized early that he had no father, and even though he was aware of what people meant when they referred to his mother as a tart, those years glow for him with an aura of warmth and happiness. Like Oedipus, Hilary wishes to return to the womb or the cave of illusion. Suddenly being thrust by the death of his mother into the world of his aunt distorts his view of reality: "I detested Aunt Bill forever with a hatred which can still make me tremble" (WC 17).[8] Murdoch is quite good at achieving this visceral response in words and eliciting a similar response from the reader. Hilary says that he became unlovable because no one gave him attention. Eventually sent to an orphanage, he found an outlet for his frustration: "I liked hitting people, I liked breaking things. Once I tried to set fire to the orphanage. I was in a juvenile court before I was twelve" (WC 20). The elementary, horrific anger that can engulf children broods over the pages of this dark comedy; Hilary never really grows beyond that anger.

A significant change in the holograph notebooks of *A Word Child* (1975) in the University of Iowa Libraries demonstrates Murdoch's method of invention. In her notebooks Murdoch develops her characters—adding, deleting, and changing the relationships between the first-person male narrators and the female characters. For example, the notebooks for *A Word Child* demonstrate Murdoch's early indecisiveness and reversal about the creation of three women characters; eventually she truly allows the characters to take control. Lottie, the nanny, whom Murdoch eventually eliminated from the novel, was apparently playing herself out too freely, taking the novel in a consoling direction. As Murdoch removed Lottie from the novel, she wove some of Lottie's characteristics into Laura Impiatt. At the same time Murdoch compressed Aunt Bill, the cruel surrogate mother, so that she becomes only a disturbing mystery. Murdoch has said: "Very often I find two characters coalesce into one. . . . Sometimes one does the other thing; one divides a character into two separate people and sets them going in opposite directions as it were" ("Now Read On," Nov. 27, 1971, Radio 4; quoted in Conradi, *Saint*). The distilling of these two motherly characters into Laura, a comic figure, gives the first-person male narrator fewer stable people on whom to rely. This change allows the narrator much less consolation and control. What is more important for the character Hilary is that he has more space in which to play.

Like Freud, Murdoch critiques self-presence and self-possession. Before he learned to order his rage with words, Hilary used two methods of survival less violent than arson: depending on his sister and escaping into sleep. "A talent for oblivion is a talent for survival. I laid my head down and merciful pain-killing sleep covered me fathoms deep. Not to have been born is undoubtedly best but sound sleep is second best" (WC 16). Hilary attempts to reclaim his missing mother. Her loss is responsible for the empty space inside. His only security outside himself is the love of Crystal, who buoys him up. At first he attempts to replace his mother with Crystal, but then the rules of the family or the law teach him to search outside the family. His love for Crystal does not reach the depth or brightness of his Platonic remembrances, as does his later love for Anne and Kitty, but brotherly love does save him from total self-destruction: "My younger sister had to be my mother" (WC 18). He tells the reader that when he was not in Crystal's presence he was "brimming with anger":

> I had a cosmic furious permanent sense of myself as victimized. It is particularly hard to overcome resentment caused by injustice. And I was so lonely. The bottomless bitter misery of childhood: how little even now it is understood. Probably no adult misery can compare with a child's despair. However I was better off than some. I had Crystal, and I lived in and for the hope of Crystal as men live in and for the hope of God. When we parted from each other, mingling our tears, she used always to say to me, "Oh be *good!*" (WC 19)⁹

Is his belief that his pain comes from the universe, the cosmos, a fantasy? He acts out the terror of being alive in terrorizing others.

Hilary's birth is mysterious enough to evoke Oedipus's status as an illegitimate foundling. Hilary has searched for lost mother love for thirty-four years. Ironically, he finds a substitute for mother love where he least expects it: Oedipus found it in his mother-wife, and Hilary first finds it in his sister-mother. But he also establishes that he was saved at the end of two seven-year cycles, at the age of fourteen, by a language teacher. This lonely scholar did not supply the "state of being loved," but he did develop Hilary's talent for words: "I learned from Mr. Osmand how to write the best language in the world accurately and clearly and, ultimately, with a hard elegance. I discovered words and words were my salvation. I was not, except in some very brokendown sense of that ambiguous term, a love child. I was a word child" (WC 21). During his thirty-fourth year, Hilary discovers that this savior, who gave Hilary the gift that has the potential of making him independent, has committed suicide because he was rejected as a homosexual.

Because of the love of this teacher, the word was made flesh in Hilary's life; he begins to recognize a sense of order when he begins to learn language. He reveals expressly that words gave order to his life in the past, just as daily scheduling gives his life additional order in the present: my days "gave me identity, a sort of ecto-skeleton" (WC 28). He also explains his psychological growth: "I relied upon routine, had done so perhaps ever since I realized that grammatical roles were to be my salvation" (WC 27). As Hilary's energies erupt into the lives of the other characters, the novel focuses more on the relationship of his inward obsessive-compulsive energies to his public conduct.

When Hilary's repressive energy lapses and the neurotic energy erupts, the hidden information from the unconscious reveals itself in a disguised form of dreamworld fantasies. Approximately seven years later, when Hilary is a young don at Oxford, he once again experiences a state of being loved. This cataclysmic moment of enlightenment has the potential of moving him closer to the Good, but he is not stable enough to weigh the prospects for good in the love relationship in conjunction with another reality: Gunnar Jopling, his mentor, is Anne's husband. Falling in love with Anne both adds joy to Hilary's life and sets in motion his disastrous recurring life cycle. The absurdity of accidentally killing her and her unborn child, Gunnar's child, in an automobile accident is the kind of pattern that Murdoch uses to picture real life.[10] A pattern begins to emerge, and the reader finds that Hilary will continue to repeat it: love, death, aimlessness, and momentary order.[11]

Hilary could have reduced his disorientation by asking for Gunnar's forgiveness. Instead, he tells Gunnar only the mechanical details of the accident. He rationalizes that his wired jaw will not allow him to discuss his problem: the guilt that is to drive the remainder of his life. Being unable to attend to the reality of his and Gunnar's rage, Hilary buries his guilt, causing it to flourish. Not having the will or courage to confront Gunnar, he escapes into philosophizing about a method for achieving salvation, a method similar to that of Saint Hilary: "A hard monotonous life favours salvation, so the sages say. There must have been some other element absent in my case" (WC 3). He continues to borrow the structure of grammar to invent a pattern for his own life, one that is "hard" and "monotonous." Although this ascetic approach supposedly helped a saint achieve salvation, it does not work for Hilary; even the joyless continence that Hilary endures is not strong enough to absolve his guilt. His construction of weekly routines is his next attempt to order his life by ordering his rage. Through these weekly dinner schedules, the reader sees him arriving at the fourth stage of his cycle.

Approximately twenty-one years after Anne died, Kitty, Gunnar's second wife, asks Hilary to help her husband alleviate his pent-up rage. Hilary reveals to her that although he has not been neurotic enough to pursue a revenge fantasy, as Gunnar has, he too has "thought of nothing else ever since" the accidental death of Anne (WC 195). Instead of gaining enlightenment from the knowledge that he and Gunnar have been interlocked in an especially destructive form of internalized rage for all these years, Hilary, obsessed by guilt, is vulnerable and reenacts his familiar pattern by falling in love with Kitty. When she asks him to give her a child, to act as an intermediary for the sterile Gunnar, Hilary admits that, having killed Anne's unborn child, he owes Gunnar a child. But instead of complying with Kitty's demands, he meets her at the boat jetty to point out rationally that both of them are full of illusion, that their "love is all shot up with falsity . . . [and that] reality rejects it" (WC 369). At this point Hilary has climbed as far as he will go toward the sun. Just like Bradley's falling in love, Hilary's disorients him enough so that he breaks momentarily out of his obsessive ego to think rationally about the welfare of another human. Contemplating that his part in Kitty's plan would drive him mad with guilt, he decides to avoid disaster. Unfortunately, coming to such a responsible decision does not save him from the aimlessness of reality. In a surprising ironic reversal, Gunnar comes charging down the jetty, threatening to kill him. He knocks Hilary around the jetty until Kitty accidentally falls into the cold December mud of the Thames. Thrashing around in panic, she moves herself out into the icy river, whose current carries her downstream. Hilary, who tries to rescue her, is also carried away. Being washed ashore relatively soon, Hilary survives, but Kitty, having been in the water longer, dies. Not only the disaster—Hilary being responsible for the death of Gunnar's wife—recurs, but his response to the horror repeats itself. Although he is seemingly more mature, Hilary cannot explain to Gunnar the circumstances of his relationship with Kitty; therefore, redemption is impossible.

As the reader has learned to expect, aimlessness follows almost immediately:

Hilary says, "I had expected to go mad" (WC 380). Two pages later appears the statement that has so clearly described the cyclical nature of his life: "I wondered about the future. Was another cycle of misery, intensified, more dense, beginning for me?" (WC 382). He realizes that he is a victim; the reader realizes that his suffering cannot redeem him until he can pay undivided attention to another person and communicate his guilt. Here Murdoch reflects in paradoxical artistic form the "self-enclosed" purposelessness of reality (SG 79), dramatizing that most attempts by human beings to make sense of life are at best fabrications, bizarre escapes from reality.

This, then, is the seven-year pattern of Hilary's life. Only Tommy, his mistress and surrogate mother, is able to suggest order again at the end of this last cycle, saying to Hilary, "Yes, I'm going to marry you" (WC 391). Tommy wants to impose what Hilary so desperately needs. The novel ends on a contingent note, for what Hilary needs if he is to avoid psychic disintegration is self-imposed inner order. If his story is to be believed, the order will be only momentary. Tommy should be wary: if Hilary falls in love with her, her life may be in danger. The pattern or cycle brings Hilary back to his childhood need to find an inner order, as he had done when he learned to use language to stabilize his behavior. Hilary's excessive rigidity portends that he will never be able to love.

Just as an infant learns, through language, concepts that can control narcissism, so Hilary has learned to use language to stabilize his behavior. Introduced early to categorizing, planning, and scheduling, Hilary finds he can substitute activities to control his compulsions.[12] Anxious for substitution as a narcotic to ease his desperate pain, he creates escape through activities that make his body secrete endorphins, tranquilizing his brain. For example, he runs excessively, "keeping *perfectly* fit": "Running was a method of death, of life in death, but not the saint's marvel of living in the present, but a desperate man's little version" (WC 26). Sleep provides another way of coping. Half-sleeping on weekends is an anesthesia that gives him some control over the self he so vehemently dislikes; he lies "like a floating turtle, just breaking the surface of consciousness, aware and yet not self-aware, tormented by being a particular person" (WC 26). All of these behaviors help him convince himself that he is less neurotic than he is.

Moreover, A Word Child illustrates several of the most pervasive patterns that encourage humans simply to retrace habitually worn circuits of the brain: fragmentation, alienation, and Oedipal family struggles. More than Murdoch's other novels of the 1970s and 1980s, this one is a satire on the absurdity of deadening routine: the "patterned sameness of the days of the week gave a comforting sense of absolute subjection to history and time, perhaps a comforting sense of mortality" (WC 27). Hilary's daily rat-runs are smaller cycles that work in tandem with the obsessively circular patterns of his life and Murdoch's large cosmic cycles. Although the routines are meant to control "the phantasmagoria" of his existence, instead of slowing down the pace of his life to give him space to live, his organization increases the unending dreariness of his world.

Since Hilary cannot grapple with reality unless he structures his time, he has for years occupied his evenings with dinner parties and his days with the routines of working, sleeping, running, and learning languages (I discuss the latter in Chapter 3). Because his unchallenging work in a government department does not fulfill his need for achievement, he visualizes himself at the office as a rat in a maze. Having no power to change the rules that he must apply, he follows them belligerently. By listing the kinds of unamusing questions he is required to resolve mechanically, he makes his resentment evident: "(Should this man's 'danger money' affect his pension? Should that man's paid sick leave be extended in these circumstances? Should another man's pay-rise be back-dated in those?)" (WC 28).

Murdoch's modeling the chapter headings on the dinnertime schedule Hilary has created leads the reader to focus immediately on his daily grind and its desperateness. The chapters, labeled "Thursday" through "Wednesday" and repeating five times, suggest his desperation. Murdoch knows that such a focus can lead to neurotic identification with those routines on the part of the reader, who encounters a phantasmagoria upon entering Murdoch's world. The emphasis on vast neurotic energy relays the famous nervous tension that seems unique to Murdoch, who frequently overwhelms the reader by introducing a rush of characters and events. The weekly routine catches the reader up in the phantasm of meeting ten characters in twelve pages, doing so in order merely to see how they fit into Hilary's schedule of meals.

His weekly schedule parallels Hilary's need for safe places to hide. The calendar-like structure of A *Word Child* seems simple at first, but actually the named and unnamed days of the week become a puzzle the reader must figure out, much like John Ducane's maneuvers in figuring out Radeechy's cryptogram in *The Nice and the Good*. When Ducane finally "stared at it without thought," he saw that the central part of the square was a cross in which one could read *pater noster*, or Our Father, "forward, backward, or vertically" (NG 344). The calendar, a puzzling diagram of time, becomes a relentless vehicle for shaping Hilary's life, eliminating his control. Hilary's obsessive arrangement, ordering his life by eating at the home of a different friend each night of the week, eventually collapses, causing panic and allowing chaos to return. Hilary says that he has imposed a mundane schedule to fulfill his longing for order and meaning. Perhaps the first of Murdoch's male enchanters to be given the new kind of freedom, Hilary comes close to remarking openly about it: "Routine, in my case, at least, discouraged thought. Your exercise of free choice is a prodigious stirrer up of your reflection. . . . Week-ends and holidays were hells of freedom. . . . Beyond my routine chaos began and without routine my life (perhaps any life?) was a phantasmagoria" (WC 27–28).

Hilary's circular existence slowly becomes evident to the reader, who notices that the chapters progress through the days of the week, beginning and almost certainly ending with Thursday but eliminating Sundays during the first three weeks.[13] By setting up a pattern and then eliminating explanatory details Murdoch creates a mystery for the reader. Even more important is the unobtrusive way the novel deals with the mystery of time and the way people use it. Murdoch's highlighting of a calendar with its arbitrary connections between one day and another, one day after another, one day beside another suggests much about her world of the novel. Hilary has wasted his life by being angry and blind to the love and beauty around him. The reader sees the influence of T. S. Eliot long before Murdoch introduces the poet in St. Stephen's Church at Gloucester Road, where Hilary retreats to salve his wounds and seek redemption from his sin. Eliot's mourning for the loss of religious values in the twentieth century, which although not named is evident in the mood of the novel, becomes manifest when Hilary communes with the poet after his attempt to confess his behavior to his friend Clifford Larr. To Hilary's chagrin, he discovers that Clifford has, in his utter loneliness, committed suicide. Feeling responsible but having no priest or friend to confess to, Hilary absorbs the series of cataclysmic events by taking comfort in the church where Eliot was a church warden and in recalling the words of Eliot. On Christmas Eve he observes the nativity scene as he considers the three deaths for which he is to some degree responsible:

> At one end of the aisle under a tasselled canopy the Christ child was leaning from his mother's arms to bless the world. At the other end he hung dead, cut off in his young manhood for me and for my sins. There was also, I saw, a memorial tablet which asked me to pray for the repose of the soul of Thomas Stearns Eliot. How is it now with you, old friend, the intolerable wrestle with words and meanings being over? Alas, I could not pray for your soul any more than I could for Clifford's. You had both vanished from the catalogue of being. But I could feel a lively gratitude for words, even for words whose sense I scarcely understand. If all time is eternally present, all time is unredeemable. What might have been is an abstraction, remaining a perceptual possibility only in a world of speculation. (WC 383–84)

Hilary, remembering phrases from *Four Quartets,* thinks about mortality and wonders what it must be like for "the intolerable wrestle with words and meanings [to be] over." As a person whose chaos is controlled by knowing words, he must assume that to die is to return to chaos. After Kitty's death, Hilary understands: "There were no more days" (WC 377). There are no more days of this seven-year cycle, no more days with Kitty or Clifford, no more days in the week, as chapter headings indicate. There are now only holy days left. Now that Crystal is marrying Arthur Fisch, Hilary has no more days to depend on her. His present includes the possibilities of becoming a *word man,* or not changing, or returning to the chaos he experienced before he became a word child. "There were no more days" reverberates against Hilary's earlier "comforting sense of absolute subjection to history and time" (WC 27). Murdoch has the opportunity here to celebrate two kinds of mystery, religion and poetry. What better poet than Eliot could she have chosen for her exploration of spirituality? She has said that if one can write poetry, why would one write anything else? Arthur's line—"Who wouldn't rather be a poet than anything else?" (WC 88)—echoes her statment. Murdoch's pervasive allusions in this novel to texts that explore spirituality, from *Peter Pan* through the texts of Julian of Norwich to the New Testament, finally come to a focus in this series of changes of aspect for Hilary. But the reader sees no permanent changes

Characters Patterning Their Pilgrimages

occurring in Hilary. The ending of the novel is ambiguous; there is no closure for Hilary. The hopefulness of the potential of holy days balances the reader's disappointment when Hilary fails to climb to the sun.

Murdoch's indeterminate ending gives the reader a further reason to notice the careful plotting of Hilary's five weeks. Eliot's diagnosis of the fragmentation of spirituality pulls together and focuses Murdoch's abiding interest in the value of time, of human beings, and of art: words to affirm and to deflate. Just as Eliot's *Waste Land* revitalizes the calendars that were once crucial to the livelihood of Egyptians and celebrates the rain and flooding necessary for the growing of sufficient grain to support the population, Murdoch, in emphasizing references to calendars, saints, and eating, evokes the seasonal cycles of ancient fertility cults and the Christian calendar.

Suggesting that life gives one time to prepare for death, Murdoch leaves out Sundays for the first three weeks of Hilary's schedule to show his inability to be revitalized by the freedom of Sundays and holidays, former sacred days in the calendar. The conditions of Hilary's pilgrimage suggest those of Eliot's pilgrim: being lost in an aimless universe with no religion, no spiritual food, no potential of renewal or rebirth. Hilary's weekly dinner schedule is mundane and narcissistic. He not only believes the plan of his life is laid out in coffee spoons but acquiesces in following the pattern.

Murdoch requires the reader to make a series of hypotheses about Hilary's calendar and then reach conclusions through deduction. The reader, noticing the cyclical repetition of the chapter headings, must grope for the information that the last chapter is a Thursday, even though it is labeled "Christmas Day," because the sequence of the final three chapters follows this order: Tuesday (the day the climax occurs or Hilary causes Kitty to drown), Christmas Eve, Christmas Day. The variation of the expected pattern allows Murdoch to work in the ambiguity of potential rebirth: Sundays and holy days exist. Murdoch's variation, changing the book's pattern at the beginning—three sequences of Thursday, Friday, Saturday, Monday, Tuesday, and Wednesday—to two sequences of Thursday through Wednesday, including Sundays, convinces the attentive reader that Christmas Eve is Wednesday, and Christmas Day, Thursday. A similar kind of balancing—leaving out Sundays and holidays at the beginning of the novel but adding them at the end—suggests that Hilary's gaining insight might mean that he can see another human being clearly for the first time. Murdoch leads the reader to believe that there is hope of Hilary's growing up. The barely perceptible change in the chapter headings suggests that Hilary is acquiring the capability not only of accepting that holidays exist but of celebrating them with Christlike, or at least selfless, behavior. The tension Murdoch creates by juxtaposing Hilary's behavior and his Christlike potential, however, complicates the cycle even more by ending it with Christmas Eve and Christmas Day and by creating an ironic reversal: even though Hilary may at the end have the potential for rebirth, for becoming the "word made flesh," he remains a neurotic puppet whose fantasies and freedom have both been thwarted.

Although a mysterious and disorienting puzzle at the outset, the cyclical use of chapter headings encourages the reader to scrutinize the novel continuously; any page may hold the key that will unlock meaning. In this way the reader progresses from disorientation to orientation, even while Hilary is experiencing the opposite, losing track of days and of time. On finishing the novel, the reader begins to see the patterns that have been emerging in this kaleidoscopic text. Because Wednesdays are Hilary's unexpected days of celebration, his week begins with Thursday and ends with Wednesday instead of Sunday. On Thursdays Hilary spends his time at the home of Freddie Impiatt, an acquaintance from the office, and his wife, Laura; Thursdays include an added comic ritual—repeatedly saving his sister's virginity from Arthur. Fridays belong to Tommy, his mistress; Saturdays, to Crystal. On Mondays, Hilary visits Clifford Larr, an old friend from Oxford; on Tuesdays, Arthur, the soon-to-be fiancé of Crystal. Murdoch leaves Wednesdays open for surprises: the surprise of Hilary's falling in love with Lady Kitty replicates his having first loved Anne. Having given such compulsive ordering, Murdoch then disorders. By making his own calendar sacred, Hilary diminishes the tradition of the Christian calendar and the sacredness of the saints' days. Occasions such as Whitsuntide become merely names of school terms rather than being even vestiges of the Anglican church calendar. But the book's cyclical structure, based on the progression of chapters and their days, Thursday to Thursday, represents Hilary's struggle for sanity.

Hilary treats people as if they exist only on the day he grants to them. Murdoch has achieved a remarkable dramatization of the way an excessively egocentric person sees other people as if they existed for his satisfaction, as scenery that decorates his view. Hilary is especially interested in using the women around him to flesh out his fantasies. For example, the first and last sentences of the novel, each of which refers to a woman who is interested in Hilary, suggest that Hilary's fantasy life presumes the hovering presence of women who desire him. Biscuit, Lady Kitty's maid, reported in the opening line to have asked to see Hilary, mysteriously follows him day after day; Tommy is much more explicit at the end, informing Hilary that she is going to marry him. Because he never sees women as real people, Hilary fails to understand which women really have the power to affect his life. He suspects falsely throughout the novel that Biscuit either is sexually attracted to him or is plotting his downfall; his paranoia establishes that his egoism is excessive. Instead, the innocent, but jealous, Tommy destroys the love between Hilary and Kitty unknowingly and accidentally by telling Gunnar of their relationship. The women caught in the public cycle of Hilary's life take an inferior position to the maelstrom of obsession in his mind. As in real life, desire follows the course of the habitual rat-runs, suggesting that Hilary is responsible for the women's inferior position as decorations for his journey. His obsessions about women appear to be as carefully balanced as his weekly routines; Hilary, rather than Murdoch, seems to be responsible for his fantasy life.

His weekly cycles are important in introducing the shifting, recurrent pattern of love triangles. Murdoch's triangular scenes are significant for more than their argument for the pervasiveness of love. She takes advantage of the Freudian argument that love triangles replicate Oedipal triangles, another pattern of recurrent obsessions from the unconscious. The classical Greeks' language is a compendium of stories based on love involving human beings and gods; this tendency to impose human desires on the gods suggests that Freud has a solid basis for his hypotheses. The relation of gods like Eros and Thanatos and of the life instinct and the death instinct are ambivalent and paradoxical, suggesting that to love is the death of self. In addition, Sophocles, the first in the Greek theater to use a third actor, creates the complexity of triangular scenes to multiply the possibilities of representing the range of human tensions. In a play like *Oedipus Rex*, where Sophocles charts the geography of the mind, Oedipus moves inexorably toward the truth about himself, while the other two actors are embattled in conflict.

Murdoch uses Eros to lighten and enliven this dark comedy. A characteristically Murdochian method is to rush the reader through a series of love triangles that are as anxiety causing as the rush of characters and events. One reason for the musical beds is Murdoch's desire to dramatize the circular Freudian pattern of human beings searching for the comfort of the mother's womb they vaguely remember. Another is her investigation of the more general cultural phenomenon of sexuality, which demonstrates that the Oedipal family drama introduces, perhaps even requires, perpetual triangularity. Throughout all her novels, the play with triangles is not light humor but black humor. Sexual games are diabolical, involving issues of power, status, and economics.

Murdoch's harmonious balancing of her male characters' obsessions speaks to Luce Irigaray's contention that the patriarchy encourages men to employ gendered arrangements to work out their fears about death. The seasonal cycles of Hilary's story celebrate his ability to repress Thanatos by projecting it onto two of his lovers, Anne and Kitty; as a result, they become his place of death.[14] Irigaray says women, on the other hand, are not allowed to "work out these masochistic death drives and must . . . turn them inward" (*Speculum* 54–55). Murdoch's novel insists that since childhood Hilary has had every reason to be suicidal, but instead he finds language, beautiful language, the first way to ward off death.

Murdoch simulates the rhythm of Oedipal triangles she sees in the real world, giving the characters the freedom to indulge their obsessive-compulsive behavior. In examining the authenticity of love, she focuses on its suddenness and irrationality. Most of the characters in the novels are not comparable to M, the loving mother-in-law in Murdoch's well-known example from *The Sovereignty of Good* (see chapter 4). At the Impiatts' dinner parties, various guests insinuate that the other characters are hiding dark secrets and that the sexual configurations have recently changed or are changing before the reader's eyes. Never quite sure what is happening below the surface of the characters' game playing; the reader watches the metamorphosing pairs, threesomes, and groups meet and exchange consoling fancies: constellations are unstable; information is skewed. The triangles break up just as groups in real-life families do; secrets are rampant, but participants do not admit knowledge. For example, when Hilary eats with Clifford Larr, a homosexual once loved by Crystal, the reader learns that the men mistakenly consider Crystal a virgin; in fact, she has made love to Gunnar Jopling. The knowledge would be too painful for the two men to acknowledge: each needs the fantasy.

If Murdoch sets up the novel to experience its own aimlessness, then there is only so much recuperation she can bring about. The mysterious aimlessness in this novel emerges both in triangles that appear to exist but do not, and in *Midsummer Night's Dream* triangles that appear when least expected. She uses such shape-shifting triangles to flesh out the characters' fantasies. The order in which Murdoch introduces characters foreshadows the way the triangles will form and reform. Her juxtapositions of the people who make up the suspected triangles create a pattern that seems to supersede the traditional pattern of cause and effect; it leaves the tangled layers of deception and misunderstanding. Murdoch's ordering of the introduction of characters allows the reader to suspect that sexual liaisons actually exist that correspond to the characters' insinuations. This system of implication affirms that love triangles are always a real possibility: by focusing on relatively minor relationships that never materialize, however, Murdoch is also preparing the reader to accept the triangles that are basic to the novel's structure. This indirect preparation is all the reader has to confirm that an improbable triangle involving the protagonist will materialize, Hilary being destined to fall into his prefigured neurotic pattern. The series of surprises this climatic pattern creates puts the reader at a loss; one finds that one can judge potential relationships no better within the novel than in real life.

In the opening lines of the novel, a dialogue between two speakers, who turn out to be Hilary and his young boarder, Christopher, indirectly suggests a cyclical pattern that is a foundation of traditional comedy—the older man being attracted to the young woman whom the young man will marry at the conclusion of the story. The comedy in such cases displaces the quasi-incestuous desires, which have to fit into a socially accepted pattern. The sexual overtones in the conversation prepare the reader to expect the confusion that results from the misinterpretation of sexual signs:

> "I say, an absolutely stunning coloured girl was here looking for you."
> "She was looking for you."
> "No, I offered myself. She was uninterested. She said she wanted to see Mr. Hilary Burde." That was me.
> "Oh." It was all very improbable however. "Did she say what she wanted? (WC 1)

The reader cannot know this early what the potential pairings might be, and in fact, the reader is unaware until the end of the novel that this dialogue suggests a Shakespearean wedding convention—that all's well that ends in couples planning weddings. What the reader is not told is as important as what is told. For example, the "coloured girl," Biscuit, a woman named for food, a physically attractive woman whom Hilary wants to take to bed, is like a Greek messenger. She is also a harbinger of his return to the pain he has been working for years to numb through controlled, established methods of behavior. Neither can the reader know until the penultimate chapter that Christopher's offer has been accepted. Learning, at the end of the novel, that Biscuit had instantaneously fallen in love with Christopher on the novel's first page and is planning to marry him can make the reader feel nonplussed.

The examination of Hilary now having proved the rule, a look at each of the other three novels will focus attention on important variations. A stronger first-person protagonist, Bradley Pearson in *The Black Prince*, takes more control away from the author. Being a writer himself, he recognizes to a greater degree than Hilary, who is a word child but not an artist, that cyclical events recur because of his own conscious and unconscious obsessions. He uses writing as a method of grasping his own obsessions and those of others. Bradley more than Hilary gains perspective and eventually gains control of his behavior. Of course, Bradley has more help; Murdoch appoints Apollo-Loxias as Bradley's guide. That inspiration enables him to organize the pervasive cyclical patterns, such as the incidents of violence, for the structuring of a good novel.

In Bradley, Murdoch creates a character who, like Hilary, selects routine to structure his life. But Bradley hopes to escape the cycles of obsession that characterize Hilary's life. With his retirement from his uninspiring job as inspector of taxes and then his planned escape to the seaside, he holds out hope to readers that he can plot new creative routines. He wants to find time and silence so that he can write the great story hidden within himself, a seemingly worthy purpose. Throughout the novel he is dominated by the desire to get away from the city and the unexpected chaos of his flat in order to concentrate on this work. But because the doorbell and phone ring continually, he keeps missing his train—making him available when a real story does occur. The parade of acquaintances through Bradley's flat inhibits him from achieving the modicum of order that Hilary achieves. Hilary, of course, manifests more neuroses—neuroses that routine has helped him repress since childhood—but he is stymied by some indescribable force from outside the planet. Bradley is able to take advantage of an alien force; his obsessions are less bizarre than

Hilary's. For different reasons, he, like Hilary, seeks refuge in sleep as he remembers having done in childhood. But he refuses to let his life "degenerate into madness" (BP 210).

Looking at *A Word Child* next to *The Black Prince*, the reader understands that although Bradley's journey into illusion is similar to Hilary's, Bradley gains more insight in his search. Hilary's cataclysmic change occurs when he thinks of Kitty and Gunnar, and not of himself. But his unselfishness is only momentary. The reader can measure the quality of his rebirth by comparing it to Bradley's longer-lasting change in perception, which continues the rest of his short life. Bradley suffers enough to see clearly the reality that his editor, Loxias, insists on: the artist produces art through suffering. Bradley's novel dares to describe his life as a drama and his subject as the "unconscious mind"; bewailing that "there is no general chart of that lost continent" (BP xv), he makes the reader believe he will construct one. The quality that makes these two protagonists comparable is that both are word children—Hilary, a word child in the most primitive sense, is a kind of Ur Bradley.

Murdoch writes cyclical plots to establish that routines imposed by humans, be they neurotic or healthy, are incapable of bringing permanent consolation. All her first-person male narrators live through such trying ordeals that they require the balance of daily routine to bring order back to their lives. When the reader meets Bradley at the beginning of his novel, he is in the midst of changing his routines. Vestiges of his old life bump up against his illusion of a new life. In the midst of Bradley's disorientation, Murdoch is able to make her most thorough plumbing of the cauldron of the creative unconscious. Here the creator and the created have more in common; they get on better together. Even though Bradley is as finicky about his schedule as Hilary, he attends more to human beings and is more open to phenomena. Bradley says he has waited most of his adult years to retire so that he might dig up his "hidden treasure" (BP xvii), his artistic story. Now that he has finally retired, however, he finds that the earlier inspirations do not come. He blames this dry spell on his change of routine and his need to have total silence (a silence he later, unexpectedly, finds in prison). Murdoch gives him space at the beginning of the novel to recount his excuses in his foreword:

> The shock of leaving the office was greater than I had anticipated. . . . Perhaps I am, more than I realized, a creature of routine. Perhaps too,

with scarcely pardonable stupidity, I imagined that inspiration would come with freedom. I did not expect the complete withdrawal of my gift. In the years before, . . . I wrote steadily and I destroyed steadily. . . . Sometimes I felt at a (terrible phrase) dead end. But I never despaired of excellence. . . . And at least I found that I could always write something.

But when I . . . could sit at my desk at home every morning and think any thoughts I pleased, I found I had no thoughts at all . . . I tried to develop a new routine: monotony, out of which value springs. I waited, I listened. . . . Noise, which had never distressed me before, began to do so. For the first time in my life I urgently wanted silence. (BP xvi-xvii)

In this lengthy passage Bradley sums up the gist of his creative life. He reveals that he remains a creature of habit even though he now has the freedom to slave away at his art. His emptiness at this point makes the reader wonder whether this self-conscious writer is truly capable of producing art, or whether these rationalizations suggest that his ambition is merely a consoling fantasy. Bradley's aside here, "(terrible phrase)," is very like the notes Murdoch makes to herself on the versos of her holograph notebooks. The balance and harmony Murdoch and Bradley immediately achieve by ordering the incidents of violence pull the reader into the maelstrom of chaotic activity. As the novel progresses, it becomes clear that Bradley's reticence and insecurity, not his artistry, motivate his behavior. No doubt Murdoch has, like other artists, experienced just such feelings of frustration and anxiety about her writing. Although Bradley determines to get away and find peace, he actually finds excuses for accepting the refuge of home and sleep. Outward circumstances—the phone, the doorbell—and other people—Arnold, Rachel, Marloe, Christian, even Hartbourne—direct his life. These phenomena jerk him from one desire to another, from one motivation to another, and set up his phantasmagoria. As the novel progresses, he moves momentarily from focusing on and being distracted by the realities of the writing process to being directed by his surprising obsession with Julian. (I explore Bradley's writing in chapter 6.) He is not aggressive enough to pursue her: his inner motivation is to seek escape. His inspiration comes only when others indict him for murder, and his time to write comes only in prison. His tendency toward depression becomes manifest in Priscilla's seemingly suicidal behavior. Just as his reticence about achieving stifles his ability to get on with the task, his lack of outrage at the culpability of his friends allows him to be drowned by circumstance.

Bradley has a distinct advantage over Hilary. Being an artist, Bradley is a better reader of his environment than Hilary is. For Bradley, the inexplicable contingency that pursues human beings is the stuff of art. Bradley's fascination with plotting circular structure reflects Murdoch's own novelistic habits and philosophical insights. In Bradley's patterns the reader recognizes Murdoch's play with framing devices, with forewords and postscripts, making this plot very different from the straightforward *A Word Child*. Bradley structures his story around two crucial telephone calls: Arnold's call for help when he thinks he has accidentally killed Rachel and Rachel's call after she has accidentally killed Arnold. In the time between the two calls, Bradley's obsessive compulsions move him toward the accident of falling in love with their daughter, his godchild Julian. The new perspective he gains from this useful shock begins to motivate him finally to write his novel. Bradley's affair with Julian, the material for the middle of his novel, is also cyclical: he loses her in the same way he found her, unexpectedly. He experiences little control until he is on trial for murder, a totally unexpected scenario.

Before the reader's eyes, Murdoch, through Bradley, works on solving technical artistic problems about the power of such patterning. Murdoch identifies so closely with Bradley as artist, in his analysis of form and technique in his novel, that she lays the groundwork for the reader's uncertainty about what level of irony to assume. When readers discover the critical postscripts at the end, they often question Murdoch's attitude toward Bradley: Does she find him a craftsman? Have they focused too much on Murdoch's identification with her novelist-character? Surely the reader is meant to see ironically the reasons for Bradley's driving artistic force. Bradley's obsession with artistic framing grows out of the struggle between his need for love and his fear of dissolving the inflexible boundaries between his ego and others'. The conversation about the cabinet in the shop suggests that the concept of womb-shaped patterning comes from Bradley's unconscious memories. But in her depiction of Bradley, who considers himself an objective observer, Murdoch very carefully develops his blindness to his own subjectivity. Even though he, like Murdoch, consciously manipulates technique in order to achieve distance, he fails to understand his own psychological needs.

PATTERNED AIMLESSNESS

The Black Prince acts out the struggle to break out of inflexible ego boundaries. Of course, Bradley's ostensible goal is to solve artistic problems, making the story accessible to the reader. But another goal is his weaving of a text in which to wrap himself securely: whereas Hilary hides in his schedule, Bradley, being a writer, hides in his text, at least at the beginning. His novel is layered like an onion. Encased within the forewords by P. Loxias, the editor, and his own foreword and the postscripts by dramatis personae, Bradley's story shields its author as if in a cocoon. When he begins to communicate with the reader, he dwells on a long series of self-conscious artistic reasons for introducing the characters to the reader in a certain order. His interest in such maneuvers seems excessive, but perhaps he, like Murdoch, is employing a mode of excess. In his foreword, Bradley speculates about framing his story with a similarly obscure character, Francis Marloe, whom he calls his "messenger of fate" (BP xviii): "I mention Francis first of any of my 'players' not because he is most important: Francis is not important at all and has no deep connection with the course of events. He is subsidiary, a sidesman" (BP xiv). Marloe's postscript, however, demonstrates that he is a complex character and that he is less sympathetic toward Bradley than one might have thought throughout the novel (see chapter 6).

Murdoch emphasizes Bradley's artistic purpose by having him, in the first sentence of his story, continue speculating about which character he should have the reader encounter first. Being more creative and decidedly more healthy than Hilary, he uses his cyclical behavior to tell a story; the story releases him from his cycle. Being a more serious and more disciplined quester makes Bradley willing to see his ordeals as necessary and to see love in the most romantic light. He knows, even though he does not admit his feelings for his lost mother, that "human love is the gateway to all knowledge, as Plato understood" (BP 339). He says late in the novel that "the book had to come into being because of Julian, and because of this book Julian had to be. . . . And through the door that Julian opened my being passed into another world" (BP 339). Bradley struggles with the labyrinthine, multilayered structure that makes up reality, referring explicitly to a frame:

> A deeper pattern however [than Arnold thinking he had killed Rachel] suggests Francis Marloe as the first speaker, the page or housemaid (these

images would appeal to him) who, some half an hour before Arnold's momentous telephone call, initiates the action. For the news which Francis brought me forms the frame, or counterpoint, or the outward packaging of what happened then and later in the drama of Arnold Baffin. There are indeed many places where I could start. (BP 3)

Bradley suggests he could start with the women's reactions to the actions. Perhaps he does not because the first actor, for the Greeks, was the first struggler, not the reactor. "I might start with Rachel's tears, or Priscilla's. There is much shedding of tears in this story. In a complex explanation any order may seem arbitrary. Where after all does anything begin? That three of the four starting points I have mentioned were causally independent of each other suggests speculations, doubtless of the most irrational kind, upon the mystery of human fate" (BP 3). It would appear that Bradley's obsessions determine the final order. Bradley has the opportunity to tell his story not only to the public but to his psychoanalyst of sorts, Francis, and to his editor. Before these characters Bradley is able to unburden his emotions. As unlikely counselors as they are, together these companions help Bradley piece his life together so that he can use it in his creative effort. Francis and Loxias each mirror for Bradley different aspects of himself, creating a dialogical model. In looking for the subplots and displacements of Bradley's life, Francis bumps into his own. Francis projects his own neuroses on Bradley, reading Bradley's confessions as if they were his own and reconstructing Bradley's life to be like his own—a habit perhaps not unusual for psychoanalysts. Loxias, being a god and therefore more impersonal in a way Murdoch sees as artistically valuable, reads in and brings out the best Bradley has to offer the world. Bradley, although he is dying at the end, is joyful in nature's revived fecundity, and his pride is balanced by his capacity for good. Bradley comes to understand that human intelligence is blind; the will of the gods is inscrutable.

Writing the story two years after the fact, Bradley is obviously aware of the relativity of occurrences in time and is awed by the mystery, the contingency of fate. He is also aware that the artist, a kind of god, may imply causal relationships where none originally existed. He knows, as Murdoch does, that truth depends on one's perspective and that ordering and emphasis distort chronological truth while at the same time increasing psychological truth. At the beginning of his foreword, the reader sees Bradley cogitating about the complexity of experience and pondering the dilemma of the writer who wishes to capture life in art. He concludes that he will allow

> the narrating consciousness to pass like a light along its series of present moments, aware of the past, unaware of what is to come. I shall, that is, inhabit my past self and, for the ordinary purposes of story-telling, speak only with the apprehensions of that time, a time in many ways so different from the present. So for example I shall say, "I am fifty-eight years old," as I then was. And I shall judge people, inadequately, perhaps even unjustly, as I then judged them, and not in the light of any later wisdom. That wisdom however, as I trust that I truly think it to be, will not be absent from the story. It will to some extent, in fact must, "irradiate" it. . . . I have already by implication described this "reportage" as a work of art. I do not of course by this mean a work of fantasy. All art deals with the absurd and aims at the simple. Good art speaks truth, indeed *is* truth, perhaps the only truth. (BP xi)

This passage, and Loxias's statements, make the reader assume that Bradley's care about truth and craftsmanship will lead him to write a good book—but at this point it is easy to overlook the fact that the reader has only Bradley's and Loxias's opinions about Bradley's motives and ability.

Murdoch has a master plan for introducing the characters and then letting them go so that they may each bombard Bradley with rapid-fire intensity. But her plan is flexible enough to allow the protagonists freedom to order the introductions in their manuscripts. Murdoch's introducing Loxias first not only establishes a frame for distancing the reader from Bradley's text but also demonstrates a blindness in Bradley: his lack of awareness that his own order of introduction reveals his intense psychological dependency on male alter egos. After introducing Marloe in the foreword, Bradley fails to name P. Loxias, referring to him instead in vague terms, "my dearest friend, my comrade and my teacher" (BP xviii). By introducing these two characters first, Murdoch and Bradley frame the story proper, in which Arnold Baffin, whom Bradley later calls his alter ego, is a much more central character. Waiting to introduce Arnold within the story, Bradley devotes several pages to describing their relationship. Bradley, in justifying himself, ingenuously reveals the polarity between himself and Arnold. Murdoch's plan is to dramatize a polarity in modern art: the pure artist in conflict with the commercial artist. This climactic order of the introduction of Bradley's alter egos subtly prepares the reader for the shock in store when Bradley is indicted for Arnold's murder.

The order of introducing women is controlled initially by Murdoch's artistic consciousness, but Bradley's unconscious control and lack of personal awareness soon challenge Murdoch's control. It is certainly significant that the women in the novel, who perform most of the crucial actions, are introduced after the men. At the end of the novel it is clear that the women have been the motivating forces behind Bradley's metamorphosis: his ability to perform sexually, his inspiration to write a novel, and his acceptance of his indictment for murder. Rachel Baffin, the first to be introduced, is crucial because her unpremeditated murder of her husband results not only from her jealousy of Arnold and his extramarital affairs but from jealousy caused by the love affair between Bradley and Julian, who is the next powerful character introduced. Indirectly these circumstances help to bring about the death of Arnold. Rachel sees, no doubt, that if Bradley had renewed his love affair with his ex-wife, Christian, then Christian could not have enticed Arnold into an extramarital affair, and Bradley would not have had time to become enamored of Julian.

Even if the order of Bradley's introduction of characters in his novel is controlled as much by his unconscious needs as by the needs of the manuscript, he does control the plot pattern. The three sections set up a series of climaxes: his inability to find inspiration as an artist until he falls in love; his renewal through authentic love; and the interruption of love through his own egoism and unforeseen outside circumstances, most pointedly Priscilla's suicide and Arnold's murder.

Replicating the culture's belief in the Oedipal family triangle, Murdoch digs deeply into the complexities, the encrustations of family life, revealing family struggles as the basis of the characters' obsessions. These major novels of the decade ending in 1980 reveal a persistent critique of the middle-aged, first-person protagonists, each of whom is love-starved for his mother. The memory of the mother is intrinsic to the creation and re-creation of each protagonist's fantasies. Their social problems recur because each man is bent on reuniting with his Platonic memories of mother love. (Hilary makes the explicit point that he has Platonic memories.) These Hamlet-like melancholics not only re-create Mother in their fantasies, they also work at re-creating her womb. The safe enclosures in which these men live—rooms, flats, seaside cabins—suggest the space they need and the space they dominate. Each is generally sympathetic to the problems of his mother. Bradley's statement about his mother illustrates Irigaray's idea that men tend to displace their fear of death onto women: "My mother was very important to me. I loved her, but always with a kind of anguish. I feared loss and death to an extent I think unusual in a child" (BP 59).

Each of these protagonists is either jealous of his father or uncomfortable with the father's image, which haunts him in the form of some contemporary acquaintance. Just as sons act out father-son competition with brothers, each protagonist has a substitute brother figure with whom he plays out the classical competitive roles of Polynieces and Eteocles: Bradley and Arnold, Hilary and Gunnar, Charles and James. Hilary has had to substitute his sister Crystal for his mother; she is pathetic in her masochistic love for her brother. Murdoch has laid the groundwork for considering emotional incest by having Hilary express his overpowering, unhealthy love for Crystal: "Crystal and I were so much jumbled up together that it might be accurate to say that Crystal was me" (BP 116); "I lived in and for the hope of Crystal as men live in and for the hope of God" (BP 19). Bradley has a much different relationship with his other sister, Priscilla, a pathetic Ophelia; the horrid character trait he must overcome is his lack of loyalty to her.

Bradley appears to have further displaced his unconscious memories of the womb in his stated memories of childhood security in the cabinet in the shop. As unreliable as Francis Marloe is, he sees that Bradley and Priscilla each have problems with ego boundaries. When Francis, in his forthcoming book, applies his Oedipal theory to Bradley, he recognizes if nothing else that Bradley is highly androgynous. During Francis's first conversation with these two, what comedically could be seen as a session with a dysfunctional family, Priscilla asks Bradley if he remembers "hiding in the shop": "We used to lie on the shelves under the counter and we'd think the counter was a boat and we were in our bunks, and the boat was sailing? And when Mummy called us we'd just lie there ever so quietly—it was—oh it was exciting—" (BP 120). Why is Priscilla more positive about the shop? Is she escaping into nostalgia, or is Murdoch proposing that women have it easier than men in childhood but harder in adulthood? Bradley begins this line of exploration and Priscilla responds:

"I often dream about the shop."

"So do I. About once a week."

"Isn't that odd, I always feel frightened, it's always a nightmare."

"When I dream about it," said Priscilla, "it's always empty, huge and empty, a wooden shell, counter and shelves and boxes, all empty."

"You know what the shop means of, course," said Francis. "The womb."

"The empty womb," said Priscilla. (BP 120–21)

Bradley's response to Francis's notion of dreaming of the womb is "Rubbish! How could you remember that! And how could anyone ever prove it anyway?" (BP 121). In his escapist attempt to be scientific, Bradley has pointed to Freud's major problem: a doctor cannot prove unconscious knowledge if a patient has no memory of it. Contrary to Bradley's negative reaction, Priscilla perhaps has a moment of enlightenment that helps her see the truth of her passage. Do Priscilla's moments of enlightenment along the path out of the cave lead to her suicide, whereas Bradley's lead to his public artistic success? Her happy memories, her desire to be connected to Bradley and Francis and to Roger, act out one tendency Nancy Chodorow sees in women. Similarly, Carol Gilligan argues that women continue to value attachment and love from parents, teachers, students, husband, and they have a cultural inability to fracture relationships. Is it possible that these ideas are important to Murdoch?

There is a significant difference between Priscilla's rather beneficent portrayal of her dream and Bradley's nightmare. Why would Bradley be more traumatized by the family than Priscilla—or is Murdoch suggesting that Priscilla has always been under more illusion and that she therefore ignores the terror of her dreams or does not reveal them exactly? Is Bradley successful in becoming an artist because he fractures the relationship between himself and his family as he as a male is required to do? Is that a part of a series of insights for him? He certainly prospers for a while after he abandons Priscilla. On the other hand, is Murdoch suggesting that Priscilla fails to live harmoniously in society because she cannot fracture her relationship with a selfish husband and a preoccupied brother? Her mother gave her a way to survive, but the mother had not, in Chodorow's terms, overcome her own upbringing and fractured her connectedness to the female line of dependency.[15]

It is ironic that the great enduring plays of the Greek theater—a didactic tool ensuring the health and well-being of the patriarchy—are not about battles the state wins but about struggles within the family, often between men and women. This magnificent struggle for power in archetypal families is basic to Murdoch's mythical fictions. Just as Oedipus feels entrapped by the system of the world in which Fate seems to predestine his behavior, Bradley feels entrapped in the cupboard in the shop of his parents' store and resents his mother even at age sixty. Their problems with mothers cause these men to find women a problem.

Murdoch's combination of Platonic imagery and Freudian concepts about the unconscious and Oedipal obsession contextualize layers of Western ideology.[16] Beneath the desire of Murdoch's semitragic first-person male enchanters the reader can glimpse the images of human civilization. Perhaps the Oedipal family struggles can explain why Bradley is fascinated by Christian, a manipulative woman like his mother, or why Priscilla settles for a weak man who is like her father. Hilary is dissatisfied that his motherly sister is leaving him to marry, and Charles searches for his mother in his now-middle-aged childhood lover of forty years earlier.

Since Eros is a major but unannounced character, each woman works to be connected to a man, and each man works to find his mother and relate to her in the way he has learned, needing her ability to connect but also striving to escape from that ability. Are these fallings in love, the tiny switches of gestalt, sudden moments of knowledge? Bradley thinks the novel is built around the celebration of a deep, authentic love; seen through Murdoch's theory of love, however, the ecstasy Bradley is celebrating is only momentarily love. Although this experience takes the central position in his novel, *The Black Prince*, like *A Word Child*, dramatizes a number of shifting love triangles. These triangles, however, reveal less conventional, and therefore more humorous, behavior. The presence of homosexual triangles demonstrates what Murdoch understands—that Western culture has never been without homosexuality, even though the culture often pretends homosexuality is unusual. Her reading of Plato and Freud suggests that the family, with its binary structure, sets up a potential for homosexuality. She most emphatically juxtaposes homosexual and heterosexual love in *The Black Prince*. While there is probably no homosexual activity in the novel other than that of Francis Marloe, every major male character is accused of homosexual desire at some point.

Like the classical Greeks, these men seem to value men more than women.

The relationships between Bradley and Loxias and between Bradley and Francis remain ambiguous. The first note of this recurring theme is struck when the editor announces in his foreword that he is the "dear friend" to whom Bradley refers in *his* foreword. At this point the reader need suspect nothing, but later, when Bradley records Francis's numerous insinuations about Bradley's sexual desire, it is easy to begin to wonder whether Bradley is telling everything. Marloe, arguing in his postscript that Bradley is a latent homosexual with classic symptoms of the Oedipus complex, is unconvincing since he also generalizes that most artists are latent homosexuals. Marloe theorizes that Bradley has loved Arnold, his "protégé," for years (BP 11), and also sees Arnold as a father figure. In addition, Marloe believes that Bradley loved him: "Bradley was blessed with another more mundane and more 'real' attachment, another much simpler and less tormenting focus of emotion. I would not, and indeed need not, use his ill-concealed love for me as evidence of his perverted tendencies. (The transparent attempt to belittle the love-object is again typical.)" (BP 350–51). Marloe's insinuations, no doubt revealing his jealousy, suggest incongruous and humorous triangles involving Loxias, Bradley, and Marloe, and Arnold, Bradley, and Marloe.

A much more serious insinuation, and the one the reader is likely to trust, is Murdoch's specific questioning of Bradley's virility. She plants suspicion by dramatizing Bradley's sexual arousal only when he is touched by the image of a boyish figure—surely a form of fetishism on Bradley's part. Bradley is first aroused when he mistakes Julian Baffin for a male flower child, and is capable of sexual activity only when, at Patara, Julian dresses up as Hamlet. Because of Murdoch's suggestion, other pieces of incriminating evidence pile up in the reader's mind. Bradley's unconscious need to deal with the male characters first and his reliance on them in life reveal his unanalyzed insecurity about the completeness of his own masculinity. Instead of being direct about this dependence, he plays down Marloe's role by calling Marloe "the mascot of the tale" (BP xiv). Actually Marloe is important to Bradley's image of himself, for Marloe is the only character who believes Bradley. Bradley never explains his relationship to Hartbourne, a "typical denizen" of his years of dullness (BP xv); this mysterious voice on the telephone simply hovers in the background. For unknown reasons Bradley does not name Loxias, his inspiration, in his foreword. Furthermore, Bradley introduces no women in his foreword: he mentions no women until the plot gets under way.

Most surprising of all are Murdoch's implications regarding incestuous triangles. Why would she go to so much trouble to suggest the incest triangles unless she found the issue basic to comedy? Her candor recognizes that family relationships are sexual; in fact, most struggle is sexual. Primary in this novel is the family structure in which the god-father steals the marriageable daughter, an underlying rather than overt issue in traditional comedy. Because this fiction is a variation on an old comic motif, the reader is not unusually disturbed when Bradley hears that Julian has written from Europe that her father, Arnold, is the man she has always loved: "Everyone at the hotel thinks we are lovers! . . . I think I never made it clear enough to you how much I love my father. (Perhaps he is *the* man in my life!)" (BP 320). Rachel proposes a variation on this motif by expressing her jealous rage when she realizes that Julian has taken Bradley from her. Also running rampant are implications that Arnold is a father figure to Bradley, and the reverse. If the reader accepts either of these possibilities, Bradley becomes a symbolic relative of Julian; anyway, he is in fact her godfather.

More conventional triangles that precipitate humor and surprise include the one linking Bradley, Christian, and Hartbourne. The reader discovers only in Christian's postscript that her new name is Christian Hartbourne, suggesting that the couple met at Bradley's trial and took advantage of the occasion to become lovers. In addition, the Priscilla-Roger-Marigold triangle is important both to the comic plot and the tragic resolution: it involves Bradley in absurd situations and also brings about Priscilla's suicide and Bradley's tragedy of love. This merry-go-round of metamorphosing sexual relationships—some acted out, some only desired, some imposed by fantasy—contributes to Murdoch's depiction of the absurdities of human behavior. Furthermore, although she insists that the path toward perfection takes one beyond egoism to love the reality outside oneself, no human effort can control contingency.

Each of the first-person narrations analyzes the personal history of a creative person; each man is an enchanter or magician figure. Murdoch uses anecdotal material from the histories of these inventive men to investigate the ways obsessional patterns work in their lives. *The Sea, The Sea*, a more impressionistic and less experimental novel than *The Black Prince*, begins ostensibly as a diary and eventually becomes fiction. Murdoch, who is so much fixed on the particular, seems to want to explore the contingency of the historical anecdote in this novel, and focusing on diary writing is a good way to accomplish

Characters Patterning Their Pilgrimages

that. Murdoch puts great stock in the simple, quiet pursuit of domestic routine and the effect of beauty and love on humans. She continues in later novels to move in the direction this novel began—the accretion of particulars from nature. Here the protagonist, Charles Arrowby, a director and writer who feels even more out of control than Bradley and is also less self-aware, determines to retire to the sea to "abjure magic" and egoism (SS 2). In order to carry out his quest for goodness and move toward the sun, he must immerse himself in his past, his prehistory, the influence on him of his relatives and his first love, Hartley. Because his diary-novel examines his past, his present at sea (in both senses of that phrase), and his potential future, Murdoch labels the sections "Prehistory," "History," and "Posthistory."

Another way of describing the organization of *The Sea, The Sea* corresponds to the pattern Joel Fineman discusses in relation to classical essay form: introduction, anecdote, amplification, moral conclusion. Murdoch's language in this novel's introduction demonstrates the rhythm of the Arnoldian language that simulates the waves of the sea. The flowing and retreating patterns of sentences moving rhythmically like the waves in and out are symmetrical. Fineman says that Thucydides' narratives balance "stylistic patterns at the level of the sentence . . . [to] correspond with larger architectural patterns, . . . e.g., the balanced dispositions of one speech against another, and related contrapuntal symmetries and formal arrangements that serve to organize the narrative" ("The Anecdote" 55). If this novel's larger architectural pattern is the climb toward the sun, then the reversals and falls back into the mediocre are contrapuntal, as are the numerous fallings into water. The novel's introduction simulates the appearance and reality of the sea, calm on the surface but agitated beneath. The moral conclusion is that fantasies about escape to the sea are dangerous: the sea may be a good place to escape to after a life of being buffeted, but the characteristic it is most known for is danger.

Murdoch focuses especially on certain contingencies in Charles's family history that play a big part in his own story. Her emphasis on magic represents some of the worries about invention that she has expressed in interviews. Occasionally, especially with Charles, the Prospero of the group, magic no longer works—or works in the way he wants. While stepping back to frame her text with classical Greek allusions, as is evident in the title, Murdoch also gives Charles the freedom to choose his own framing contexts. He does bend the reader's ear with anecdote upon anecdote, and Murdoch's philosophical leanings might lead one to expect this analogical method. The exploration of the most insignificant occurrences in this former theater director's life turns out to be psychologically significant. Charles probes his own symptoms, but as is true of most human beings, he is usually blind to more objective outside perspectives. The reader must decide whether the anecdote about Charles's jealousy of James is more important than his anecdote about his loss of Hartley: the novel seems to reverberate between the two.

The Sea, The Sea is an amplification of these two major anecdotes. Murdoch understood even before there were New Historicists that she could produce "the effect of the real, the occurrence of contingency, by establishing an event as an event within and yet without the framing context of historical successivity" (Fineman, "The Anecdote" 61). She chose to call the novel *The Sea, The Sea* because she understood, like Stephen Greenblatt, that "the historical anecdote functions less as explanatory illustration than as disturbance, that which requires explanation, contextualization, interpretation" (*Learning* 5).[17] Murdoch's using anecdote or alluding to anecdote as an entrance into classical Greek history functions less as an explanatory illustration than as a framing context. Her placing the novel in the context of Xenophon's *Anabasis* certainly piques the reader's interest in digging into the novel's intertextuality. Such digging uncovers not only the challenge of an expedition to the coast but the emotion of the thrilling outburst in *Anabasis:* "The sea, the sea." "After ten thousand Greeks have been wandering and buffeted a bit, they finally make it back to the Black Sea, to safety, serenity, light after darkness" (Howard, "Eight Recent Novelists," 434). Murdoch has always demanded this kind of reader participation in the text, all the way back to *Under the Net*.

She prefers, of course, that the reader perform the function of historian. Her maintenance of patterned aimlessness requires narrative excess and contingency to destabilize the world of the novel. Being a classicist herself, she understands that she can produce this effect of the way the real world feels through references to historical contingencies. Her novels then enter history at several levels: they are the histories of her characters, they are historical events in themselves, but they are also contextualizations of all literature that she values. Whereas *The Sea, The Sea* seems to some readers to be pages of digressions, the interminable anecdotes, by fleshing out the narrator's history, give the reader the narrator's prognosis.

Charles's "Prehistory" contains the seeds of the egoism and jealousy that destroy his history in midlife. The "History" dramatizes his drowning and rebirth, echoing the metamorphoses in *The Tempest* and *The Waste Land*, and, of course, those of Hilary and Bradley. The "Postscript," subtitled "Life Goes On," indicates not only that the stream of life is very like the uncontrollable waves of the sea, but that Charles's rebirth is only temporary, or only a possibility that he cannot accept. Like Prufrock he has knowledge that cannot sustain his renewal, and he drowns again in his unconscious self-centeredness—the sea, the sea.

Perhaps Murdoch's reason for having a diary metamorphose into a novel is to emphasize the anecdotal quality of the diary-writing process and its similarity to her novel-writing process. Being a combination of memoir, diary, philosophical journal, and novel, *The Sea, The Sea* seems to ramble perpetually like the waves, seems to be as out of control as Charles. Because the language simulates the consciousness of its protagonist, the work drifts along just as language tends to do. Ostensibly investigating the basis for his egoism, Charles analyzes his past sixty years simply by addressing memories as they pop into his head. Being a much less self-conscious artist than Bradley, Charles records his story in a stream-of-consciousness style, convincing the reader until well into the text that he is ingenuous. The resulting flow of his irrational and sometimes rational thought patterns simulates the peristaltic rhythm of the sea.

Even though he retires to the sea to "repent of egoism" (SS 3) and to write about his relationships with others, Charles dominates the narrative while he is becoming familiar with the writing process. To the extent that he is immersed exclusively in his own history, he reveals his own unself-conscious egoism. Murdoch frees Charles to ramble and lets him digress to analyze his obsession with food and his preoccupation with the influence others have had on his past. His unconscious self-centeredness continues to cause him to focus on his relationship to whatever impinges on him. At the beginning of the diary, since he is alone, he reverses his usual tendency to see people as objects and personifies objects instead. He does not intend to color the reality he experiences, but his value system is so distorted that he cannot restrain an egoistic emphasis. His moments of enlightenment are more magical, and therefore more suspect, than Bradley's. Being a man lost in personal fantasy, this Prospero figure has a difficult time abjuring magic.

In the introduction, Murdoch gives Charles free rein to move from unimportant influences, like food and home, to important influences, like his father and his cousin James, back to the relatively unimportant influence of Clement, a former mistress. The memory of her sets his mind to ranging over a list of theater friends: Lizzie, a former mistress; Rosina, a former mistress; and Peregrine, Rosina's husband. Charles's series of anecdotes about these people serve as openings to pull the reader into the waves. This wavelike motion climaxes with the introduction of Hartley, the woman Charles has spent the past forty years remembering. The introduction of his father and James, virtually drowned in the wash of less important characters, reflects Charles's fear of self-analysis. It soon becomes clear that Charles must actively deny the effects on his psyche that he attributes to his father and James, each of whom helped precipitate his feelings of inferiority. Murdoch has her narrator displace these insecurities with stories of love and fantasy. His recounting of a series of anecdotes seduces the reader, who is then pulled along by the wavelike motion of the sea of details. Near the end of "Prehistory" the reader learns that it is Hartley who, having rejected him, has had the greatest ostensible influence on Charles's lack of integrity: her leaving indirectly exacerbated his lack of self-confidence. His fantasy of Hartley has haunted Charles, apparently because he has not dealt directly with the reality of his abandonment.

In letting Charles historicize his life, Murdoch helps the reader see without being told that she is again exposing, as she does in *The Black Prince*, a character's study of the past only partially grounded in reality. Just as readers are uncomfortable about believing Bradley after the postscripts expose others' views of him, the reader begins to realize that comparing Charles's anecdotes with the various versions others tell about the same incidents is a crucial part of the process of reading this novel. The history he tells the reader is contradicted by the reaction of the other characters, especially Hartley: after Hartley escaped from Charles, he immediately displaced the pain by turning to romantic love to avoid dealing with his feelings of inferiority. Here Murdoch seems to be dramatizing a male fantasy that the creator insists is history. Even though readers worry that they do not have correct versions of Bradley's past, he at least comes through as a good artist. Charles, on the other hand, does not.

The reader sees from the order in which Charles introduces characters that the perpetual shifting of love relationships is a pattern common to his world: the world of the theater, the world of Shakespearean romance. Murdoch's plot includes the tradition of the midsummer night's fantasy; most of the characters, other than Hartley and her family, accept partner swapping as normal behavior. The triangles become an excuse for Charles's rattling off anecdotes about love affairs, a device for making connections as he moves through his material and opens up new periods of history. He does not get to his deep-seated early problems until he has worked through the more theatrical love interests.

Charles has come to the sea to work magic on Hartley. He has no compunctions about destroying her relationship with Ben, the man who won her from Charles long ago and married her. Knowing of Hartley's past and having an obsessively jealous nature, Ben has for many years believed Titus, his adopted son, to be Hartley's son by Charles. The reader has no reason to think this story of Ben's jealousy is Hartley's fantastic concoction. Since Charles retained his love for Hartley, he fancied himself involved in a comparable triangle with Hartley and his first mistress, Clement, during his early days in the London theater. Charles has always regretted that Clement, an actress many years his senior, convinced him to give up his search for Hartley. Perhaps his early attachment to Clement, representing a return to the Oedipal family, helped him temporarily displace his feelings of insecurity.

The triangles become awkward gears that run the merry-go-round of obsessive love from Charles's past. Between his on-and-off life with Clement, Charles was able to convince another mistress, Rosina, to leave her husband. Charles, being oblivious to the plight of others, never marries her, of course. This situation turns another gear of the machine, and Peregrine immediately marries Pamela. This relationship metamorphoses later when an intruder takes Pamela from him. These results help Murdoch argue that each individual's experience in a family prepares that individual to act out a certain series of behaviors in the family he or she goes on to create. Obsessive Charles does not leave out any possibilities in his account of relationships that characters act out—or imagine. The "History" plots a Lizzie-Charles-Rosina triangle in which Rosina fantasizes taking Charles from Lizzie, who actually has no power over Charles; a potential Hartley-Charles-Rosina triangle (of which Rosina is unaware); and insinuated Charles-Titus-Gilbert and Charles-Titus-James triangles. This merry-go-round of romantic love not only simulates life in the London theater but also reinforces the impression that Charles, a participant in each absurd relationship, is not as effective a lover or a director as he convinces himself that he is.

Being a director of plays, Charles has, in a sense, been a public figure; his work affects the psyche of his audience. The job Murdoch chooses for him has evolved from the Greek choragos, the wealthy man in charge of directing the Greater Dionysia. When Charles retires to the sea to eschew his former behavior and search for morality, he has a difficult time extricating himself from the patterns of his public life and concentrating on domestic routine. Hoping to live like a monk, a seemingly worthy intention, he has failed to recognize or give credit to the ordeals involved in the saintly life. His attempt to become a new man through domestic routines hardly makes Charles a Brother Lawrence.[18] The space at the beginning of the diary that he takes to describe his routines develops his obtuseness.

Unlike Hilary, Charles considers himself a man who deserves "continuous small treats" (SS 8). Where could this idea have come from other than self-actualization psychology? One routine he practices in his new home is also a joy: preparing simple meals. For years he has planned to publish the *Charles Arrowby Four Minute Cookbook* so he might share with others his philosophy for a happy life, and he now shares his recipes with the reader. As he examines cooking—instead of thermodynamics, as Wittgenstein does—Murdoch allows him to get under the net of generalization and supply the reader with anecdotal reality: even when he is anticipating writing a cookbook, he values particular details. Fussing about the way cookbook writers miscalculate the amount to time necessary to prepare the food, their lack of elementary definition and basic steps for novices, he berates the cookbook that generalizes "make a light batter": "The sturdy honest persons to whom my book would be addressed would not necessarily be able to make a light batter or even to know what it was. But they would be hedonists. In food and drink, as in many (not all) other matters, simple joys are best, as any intelligent self-lover knows" (SS 8).

This self-lover's obsessively thorough and charmingly concrete diary raises the important question of the writer's audience. Charles's fanaticism about daily meals (at least twenty-two meals are laid out for the reader) is Murdoch's way of making fun of her own accretion of particulars in a novel. Murdoch has said that she dislikes cooking and domestic routine, so her play with so many recipes is not self-indulgent, as might be true with her descriptions of nature. At regular intervals throughout the day, he sets before the reader the items and explains his reasons for such combinations. After describing "anchovy paste on hot buttered toast . . . kidney beans with chopped celery, tomatoes, lemon juice and olive oil," he insists the bananas "should be cut, *never* mashed, and the cream should be thin. . . . Then hard water-biscuits with New Zealand butter and Wensleydale cheese" (SS 7). Such specificity shows the reader that Charles's writing process is less tied up in aesthetic theories than Bradley's. The subject matter raises the question of whether he has forgotten his diary and is inadvertently writing a cookbook. Murdoch is no doubt preparing the reader for a surprise. This diary-style cookbook reveals a much simpler, more likable protagonist than the man the reader encounters later. Actually, Charles fails to see the difference between using olive oil in kidney beans and using people as simple ingredients for one of his magic potions.

His seeming satisfaction with simple domestic routine creates the impression that he sees himself as a kind of mystical monk. Having found no laundry in the village, Charles says, "So far I have washed everything myself, including the sheets which I lay out to dry upon the lawn. Perhaps I will continue to do this; there is a remarkable satisfaction in the performance of these simple tasks" (SS 24). Perhaps the superficiality of Charles's work on his old, rundown, badly constructed, damp, possibly haunted bungalow is simply a preview of the superficiality of his moral search; however, he concentrates on the superficial when trying to put his house in order and make it livable. His cleaning routine is a game that creates order only on the surface: he does not, for example, even continue doing his own laundry. In the following passage, his focus on the frame of the mirror and his seeing the mirror as "a source of light" prepare the reader for his fall into the cave later:

> I have been cleaning and tidying up the house. What an extraordinary satisfaction there is in cleaning things! (Does the satisfaction depend on ownership? I suspect so.) I swept the hall and stairs. I washed the big slate flagstones . . . [and] the big ugly vase on the landing. . . . I started to dust the drawing room chimney piece but some spirit that dwelt therein resisted me. . . . And I have now been polishing the big oval mirror in the hall. . . . A lot of dirt certainly came off on the cloth. Since I have just spent a little while gazing at myself in this mirror it is perhaps time to attempt to describe my appearance. (SS 31–32)

His attempt to replace his egoism with domestic routine fails: even his effort to focus on the polishing of the mirror results only in him gazing at himself. Murdoch subtly leads the reader from Charles's obsessive ways of dealing with the world outside him to his dominating obsession—himself, his much-photographed self.

Murdoch argues in "The Sovereignty of Good over Other Concepts" that human beings can eschew such vanity and egoism by paying attention to the beautiful reality outside themselves. The reader of *The Sea, The Sea* would expect, therefore, that the time Charles spends collecting pretty stones and arranging them in a border around his lawn while he observes the wildflowers, the birds, the clouds, the breeze, and the "strange coffee-coloured light over the sea" would make him susceptible to change (SS 31). Murdoch does convince the reader that Charles enjoys every minute detail of the patterned rocks along the coastline, just as he relishes incorporating the cooking metaphor involving *folding*: "The rocks, which stretch away in both directions, are not in fact picturesque. They are sandy yellow in colour, covered with crystalline flecks, and are folded into large ungainly incoherent heaps. Below the tide line they are festooned with growths of glistening blistery dark brown seaweed which has a rather unpleasant smell. Up above however, and at close quarters, they afford the clamberer a surprising number of secret joys" (SS 5). Charles also feels in control of himself when he, a strong and skillful swimmer, is observing nature from the sea. Swimming is arguably Murdoch's favorite metaphor: "Looking down from my cliff before I dived in I could see tall dark trees of seaweed gently waving and fishes swimming between them. I swam about quietly, looking at that special 'swimmer's view' of the sea, and feeling, for the time, possessing and possessed. The sea was a glassy slightly heaving plain, moving slowly past me, and as if it were shrugging reflectively as it absent-mindedly supported its devotee" (SS 139–40). But Charles is only teasing the reader with his potential for good. Even though he observes beauty minutely, he does not immerse himself in what he sees—as attentive readers noticed in the first paragraph of the novel. He is never able to get beyond his self to see, as Murdoch says, "the unself, to see and to respond to the real world in the light of a virtuous consciousness" (SG 93). Therefore, his consciousness is not altered by the beauty surrounding him and the placid routines in which he engages. The reader never feels the shock of the innocent eye trying to absorb a shift of gestalt, or a moment of misseeing.

Although his decisions to retire and to plan a moral life based on simple routine are rational choices that have the possibility of enlarging his vision, these patterns do not stay the fury of the world when it finds its way to his seaside haven. The aimlessness of the universe, which for Murdoch acts mysteriously in tandem with Hilary's and Bradley's uncontrollably selfish drives, impinges on Charles's fantastic plans of capturing Hartley. Never being aware of the extent of his egoism, he drowns when all his past sins converge at the sea to haunt him. His painful moment of enlightenment, a magical death and rebirth, fails to last. He reverts to his old life, never realizing his culpability. Refusing to accept the fact that Hartley never loved him as he wished, he loses her at the end of his life just as he lost her in the beginning; she simply disappears.

Having learned virtually nothing from his tragic experiences, Charles looks a fool when he melodramatically asks himself the crucial question—"Who is one's first love?" "Aunt Estelle?" (SS 502). He misses the significance of James's sacrificial act of love when he, Charles, drowns in a whirling vortex where "the sea has . . . composed an arched bridge of rock under which it roars into a deep open steepsided enclosure" (SS 5). James revives Charles but dies himself as a result of his great effort, and Charles never sees the obvious. On the last page of the novel, when James's mysterious casket of demons falls to the floor, releasing its contents, Charles can manage only shallow speculation: "Upon the demon-ridden pilgrimage of human life, what next I wonder?" (SS 502). The accidentalness of so small a mishap renews his self-conscious sense of agony, and his life cycle begins again.

I ended chapters 5 and 6, chapters about characters' cave pilgrimages, with a suggestion of where this pattern had taken Murdoch by the end of the 1980s. Writing novels apparently sometimes seems to her like working one's way out of the cave. Like *The Sea, The Sea*, *Nuns and Soldiers* demonstrates the baroque layers of contextualization toward which Murdoch has moved. In *Nuns and Soldiers* she delights in weaving into the text historical, literary, operatic, and philosophical contexts. Murdoch has no qualms here about being labeled a philosophical novelist. By the time she wrote *The Sea, The Sea*, she had the audacity to focus directly on the cave myth, as she had in her philosophical work *The Fire and the Sun*, in addition to calling the protagonist's writing at one point a philosophical journal; and by the time she wrote *Nuns and Soldiers*, she apparently felt free enough to go on and on about Wittgenstein.

Nuns and Soldiers opens with Guy Openshaw having philosophical dialogues with the Count, as Murdoch creates dialogic play among traditional but unidentified ideas. Not inhibited about giving her critics ammunition, she employs the cave metaphor with all its paraphernalia to focus on the artist's writing process, suggesting to her audience that writing is dangerous in numerous ways. In a crucial passage from *The Sea, The Sea*, Charles compares writing his book to living in a cave (this quotation appears in chapter 3; I repeat it to demonstrate the numerous levels at which it permeates the issues in this novel and the world of Murdoch's novels):

> Since I started writing this "book" or whatever it is I have felt as if I were walking about in a dark cavern where there are various "lights," made perhaps by shafts or apertures which reach the outside world. (What a gloomy image of my mind, but I do not mean it in a gloomy sense.) There is among those lights one great light towards which I have been half consciously wending my way. It may be a great "mouth" opening to the daylight, or it may be a hole through which fires emerge from the centre of the earth. And am I still unsure which it is, and must I now approach in order to find out? This image has come to me so suddenly, I am not sure what to make of it. (SS 77)

Charles's meditation reminds the reader that living so much in one's head is ominous. The monsters that lurk in Charles's mind are a writer's dangerous potential for either failure or success. In this analogy the mouth of the cave is the entry into the world; the various lights come from the world, which may or may not be dangerous. The great light seems to become clear to the viewer over time, perhaps with help from the unconscious. What precipitous openings await? The light the writer is groping toward may be a mouth or a cavern that can suck the writer under. If the writer does not complete the ordeal, he or she remains in the dark ignorance of the mind or may mistake the fires in the center of the earth for the sun. In the early stages, when the writer wends "half consciously," there is the fear of losing contact with the original goal or never discovering the pattern with which to order the ideas. In interviews, Murdoch talks about the danger of a writer's finding a pattern and then letting it take control; she claims not to write down any of the novel until she has it all worked out in her mind (Heusel, "Dialogue" 4). In *The Sea, The Sea* she seems to be exploring the dilemma that occurs when the pattern has ordered the chaos in the writer's mind but is still flexible enough to allow the characters to continue to press out against the form. Undoubtedly, the characters may have different goals from those of the writer. Here the cave parable carries with it the paraphernalia of the birth trauma and brings to mind the world that human beings enter bawling and screaming, as Shakespeare records in *King Lear*. A kind of creation myth, the fertility and sexual imagery includes the upward thrust Irigaray discusses in addition to the erotic hole and mouth. Readers will recall the dangerous pink mouths of the women who are feared by Charles and even Bradley; the mouths suggest mouths to the womb.

In addition, the cave myth represents the movement toward insight and toward the rationality that will bring order to chaos. The light is both the good and the knowledge of abominable horror rampant in the world. This horror is similar to the horror in the heart of darkness that Marlow traffics with in cavelike Africa but manages to climb out of. The only reality that keeps Marlow from jumping overboard is the ordeal of keeping his craft on course. Charles's dilemma as a writer who never seems to produce anything useful is imaged on page 1. The scene is bright with golden-fretted splendor, but the sea is dark. In this place of paradox, a monster (perhaps of the mind) jars the placid exterior that the eye contemplates. Submerged below the skin is a dark secret, a horror: "a kind of crested snake's head, green-eyed, the mouth opening to show teeth and a pink interior. . . . Then in a moment the whole thing collapsed, the coils fell, . . . indulating back" (SS 19). Charles's vision of the "*monster rising from the waves* . . . [significantly arching] itself upward" (SS 19) and its phallic quality corroborate the sexual dimension of the unconscious for Murdoch. Charles writes down his experience of shock only after his heart has returned to its normal beat, his terror having abated.

Why would Charles's psyche endanger his welfare now that he has escaped the responsibilities and lures of his workaday theatrical life? Routine has been an instrument he necessarily used for denying his obsessive psyche. At his new stage of development, his mind works overtime to convince himself that he can abjure the magic of the theater and continue to believe that in retirement he can live a fairy-tale existence. His fantasy about Hartley is destined to self-destruct, leaving him at the end alone and afraid. When someone apparently tries to kill him by drowning him in Minn's cauldron, Charles is able to reach further down in his unconscious than he has ever reached. Like Effingham Cooper in *The Unicorn*, Charles gives up his control and recognizes the vulnerability of the animal creature against the cosmos.

The disorientation that results from Charles's buried fears maps one of the perceptual and cognitive processes of the human mind that Murdoch reproduces so well. For example, Murdoch's crafting of Hilary's cycle repeated four times aspires to dramatize this human movement from disintegration back to the illusion of order. In *The Sea, The Sea*, Murdoch has Charles reflect on the vulnerability of the human form:

> Falling, what the child fears, what the man dreads, is itself the image of death, of the defencelessness of the body, of its frailty and mortality, its absolute subjection to alien causes. . . . [H]e has been taken over by a relentless mechanism and must continue with it to the end and be subject to the consequences. "There is nothing more I can do." . . . The enmity of matter is unleashed against the frail breakable crushable animal form, always perhaps an alien in this hard mineral gravitational scene. (SS 365)

When he tries to record the incident, he recalls being in a vortex and seeing a dome above him. His references to *vortex, dome, fear,* and *child* work together to re-create the trauma of the birth experience.

Whereas Tim Reede in *Nuns and Soldiers* uses his double near-drowning crises to move further on his pilgrimage, Charles never produces anything out of his trafficking with the monster in the cave. Tim's first near-drowning, however, is in his imagination, and his second is a mysterious kind of attempted murder and rebirth. His first episode includes a metaphorical demon, but one unlike Charles's horrible unconscious fear. Tim's is more a demon of the unexpected deep. During his first baptism, Tim keeps his head and saves himself from being sucked into the canal, but the second time he is unable to avoid the "dark hole of a subterranean tunnel" (NS 158). His first near-drowning occurred when he sat down on a "grassy verge and slid down into the moving stream. Instantly he was seized by a water demon. It was as if two firm light grey hands had gripped his waist, lifted him and conveyed him firmly along, turning him over and ducking him in the process" (NS 156). When he nearly drowns in the same canal again, it is because he identifies with an English collie being swept away by the torrential water and falls in trying to save it. Coming much closer to death in this second incident, he also gains more insight:

> When Tim's head rose above the surface of the raging foam he was already close to the tunnel. He could see the waters contending, boiling, stooping as they constrained themselves into the tunnel whose entrance was below

the surface. . . . [The waters finally suck him into utter darkness.] With the realization that he was still alive came [first] an instantaneous absolute death-fear identical with hope . . . [and then the conclusion] [h]e would die indeed like a rat. (NS 422–23)

But he escapes from drowning only to go through equally difficult psychological ordeals. Perhaps because Murdoch stands at a greater distance from Tim, his recovery is more hopeful, more rational. In *Nuns and Soldiers*, a less psychological, more open novel, Tim fares better. Tim, who is childlike in his affinity for animals and who has never been a director of anything, can intuitively deal with the contingencies of life more easily than Charles can. Tim's near-drownings result from innocence. He evokes new love and new art; Charles does not.

In a novel full of near-drownings, Tim's seem in many ways the most beneficial to society. By laying a foundation early in the novel, Murdoch carefully prepares the reader for Tim's seemingly sudden ability to order his imagination with "abstract 'network' pictures." Actually the sudden fanaticism about abstract painting manifested itself when "his companions at Slade laughed him out of his life class" and he began to focus on abstract art (NS 125). At Slade he had proved to have a natural bent for mathematical ordering with diagrams:

> He lived in a sea of graph paper. His squares became dots, pinpricks, then something invisible. It was (as someone said at the time) like a not very gifted savage trying to invent mathematics. It was as if he wanted to decode the world. His paintings looked like elaborate diagrams yet what were they diagrams of? If he could only cover everything with a fine enough mesh. . . . If he could only *get it right*. Sometime in dreams he thought that he had done so. No one liked these "fanatical" paintings, and in the end for Tim they became a sort of sterile torment. Then one day (he could never explain how) it was as if the mesh began to bend and bulge and ever so quietly other forms came through it. When he returned to organic being it was as to something which had been vastly feeding in captivity. Everything now was plump, enlaced, tropical. Live existence which had been nowhere was now everywhere. (NS 125–26)

Murdoch is exploring here the way her own writing process has developed over the years; the exploration makes an excellent allegory. The paragraph above quotes the statement she has made about the Demiurge in *The Fire and the Sun*, and it alludes to Wittgenstein's statement, "If I cover the surface with a sufficiently fine square network" (see *Tractatus* 6.341). Elizabeth Dipple, pointing out that "meshes and nets abound [and] connect . . . Tim's early and late painting," concludes that Murdoch is not using Wittgenstein here: "Certainly it would be wrong to connect the nets to Wittgenstein whose directions were quite other than what is obliquely indicated here" (*Work* 338). Dipple includes no citation when she attributes Tim's new work to his having "roots in Mallarmé," and perhaps because of this simple lack of information I find her argument a mystery.[19] Wittgenstein was never so monological as Dipple indicates.

Murdoch's allusion to the Demiurge and to Wittgenstein, an architect, is helpful. Tim's pictures seem to be frames for ordering the unpredictable, animalistic behavior of human beings. His fanaticism about his painting is similar to that exuberant energy of the Demiurge, insisting on getting it right. Is Tim perhaps the metaphorical Holy Spirit to Anne's Christ, albeit a holy force she fails to recognize? Murdoch seems to be deeply involved in expressing the freedom an artist feels when the unconscious spills out pell-mell in so many particulars.[20] At the same time, the artist who cannot find a pattern to control the excess fears chaos. On the other hand, once the framing devices appear in the mind's eye of the author, there is a danger that the characters will be imprisoned in the frame: toward the end of the novel, Tim is not immediately satisfied with one pattern or network because of its inhibitions and adjusts it and readjusts it. Murdoch is exploring here the artist's need for a mode of excess. By placing humans in a scheme bigger than the Freudian mechanistic model allows for, Murdoch is quite willing and very much able to evoke mystery for the reader.

Tim begins to feel, when he paints, apparently the way Murdoch sometimes feels when her characters keep multiplying in her mind:

> [He started] drawing funny animals and strange half creatures which amused Gertrude [his wife], sometimes frightened her, and which she regarded as jokes. But for Tim it was as if these beings were coming to him out of a faintly discernible background of relentless form which he could apprehend as taking shape behind them. Sometimes he filled in mathematical patterns of which his "animals" were part. He had painted on big

wooden panels with bright acrylic paint some purely abstract "network" pictures which did not displease him. But then how did these networks connect with the organic forms which also spontaneously appeared? His thoughts about this were nonsense, and he never spoke of these deep things to Gertrude, but he lived calmly and patiently with the nonsense in expectation of, if not clarification, at least change. He began, drawing them out on graph paper, a series of compositions of Leda and the swan. (NS 475)

No doubt there are some deep experiences that an artist can express only in art.[21] Tim, with his "nice animal" aspect, seems to be freed by his new position as commercial artist. He appears to be allowing his imagination to play with impulses from the unconscious. The resulting experiments are in the vein of Escher—animals form and search for the other side of reality or adjust to indeterminate spaces (NS 459). The "funny animals and strange half creatures" evolve until they metamorphose into the struggling bodies of Leda and the swan. Tim, through Murdoch, is taking advantage of some of the implications of W. B. Yeats's poem. Yeats saw that since antiquity humans have used animals as vehicles of their own illusions. The metamorphosing that Tim observes, of animal to human or human to animal, is quite traditional. Tim's new art would seem to justify my comparison with the Escher engraving *Moebius II*, an identification I made in 1983.[22]

Before his sudden burst of creative energy, Tim goes through an ordeal of pain and preparation. Because he lied to his wife and did not tell her about his mistress, Daisy, he has to experience the pain of deciding to "lay down the burden of Daisy forever" (NS 402). Murdoch not only puts stock in the benefits of domestic routine, as she has in other novels, she uses it as a prelude to creativity. She paints a portrait of a man staving off imminent madness with imposed routines: Tim needs to restructure his life after he thinks he has lost Gertrude. In his "strange mixed up unstable frame of mind" (NS 401), he makes peripatetic journeys to London, visits new pubs, tidies and rearranges his studio, cleans skylights, sorts paintings and wraps them in cellophane, visits additional pubs, scrubs floors, and washes his summer clothes. Eventually the mundane routine works as a charm, calming his anxiety, and when a quietness begins to pervade his psyche, he hits on a simple, creative idea—one that prepares him for his later rich spell of creativity. The beautiful autumn leaves suddenly register on his consciousness. His obsessiveness takes a new form: he gathers leaves, varnishes them, and produces collages. Surprisingly, these little works of art sell. Receiving his first real notice as an artist, he is commissioned to produce "a sumptuous series of tableaux" for a fall festival (NS 401). Ordinary routine carries Tim one step further than it carries Charles. Time progresses from virtual madness to renewing sanity: "He did not go mad" (NS 403).

Murdoch uses the *Odyssey* and *Hamlet* as framing contexts for this story. The welfare of the nuclear and extended families also reverberates in these two texts. On a personal level, the plot echoes Odysseus's return to Ithaca. The men in Gertrude's life hover while Guy is dying so that they might have the first chance at the widow's hand. The unlikely and unexpected suitor is Tim. Murdoch does not analogize the years of Gertrude's waiting; in fact, she ironically makes Gertrude's marriage look like Hamlet's mother's rushing to find the traditional heterosexual security. Because there is no waiting, Gertrude creates no tapestry; she is, therefore, silent and enigmatic. If the novel has a protagonist, it is she, although Tim, who becomes her unconventional second husband, is a more dynamic character.

As in most Murdoch novels, love's labors are not all lost. Arrayed around the major sexual triangle, in which Gertrude and Daisy vie for Tim, are hints of many possible triangles. The relationship between Tim and Daisy seems to be valuable to each partner; Tim, however, may have a need for an older, more stable woman to balance out his instability. Gertrude's stability and warmth have the potential to turn Tim's chaotic life around. Before his death, Guy tells Gertrude that he wants her to remarry, proposing that the Count, who has loved her for many years, would make a worthy partner. Although Guy did all he could to free her, Gertrude's thoughts reveal her incomparable egoism: after Guy's death, she wonders if at the time Guy was trying to shut out Manfred, his cousin, as a contender for her hand. Guy's competitive relationship with Manfred reminds the reader of Charles and James in *The Sea, The Sea*. Triangles that complicate the plot, build up tension, and provide contingency but are given no real credibility include several last-minute surprises: a Peter-Anne-Ned triangle and an Anne-Manfred-Veronica triangle.[23] More important, Murdoch teases the reader into hoping that Anne's love for the Count (Peter) will precipitate an exceptional unselfish love, one that readers have been waiting for, but he continues to love the much shallower Gertrude.

Characters Patterning Their Pilgrimages

Murdoch brings nature into *Nuns and Soldiers* by using extreme weather conditions to echo the characters' inner storms and eventual inner calm. This is a Shakespearean technique used to especially good effect in *Othello*. While Gertrude is trying to assimilate Guy's impending death, she desires "tempests, mountains of snow, . . . screaming winds and floods, a hurricane" to obliterate her grief (NS 14).[24] Anne, Gertrude's friend distressed by her inability to find God, is almost drowned by the sea (NS 43).[25] Tim, disintegrating because he is not good enough for Gertrude, is almost drowned by a torrential stream. A hellish mistral destroys sections of Gertrude's French cottage while Gertrude suffers her loss of Tim's attention, and Anne, her loss of the Count's attention. At the end, when Anne has decided to leave the social set she has recently joined, the abundantly falling snow reflects her resolution: "[The snow] looked like the heavens spread out in glory, totally unrolled before the face of God" (NS 504). Struggles with weather conditions bring enlightenment to these characters, if not to Charles Arrowby.

Tim's history changes the stultifying, sterile group his wife belongs to. He moves the greatest distance toward the sun, climbing from being a thief of sorts to being a creative artist. Tim is very different from the other three male characters—Charles, Bradley, and Hilary—in that he is more lovable and not so forbidding. Lacking the neurotic drive of the others, he does not try to redirect Murdoch's goal. Murdoch needs an omniscient narrator here, rather than someone who is participating in the story, to keep the novel open so that many characters can participate fully. A very few of these characters participate as "nuns," selfless lovers; most participate as "soldiers," selfish survivors of the patriarch Guy, whose imminent death sets the stage for the novel.

For Murdoch, art happens when chaos comes and destabilizes the carefully patterned order. My exploration of the patterned aimlessness in *A Word Child*, *The Black Prince*, *The Sea, The Sea*, and *Nuns and Soldiers* analyzes both Murdoch's and the characters' reasons for fabricating "falsifying *veil*[s] which partially [conceal] the world" (SG 84). As Murdoch lifts the veils of illusion, enlightenment gives the characters the opportunity to change. Murdoch's affinity for bizarre patterning balances the orderly, Platonic structure of her novelistic world. Ranging all her characters along the route of a pilgrimage up from a cave, she employs analogies and ironic juxtaposition as vehicles for contingency. In giving the characters freedom to escape her authorial grasp, she takes the risk of confusing readers who are looking for simple, univocal novels. The characters' domestic routines, love relationships, and cyclically obsessive lives manage to flow along habitual rat-runs without much manipulation from Murdoch. She believes that the good novelist has "a natural gift," a "blessed freedom from rationalism," and she understands that "human reason is not a single unitary gadget the nature of which could be discovered once and for all"; she has her "eye fixed on what we do," a Wittgensteinian position (ix–x). As she proposes in her first preface to *Sartre, Romantic Rationalist*, the artist describes rather than explains.

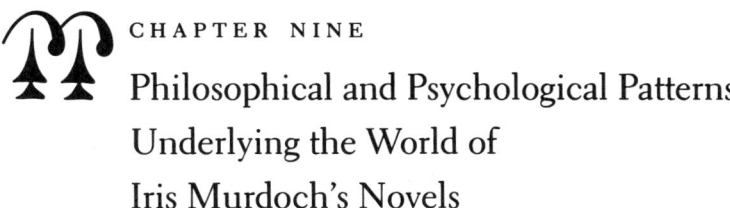# CHAPTER NINE
Philosophical and Psychological Patterns Underlying the World of Iris Murdoch's Novels

This chapter explores an issue that is worthy of major emphasis in Murdoch criticism: the way the visual patterns of her world of the novel reflect underlying conceptual frameworks and embody her philosophy and psychology. Her world of the novel, complete with its Platonic base and cosmology, erupts out of a struggle central to Western culture, the conflict between the centrifugal force of desiring to see the light and know Good and the centripetal force of desiring to know the dark of the unconscious. Murdoch not only juxtaposes these forces but often defies Aristotelian logic, going beyond this binary opposition to dramatize the plurality and multiplicity of reality. Most readers will agree that Murdoch's world is different from the world of any other novelist. Murdoch's own perceptions reach out into the "vast space" beyond formal logic. Perhaps her character Marzillian in *The Message to the Planet* (1989) speaks for her when he argues that the psyche is large and most people crouch in a tiny corner, "living the life of a beetle in a hole" (MP 431). With her ability to visualize and pay attention to particulars, she expands binary thinking into spectra of possibilities, demonstrating the kind of subversion Julia Kristeva attributes to Menippean satire: "break[ing] out of the framework of causally determined identical substances and head[ing] toward another modality of thought that proceeds through dialogue (a logic of distance, relativity, analogy, nonexclusive and transfinite opposition)" (WDN 86).[1] Murdoch's experience with Plato has prepared her to move toward enlightenment by way of the Socratic method rather than through formal logic; moreover, her experience with Wittgenstein has shown her diverse deployments of language for the purpose of understanding.

Exploring the visual and spatial characteristics of Murdoch's form as the embodiment of her philosophy and psychology raises certain questions.[2] In what ways, for example, do her choices regarding fictional form—both the structures of her world of the novel and of the individual novels—reflect specific philosophical and psychological patterns that order or do not order chaos? What are Murdoch's shaping patterns? Murdoch understands that if readers are to comprehend the world of her novels, that world must be less aimless than the real world. In imposing a macro-order on a world that resembles a Platonic cave allegory, she assumes that the Apollonian characteristics of rationality, light, order, and harmony are positive. But because her purpose is multidimensional,[3] she values and celebrates just as vigorously the Dionysian tendency to disrupt that order. In recognizing the interrelationship of these two opposing ways of moving to consciousness (knowledge of the world and knowledge of the self), she arrives at a synthesis of the two. Then, with help from what may be called a Nietzschean perspective—acceptance of paradox and the occasional reconciliation of opposites—and from a Wittgensteinian perspective—ironic juxtapositions and analogical thinking—she veers away from that tradition of binarity.

Why does she favor certain patterns borrowed from Plato and Wittgenstein over other patterns? Like Murdoch, Plato and Wittgenstein are visually oriented and are, moreover, enamored of spatial configurations. Some of the perceptual and cognitive patterns that help Wittgenstein investigate the connections between perception and cognition, such as gestalt, also give Murdoch the opportunity to dramatize the power of occasional moments of enlightenment that unveil reality, in addition to dramatizing her characters as puppets manipulated by illusions. Sudden moments of enlightenment are epistemologically necessary to her concept of "reproducing the accidental, the idiosyncratic happenings of life" (AD 9).

Murdoch's goal, as I see it, is to spin out the stable patterns of her fictional cosmos—the necessity—and to allow the characters to weave the contingent: what may come to pass but may not. From Plato she selects patterns, concepts, and metaphors to establish the former, the necessity of the cosmos that grounds and structures her fiction; from Wittgenstein she selects patterns, concepts, and methods to foreground the latter, the possibility or chance of contingency in the events of the characters' lives.[4] The patterns Murdoch controls—her cosmology, her cyclical patterns of fate, her shifting of gestalt, her juxtaposition of bizarre incidents, her stepping down to be on a level with the characters—bring insights to her characters. Discussing such patterns helps in understanding the question of who controls her characters.

In her novels of the 1970s and 1980s, Murdoch relieves her omniscient voice of some of its authority and allows the characters to be a part of the dialogical play of the text, thereby embodying contingency. The characters have the responsibility of surviving amid Murdoch's assumption that people in general are lost in illusion: "We live in myth and symbol all the time" ("Mass, Might and Myth" 338). The characters prefer that their routines, or "rat-runs" (SG 86), daily schedules, compulsive life cycles, and love triangles not be frustrated by accidents, for accidents break up the safe patterns and provide disorienting opportunities for change. Murdoch's characters are often more comfortable when lost in illusion.

Plato has had an obvious influence on Murdoch's cosmology, and the moral values in her fictional world are greatly influenced by his cave myth drama [5]—the upward movement within a hierarchy, from false images toward true forms. Chapter 8 shows that along that pilgrimage Murdoch allows her characters moments of insight achieved through cataclysmic changes in perspective and juxtaposition of incidents.

One reason Murdoch might have chosen the pattern of the cave from a traditional philosopher who feared patterns is that its remoteness defamiliarizes the contemporary material and therefore fails to console the reader. Another challenge to consolation lies in Murdoch's use of Wittgenstein's concept of getting under the network of language or logic. This conceptual framework underlies Wittgenstein's and Murdoch's rejection of the scientific method. Wittgenstein draws on one of Plato's images to demonstrate that logic is only a small part of cognition. He refers metaphorically to the network (language or logic or theory) that thinkers must get under in order to touch the particulars of reality, and his resistance to stopping at such a network is a major illustration of his need to celebrate the mysterious. The concept of the network helps Murdoch dig down into the level of the particular and resist generalizations. In her early analysis of Murdoch's work, A. S. Byatt says that Murdoch seeks an experience and a language "independent of our ordinary modes of understanding" (*Degrees of Freedom* 15n).[6] Murdoch's grounding in the ideas of Plato and Wittgenstein allows her the freedom to examine mystery from multiple perspectives and at the same time to find the particular. She has called herself a "Wittgensteinian neo-Platonist" (Chevalier, *Rencontres* 90).

To emphasize that Western philosophy since Plato has been moving in two directions—toward Aristotelian science and toward discovering ways to get past theory to the particular—it is helpful to draw attention again, as I did in chapter 3, to a central passage from the *Tractatus* (6.341). Wittgenstein, speaking of Newtonian mechanics, distinguishes between humans' need to see the universe as unified and the danger inherent in imposing a one-grid pattern on the complexity of life: "Let us imagine a white surface with irregular black spots. We now say: Whatever kind of picture these make I can always get as near as I like to its description, if I cover the surface with a sufficiently fine square network and now say of every square that it is white or black. In this way I shall have brought the description of the surface to a unified form" (quoted in Byatt, *Degrees of Freedom* 16).[7] This highly visual passage, with its evocation of Plato, suggests Murdoch's reasons for employing multiple patterns to avoid the mistake of looking at reality through an insufficient number of grids. Wittgenstein sees the "fine square network" as arbitrary; Murdoch creates innumerable patterns to achieve multiple views. So that each perspective, or lens, supplies a small piece of reality, she searches for new patterns, even genres, to lay over the changing reality she discovers daily. The fine square networks, or triangles or octagons or various other combinations of lines, generate different meanings in different contexts. This attitude is one that Wittgenstein did not eschew later, when he revised his philosophy. Like the later Wittgenstein, Murdoch struggles to avoid any kind of blindness, however bizarre the resulting method of communication becomes; she is always searching for methods and patterns unfamiliar to her reader.[8] An analogy she uses is Tim Reede's making "purely abstract 'network' pictures" in *Nuns and Soldiers* (475): when stress and anxiety push Tim to find creative ways to order his own private chaos, he grows beyond superficial artistry toward maturity. This ordering, using the network metaphor, is a complicated maneuver that has complex implications for Murdoch's exploration of form, as Elizabeth Dipple points out (*Work* 347). Perhaps Murdoch is invigorated by the tension of getting beyond the network pattern Wittgenstein has superimposed over Plato's Forms. She asks herself, "Is it possible to *see* beyond the 'formal network'? (Instinct says yes.)" (FS 47).

Murdoch's skepticism about the arbitrariness of theories comes from a synthesis of ideas from Plato and Wittgenstein, resulting in a Platonic position that is not easy to understand. As I show in chapter 1, she has no problem synthesizing Platonism and empiricism. Her work on Plato demonstrates the way she sees the relationship of Plato's network to Wittgenstein's. She depends on Plato's metaphor of the forms but interprets them in what George Steiner calls an unorthodox way.⁹ In *The Fire and the Sun: Why Plato Banished the Artists*, she explains Plato's argument about the Forms:

> The world is neither a dense unity nor an inapprehensible flux, but an orderly network of sameness and difference (249). This network . . . makes possible falsehood and deception, and also truth and language. What are thus systematically connected are the Forms, here figuring as classes. "We derive significant speech from the inter-weaving of the Forms" (259e). This interweaving depends upon the pervasive presence of certain "great kinds," very general structural concepts or logical features: existence, same, different, rest, motion. (29)

Moreover, not only is her interest in Plato's Forms and his mathematical diagrams pervasive and continually fine-tuned, but she periodically weighs that interest against her growing skepticism vis-à-vis Jacques Derrida. Her play with the Forms as a living force is quite different from Derrida's: "Derrida and Heidegger and Nietzsche misunderstand Plato. The Forms are not a static separate world, but living forces in our world" (Letter to the author, Sept. 3, 1990). Since 1953 she has been tracking Derrida's development away from her own understanding of Plato. Her belief that human beings must recognize the reality of something outside themselves does not make her a determinist or a mechanist, and, as she says in *The Sovereignty of Good*, her view is not existentialist, technological, or behaviorist.

Knowing she can never get close enough to the particulars does not daunt Murdoch. She focuses on discovery, using patterns "to isolate, to explore, to display" (SG 65), the process her artist-character Tim Reede tries. She takes up each novel as a new lens, a living force with which to focus on a new, as yet unexplored section of an earlier grid or on a new grid, such as a new genre. She does not employ the new lens fervently, to fight a battle, but dispassionately, in the sense that Plato's Demiurge allows events to play out necessity or contingency, to engage a mode of experience or of language.

This chapter examines the ways Murdoch, in the role of that Demiurge, demonstrates her religious sensibility and tells her love stories or parables of her love affairs with art. If Eros is at the base of all human motivation and creativity, then life is a kind of love affair as the classical Greeks understood it. What many consider Murdoch's best novel examines this issue: *The*

Black Prince discusses at length the work of art as a love story, and its artist-protagonist, Bradley Pearson, is able to create because he eventually opens himself to a visitation from Eros. This incredibly lucky second-rate artist, in describing his conscious process of creation, prattles to the reader about the need for superficial patterns and the deeper patterns. The reader can watch, through Bradley's creation of his novel, the formation of Murdoch's configuration at a deeper level. Even though Murdoch began her writing career using traditional plots, her process became more indirect and her mythology more complex during the 1970s and 1980s; and when she began to move in a unique direction, she began to craft her own version of the peripeteia of classical Greek drama. Some critics think Murdoch is a better novelist when she is patterning boldly, while others, sometimes including Murdoch herself, think she is better when she relaxes her tendency to pattern (see Bellamy, "Interview"). The dependence of the artist on pattern appears to be self-evident to Murdoch: "Of course, too, artists are pattern-makers. The claims of form and the question of 'how much form' to elicit constitutes one of the chief problems of art" (SG 65). Being an unorthodox neo-Platonist, Murdoch instinctively struggles with form, knowing how easily she creates form and fearing, as does Plato, its consolations.

Murdoch fits her own description of the Demiurge, who "is moved by love for the Forms to attempt to imitate them in another medium. Like the mortal artist he fails, both because the other medium cannot (as he is well aware) reproduce the original, and because the material resists his conceptions and his powers. The result is a quite different entity, which is the 'best possible'" (FS 52). Her understanding of the gap between the ideal and the work of art explains her almost unbelievable humility, her lack of fear of failure,[10] and her willingness to begin preparing a new novel immediately after having just finished one. She distinguishes this tendency—the dependence of artistic inspiration on unconscious processes that battle with the necessity of form—from the human tendency toward private fantasy. In addressing this artistic problem Murdoch reveals how empirical and utilitarian she is: "It is when form is used to isolate, to explore, to display something which is true that we are most highly moved and enlightened. Plato says (*Republic* 7:532) that the *technai* have the power to lead the best part of the soul to the view of what is most excellent in reality. This well describes the role of great art as an educator and revealer" (SG 65). Great artists like Shakespeare, Murdoch goes on to say, are not dramatizing their own private fantasies in order to justify them—a role many critics, especially critics like Carolyn Heilbrun, seem to want Murdoch to play (see, e.g., *Reinventing Womanhood*). Murdoch is straightforward about wanting the public to see her product. She is unusually vocal about the general plight of human beings, including herself: even though people continually attempt to absorb the reality surrounding them, they are prone to connect the details they discover to a myth existing in their minds.

Murdoch describes her aesthetic process as a struggle against this narcissistic tendency in life. One way she talks about the artist's inspiration is through the metaphor of Apollo, the god of poetry, flaying Marsyas, the satyr audacious enough to challenge perfection. The metaphor of flaying is closely related to other classical concepts, such as the artist being "analogon of the good man . . . the lover who, nothing himself, lets other things be through him" (SBR 270) or "the continual expelling of oneself" from the prose (SBR 269). Murdoch sums up these two concepts using the term "negative capability" (SBR 270). She willingly reveals her own flayings, or what she considers her failures, in interviews. Feminists might argue that by the end of the 1980s she had still not found it appropriate to create characters like herself. Should one conclude from Murdoch's comments that she has no control over her imagination as it creates vehicles for her unconscious materials? Is the artist, for her, to be a metaphorical vessel like Apollo, conveying the reality of life? This competition between Marsyas and Apollo, which appears in many of her novels, is a mythical displacement for Murdoch's own struggle with inspiration and creation. Her use of this myth raises the issue of her suffering as a writer—an issue she is reluctant to discuss. She describes her inspiration this way: "For me a novel begins in a great cauldron of ideas and images, impulses and feelings" (Heusel, "Dialogue" 9). She talks lovingly about the time of contemplation before she writes anything down: "I think the period of reflection—when one has nothing, except notes, of course, to remind one—is very important; it's a kind of deep free reflection which may be more difficult later on" (Heusel, "Dialogue" 4).

Seeing herself as a medium—instead of seeing her ego as the message of the discourse—inhibits her from taking a platform to rationalize her mistakes. Murdoch addresses her fears and idiosyncrasies in jokes and perhaps in slips of the tongue. For example, she jokes about her writing in her remarks on Arnold Baffin, Pearson's artistic rival in *The Black Prince*. Arnold's statement that he must get on to the next book suggests the Platonic stance that each attempt is only a movement toward perfection, only practice at imitating the forms. Perhaps in addition to making a joke on herself, Murdoch is doing what Peter Conradi calls "caution[ing] against competing with the divine" (*Saint* 188), another indication of her humility about her own writing. Furthermore, Conradi recounts Murdoch's saying that "Bradley can be seen as a minor artist whom the god rewards and comforts for his patient zeal and longing" (*Saint* 188). To Murdoch, the unconscious is both crucial to creativity and a source of danger.

Part of the danger is that the Demiurge makes a connection in the unconscious with Eros, the "ambiguous spiritual mediator and moving spirit of mankind" (FS 34). Murdoch finds that Plato's understanding of the beautiful "gives to sexual love and transformed sexual energy a central place in his philosophy.... Sexual love (Aphrodite) [is a] cosmic power" (FS 33). Murdoch as mediator sees Plato's Eros as "a principle which connects the commonest human desire to the highest morality and to the pattern of divine creativity in the universe.... The Eros described ... in the *Symposium* is not a god but a daemon, a mediating spirit of need and desire, the mixed up child of Poverty and Plenty" (FS 33). Murdoch seems much like the Eros she describes. In the following passage Murdoch reflects the concern of critics like Harold Bloom and David J. Gordon that she might become too much the magician: "a sort of magician and sophist, always scheming after what is good and beautiful, neither wise nor foolish but a lover of wisdom. We desire what we lack" (FS 34). "This Eros," she continues, "who is lover not beloved, is the ambiguous spiritual mediator and moving spirit of mankind. Eros is the desire for good and joy which is active in all levels of the soul and through which we are able to turn toward reality. This is the fundamental force which can release the prisoners and draw them toward the higher satisfactions of light and freedom. It is also the force which finds expression in the unbridled appetites of the tyrant.... Carnal love teaches that what we want is always 'beyond'" (FS 34). Indeed this analysis of Eros's work describes Murdoch's fictional path; she is continually arousing desire that leads beyond the text. Her patterns serve as networks that establish order by laying out boundaries for investigation, but they are boundaries she goes under or beyond. She challenges readers to use her patterns as measuring devices to discover optional choices for particular decisions along their pilgrimages—but never simply to stop with the measuring devices she furnishes.

Conradi asserts that, for Murdoch, Eros in its rational form can release prisoners from the cave, while in its lower forms it chains them (*Saint* 85). He relates Murdoch's and John Bayley's understandings of the relationship between love and sex, quoting a bit of the following statement by Bayley from *Characters of Love*: "Love has fewer preconceptions than sex, for the latter is a highly conservative instinct operating in terms of stock responses. We desire in obedience to the fixed patterns of our sexual imagination, but we fall in love because we are really seeing another person. Love is the potentiality of men and women which keeps them most interested in each other. . . . Love is not only more complex and intriguing than sex but more absorbingly local" (5).[11] Here Bayley suggests that love is a breaking up of stereotypical patterns while sex is dominated by patterns, presumably imprinted by culture. His comments raise the question that if sex is a stock response or unconscious pattern, how can people in the real world, let alone characters in a Murdoch novel, guard against or control it? Since most of her characters cannot control it, does Murdoch then agree with Bayley's theory; does she see the behavior of these characters as usual? I am more skeptical than Conradi about being able to distinguish Murdoch's characters drawn toward sex from those drawn toward love—that is, defining love as Bayley does. Because so much in Murdoch's novels that is called "falling in love" seems less than love, I am not sure Murdoch believes all so-called falling in love necessarily comes from "really seeing another person" (*Characters of Love* 5). Some falling in love is mistaking the ego for the sun. In *A Word Child* a comparison between Hilary, the protagonist, and his sister Crystal demonstrates the difference. Crystal, who has established in her relationship to Hilary her ability to see the reality of another, cherishes Arthur Fisch, her fiancé; Hilary, on the other hand, who has used Crystal to complete his own ego, cannot really love the people around him because to him they are never complete and separate persons. In other words, Murdoch creates a great gulf between Crystal's seeing Arthur's real personhood and Hilary's failing to see Crystal's—let alone that of Kitty, the woman with whom he is obsessed.

As Demiurge, trickster, and pattern maker, Murdoch tries to see others from a distance as separate beings. Such a perspective gives her this aesthetic: "The greatest art is 'impersonal' because it shows us the world, our world and not another one, with clarity which startles and delights us simply because we are not used to looking at the real world at all" (SG 65). Murdoch uses quips about the relation between the subjectivity of the writer and the desire for distance in *The Black Prince* when she weaves aspects of the protagonist's small-mindedness into his complexly patterned insights. Bradley tells Julian Baffin, his godchild, that Hamlet is Shakespeare and that because of this mirroring, all readers identify with Hamlet.[12] Murdoch is creating a comic discrepancy, and most likely Bradley's tongue is in his cheek, too. Murdoch does not want the reader identifying with her; the characters she creates are not her. On the other hand, she cannot always gauge the extent to which her experiences have entered the cauldron of creation at some unconscious level and have identified her with her character.

Murdoch supplies her characters with personal as well as physical space so that the author is just one among many. Again, to guard against being controlled by her own private fantasies, she establishes a spacious playing ground, a big plot with exaggerated diachronic and synchronic spaces. Characters participate in the progression of the time sequence of the plot the author has established, but their compulsions determine the way they pattern their own time. This plotting of their repetitious routines, as if being viewed through another lens, metamorphoses into a spatial construct (e.g., the calendar, be it tangible or simply mental, by which Hilary keeps track of where and with whom to eat each evening). Through such metamorphosing, the planes of temporal and spatial language become interdependent.[13]

Murdoch's interest in and adherence to spatial metaphors and patterns naturally follow from her grounding in Plato's imagery, her visualization of Plato's cave allegory energizing her exploration of the history of Western consciousness. Even though humans cannot get outside the world to look at it, being stuck in our perceptual apparatus, Murdoch attempts this getting outside her imagination, and perhaps that is what she means when she says, "Art is playful, but its play is serious" (FS 84).[14] She has used theatrical framing in her twenty-five novels to scrutinize the human pilgrimage.

First-time readers can immediately value the complexity of a Murdoch novel if they can visualize the layers of verbal pentimento she builds. She superimposes the layers of her fictional world over cultural strata from Ovid's Greek labyrinths to the catacombs of Rome. These metaphorical novelistic spaces suggest underground networks of Western values such as justice, creativity, balance, and harmony that hide historical concepts of weakness such as hubris and hamartia. For example, the first-time reader might be too involved in the plot of *The Philosopher's Pupil* to see immediately the relationship of the cavelike waterworks to the *omphalos* at Delphi, to Daedalus's labyrinth, or to the underground Roman baths in Bath, England; or to see the significance of the town's multileveled representation of the history of England. Such pentimento recalls Joseph Conrad's in *Heart of Darkness* when he has Marlow "evoke the great spirit of the past upon the lower reaches of the Thames. . . . What greatness had not floated on the ebb of that river into the mystery of an unknown earth! . . . The dreams of men, the seeds of commonwealths, the germs of empires" (8) all the way back to the Romans.

Underlying the diagrams in Murdoch's holograph notebooks at the University of Iowa Special Collections, as well as her philosophical hierarchies of Good in her fictional world, are images she discusses in *The Fire and the Sun*, images of Plato's cosmology and his diagram of four stages of cognition, the Line that parallels his cave myth allegory. In attempting to distinguish Murdoch's world of the novel from other cultural worldviews or visual paradigms—such as the great chain of being; Shakespeare's, Milton's, or Swift's three-story universe; Donne's neoplatonic cosmos; or Yeats's mythology—Murdoch's reader must first visualize a series of metaphors that Murdoch employs.[15] It is helpful to think of thin, transparent overlays similar to the ones an encyclopedia uses to diagram the body's circulatory and respiratory systems. The first layer of the landscape of Murdoch's world is, like Plato's labyrinthine cave, made up of cavities and hierarchies of geological strata that are inhabited by pilgrims. All of her character types, each of whose personalities have an effect on their respective potential moral choices and who are at different distances from the sun, prepare within specific strata to go onstage and discover the ordeals awaiting them. Some characters will move far toward the sun, exiting the cave and being disoriented by the light; others, as they climb, may confuse their egos with the reality of the fire; and others will sit chained in the labyrinthine chambers of the cave below. Murdoch's goals being complex, her characters' movements are more paradoxical than those of Plato's pilgrims.

Another series of overlays, illuminating the geography of particular novels, might consist of the ancient Greek city of Athens overlaid by Murdoch's diagram of the plotting of her London bedroom community in *The Philosopher's*

Pupil, an ancient-modern imaginary city consisting of the Greco-Roman system of the agora surrounded by baths and environs. An overlay of modern London as it is set in *The Nice and the Good*, with its Underground built over the bomb shelters of World War II and the ruins of Roman roads, would make visible Murdoch's layers on top of layers of culture. In the mysterious and dangerous labyrinths below the streets of London, the nice, but not quite good, protagonist investigates the mysteries of bizarre cult worship.[16]

First-time readers touring Murdoch's fantastic labyrinths—literal caves in the novels and labyrinthine constructs that have apparently arisen from her unconscious—will find it useful to tie these abstractions to real caverns like the mammoth labyrinth of Carlsbad Caverns in southeast New Mexico, which she has seen. A more original overlay might superimpose Murdoch's playful metaphor of the world as a pot at the bottom of the ocean, where fish swim in and out through the holes (from a conversation between Conradi and Murdoch). This image is similar to the fishbowl she uses to describe a party in the conclusion of *Flight from the Enchanter* (1956). Many of her characters are caught by waters that flood caves, as in *The Nice and the Good*, *The Sea, The Sea*, *Nuns and Soldiers*, and *The Philosopher's Pupil*—a drowning or near-drowning occurs in almost every novel (I discuss the feminine implications of *water* and *cave* in chapter 8).

Murdoch chooses certain types of characters who play certain roles in this fictional environment. Apparently, as she herself suggests, she selects these characters from a storehouse in her mind. Perhaps these archetypal, stereotypical, and/or unique characters wait in their respective strata along the edges of the cauldron of her imagination for a summons to inhabit the next novel. As they strive to get to the sun, they congregate in their strata, emerge or fail to emerge from the cave, or drown and return (cf. Minn's cauldron in *The Sea, The Sea*). Murdoch's description of Plato's characters can apply to her own characters as well:

> The prisoners in the Cave are at first chained to face the back wall where all they can see are shadows, cast by a fire which is behind them, of themselves and of objects which are carried between them and the fire. Later they manage to turn round and see the fire and the objects which cast the shadows. Later still they escape from the Cave, see the outside world in the light of the sun, and finally the sun itself. The sun represents the

Form of the Good in whose light the truth is seen; it reveals the world, hitherto invisible, and is also a source of life. (FS 4)

Determining how far characters progress toward the sun is problematic since they have so many choices and since the reader can misinterpret ego for the sun, as can the characters.

Superimposing Plato's Line over the cave image makes it easier to see the characters' progress up through the hierarchy.[17] The editor of the Oxford edition of the *Republic* explains that Plato divides a simple straight line *"into two parts, whose inequality symbolizes that the visible world, has a lower degree of reality and truth than the intelligible. Each part, the lower visible world and the intelligible world, is then subdivided in the same proportion as the whole line, (thus A + B : C + D = A : B = C : D). . . . The four sections this division creates correspond to four states of mind or modes of cognition, each clearer and more certain than the one below."* The diagrams and models are *"a sort of bridge carrying the mind across from the visible thing to the intelligible reality, which it must learn to distinguish"* (Cornford, *Republic of Plato* 221, 223). "You also know," Plato writes, "how [students of mathematics] make use of visible figures and discourse about them though what they really have in mind is the originals of which those figures are images: they are not reasoning, for instance about this particular square and diagonal which they have drawn, but about *the* Square and *the* Diagonal" (*Republic* 225). Cornford explains: "That the mathematician can use visible objects as illustrations indicates that the realities and truths of mathematics are embodied, though imperfectly, in the world of visible and tangible things; whereas the counterparts of the moral Forms can only be beheld by thought" (*Republic* 225n). This explanation helps the reader of *Nuns and Soldiers* understand the progress of Tim Reede. Tim exemplifies the mathematician who moves through the first two stages of the visible world, but he does not move to the level of abstraction in the intelligible world. Cornford's relating of the allegory of the cave to a poem by Empedocles informs Murdoch's choice to have some good characters blinded by the sun. In Empedocles' "poem the powers which conduct the soul to its incarnation say, 'We have come under this cavern's roof'" (*Republic* 227). Cornford describes ceremonies in which religious objects were suddenly revealed to initiates by a blinding light, after which they exited the cave's dark chambers. The image is similar to the reference of Charles Arrowby in *The*

Sea, The Sea to the light in the cave as a "hole through which fires emerge from the centre of the earth" (77). Murdoch's use of former bomb shelters in the bowels of London to house the mysterious sexual rituals of a cult in *The Nice and Good* harkens back to Plato, who attributed images of imprisonment in the underworld to the Orphics (*Republic* 227).

Another version of Murdoch's interpretation of the cave allegory reveals much about her personal values. Murdoch suggests in *The Fire and the Sun* that she agrees with Cornford's comparison of the Eros of Plato with that of Freud. Murdoch's "Art and Eros: A Dialogue about Art" focuses on the idea that dealing with Plato's Eros is an integral part of the pilgrimage toward the sun. In addition to describing spatial levels, she explains the courage and determination necessary to look closely at reality. The dialogue demonstrates that the dark unconscious, the dark Eros, is part of Murdoch's conception of good, that the concept of *down* is no less valuable than the concept of *up* and *out* to the sun. More complex than Plato's and much less spatially grounded in the concept of up being good and down bad, Murdoch's character Plato in *Acastos: Two Platonic Dialogues* makes these statements paradoxically celebrating dark and down as good: "I think—I think that the human mind, the human soul is a vast region most of which is dark. There are different parts, different levels. There are dark low levels where we are hardly individual people at all" (55). The character Plato explains the epiphany, or blinding flash, that some people experience in escaping into the realm of light—"perhaps it's only for a short time, because the light of the sun dazzles you" (*Acastos* 36)—and describes several layers of wisdom, ranging from low to high Eros. The reality that Deximines suggests by his question" Are we all living at these different levels all the time?" (*Acastos* 58) is important to this exploration. The movement from dark to light takes a lifetime of simultaneous pilgrimages.

As the structuralists have long since demonstrated, the concept of the layering of cultures, basic to anthropology, is also basic to the stories that Western culture produces.[18] Anthologies of Western literature often begin with simple, ancient stories of a temporal conflict taking place on a plot of ground, often a cave or cavity. The ancient Greek theater was itself a cavity in the ground; the first Roman play, *The Widow of Ephesus*, by Petronius, and the first extant Christian play, *Quem Quaeritis*, take place in caves or cavities. Perhaps the Greek concept of omphalos is explained by the incidence of the spatial cavities in stories. Narratives put together spatial elements, such as in prehistoric

Philosophical and Psychological Patterns

cave drawings, and temporal elements, such as prehistoric dance. In more recent history, a Navajo story includes spatial levels of a labyrinth with insects working their way up and out of the ground. While modern stories tend to be more urban, they still involve excavations of complex labyrinths, often including a trickster figure. Many modernist writers have explored the panorama of labyrinthine cities: James Joyce's Dublin, Virginia Woolf's London, Andrey Biely's St. Petersburg. In Stephen Dedalus, Joyce creates a protagonist who apparently considers himself the Demiurge, "Los *demiurgos*," and who also makes much of the spatial and time modes: "*Nacheinander* and *Nebeneinander*" (*Ulysses* 31), dutifully contemplating how human beings know the world: through time and space.[19] Writers, in recording reality as they see and feel it, impose time and space perception on literature, assuming literature is a reflection of such reality—the crossroads for Stephen and Leopold Bloom, whose paths cross in a parallactic diagram on June 16, 1904, in Dublin.

Murdoch is both more abstract and more concrete than many writers. It is fruitful, for example, to compare Murdoch's world with the labyrinth of Dublin in *Ulysses*, which includes Dedalus and Icarus and the Minotaur. Although her work does not depend tangentially on a Greek source in the way that *Ulysses* does, it is easy for one to imagine her world as much more Greek than Joyce's because of her use of archetypal patterns. Her labyrinths are in the mind, as her *Acastos* suggests, but they also occupy physical space in the world of her novels. Joyce's labyrinths are of a real, tangible Dublin, Murdoch's are of an equally real London; Joyce's *Ulysses* draws elaborate analogies with Greek myth, but Murdoch has attended more to Greek myth and has created a more complex, multivalent cosmos.

Calling Murdoch's universe a cosmos is not, however, quite accurate: it is not ordered, harmonious, or whole, as, for example, Hesiod's is.[20] She does take advantage of the capacity of cosmology "to provide an ultimate frame for occurrences in nature, and to offer a demonstration of where the limits of the spatio-temporal world are, and how they might be transcended" (Runes, *Dictionary of Philosophy* 69). Her choice to pattern her world of the novel within a chaotic universe, like her choice to allow her characters to pattern their lives, causes disharmony and discontinuity. In sustaining this perpetual lack of order, she carries out her strategy to sustain dramatic tension between the centrifugal desire to reach the sun and the centripetal force to know the contents of the psyche. Murdoch's analysis here suggests, if anything, that she does not assume the universe is mechanical, especially since she refers her reader to Cornford's commentary of the *Timaeus*, remarking that the "Greeks were familiar with tools, not with machines.... The purposeful Demiurge is not omnipotent and cannot subdue the wandering causes, but *persuades* them, so as to create the best possible world. In this process the Forms remain entirely separate and untouched as they have always been. Their copied reflections appear ephemerally in the medium of space which is eternal and uncreated. (There is no Form of space, though there is a Form of time)" (FS 50). Furthermore, Murdoch appears to assume that the artist, a version of the Demiurge, inevitably introduces nonrational order into his or her design.[21]

A pivotal protagonist, Bradley Pearson, is only one of Murdoch's artist-characters who talk often of cosmic circumstances. When justifying his love for the twenty-year-old daughter of his best friend, Arnold Baffin, Bradley explains to Arnold: "There are huge cosmic forces here. Maybe you don't know about them" (BP 281). But can the reader suppose that Bradley at this point in the novel speaks for Murdoch? Is Bradley not rationalizing? In describing to the reader his situation as he drives away with his love, escaping from her family, Bradley broods over two elements that bother him:

> One [is] vast and cosmic, the other horribly precise. The cosmic trouble was that I was feeling in some way quite unconnected with ordinary speculations about what might happen, that I should certainly lose Julian. ... I felt a kind of absolute despair, as if we had loved already for a thousand years and were condemned to become weary of something so perfect. I raced about the planet like lightning, I put a girdle round the galaxy, and was back in the next second gasping with this despair.... A great loop had been made in the continuum of time and space. (BP 306)

Quite obviously, Murdoch is revealing the comedic side of this kind of romantic fantasizing. The more pressing trouble, the more practical question, was whether Bradley *could* make love to young Julian.

Earlier Bradley had thought he and Julian had "all the time in the world": "This morning I had felt like a cave-dweller emerging into the sun. She was the truth of my life" (BP 285). Murdoch is working hard here not to play the part of a god pulling strings. Toying with a Platonic-Freudian truism, she watches the characters maneuver in their obsessive-compulsive patterns, which pull the strings the gods once pulled. In incorporating Greek concepts of the mysterious ways the universe works, Murdoch appears to be doing what the Greek playwrights did. The universe creates the gods, and then the gods control—erratically. This open playing field, though Murdoch does not mention it explicitly, seems consistent with her world of the novel: she creates characters with obsessions, and their obsessions control the novels.

Viewing Murdoch's cosmos, the reader perceives a layered effect similar to that of physical reality—a universe, a world, and a geography, somewhat the way young Stephen Dedalus perceives Clongowes Wood College. First exists the representation of the modern world superimposed over the Christian world, which is itself inscribed over the ancient Greek world of tragedy. Murdoch discusses here her relationship to that stratum of Western culture: "My connection with the Greek world runs through Plato, of course, and through Aeschylus and through Homer and belongs to a . . . solemn, godridden world. . . . My ancient world ends with the death of Plato" (Heusel, "Dialogue" 7–8). For Murdoch, the secular and the religious are not separate, any more than they were to the ancient Greeks. Apollo in the guise of an editor brings aid to Bradley in *The Black Prince*; Jesus, a presence in *Nuns and Soldiers*, is able to communicate with Anne Cavidge; in all the novels, Eros, "the daemonic negotiator between God and man" (FS 38), is always present among the characters, as is Aphrodite when humans see earthly copies of Forms (FS 35). Through works of art, such as paintings, other gods make contact, as in *The Nice and the Good*: an allegorical painting by Agnolo Bronzino (1503–1572), *Venus, Cupid, Folly, and Time*, becomes instrumental in bringing the Birannes back together as a couple (NG 328).[22]

Murdoch's Christianizing of Plato's cave myth, or her Platonizing of the Christian myth, is another example of creating pentimento. The reader can see in the following statement that Murdoch finds Plato's cosmology both profound and palpable: "The cosmos is in the highest and exemplary sense an aesthetic object, and indeed the only one. The Demiurge's satisfactions and his relation to his material are those of an artist. The material resists organization not as a scientist's material resists, when systems cannot yet be discerned, but as an artist's material resists, because it is in part fundamentally a jumble of which nothing can be made. (Possibly modern physics feels itself closer to the situation of the artist.)" (FS 53). The idea of being parts of the whole, in balance with the rest of creation, is difficult for modern audiences. The Greek model of the cosmos is not human centered or individual centered.

Seeing the Christian trinity as a romanticized version of the Platonic trinity, Murdoch prefers a trinity that is much less patriarchal, there being no father figure. Turning her attention to the trinity that Plato describes, she refers to the "mysterious" World Soul as

> an incarnation of the spirit which pervades the whole sensible cosmos and is created for this purpose by the Demiurge. At 44 a–b [in *Sophist*] it is hinted that the World Soul may not be entirely rational, and it is certainly the most junior and least authoritative of the trio, its two partners being uncreated. In terms of the (not unrelated) Christian trinity the artist figure, the creative Demiurge, occupies of course the position of the Holy Ghost, not of God the Father. The Demiurge is active . . . , best translated here as "mind." Absolute original authority rests in the Forms, and the World Soul, incarnate spirit in the realm of sense, is, it is implied, somewhat "fallen" thereby (as the incarnate Forms are "fallen" in the *Phaedo*). (FS 51–52)

Murdoch breaks in here and does what Jane Tompkins or Marianna Torgovnick might say is characteristic of feminist critics. She speaks of her feelings: "If one may here respond simply and naively to something so complex, I confess that I find Plato's Trinity more morally radiant than that of the Church" (FS 52).[23] The Platonic Trinity "relates Eros to Cosmos, and expresses in an alternative and more complex way the idea that Good attracts"; the Demiurge is "the mediating figure between Being and Becoming," a "live force [that] moves through the created world towards Good" (FS 52). Murdoch's interest in cosmology evokes an attitude toward the external world reminiscent of the seventeenth century. But more important, like the Demiurge she also knows she cannot reproduce the original but proceeds to do what she can to achieve the "best possible."

In saying that her "subject lies on the borders of literature and philosophy" and that "although what follows may sound like a manifesto and may imply a dogmatic tone of voice, I am not all that sure that what I say is right" (SBR 247), she reveals her humble position among her characters. Finding that Jesus Christ has a more vital, more central role in the Judeo-Christian sacred text than God, Murdoch chooses a position in her text for herself that is more Christlike than Godlike, a position consistent with her philosophy but disturbing to some of her readers.[24] She makes a more explicit statement of her view that the universe is decentered: "Form in art is properly the simulation of the self-contained aimlessness of the universe" (SG 86). If this statement describes the kind of reality she conveys in the novels, then Murdoch is obliged to discover forms for displaying and depicting such aimlessness in the universe and in human personality. Perhaps she is comfortable remaining in a condition of ambiguous suspension, creating temporary forms out of the chaos around her.

Being an author who finds no God in charge but who searches for moral direction, she takes a position in her novels similar to the one Fyodor Dostoevsky takes in his, a position Bakhtin says is like Christ's position in the world. By not wanting all the power and not taking control of all the text, Murdoch is like one of her good characters, one of the few who is dynamic. Like Tallis in *A Fairly Honourable Defeat*, she absorbs evil instead of "transmitting suffering," as the Satanic figure Julius does (Conradi, *Saint* 169).[25] That some of her characters insist on the sovereignty of good over other concepts—and do good while having so little power and prestige—points toward a horrific reality: the ubiquitous powerlessness of good in the universe. Her dramatic Miltonic streak leads Murdoch to create a theological allegory in this novel. She explains in *Rencontres* that Tallis is "the 'high incarnation' [of Christ] to use a sort of Eastern term—Julius is of course the Prince of Darkness, King of this World—Morgan is the human soul over whom they are disputing,"[26] mentioning that the allegory is "so concealed that it doesn't in a sense matter" (75). The polarization of good and evil is a comment on theology and does not reflect her philosophy. In actuality she finds a graduated range between good spiritual people and those who fail to tap their goodness.

Patterning good and evil often looks old-fashioned to critics. Because some of Murdoch's critics complain that her texts are plot-bound or pattern-bound, a close look at the relationship of the plot to the novelistic space is valuable. She says herself in *Rencontres* that she is "interested in plots and patterns" (74). The ancient Greek idea of plot is also a helpful way to visualize the cave myth drama belowground and the cosmology aboveground, all parts of Murdoch's fictional world. Murdoch's explanation in her interview with me about the writing process demonstrates what Peter Brooks has pointed out about a "subterranean logic connecting the meanings" of the ancient word *plot*.

Murdoch's holograph notebooks show that her ground plans include charts and diagrams; Plato had a similar habit, as is evident in his Line diagram. Wittgenstein, too, being first an engineer and architect and then a philosopher, gravitated toward the spatial. Stuart Hampshire corroborates that Wittgenstein used notebooks continually and thought out ideas in diagrams. Because few readers have seen Murdoch's holograph notebooks in the University of Iowa Libraries, few know that she often uses diagrams. Her spatial sketches and cryptograms, drawn in her notebooks during the writing process, show how she visualizes space in enclosure and the relation of space to enclosure, making it easier to discuss what was before only an abstraction.

It is much easier for a reader to appreciate the purpose of the agora in *The Philosopher's Pupil* if criticism calls attention to the relation between the spatial and temporal elements in the novel. For example, the narrator's description of the Bath Institute illustrates the qualities readers of Bakhtin recognize from his descriptions of the carnivalesque, qualities that eliminate the "impenetrable hierarchical barriers between people and [allow] them to enter into free, familiar contact on the carnival square" (PDP 101). The novel's narrator explicitly links this square to those of ancient Greece: "Its role has been compared to that of the agora in Athens. It is the main rendezvous of the citizenry where people idle, gossip, relax, show off, hunt for partners, make assignations, make business deals, make plots" (PP 23). As a metaphor for interaction in the community at all levels of age and gender, the agora comprises hierarchies that seem always to be moral and ethical, with no emphasis on class consciousness.[27] The Greeks saw the stage as a holy ground on which to teach fellow citizens how to behave; they considered the agora a meeting ground on which citizens would determine the direction of the city. The standard definitions of *plot* not only call attention to the cultural issues of plot, drama, and represented conflict created by the Greeks but also tie those issues in with the tone and atmosphere of fate: necessity and contingency.

In a less explicit way, Murdoch replicates these spaces or places as metaphors, in addition to using them literally in *The Philosopher's Pupil*. She begins early with the stage metaphor in *Under the Net*, a novel whose paperback cover or dust jacket is often decorated with Greek masks, but she does not really make the idea of stage and control integral to a novel until *The Sea, The Sea*, in which the protagonist, who envisions himself Prospero, wants to be forever a director of the play of life. In addition, Bradley Pearson's preoccupations in *The Black Prince* include allusions to playacting, references that also address the subjecthood of women: "Of course men play roles, but women play roles too, blanker ones. They have, in the play of life, fewer good lines" (BP 34).

Bradley's analysis of Francis Marloe as "subsidiary, a sidesman," as opposed to a hero, and his reference to the fact that "in a purely mechanical sense he opens the tale" suggest that Francis is the messenger bringing the news that begins the "absurdities of chance" (BP 14). Although critics have used such labels as *melodramatic* and *sensational* to describe this kind of focus on the techniques of the Greek play and Murdoch's focus on low Eros (incest, homosexuality, lesbianism, adultery) and on murder and death, Bakhtin's work has revealed that such techniques do not blaspheme the sacred taboos of the novel form.

Examining Murdoch's diagrams is a way of excavating the layers of detail that represent the stages of her creative process. The Greekness of the diagrams demonstrates the emphasis on space and on balance and harmony within the spaces. Her diagrams reveal and reinforce her bent for architecture, for what Edith Hamilton suggests is a necessity of the Greek mind: to see parts in relation to a whole. As a contrast to the Greeks' need to see all, Hamilton describes medieval architects' habit of building cathedrals down low in the middle of old houses. Such architects did not consider the building's relationship to the landscape, so basic to the Greek architect's placement of a temple. Being more than a building, it must dominate the scene: the architect conceived of it in relation to the "summit of a hill overlooking the wide sea, outlined against the circle of the sky" (*The Greek Way* 68). In its comprehensiveness, this conception resembles Murdoch's architectural plots and the spaciousness of her imaginary worlds.

One can see through her diagrams that she carefully thinks out balance and harmony and spatial relationships, in addition to mapping visually where the characters tread. For example, her diagrams in the manuscripts of *Henry and Cato*, a novel Lorna Sage calls particularly visual ("Pursuit of Imperfection" 112), record the balanced and harmonious layout of the family estate Laxlinden (see figures 2 and 3). Henry Marshalson comes home to be immersed in a sense of place, of space, and of class and culture: "The drive curved and the trees receded. A blackness upon the left, like a huge wall, was a yew hedge where there had once been statues" (HC 51). Murdoch's diagram on the verso opposite this passage (figure 3) includes two north-south pointers, with one at a forty-five-degree angle to the other, and a question mark that suggests the importance to Murdoch of orienting the spatial details precisely. The drive by which Henry enters appears stately, even in the two-dimensional diagram, due partly to the distance between it and the yew hedge (with former position of

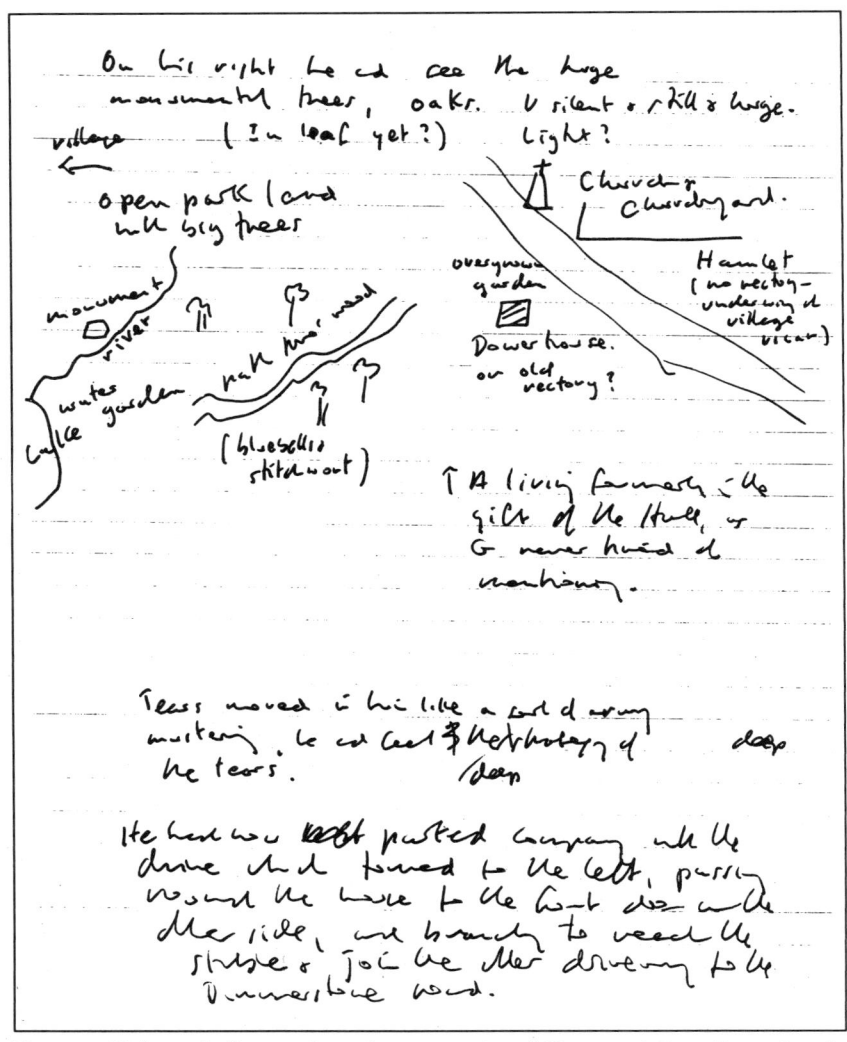

Figure 2. Holograph diagram from the manuscript of *Henry and Cato*. Reproduced with permission of Iris Murdoch; copy courtesy of Special Collections, University of Iowa Libraries.

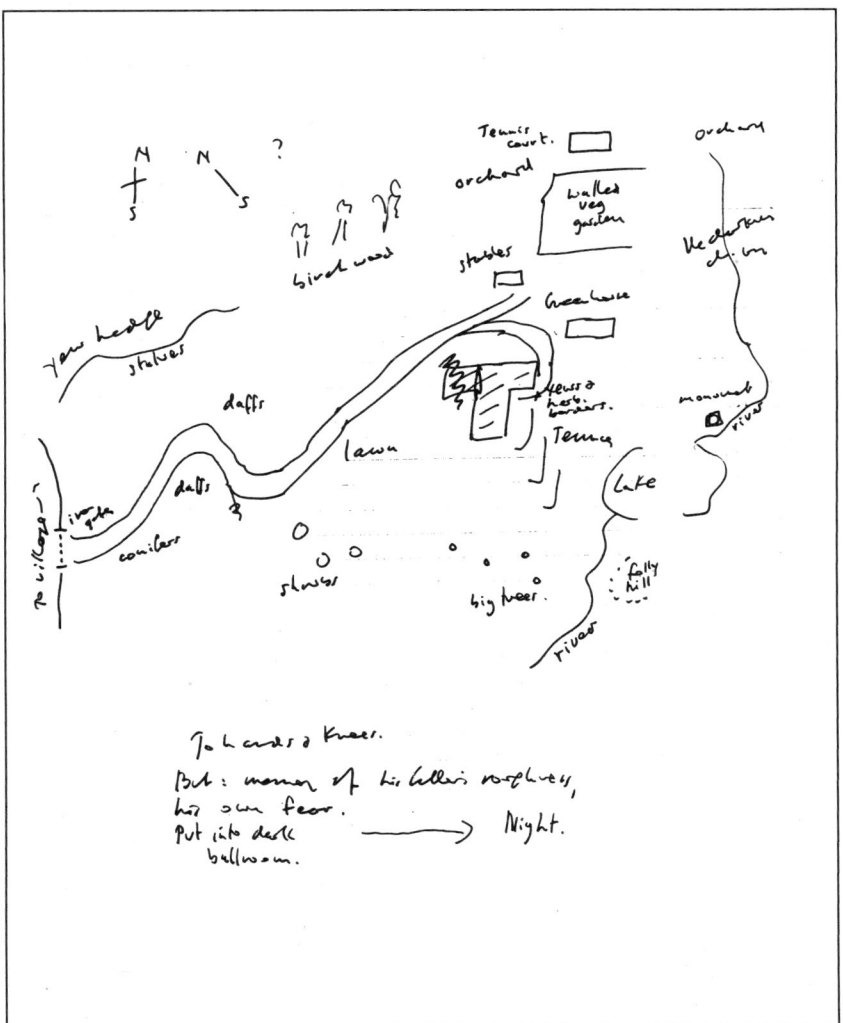

Figure 3. Holograph diagram from the manuscript of *Henry and Cato*. Reproduced with permission of Iris Murdoch; copy courtesy of Special Collections, University of Iowa Libraries.

the statues noted) and the birch wood; on the opposite side, bordering the large lawn in front of the ancestral house, Murdoch has drawn small circles representing "shrubs" and "big trees." The diagram shows Murdoch's rethinking of the direction in which the house faces: "The Hall was L-shaped, the foot of the L being a remnant of a brick-built Queen Anne house onto which about seventeen forty a longer slightly lower stone house had been added at right angles" (HC 51), showing that Murdoch thinks in terms of the kind of layering I have been formulating in this chapter. The concave side of the L faces away from the drive and toward the lake that the narrator will describe in the following sentence. The L-shape had originally faced the opposite way—away from the lake—but Murdoch apparently changed her mind before completing her simple outline, marking out the section that would have faced the drive and adding a branch of the drive that curves between the greenhouse and the house proper. The narrator begins by describing the outside of the estate: "Beyond the house, invisible, the land sloped to the lake. . . . A bright half-moon was now making its presence felt from behind the grove of conifers, shining over Henry's shoulder, silverpointing the slates and making pendant shadows beneath the far-projecting eves" (HC 51). Inside the house Marshalson encounters "Victorianized sash windows" and a "tapestry with the outstretched hand of the goddess buried in the hero's copious hair" (HC 52). Such attention to details of rooms and accoutrements is characteristic of Murdoch's novels.

In the same way that Murdoch's diagrams fit together in a hierarchy of universe, world, geography, and houses, Hamilton shows that each unit of an ancient Greek structure, even one as small as an individual house, fits into a complex hierarchy: "each room [is], indeed, made up of many things; but, if it is considered as part of a block or part of a city, the details sink out of sight. Just as a city in itself is a mass of complexity but is reduced to a few essentials when it is thought of as belonging to a country. The earth shows an infinite diversity, but in relation to the universe it is a sphere swinging in space, nothing more" (222). It is not until *The Philosopher's Pupil* that Murdoch explicitly re-creates Greek architecture, focusing on it predominantly. Her note to herself on page 55 of notebook 1 reflects her interest in architectural configurations: "(Space!)."

At the stage of composition when the notebook's title page reveals her progressive play with working titles (*Hot Springs, Dragon's Riddle*, and then *The Philosopher's Pupil*, in that order), her conception of the town and its accoutrements progresses from a rather vague diagram to a much more specific one in notebook 3—and even more so in notebook 9. Ennistone, like Bath, is beyond the outskirts of London. The first diagram, on the verso opposite manuscript page 55, notebook 1 (June 20, 1980), shows the baptistery, promenade, and indoor bath (see figure 4). She considers "cut[ting out] iron palace, dancing floor, corridor, etc." There is evidence of crucial decisions immediately below the diagram, opposite the narrator's reference to *Ennistone, Its History and Antiquities*—"I think the book is out of print but a copy survives at the public library. There used to be 2 copies but one was stolen"—Murdoch's note is "stolen— by——? George obviously!" The narrator's next sentence begins, "At the time of this story," and the comment alongside the diagram reads "Today," helping the reader see Murdoch's tightening process. Murdoch's comment at the top of this page is "Tiny water snails to keep pool clean? An early idea noted," with an arrow pointing toward the facing manuscript page. At the bottom of the same verso, notes describe the contents of the local museum ("postcards & polished bits of local stone") and add comments she has circled: "FEW PUBS—Methodism" and "No alcohol in Baths." If one compares the floor plan at the center of this page with the one on the verso facing page 52, notebook 3 (see figure 5), the repeated parts are the rooms, promenade, and indoor bath, now labeled a pool. Here she has diagrammed across the top a walled courtyard between rooms and a garden, with an arrow pointing past the garden toward the Hall. The courtyard includes a lawn, the main pool, a children's pool, and the stews—the hot tubs; below the diagram she asks herself, "where stews?" and she has moved the latter and crossed out their first location. The layer of rooms across the bottom includes the promenade, dancing floor (with service area between it and the courtyard, and corridor along the opposite wall), changing rooms between the courtyard and the indoor pool, infants' pool, offices, and an area marked "Annexe." Having the diagram allows her to substitute a more detailed description of characters' movements in a more specifically conceived spatial area: a paragraph of manuscript that she has marked out includes the sentence "Gabriel & Bill went toward the changing rooms," followed by a caret, and on the facing verso—below the detailed diagram—a caret appears with this more detailed version of the same statement: "went out thro' the doorway & turned down the edge of the hill toward the changing room" (notebook 5:52).

Such architectural patterns are clearly important to Murdoch's replication of cultural sediments in the world of her novel. Endlessly critiquing the pull

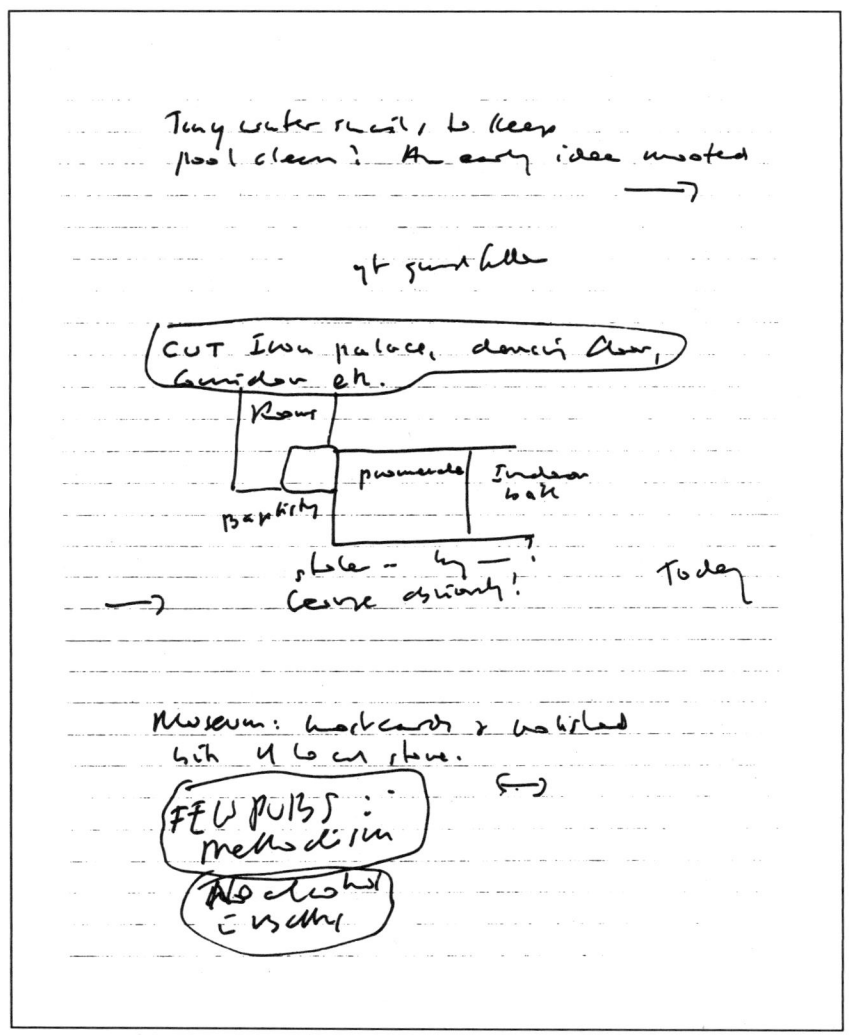

Figure 4. Holograph diagram from the manuscript of *The Philosopher's Pupil*. Reproduced with permission of Iris Murdoch; copy courtesy of Special Collections, University of Iowa Libraries.

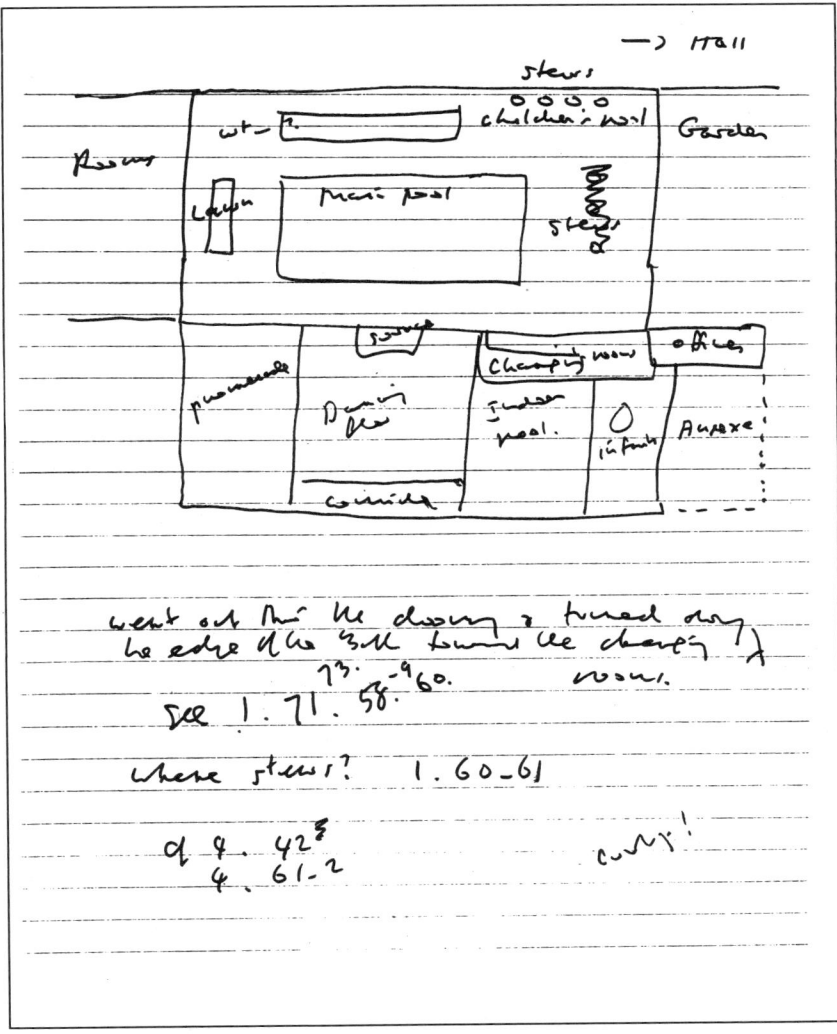

Figure 5. Holograph diagram from the manuscript of *The Philosopher's Pupil*. Reproduced with permission of Iris Murdoch; copy courtesy of Special Collections, University of Iowa Libraries.

of ideological discourses that religious institutions have superimposed on most other social institutions, Murdoch records scrupulously throughout the body of her work the effects of religion on such interlocked institutions as philosophy, economics, class struggle, education, marriage, family, and the individual. Beginning perhaps with *The Bell*, and more blatantly in *The Time of the Angels*, Murdoch has foregrounded spaces and enclosures to demonstrate women's potential entrapment in Western culture by religion. A simple architectural diagram on the verso of the first notebook (June 3, 1957) for *The Bell* seems to have multiplied in importance since the day Murdoch drew it for her own spatial mapping in the novel (see figure 6). Deborah Johnson, a feminist critic who had not seen the diagram, applied French feminist theory to the symbols of the novel, symbols that have continually inspired critical interest since A. S. Byatt referred to them as "planted."

Relying on the work of Luce Irigaray to establish the possibility of seeing all womb-shaped enclosures as "female-centred," Deborah Johnson reads the convent garden and the church bell as "liberating and enhancing symbolism [and finds *The Bell* unsurpassed] in its subtle yet insistent feminism" (*Iris Murdoch* 96). From a female-centered perspective, Johnson analyzes the following passage as a long line of allusions reaching back to Eve, dynamic references to female sexuality:

> [Dora] pushed open a heavy wooden gate in the wall, and [she and the mother superior] came into the fruit garden.
>
> The old stone walls, dry and crumbling with the long summer, covered over with brittle stonecrop and fading valerian, enclosed a large space crammed and tangled with fruit bushes. A wire cage covered an area in the far corner, and there was a glint of glass. A haze hung over the luxuriant scene, and it seemed hotter than ever within the garden. Disciplined fruit trees were spread-eagled along every wall, their leaves curling in the heat. (B 73)

Johnson uses what she calls a "Dora-centred perspective" to show that several elements are all part of one path that leads to the emergence of Dora as a human being: Murdoch's incorporating Dora's entering the gates of the convent, and then the gates of the fruit garden at Imber; restoring the bell and ringing it; and uncovering the sexual secrets.

In her notebooks, Murdoch has Dora leaning on "the balustrade between

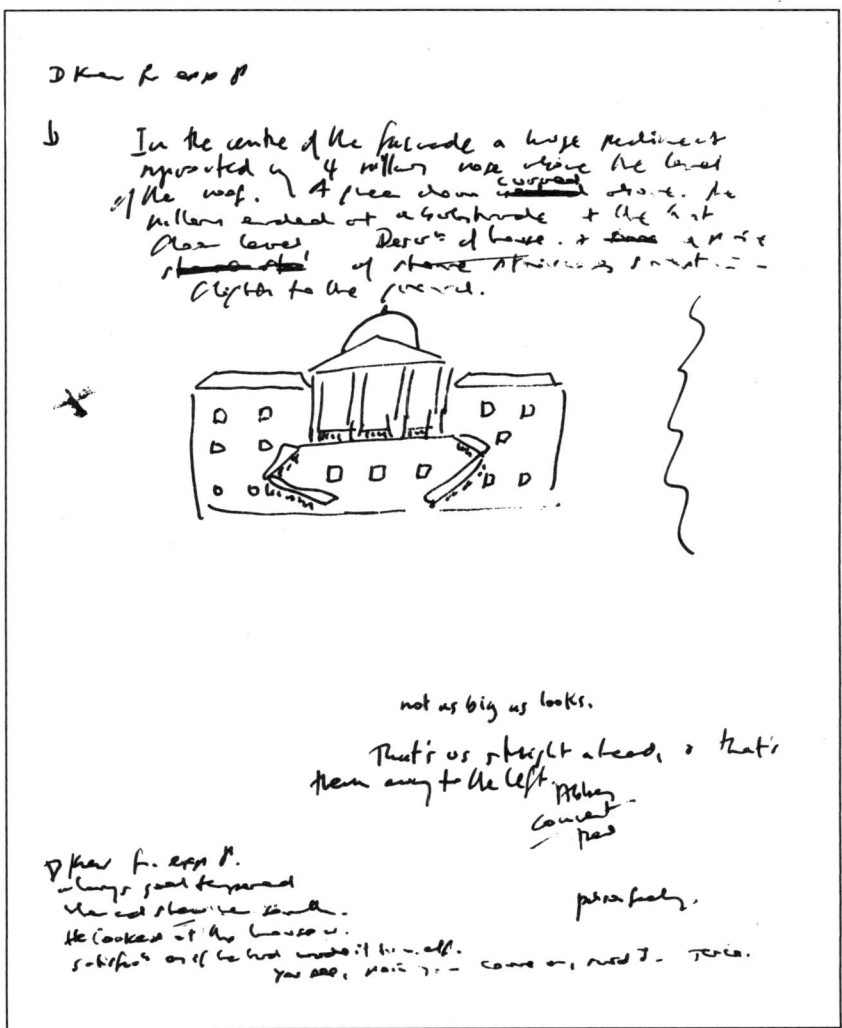

Figure 6. Holograph diagram from the manuscript of *The Bell*. Reproduced with permission of Iris Murdoch; copy courtesy of Special Collections, University of Iowa Libraries.

PATTERNED AIMLESSNESS

the pillars, looking down across the terrace to the lake. The sun had gone but the western sky to her right was still full of the orange murky glow against which a line of trees appeared black & jagged. . . . She could also see the silhouette of a tower which must belong to the Abbey. The lake too was glowing very [silvery], darkened almost to blackness, yet holding here and there up on the surface a skin of almost phosphorescent light. Dora began to descend the steps" (notebook 1). On the verso, Murdoch has drawn a picture of Imber Court (*imber* suggesting "liquid"), the religious establishment that Dora visits. Dora's first sight of Imber Court, soon to be the place of her enlightenment, inspires the kind of childlike awe that the almost-six-year-old James Joyce must have felt the first time he rode into the driveway of Clongowes Wood College. In *The Bell*, awe pervades the scene:

> Dora turned back to the front and gave a gasp of surprise. An enormous house faced them, from a long way away, down an avenue of trees. The avenue was dark, but the house stood beyond it with the declining sunshine slanting across its front. It was a very pale grey, and with a colorless cloudless sky of evening light behind it, it had the washed brilliance of a print. The facade was in three segments, a high pediment in the centre behind which a green dome could be seen, and a soberly windowed square of wall on either side with a lower roof. Beneath the pediment were four large pillars which ended at a balustrade half way down the front of the house. From here a pair of staircases descended in two flights to the ground. (notebook 1)

Murdoch's irony captures Dora's know-it-all academic husband, who not only explains that the architecture is Palladian (that is, in the style of the Renaissance architect Andrew Palladio), but points out glimpses of the Abbey wall "hidden in the trees," behind which women of the order are confined, and the tower, which is in full view, as are the men of the religious community. Dora, on the other hand, has an artistic nature that makes her reaction to the pervasive balance and harmony overwhelming.

These diagrams demonstrate the visual intensity of Murdoch's imagination as well as the thoroughness of her visual plans. Murdoch's comments below on the verso, apparently referring to Abbey Convent on the grounds, remind her that the convent is "not so big as it looks."[28] Murdoch explains in her interview on the Booker series that she once considered being a painter.

Continually disrupting Murdoch's carefully planned architecture of balance and harmony, her characters accomplish her goal of representing the contingencies of real life. According to Murdoch, the good artist frees characters to do what they must do; even though the author does not command their activities, other forces do. Like Greek characters, Murdoch's characters have the propensity Plato describes in humans: to be marionettes, "abject creatures," "dangling from strings of pleasure and pain" (FS 61). Charles Arrowby illustrates this generalization when he says that Minn's cauldron is "a maelstrom of powers which seemed about to dismember me" (SS 66). Murdoch, not wanting to rely heavily on psychological paraphernalia but drawn to the obsessions of contemporary human beings, uses mythological vehicles to explore the idiosyncrasies of her characters. She enlarges their boundedness in time as well as space by allowing them the spaciousness of the myths of Western culture, which she crowds into her novels along with characters and rapid-fire time sequences. And she constructs necessities, assuming that human beings need to recognize that there is "something outside" themselves—a continually spinning world, nature, death, love, and disease. The choices she makes create the cultural norms for her novelistic world.

Murdoch's allusions to Greek theater and mythology focus on the human condition, in effect tapping a cultural unconscious in her readers and making room in her novels for the unseen forces that moved freely through the world of classic drama. Freud made clear to the twentieth century that "that Necessity" underlying the world is sexuality—a vestige of animal need, a necessity for the continuation of the species, a sign of the cycle of birth and death that controls reality. This chapter's earlier explorations of cosmos and beginnings make it clear that all beginnings come from chaos; at a practical level, all worlds are created out of the chaos of sexuality.[29] Murdoch's novels recapture the mystery of how creation works: the novels put into play more forces than meet the eye. They do not insist on housing only contemporary characters—mythological Greek characters are free to enter if the investigation Murdoch is pursuing demands such excess. This multilayeredness requires allusions to creation myths and procreation myths. Perhaps this is why her characters are sometimes like those in Greek drama, stylized but not simplistic. If readers saw the drama of Murdoch's world as a whole and saw that there is a necessity that must be played out, they would be less likely to complain that her characters are too much alike or are not memorable.

For the Greeks, the gods as well as the characters inhabited the stage, and the space of Murdoch's stories is also inhabited by vestiges of the gods. Murdoch relies on the power of well-established cultural icons to challenge the unwieldy and uncontrollable characters she bodies forth. Her creative process takes into account certain ancient deities and powers, such as the Demiurge, Eros, Venus, Narcissus, Persephone, and Christ. *The Black Prince* is unusual in including Apollo-Loxias as a contemporary character, but Murdoch's novels in general take the opportunity to reactivate literary ghosts and cultural concepts, fleshing out the novels' intellectual and psychological worlds. Such characters as Hilary Burde in *A Word Child* express fears that destructive patterns will appear again if they provoke fate. In using gods, Greek characters, Christian historical figures, and ancient beliefs in this way, Murdoch never lets the reader forget that her god-ridden world is forceful, mysterious, and dangerous. Natural forces often accompany Murdoch's cosmic patterns (FS 49); for example, the storms and hurricanes in *Nuns and Soldiers*. Sometimes a god manipulates the characters, but more often their own psyches reflect the concepts and activities of ancient heroes and saints. For example, the narrator and characters in *The Sacred and Profane Love Machine*, a title with a direct link to Greek drama's version of deus ex machina, allude to Homeric characters: Achilles, Agamemnon, Ajax, and Clytemnestra (100); Greek philosophers: Anaxagoras, Anaximander, and Anaximenes of Miletus, Aristotle, Heraclitus, and Empedocles (101); and gods: Hera, Hermes, Atlas (67), Artemis (207), and Athena (101) to contextualize the characters who are heroic or wise or powerful or egoistic.[30] *The Black Prince* alludes to Aeneas, Achilles, and Agamemnon, in addition to making Apollo the protagonist's editor. Characters are often imitating or taking on the features of mythological creatures or reading the *Iliad*, the *Odyssey*, or the *Aeneid* and quoting them to other characters; and figures such as Hermes often listen in from niches. The novels' references to the classical Greek have the ambivalence of being both sacred and profane.

This literary, psychological layering of Western culture makes some readers uncomfortable with Murdoch's plots; the intertextuality can be disturbing. But feeling privy to her plan or scheme allows readers to textualize the fleshy pentimento of their own culture. The reader's uneasiness, carefully nurtured by the allusions to so many characters and events from the past, prepares him or her for the sudden unveilings of reality. Crowdedness is an effect Murdoch is quite skilled in producing. Murdoch's novels reenact for the twentieth century Plato's pilgrimage toward the consciousness of Good. In addition to using the cave myth allegory to search for the history of consciousness of her culture, she insists on reproducing the pervasiveness and the power of sexuality in the lives of human beings. In this world of the novel, Murdoch weaves a series of many-layered movements, including the centrifugal motion up toward the light and the centripetal motion down toward the dark of the psyche. This endeavor requires that she use some of Freud's conclusions to update the Greeks' understanding that sexuality is a human necessity and to probe the unconscious in order to tap sexual energy.[31]

Freud drew on Greek myths, archetypal stories, to make concrete his conceptions about the psyche. The stylized but not simple characters of Greek drama act out for the audience the archetypal actions of the human mind; the Greeks, being knowers and teachers above all, gave subsequent ages believable generalizations about basic human qualities. To diagnose his case histories, Freud conceived a model of the mind, a multilayered labyrinth that appropriated Plato's use of spatial levels in referring to the mind, conscious and unconscious. Being a Freudian to the extent that she believes Freud is the modern exponent of Plato's three-tiered mind, Murdoch no doubt sees her characters as reenacting the cultural family dramas.[32] Françoise Meltzer speaks of these

> "topographic" metaphors found throughout Freud's writings: spatial notions of place and of "layers" in the mind. It is when Freud is alluding to the "descriptive" unconscious . . . that we get metaphors such as "regions of the mind," "map of the mind," "uncharted terrain," "unknown regions," the dream as the "royal road to the unconscious," and the unconscious itself as an antechamber leading to a sitting room (consciousness) which is carefully guarded by a sentry (the sentry is the personification of the repression barrier—the barrier that refuses unconscious thoughts entry into consciousness). ("Unconscious" 150)

Meltzer's explanation that the unconscious is unknown and must be described in "analogies, metaphors, similes, etymological play, and anecdotes" ("Unconscious" 149) and Freud's understanding that the unconscious is sexual both buttress an argument by Barbara Johnson in *The Critical Difference* that literature is sexual and is about sexuality (13). The creative impulse comes from unconscious influences, not only the diagnostic desire of psychoanalysts to know the patient's story but the artistic desire of writers to produce literature.

Stories, and particularly anecdotes, serve New Historicists in much the same way they have served physicians and psychoanalysts in writing case histories. Each of Freud's case histories is a personal history of a patient's sexual experiences. Indeed, Joel Fineman's metaphors for discussing the advantages of the anecdote as a descriptive and diagnostic tool argue for the basic sexual nature of narrative.[33] Using the language of psychoanalysis, he argues that the anecdote is "the hole" that seductively opens the "rim" of history.[34] There is a sense in which Murdoch's novels are openings into historical contexts. For her texts, the relation between historicity and sexuality also becomes an issue whenever a first-person narrator relates his personal history.

For example, in the three first-person novels I explored in chapter 8, each protagonist is unable to detach his creative impulses from his sexual history; perhaps the combination contributes to the particular dynamism of each text. Murdoch gives her three first-person narrators the ability to use anecdotes seductively. Because his personal history has been negative, Hilary's attitude toward history is negative: "History was a slaughterhouse, human life was a slaughterhouse" (WC 28). He has, after all, accidentally killed two women he loved. In *The Sea, The Sea*, Murdoch creates a narrator who tells a story about the events of the past, probing his experience as a director in the theater. Charles Arrowby's descent into a womb-shaped cave, called Minn's cauldron, introduces him to the Buddhist perspective of his cousin James. As he constructs his history, Charles is too blind and egoistic to conceptualize the contradictory views of other characters' mutual histories. The form of the novel, a diary divided into "Prehistory," "History," and "Posthistory," explores connections between Charles's history and his sexual obsession. Charles at first captures the reader with his joy in the beauty of nature and then with his seeming naiveté before he alienates the reader with his monological tirade on his first experience of love; he repeats an earlier search, perhaps for a lost mother love.

In my interview with Murdoch, she images descending into the cave of the imagination as a way of tapping the energy of Eros (Heusel, "Dialogue" 9); in Western culture, the imagery of the cave, the indentation, the omphalos, signifies the biological function of the female. Murdoch's texts suggest a relationship between the cave as a haven of illusory consolation and the cave as a metaphor for the female womb. Numerous womb-shaped enclosures in the novels argue that, for Murdoch, relations exist among sexuality and religion, philosophy, literature, and history. For example, the baths and dome Murdoch draws in her notebooks illustrate community and religion, respectively. In *The Philosopher's Pupil*, young Tom McCaffrey's search for the source of the Institute, literally the hot springs, suggests his need to get back to his own source, his mother: "A flood of excited physical fear took possession of the lower part of his body, a painful vertiginous thrilling urgent pressuring feeling, like sexual desire. Then Tom thought, it's not like sexual desire, it *is* sexual desire. He moved quickly now, his mouth open, his eyes wide. He padded on his toes toward the source of light, which was the partly open door of the Baptistry, which housed the descent to the source, and led also to the long downstairs corridor of the Rooms" (PP 519). In *The Bell*, the Abbey, bell, and garden analyzed by Deborah Johnson represent religion, philosophy, and history. Johnson argues that Luce Irigaray in *Speculum* suggests the possibility of seeing all womb-shaped enclosures as "female-centred." Irigaray's study of the philosophers of Western patriarchy establishes the point that Plato's cave is a metaphor of masculine representation for the woman. It is easy to agree with Johnson's reading of the character central to this novel: "[It] is perhaps not over-fanciful to see in Dora certain analogies with the female text as described by Cixous, Irigaray and Kristeva; like the female text Dora [reminiscent of Freud's Dora] subverts patriarchal, logical expectations, possesses a multitude of meanings, and is characterised by the presence of *jouissance*, female pleasure" (*Iris Murdoch* 75). Murdoch consciously uses Plato's cave imagery and the subsequent Renaissance architectural dome imagery to undergird her explorations of the human being's preverbal memory of and need for a haven like that of the mother's womb or arms.

Murdoch understands that many people find consolation in considering goodness a pervasive quality that one can sometimes almost recall from early childhood. Some of her characters use such comforting memories to wrap themselves in dreamworlds. In her diagrams, Murdoch demonstrates how much she immerses herself in fleshly particulars. The dome in *The Bell*, a metonymy for the supposed safety of a religious haven, and the agora at the baths in *The Philosopher's Pupil*, likewise a metonymy for community, evoke the mythical warmth of the female body. In the same way that the baths evoke the potential of rebirth, the harmonious Renaissance architecture elicits unconsciously the memory of the fullness of life in the arms of the nursing mother and the liquid womb. Both metaphors flesh out Murdoch's imaging of the institutions of church and city. *The Bell* also emphasizes withdrawing into the consolation of religion, as embodied by Renaissance architecture: characters at all levels of the cave pilgrimage seek out the religious retreat to find what they have lost in the past. Furthermore, the baths at Ennistone hold the community together: even when recalcitrant men like George McCaffrey become destructive, the baths provide numerous avenues for the relief of anxiety and redirection of energy.

Specific links exist between Murdoch's writing process and such vestiges of Greek culture as the structure of the cave, the Greek theater, the omphalos, and the oracle at Delphi. One way to recognize such links is to explore Irigaray's validation of female sexuality and its bearing on woman's epistemology, as Deborah Johnson does: "The Cave stands in this masculine representation for the womb, the matrix, also the earth. It is described as a *theatrical* enclosure (*enceinte theatrale*)—where the representations, the images proposed by the inherent metaphoricity of Western thought are deployed" (*Iris Murdoch* 87–88). Furthermore, Irigaray's treatment of Plato in *Speculum of the Other Woman* deals with two issues that have to do with gendered difference: the upward thrust of the pattern of the cave as grounded in patriarchy and the roundness and enclosure of the Greek theater in relation to its beginnings in the fertility cults in which the omphalos and oracle at Delphi figure prominently. In discussing Irigaray, Johnson argues that the cave image of progress upward, being male centered, is a metaphor that "underline[s] the course of Western metaphysics": "The Platonic image of the Cave proposes a set of oppositions, differences, discontinuities between outside and inside, high and low, daylight and earth-fire, escaped man and prisoner, truth and shadow, truth and veil, reality and dream, the intelligible and the sensible, good and evil, the One and the many. These oppositions, Irigaray goes on to say, 'always assume a *leap* from worse to better. An ascension. A displacement (?) towards the heights, a progression along a line. Vertical Phallic?'" (quoted in *Iris Murdoch* 88).

In her use of metaphors, anecdotes, and analogies, and in her etymological play, Murdoch employs, some think indiscriminately, the orthodox genres—the biblically canonized parable and allegory and the less orthodox joke and anecdote, especially when it includes peripeteia. Murdoch turns more and more in the novels of the 1970s and 1980s to the psychiatrist and philosopher whose investigations depend on manipulating the anecdote in order to probe reality; the manipulating and probing are grounded in sexuality. For example, *The Good Apprentice* blatantly uses the parable, perhaps to write an allegory about the creativity and sexual fertility of patriarchs and the incredible pain they pass on to their sons, suggesting Irigaray's statement in her title chapter: "The Vengeance of Children Freed from Their Chains." The novel's opening narrative poses the questions of good and evil and the consequences of selfishness and selflessness, a prodigal son recalling the way he childishly urged his friend to eat a sandwich laced with drugs while he left to make love to a young woman.

Murdoch's fear of being encaged by formalism, whether spatial or temporal, balances her love of patterning; it is as if she has created her own cage out of her interpretations of Plato, as a sonneteer learns from and draws energy from the inhibition of the form. What interests her about invention is to a large extent the same as what she describes in the following passage from *The Fire and the Sun*: "What interests Plato in nature is pattern, necessity which is the test of truth: what turns opinion into certainty" (43). When Murdoch argues that patterns are every artist's medium, she includes herself and Plato as well as some of her artist-characters. Again, Murdoch talks about her novel writing as if she were a kind of Demiurge, saying, when asked about her use of the Greek,

> There is plenty in Greek tragedy and in Plato and in the myths. . . . For me a novel begins in a great cauldron of ideas and images, impulses and feelings. . . . I don't write anything until I have invented the whole thing. Until it is *all* there, I would not write the first sentence. . . . I would have . . . [an understanding of the way it is going] in my mind very early on. But I think the period of reflection—when one has nothing, except notes, of course, to remind one—is very important; it's a kind of deep free reflection which may be more difficult later on. (Heusel, "Dialogue" 8–9, 4)

Her process of writing a novel requires both a Dionysian condition and a controlling spirit of inspiration. She says that the artist experiences the "conflict between the form-maker and the truthful formless figure" (Bellamy, "Interview").[35] Like a potter allowing the clay to act out all its potential or Michelangelo letting the figures out of the stone, she invests her medium with sometimes tremendous intensity—hurricanes, perhaps, or a void or vortex or chaos—and then struggles with that medium to give her characters every opportunity to escape its grasp—and hers. She has learned that "if you get hold of a good character, he will invent himself, will invent his mode of speech and his past, make his jokes, and so on. The thing is to get the fundamental patterns right, the basic idea of what it's all about and who the people are. It begins for me with a very small, but one hopes a very powerful, nucleus of two or three people in a situation" (Heusel, "Dialogue" 4). For there to be art, she has also learned, the play of the imagination must halt and the work of ordering must begin.

Murdoch's characters have real freedom during the time between her plotting a novel in her imagination and her writing it down. When the characters and the author are given freedom to work at their respective jobs, the men, more than the women, demand to take over: survival is no easy task for the characters because the author imagines egoistic enchanter figures who threaten the weaker ones. Once Murdoch has structured the parameters—the time sequence and whatever the protagonists, particularly the males, will fail to control, the plot of the story—she can let them proceed as they wish, without her needing to manipulate them. She gives her enchanter figures free rein, allowing them to participate even more actively in creating the text. Being more independent than the other characters and having more literary testosterone, these powerful figures (some of whom are first person, some third) often help work out the structure of the text.[36] She gives them personality traits that make them self-starters, characters with exceptional drive and deep-seated obsessions.

Three of her first-person male narrators demonstrate this possibility most cogently: in general the more each one's routines are rigidly derived from obsession, the more he manages to take over the story. By imagining characters who are jerked about by compulsive behaviors, Murdoch builds up palpable evidence that characters can get out of her control and run riot: her abstract notion of giving characters their own freedom becomes a reality. Murdoch works like the hands-off gods in Greek literature, models of agents who do not make the literary archetype act as he does. They do not, for example, make Oedipus attack his father where three roads meet; the gods simply see the entire history of time and, therefore, see Oedipus's behavior on the road. In a similar

Philosophical and Psychological Patterns

way, Murdoch watches her characters climb or fail to climb toward good; some are compulsive like Oedipus and are pulled by unconscious strings. She can see what her characters will of necessity do, but she does not make them do it. One possible explanation of why Murdoch repeatedly uses powerful male enchanters is simply that they survive the evolutionary battle during the first days of the novel's conception as her mind sorts out the cast of characters.

Would female narrators portray the characteristic obsessions in our culture as well? Could a Rachel Baffin or a Christian Hartbourne, each as neurotic as Bradley Pearson but in decidedly different ways, provide a believable series of trivial incidents like Hilary's quarrel with his boarder or his driving so wildly or his rushing out like a bison to save Kitty, his lover? Would readers laugh at the neuroses of these women? Murdoch's novels suggest that the culture is not distanced enough from the spectacle of neurotic women to see them as comic figures in the same way it sees neurotic men. Does this possibility further suggest that certain stereotypes of neurotic men have been proffered by society to relieve the pressure of cultural guilt? Women do not demonstrate the same kind of seductive obsessional patterns, especially in relation to sexuality. Murdoch's statement that men rule the world is corroborated in her renditions of how the world works; she seems not to be interested in writing utopian fiction.

Her characters' routines are their patterns rather than simply Murdoch's. For example, when Hilary Burde keeps repeating similar disasters, the reader sees that the wheel of fortune is indeed circular and that the fates do keep striking. Murdoch gives Bradley Pearson the kind of bumbling personality that can create the lengthy time lapse between the moment he plans to leave London in order to write and the moment he leaves. And, of course, fate has five people arriving at Bradley's front door within two minutes, just at the instant he discovers that his sister has swallowed a bottle of sleeping pills (BP 76–78). Murdoch's choreography—five stooges knocking into each other in their efforts to call the ambulance, find the empty bottle of pills, and clean up the vomit—establishes a wonderfully slapstick pattern that will recur throughout the novel, enabling the compulsive energy of this protracted scene to reverberate like fate.

Several times at the beginning of the novel he is writing, Bradley himself discusses the invention of patterns; he is a man with Greek intimations of order. He immediately thinks that he could make a choice whether to begin his novel with the "deeper pattern" of Francis "as the first speaker, the page or house-maid . . . who, some half an hour before Arnold's momentous telephone call, initiates the action" (BP 21). Because Bradley is a man to whom people flock for help, he cannot get away to write his book: inspiration cannot penetrate the hectic atmosphere of his life. Murdoch as author is like Bradley trying to control the Dionysian wildness and lack of control of the beings that invade his privacy. On the other hand, Bradley finally, with the help of the change of aspect that love gives him, manages to continue his journey toward the work of art he is finally inspired to write.

The fantasies that go on in these three narrators' minds about the way each would like others to behave give Murdoch a way of categorizing her characters in certain strata of her labyrinth. Each character's success is determined by his interest in his pilgrimage, his energy, and his luck. Hilary, for example, is the least capable of getting outside himself: when it comes to attending to the mystery of other human beings, he is quite dense. Charles is like most of Murdoch's other characters in wanting people to be his puppets. Of the three, Bradley is the most likely to want to escape responsibility, but the possibility of being greatly inspired to write forces him to attend to others.

If obsessions have, for Murdoch, taken over the power of the gods, then might she find the enchanters the best sort of instruments to jerk the obsessional strings of the abject creatures that surround them? Perhaps she learned through her early novels that each time she gave a more powerful enchanter more power, she had to expend less and less energy on inventing the character, leaving her free to control other matters. These vital and dynamic first-person male protagonists who combine some of the characteristics of the early enchanter figure with a carefully developed repertoire of major obsessional weaknesses are an important achievement.

One of this obsessed group wants to partake in the divine nature: like Oedipus, Bradley is able to achieve a degree of perfection. Bradley's most important characteristic may be his understanding of inspiration from the unconscious. Because Bradley as artist, even at the beginning of his novel, understands the relation between Eros and Thanatos, he succumbs to the enlightenment awaiting him in sexual love. Without this giving in, Bradley would have been unable to communicate with Apollo. All the enchanters, including old Bradley, use sexuality negatively as a control over others. But in addition he moves closer to the sun and gets more good work done than most characters because he is open to inspiration. All the enchanters understand that other characters lose control when Eros, the demonic negotiator between God and man, is rampant. But they do not always understand that Eros, mystery that it is, must also engulf them. They must love, but for no reason—for nothing. This kind of loving is often accompanied by cataclysmic change.

During the 1950s and 1960s Murdoch worked at creating, developing, and perfecting two dynamic narrative strategies for recording her free characters as they experience momentary insights, larger revelations, and rebirth—as they *see*, in the sense of gaining understanding. Seeing and understanding, seeing and appreciation, seeing and loving, seeing and good are all related, for Murdoch, to removing the veil of illusion. She is well known for her ecstatic love of paintings, commenting that one of the reasons she likes to visit New York, or almost any city, is to see "the pictures," her metonymy for visiting art museums.[37] Her narrative effects determine that the abrupt change most often comes through the visual. As she has Plato explain in "Art and Eros," insight blinds momentarily as it enlightens: "perhaps it's only for a short time, because the light of the sun dazzles you" (*Acastos* 56).

Murdoch's play with visual perspectives thus goes beyond the obvious metaphorical analogies such as world as cave, network as logic, movement up and out as good (light), and movement in and down as evil (dark). For Murdoch, seeing requires the mind to participate in being and becoming. Using methods that were also important to Wittgenstein, Murdoch reveals her characters' moments of enlightenment as they climb toward the sun. Both epistemologically and ontologically, these moments are necessary to her concept of the unveiling of reality and to her insistence that the contingency of misseeing and misunderstanding defamiliarizes certain realities for the character and the reader;[38] she also insists that such defamiliarization often leads to reseeing and understanding. Her use of these methods to create accident and elicit surprise is an important element missing from current discussion by Murdoch's critics.

Murdoch's goal in the slight revising she does is to create inconsistencies, to allow for cacophony, thereby destabilizing the form of her novels. For example, her note to herself in the manuscript of *The Black Prince* to "Absurdify Francis" shows she does not want the reader to take anything for granted. Her goal is to place side by side a series of disjunctive ideas to give them the opportunity for dialogic play. Such juxtaposition assumes either a gradual continuum, as in the cave myth, or an abruptness. Throughout Murdoch's oeuvre there are analogous relationships between the pilgrimages of various types of characters that allow the reader to place the characters on a continuum. Throughout a particular novel, Murdoch achieves defamiliarization through abrupt juxtapositions, through modulating abruptly between two visions to achieve dramatization of inconsistency and/or exploration of paradox. Murdoch's novels are unique products of her eclecticism. Her goal is in part to evoke and elicit a fresh vision, especially when she is attempting to get the reader to attend to the ways her characters learn to attend to the ultimate realities of love and death. Familiarity with the world and with human perceptual mechanisms deadens perception.

Basic to her moral philosophy, or psychology, are the necessary moments of surprise, trompe l'oeil and tricks of the brain, that help the reader *see* for the first time. In juxtaposing divergent materials, some realistic and some fantastic, she plays with learned responses in order to subvert them. In order to shock characters—and readers—into seeing,[39] Murdoch utilizes a perceptual phenomenon analyzed in Gestalt psychology and discussed by Wittgenstein in *Philosophical Investigations*, because it explicitly names the pattern of sudden disorientation she finds basic to vital human experience: a switch or shift of gestalt. Her use of the term in *The Black Prince* suggests her search for evidences of visual misinterpretation so that she can use them to dramatize growth or movement toward the sun. By repeating this concept of sudden disorientation on two successive pages, Murdoch demands that the reader notice it. For Bradley, a switch in gestalt precedes his falling in love, serving as a signal he fails to recognize. Noticing a young fellow behaving in a particular way—"strewing flowers upon the roadway" like a Hindu priest (BP 54)—Bradley accepts this sensory information for a page before he realizes that he has been "pondering a young woman": "I had paused and had been watching him for some moments . . . when, with one of those switches of *gestalt* which can be so unnerving, I realized that the light had deceived me and that this was in fact no young man but a girl" (BP 55). A page later, Murdoch makes it impossible for the reader to have missed the term: "Only now I realized, with yet another shift of *gestalt*, that the whirling white blobs were not petals at all, but fragments of paper" (BP 56).

Murdoch would have been familiar with such concepts as figure versus ground and gestalt because of Wittgenstein's interest, if for no other reason.[40] Wittgenstein's use of the duck-rabbit figure in *Philosophical Investigations*, which I discuss in chapter 3,[41] evokes a pattern that has become extremely

Philosophical and Psychological Patterns

familiar in twentieth-century novels, a pattern that an innovator such as Joyce gets at through metaphors that call up visualizations of parallax or the stereoscope. Julian Hochberg describes gestalt as "a figure or pattern which can be distinguished against the background or field of perception. . . . The term applies whenever a significant pattern or construct (the 'figure') emerges against the background scene or noise (the 'ground')," explaining the figure-ground phenomenon as "i.e., that the same outline can be perceived as different alternative figures, with very different shapes" ("Gestalt Theory" 291, 288). Furthermore, if the human mind perceives the energies of the physical world not as atomistic sensations but as configurations, in the way that Gestalt psychology proposes, then each work of art is a configuration of ideas, themes, and details organized in potentially meaningful wholes that viewers will perceive differently depending on their perspective and their proclivity to look at the figure or at the ground.

Murdoch finds the switch of gestalt significant at visual, mental, and moral levels.[42] For Murdoch the purpose of art is to elicit reaction from the reader so that he or she sheds the dead skin of perception, narcissism, or preoccupation with ego, all of which make human beings oblivious to the realities of the world. Murdoch creates a world that shocks her characters not only into seeing visual phenomena but also into what she calls "unself[ing]," when a sudden, often beautiful reality impinges on them. By *unselfing* she means "see[ing] and . . . respond[ing] to the real world in the light of a virtuous consciousness" (SG 93). Her characters do not simply trudge up to the entrance of the cave; they experience degrees of insight and occasionally fall back to where they had trudged earlier. Murdoch's exuberant comedic insight suggests ways to use switches of gestalt and moral switches or unselfing to adjust and finetune the "falsifying *veil*[s] which partially [conceal] the world" (SG 84). Her narrative effects encourage the reader to search for such concealed reality, for such mystery.

To some degree a switch of gestalt is a less significant version of a moment of moral enlightenment. In "Existentialists and Mystics," Murdoch describes the shock of suddenly encountering good: "Virtue standing out gratuitously, aimlessly, unplaced by religion and society, surprising us as it so often does in real life: the gentleness of Patroclus in the middle of a ruthless war . . . something gratuitous, something which belongs in the absolute foreground of our existence, along with self-evident goods such as eating enough and not being afraid. . . . Goodness is needful, one has to be good, for nothing, for immediate and obvious reason, because somebody is hungry or somebody is crying" (182). A well-known scene in her fourth novel, *The Unicorn*, illustrates the phenomenon of unselfing. This archetypal scene demonstrates what a switch of gestalt becomes when Murdoch expands the moral, epistemological, and ontological implications. Effingham Cooper moves closer to the sun when he almost drowns in a bog; his moment of enlightenment reveals that life reaches toward selflessness, whether or not human beings notice. This soul wrenching is, for him, more cerebral than perceptual. As he struggles not to go under, he sees the sun and realizes that death is perhaps the only fact there is:

> If one had realized this, one could have lived all one's life in the light. Yet why in the light, and why did it seem now that the dark ball at which he was staring was full of light? Something had been withdrawn, had slipped away from him in the moment of his attention, and that something was simply himself. Perhaps he was dead already, the darkening image of the self forever removed. Yet what was left, for something was surely left, something existed still? It came to him with the simplicity of a simple sum. What was left was everything else, all that was not himself, that object which he had never before seen and upon which he now gazed with the passion of a lover. And indeed he could always have known this, for the fact of death stretches the length of life. Since he was mortal, he was nothing, and since he was nothing all that was not himself was filled to the brim with being, and it was from this that the light streamed. This then was love, to look and look until one exists no more, *this* was the love which was the same as death. He looked and knew, with a clarity which was one with the increasing light, that with the death of the self the world becomes quite automatically the object of a perfect love. He clung to the words "quite automatically" and murmured them to himself as a charm. . . . [He had] been depersonalized, abandoned by his self. (U 188–90)

This lengthy passage is an exquisite description of a change of aspect at a moral level. Momentarily, light streams from all being that is not himself; he is nothing. Before the experience in the bog, he had assumed that his being was filled with life and that what was around him was nothing. What was background space to him is now foreground, and he recedes into the background. Bloom is right that Murdoch's sun—the truth to which her characters are climbing—is, as she describes Effingham's, death. Perhaps Bloom's remark about death's being the center of Murdoch's philosophy comes out of passages like this one in *The Unicorn*. Bloom comments on the way Murdoch dramatizes a post-Christian world in which the center is death or nothingness: "[Murdoch's] version of a post-Christian religion is marked by violence and deathliness. Whatever Socrates meant by saying we should study dying, Murdoch harshly means that death is the truth, since it destroys every image and every story" (*Iris Murdoch* 5).

Perhaps a few historical lenses can put this argument in perspective. Clearly modernist artists' dependence on figure-versus-ground switches of gestalt is not new. Thinkers have been considering the phenomenon and artists have been simulating it since at least the beginning of the modern period. Modernist artists have perfected the techniques for emphasizing it. For example, this visual phenomenon is central to Joyce's epiphanies. Since much of Joyce's fiction consists of a series of exercises in narcissism, his epiphanies focus directly on the artist's ego. The quotation from *The Unicorn* demonstrates that Murdoch's reason for using the figure/ground gestalt phenomenon is quite different from Joyce's.[43] Since the Romantic movement, artists have been trying out ways to record such experience—William Wordsworth's "spots of time," Poe's retracing of an emotion, Proust's "moments of time." No artist, however, except perhaps Gerard Manley Hopkins, dramatizes characters moving toward selflessness. In general, authors' use of perceptual shift is predominantly phallocentric and scopophilic or visual. Joyce used the concept of epiphany when he wanted to show the final stage of cognition,[44] and parallax and stereoscope when he wanted to place in conflict his fictionalized visions of his young self and his mature self and determine if any resolution was possible.[45] In Sophocles' and Joyce's texts this phenomenon is less subtle, and the epiphanic moments become part of the foreground—for Sophocles, a message; for Joyce's Stephen, an aesthetic theory.

Murdoch, however, conjures visions that are not so monstrously personal nor so gigantic. Rather than use parallax to demonstrate the relationship between the extreme point of view of her young self and the opposite point of view of her older self, as Joyce does with Stephen and Bloom in *Ulysses*, Murdoch chooses to show numerous characters having such experiences. Her oeuvre analyzes various continua, a group of first-person male narrators, a group of artists, and, as Bloom points out, a group of "fierce, very young women, . . . narcissistic charmers [who are weak, older men], 'alien gods,' . . . unfulfilled older women" (*Iris Murdoch* 2). Since many of these characters experience insights, and since metaphors such as parallax and stereoscope are reductively binary, Murdoch chooses to use a multiplicity of switches of gestalt. One could argue that Murdoch uses the phenomenon in a traditional way if one thinks of Sophocles. The classical Greeks emphasized change of aspect for purposes of showing moral enlightenment. Their scopophilia is also basic to their scientific and artistic methods. Greek tragedy structures the events to move toward a sudden moment of enlightenment and the stark juxtaposition of previously unbelievable revelations; in Murdoch, however, the seeing better does not usually involve such gigantic consequences as those understood in classical tragedy.[46] She uncovers reality suddenly for the characters in order to create the same experience in her reader, simulating what Poe proposes: that a work of art is a retracing of an emotion for the writer and then for the reader (Heusel, "Escher" 395, 405). Whereas Joyce was interested in the end product, the work of art, Murdoch is more interested in the process. She does not expect each product to change the world, as Joyce might have expected; she has no problem with returning to the drawing board to have another try at it. Her focus is more directly on the earlier stage, on the shifting of the veils of illusion; perhaps this is why some call her a magician.

Being eclectic, Murdoch surprises readers by using postmodernist practices: indeterminacy created through irony and contingency, openness, and improvisation. For example, Murdoch combines modernist fragmentation of characters and truths and postmodernist indeterminacy in *The Black Prince*. She structures the novel so that a reader must analyze Bradley's life and/or his novel in discrete pieces; the resulting conclusions can be distorted in bizarre ways, as the postscripts demonstrate, each added one presenting new configurations of reality. None of these perspectives of the dramatis personae can be trusted, although each may be partially valid. Each has a unique way of producing a mysterious reality about Bradley while distorting other realities, such as his potential for homosexuality. The different voices employ devices that dramatize the relationship between the phenomena of seeing and representation. In addition, Loxias has an indeterminate identity, similar to the polymorphous perversity in *Ulysses*.[47] Furthermore, Murdoch disturbs narrative continuity in *The Philosopher's Pupil* when she punctures the myth of authority of the narrator, N.

Because each of these writers is willing to mix conventions, their unorthodox methods teach readers to see, to listen, and to read in a new way. When she discusses ways in which *The Black Prince* is more modern than *A Word Child*, Murdoch reveals that she feels free to switch back and forth between modern and more traditional conventions. For example, she sees no reason why Hilary should not be presented through an older convention. She says the modern novelist often "situate[s] the first-person narrative within some kind of hint of how it has been written, or when it has been written, or why" (Chevalier, *Rencontres* 73), a method she decided not to use in *A Word Child* but did use in *The Black Prince*. She no doubt has a similar reaction to people who ask how a novelist writing a realistic novel can include a character who dares to raise another character from the dead. In *The Message to the Planet*, she explores the mystery of the mind of genius; some of the characters and some critics assume that this enchanter figure is insane. Both she in this novel and Joyce in *Finnegans Wake* investigate and problematize the human desire for centeredness.

Perhaps Murdoch, like other writers, has learned from *Finnegans Wake* to play with the introduction of characters. Her introduction of characters is most often noticeably patterned. Of course, Murdoch retains more of the conventions of realism than Joyce does. It is when she works these methods into otherwise realistic fiction that readers have problems. Murdoch does occasionally use initials and abbreviations for characters—N, for example, the narrator of *The Philosopher's Pupil*—as Joyce does in *Finnegans Wake*; and her characters and their "names emerge slowly," as Margot Norris says Joyce's do ("Consequence" 210). Both of these Anglo-Irish writers of comedy introduce characters mysteriously. Both apparently savor wild incongruity and narrative excess. Perhaps gender causes critics to question Murdoch's excess and not Joyce's because hers seems more incongruous, juxtaposed as it is to realism. The poet figure raised from the dead in *The Message to the Planet*, like the late Finnegan, is an Irish alcoholic. This play with reality in the novel might be her Joycean joke. But more important, the two novels reflect—albeit in different ways—a postmodernist contingency that wrenches the reader. Whereas the shock reviewers experienced in reading Murdoch's novel could not have been so great as that of the first readers of *Finnegans Wake*, back in the days of *Works in Progress*, reviewers were nevertheless disoriented by Murdoch's interest in such magic. Even though she creates what appears to be a traditional novel, the traditional worldview of Aristotelian identity, substance, and causality are not at its center.[48] Like *Finnegans Wake* her novel simulates some of the characteristics of prose without a center. The characters, especially philosophers and psychoanalysts, are looking for magic; only magic, which no one finds, can fill the void. *The Message to the Planet* reveals Murdoch's interest in postmodern art, art that copies another kind of reality, reality that does not have a formal wholeness or refer back to a center.[49]

Murdoch's sense of comedy and her sense of drama, however, demand a juxtaposition of many views, making the reader experience and recognize the contingency basic to existence. As disconcerting as her methods can be, their purpose is to prepare the reader for the bizarre unveilings of reality that do occur in real life. For example, she addresses this kind of aesthetic and stylistic problem in *Rencontres* when she considers whether she tied up too many loose ends in *A Word Child*. She argues for her own narrative decision and then questions its effectiveness:

> I think this is always a temptation that a novelist has (particularly a novelist like myself who is interested in plots and patterns), that he must relate everybody to everybody, and that I related Crystal to Gunnar through that rather odd incident. I don't mind the incident itself because this is the sort of odd thing that seems to me not impossible to tell in such a context—how Gunnar seduces Crystal on the night that Anne dies—but this very close connection of Crystal with Gunnar was perhaps a mistake. (Chevalier, *Rencontres* 74)

I disagree with Murdoch. She has revealed mysterious and indeterminate phenomena that the reader would have otherwise ignored. Her illustration manifests "the conflict" that she says she always feels "between character and plot" (*Rencontres* 74).

While both Joyce and Murdoch deal with the disturbing cultural paradoxes of birth, death, and rebirth, and while Murdoch's texts create excess in uncategorizable visions enclosed in uncategorizable forms, as Joyce's do, Murdoch's novels are experimental in ways that Joyce's are not. For both, masochism is a crucial issue. Joyce is so enthralled in his own battle with masochism and sadomasochism that he is unable to offer or examine many perspectives on this subject.

A useful cultural icon Joyce misses but Murdoch resurrects is the myth of the slaying of Marsyas. Appropriating this myth, Murdoch makes her characters more poignant in their desire to escape the slavery inherent in their system, an imitation (simulation) of human life, and to escape the masochism that results from total acceptance of any culture's ideology. Helping to cement my understanding of her reasons for celebrating excess and for creating potential cacophony in her forms, her interview with A. Wilson on the BBC TV Booker program reinforces the paradoxical complexity she achieves by having Bradley Pearson's skin flayed. By recording her animation upon seeing the Titian painting *The Slaying of Marsyas*, the program demonstrates the many conflicting desires that she as an artist holds in suspension (see chapter 8, n. 1).

She reveals the Faustian searches in life and leads the reader into comprehending them, if not dabbling in them. In this sense her novels can be dangerous. Conradi comes the closest to alerting the reader to the chaotic energy Murdoch taps into. He points to the negative sublime in the philosophy of Carel in *The Time of the Angels*:

> Suppose the truth were awful, suppose it was just a black pit. . . . Suppose only evil were real. . . . Who could face this? The philosophers never even tried. All philosophy has taught a facile optimism, even Plato did so. . . . All altruism feeds the fat ego. . . . We do not know the truth because as I told you it cannot be endured. People will endlessly conceal from themselves that good is only good if one is good for nothing. . . . One must be good for nothing. . . . [T]hat is why goodness is impossible for us human beings. (TA 163–65)

Murdoch dares to give her characters free rein in this dangerous world of the novel. To achieve the paradoxical and cacophonous, she experiments with form and narrative effects. As I have demonstrated in earlier chapters, her subversive philosophy and her writing process lead her to create dialogic novels, not monological totalities. Perhaps Bloom prefers monologic novels and wants Murdoch to fit his vision. Murdoch has no desire, however, to cover over contradictions: she is intent on empowering inconsistency and contingency.

Attending to the whole configuration of Murdoch's world of the novel demonstrates that she creates narrative strategies to record mental and perceptual changes in her pilgrims, strategies that some critics look at atomistically. But using such atomistic methods exclusively to analyze Murdoch's texts fails to deal with her philosophical and psychological goals. Using a holistic approach to explore the novels is more valuable than condemning her techniques, like the critic who decries her "cloak and dagger violence and shock tactics" (Kuehl, "Iris Murdoch" 353). It is a mistake to assume that Murdoch uses these conventions or clichés of the novelist's trade merely to create sensational effects rather than to create serious fiction. On the contrary, she employs these methods to demonstrate that good artistic form reflects life's inexplicable complexity.

 Conclusion

Dame Iris Murdoch's novels mirror British and Anglo-American society at the close of the twentieth century, a society that echoes Dostoevsky's "All is permitted" (quoted in Conradi, *Saint* 91). Such freedom demands a moral philosophy. Readers conditioned to seeing well-known authors as egotistical celebrities can be caught off-guard by Murdoch's humility. Her moral vision, her intellectual tough-mindedness, and her remarkable success as a storyteller argue for her candidacy as a Nobel laureate in literature. She is audacious in retracing the history of the novel form, revitalizing techniques now considered out of fashion, if not illegitimate—techniques that evoke the ineluctable fears, desires, and hopes of her sometimes puzzled readers. Unlike many contemporary novelists, she refuses to console readers by fulfilling their expectations, whether those expectations be modernist or postmodernist. In her essay "Against Dryness," she reminds the reader that only the "greatest art invigorates without consoling, and defeats our attempts . . . to use it as magic" (20). Instead, she uses the novel form in all its richness and variety as the best novelists always have, to make palpable the multiple layers of human experience, the contradictory arguments in each person's mind. In addition, she undermines what she represents, teaching readers to unlearn their ways of perceiving.

Her independence and her security as a thinker give her the authority to subvert and enrich the realistic novel with forms from other genres. This former Oxford philosophy don has written twenty-five novels, three books of philosophy, five plays, a libretto, and a philosophic dialogue, as well as criticism, verse, and numerous uncollected philosophical and critical essays. She has not only published in many genres but is an expert at mixing modes that until recently struck critics as incompatible. Drawing from British intellectual discourse as well as from such genres as fairy tale and psychological drama, Murdoch interjects a strong, irreverent, carnivalesque flavor into her texts. Furthermore, when she mixes genres, and mixes techniques within genres, a chemical rather than a physical change occurs.[1] Indeed, she has been breathing new life into the novel form for nearly four decades by using the analogical to destabilize Aristotelian logic.

Since she began publishing fiction in the mid-1950s, academics, identifying with the canonical hierarchy, have been sniping at Murdoch for clinging to old-fashioned ways. Some critics have severely criticized, even belittled, her novels for depending on sensational effects, for lacking depth of characterization, for imitating nonstandard language, and for achieving frivolous ends. Nor do readers always value her surprises, the erratic movements of her plots. The controversy about Murdoch's fiction is so great that Robert Detweiler's little book *Iris Murdoch's* The Unicorn begins with the following quotation from John Fowles's novel *The Magus:* "every year the critics revive the argument of whether her fiction is erratic ladies' magazine caliber or genuinely first-rate, whether she is a philosopher addicted to slightly old-fashioned narrative or an authentic intellectual novelist." Fowles's novel, Detweiler explains, includes a

> dinner-party conversation among some Englishmen living in Athens:
> "Has anyone read Murdoch's latest?"
> "Couldn't stand it."
> "Oh, I rather enjoyed it." (*Murdoch's* Unicorn 5)

Fowles's use of untagged stichomythic dialogue, a device now considered Murdochian, is a playful way of poking fun at Murdoch. The label *Murdochian* reflects Fowles's irony—and her own. Similarly, a running gag in the 1990 BBC film *Antonia and Jane* involves a character's aversion to Murdoch's novels—and to the beau for whom foreplay amounts to having his partner read the blurb of *The Sandcastle* aloud in bed.

Many factors cause critics to be flippant about Murdoch's novels. Some critics do not notice how formidable the texts are because they accept Murdoch's humble, self-deprecating comments about them as straightforward evaluations. Having listened to her stated goals over many years, they look for those goals in her novels to remain unchanged, as if in the 1950s she could have articulated her goals for the 1970s and beyond. Murdoch is so gently ironic that readers can miss her humor, sometimes finding the novels depressing or taking jokes as serious statements. The many violently different responses to her novels demonstrate that they are visceral as well as cerebral works. The magnificent complexity of the novels is a problem for some; her multigenre approach can be distracting to others. Often readers of Murdoch do not know that they are being lovingly flayed. The British middle class, in whom Terry Eagleton thinks Murdoch is overly absorbed, are most decidedly the intellectuals whose skin she is peeling back in her comedies.

As the preceding chapters argue, Murdoch's goal is to create "a house fit for free characters to live in" (SBR); furthermore, she has worked toward finding methods of patterning that give her characters maximum freedom and that challenge her own authority. Requiring narrative methods that encourage contingency, and knowing, for example, that Wittgenstein's analogical methods were in part intended to preserve mystery, she eschews a logical approach for an analogical one, focusing on the correspondence between equivalent entities. Murdoch is exploring what Kristeva calls "a logic of relations and analogy rather than of substance and inference" (WDN 85). She learned from Shakespeare and other writers certain conventional methods that allowed her as a maturing writer to find her individual rhythm: repetition of parallels and ironic and parodic juxtapositions, jarring allusions, and surprising syntax. Perhaps she and her characters have irreconcilable wishes that generate further contingency.

Several of Murdoch's understandings of the world are tied to paradoxical forms. In her stance as religious agnostic, she explores the possibility of morality in the twentieth century. Because she has so long been a sedate revolutionary, many mistake her critique of the twentieth century as unquestioning acceptance. Because she is a loving person, some mistake her kindness for approval of the status quo. She, however, appropriates the metaphor of Apollo's lovingly flaying Marsyas as a cultural myth, demonstrating that she has always identified with elements that would subvert the status quo. Conradi suggests Murdoch's position when he says that her novels are original in addressing "what it means to come from one of the luckier, stabler societies or sections within that society, in an unlucky century, but avoid false piety about either that luck or that misfortune" (*Saint* 13). He and many others insist that Murdoch's work will last because it reveals something new about the novel. Conradi, seeming to respond to Frank Kermode's suggestion that Murdoch is the heir to E. M. Forster, argues against drawing any narrow parallel: "Murdoch is a better novelist than either Forster or Woolf" (*Saint* 284). Harold Bloom praises her while questioning the stance that makes her unique: "The aesthetic puzzle is whether the comic story and the Platonic kernel can be held together by Murdoch's archaic stance as an authorial will. And yet no other contemporary British novelist seems to me of Murdoch's eminence" (*Iris*

Murdoch 7). If she is "the most intelligent novelist the English have produced since George Eliot" and "the only Henry James our age deserves or is likely to produce" (Fletcher, "Iris Murdoch" 547, 560), then critics must take a more exacting look at her goals. The point Elizabeth Dipple made so astutely at the beginning of the 1980s is still true: "criticism of Murdoch is still at a naive stage" (*Work* x). I believe that, taking a cue from Murdoch's *The Sovereignty of Good*, readers can move beyond such a "naive stage" by examining the quality I describe as "patterned aimlessness." She uses both terms but not together. In *The Sovereignty of Good*, she says that "form in art is properly the simulation of the self-contained aimlessness of the universe" (86). Her expression names the macrocosm; mine, the microcosm of her carefully crafted art.

Rather than lumping together all twenty-five of Murdoch's novels, I have chosen to focus on the later ones, emphasizing those from the 1970s and 1980s. During these two decades of this postmodern era, Murdoch redefined the boundaries of the novel of formal realism to address moral issues that are still unresolved at the end of the twentieth century. Murdoch has always defied categorization. Her willingness to struggle against Aristotelianism and to use analogical thought allows her to ignore the expectation of clear causes, fixed referents, and essence. Her daring to set items side by side with no causal connection—the sacred and the profane, the ugly and the beautiful, the good and the bad—shows that she does not settle for binary oppositions. Being a "Wittgensteinian neo-Platonist" (Chevalier, *Rencontres* 90), she instead puts each item in a continuum beside something else, multiplying the series of choices for author, characters, and readers. In *An Accidental Man*, an anti-Aristotelian fairy tale, the kind and beautiful Dorina Grey escapes the harassment of her irresponsible husband to relax alone in a bathtub and dies when the hairdryer electrocutes her; the same husband, driving drunk, kills an innocent child; at the close of the novel, he marries Dorina's beautiful sister and lives ever after. In *The Sea, The Sea*, a powerful theater director lures a youth from his mother but does not pay attention to his safety and allows him to drown. In *The Severed Head*, a sophisticated wine merchant has the responsibility of chauffeuring from the airport a woman whose ugly, fat legs distract him from her other attributes, but later, when he falls down the steps into the lap of this seemingly unattractive woman, he instantly falls in love with her. Such instances illustrate that Murdoch's characters are free to act their parts without the help of logic. In her interview with W. K. Rose, she explains that she tries to create characters with "depth and ordinariness, and accidentalness" ("Interview" 11), characters who escape from the planned structure and create a reality of their own. Since she lives with her characters for a long time before she actually writes their novel, she allows them to work out their own problems in her imagination.

Insisting that the reader participate also in the chaos of existence, Murdoch supplies surprising data, and descriptions rather than explanations. Setting in conflict absurd human actions and equally mysterious movements of the universe, she makes the reader pay attention to the drama. Murdoch allows the reader to absorb her view of reality at his or her own rate. Her novels capture the terrifying contingency of life so that the reader recognizes that explanations are not usually available. Her method serves this purpose by revealing the confusion, the pathos, and the incompleteness of reality.

Readers can see better if they take the time to learn to compare differences as the artist does, to see what the artist sees. In discussing how crucial vision is, Murdoch suggests that training in seeing is valuable: "The art critic can help us if we are in the presence of the same object and if we know something about his scheme of concepts." Murdoch argues that the art critic helps "our ability to move towards 'seeing more,' towards 'seeing what he sees'" (SG 32). In *Philosophical Investigations*, Wittgenstein insists that the mystery of life can only be shown, not explained. He left *Philosophical Investigations* as a series of disconnected notations because he humbly believed that attempts at synthesis would distort the process being recorded. In his view, a philosopher's job is to place examples of reality before the public; the philosopher distorts reality when he pigeonholes the data into logical categories: explanations are illusions.[2]

In her vast novelistic scheme, Murdoch seems to view each novel in a way similar to the way Wittgenstein sees his philosophy, as "a number of sketches of [mental] landscapes which were made in the course of these long and involved journeyings. The same or almost the same points were always being approached afresh from different directions, and new sketches made" (PI ix). In providing a series of stories that grind away at some of the same human dilemmas, Murdoch is like Monet painting the cathedral at Rouen over and over in varying lights to "get it right." Her own fictional process and style reflect her abiding interest in Wittgenstein's conviction that a writer reveals bits of truth through showing transactions rather than through explaining. Her process, a way of helping readers "move towards 'seeing more,'" requires the reader to experience repetition, similarity, and contiguity—the repetition of themes, characters, and incidents. Murdoch achieves labyrinthine parallels by situating her character types, both side by side in strata with others like them, like the ants in Escher's print, and vertically, along the deep structure of the cave analogy in her world of the novel. The character types, each of whose personalities determine their potential moral choices, have the potential of moving toward the sun: some exit the cave and are disoriented by the light; others, as they climb, become confused upon seeing the fire; and others remain chained in the cave. The inevitable comparing and contrasting of dilemmas that characters experience from novel to novel give the reader a broad panorama of perspectives. In using the laws of association—contiguity and similarity—she is like the Demiurge. She is free to re-create patterns similar to those she created earlier because her goal is to "get it right" and to visualize an aesthetic continuum and a moral continuum.

The advantage of this model is that it allows Murdoch to achieve a continuum of perspectives, much like looking at the consecutive frames in a piece of film. The pieces of Murdoch's film are stylized; her divisions seem arbitrary. She need not adhere to the rubrics of formal logic; nor does she have to limit herself to one perspective or one voice or one conclusion. She juxtaposes a series of bizarre events in order to reveal jarring unveilings of reality. She is like the self-reflexive artist in Peter Greenaway's film *The Draughtsman's Contract*, setting up her easel and viewing and framing the potentialities of each scene.

Murdoch's interest in diagnosing the symptoms of a universe without God, and her insistence on working out ethical imperatives in such a universe, are undeniable. Putting on alternatively the masks of the Demiurge, Eros, and Prospero, Murdoch creates cacophony by juxtaposing suffering and comedy. She finds Grunewald's Christ an accurate depiction of suffering, not romanticized and prettified. Perhaps the same otherworldly grotesqueness draws her to Simone Weil's experience. The ascetic holds a magnificence for Murdoch as a result of Weil's understanding of suffering and affliction, the symptoms of which are "difficulty of breathing, a vice closing about the heart" (MGM 502). Murdoch is an expert at discovering whatever techniques can produce a wrenching—the clashing of the human mind against such mysteries. Murdoch's complex perspectives on life inspire her multigeneric approach, and her classical background, of course, contributes further to that complexity.

Conclusion

She seems inevitably drawn to periods of history when drama held sway. Her novels manifest some of the characteristics of Greek tragedy, such as pervasive irony of all kinds, rushing of peripeteia, moral crises, family triangles, fated cycles, and the sublime. She works to create or pattern a jumble in order to capture "the accidental, the idiosyncratic happenings of life" (AD 9). Charles Arrowby's use of the theatrical reflects Murdoch's as she calls on her imagination to represent and critique the contemporary world's excess.

In addition, her emphasis is on the varying shades of illusion. Her aesthetic goals require that she employ, among other kinds of disorientation, sudden visual change. Visual metaphors are necessary to her description of her concepts about love, art, and language. Her belief is that "human beings are obscure to each other, in certain respects which are particularly relevant to morality, unless they are mutual objects of attention or have common objects of attention. . . . We develop language in the context of looking" (SG 33). If she wants to give the reader the opportunity to experience her multiple positions, she must find techniques for demonstrating the truism at the level of human visual apparatus and then at a visceral level. *The Black Prince* is expressly about this issue. Her emphasis on gestalt in the novel, when Bradley mistakes Julian for a Hindu priest and mistakes pieces of a love letter for flower petals, illustrates the problem from a perceptual standpoint. One sees, then, how the two methods of switching gestalt and juxtaposing items work together: to be vital, humans must pay attention.

Murdoch's novels are attempts to show the reader the possibilities of the future that erupt from the cauldron of her imagination into her conscious mind. The reader does well to attend to the novels, to see what Murdoch sees. She experiments with certain methods to create the moods and sensations necessary for that participation. Because of the discrepancy between the human visual apparatus and the human capacity to pay attention, people often missee and misinterpret. Perhaps like the Greek tragic heroes, readers would do well to be shocked into reality. Murdoch's patterned aimlessness breaks in on the reader's presuppositions.

 Notes

PREFACE

1 What interests her about invention is to a large extent the same as what she describes in this passage from *The Fire and the Sun*: "What interests Plato in nature is pattern, necessity which is the test of truth: what turns opinion into certainty" (43). When Murdoch argues that patterns are every artist's medium, she includes herself and Plato as well as some of her artist-characters.

CHAPTER ONE *Metaphysics as a Guide to Morals* and Iris Murdoch's Ongoing Dialogues with Other Philosophers

1 Letter to the author. Murdoch continues: "My books are just about the jumble of the mysterious world as we know it."
2 Murdoch says art and philosophy uncover the same reality: "The artist makes us see what is, in a sense manifestly and edifyingly open to discussion, *there* (real), but unseen before, and the metaphysician does this too" (MGM 433).
3 Murdoch does not distinguish in the usual way among structuralism, deconstruction, modernism, and postmodernism. She chooses to use the "old original term [structuralism] as it is informative and less ephemeral" (MGM 5).
4 Murdoch says that Derrida employs "the old idea of total coherence . . . to inspire a way of life which excludes the value of individually establishable truths" (MGM 197).
5 Paul de Man said in 1986 that "the real debate of literary theory is not with its polemical opponents but rather with its own methodological assumptions and possibilities . . . ; resistance to the introduction of linguistic terminology in aesthetic and historical discourse about literature is only one particular version of a question that cannot be reduced to a specific historical situation and called modern, post-modern, post-classical or romantic" (*Resistance to Theory* 12).
6 Murdoch says she is "aware of the danger of inventing [her] own Plato" (MGM 510–11).
7 For Murdoch, art and language point to a reality, or value, beyond themselves. For example, impressionism, as well as cubism and abstract painting, she insists, have demonstrated that the artist is "not a demythologising 'ironist' . . . [but] authoritatively asserts the presence of the *transcendent object*." She values "the familiar

concepts of individual object, individual person, individual meaning, those old and cherished 'limited wholes'" (MGM 5).

8 Ved Mehta categorizes Murdoch in the late 1940s as a part of Oxford's squadron of feminine philosophers along with Anscombe and Foot: "they and Richard Hare make up the constabulary of moral philosophy at the university" (*Fly and the Fly-Bottle* 53). The three women were "united," however, "in their objection to Hare's view that the human being was the monarch of the universe, that he constructed his values from scratch" (*Fly and the Fly-Bottle* 56). Murdoch began to lecture at Oxford as a Fellow of St. Anne's College, and she served until 1963 as university tutor in philosophy (Tominaga and Schneidermeyer, *Murdoch and Sparks* xi).

9 Also marked "Chapter IX," this portion (125–36) survives in the *Sartre* manuscript housed at the University of Iowa Libraries.

10 Jacques Lacan writes that there is no sense of a separate self until a third party breaks up the symbiotic relationship of the child to its mother. He thinks the Other is the locus of the constitution of the subject. The deconstructive act uncovers in a text the *aporia*, or gaps, that reveal the author's blind spots. Paul de Man writes that deconstruction is unearthing "hidden articulations and fragmentations within assumedly monadic totalities" (quoted in Lentricchia and McLaughlin, *Critical Terms* 215).

11 Preferring "the language of encounter or dialogue, not contemplation," Buber charges Plato with "opticis[ing] thought" (quoted in MGM 463).

12 For proof that good exists, Murdoch recommends the use of common sense and intuition rather than the arguments of philosophers, which are most often circular arguments for what is already known. She suggests that individuals look empirically at their own conscious activity: "the idea of perfection haunts all our activity, and we are well aware of how we try to blot it out." Showing great respect for the nonphilosophical person, Murdoch believes that "the ordinary fellow 'just knows,' for one is speaking of something which is in a sense obvious, the unique nature of morality" (MGM 428).

13 Murdoch even attributes moderation to Wittgenstein, who says that philosophy "leaves everything as it is" (quoted in MGM 2).

14 Murdoch's use of the word *ordinary* does not imply a hierarchy of value on which philosophers or thinkers inhabit higher rungs than other people. Human beings are ordinary when they are not occupying a particular role. For example, Murdoch says that a male represents ordinary humans and that ordinary human beings continually compare and contrast "language with the *extra-linguistic* world" (MGM 195).

15 Murdoch's method in *Metaphysics as a Guide to Morals* is similar to Wittgenstein's in *Philosophical Investigations*: "traveling over a field of thought criss-cross in every

direction" (PI ix). For instance, Murdoch returns to a subject, and sometimes to a specific example, at various places in her text. In chapter 3 she cites Wittgenstein's *Culture and Value* to make a point about transcendence (MGM 75); ten chapters later, she cites the same page of the same text (MGM 415) to make a similar point.

16 Murdoch foregrounds the similar optical view of theologian Martin Buber that "the Greeks established the hegemony of sight over the other senses"; the optical world became the world (MGM 461), and the optical character became part of philosophy. Her only complaint about Buber's stance is his blindness to Plato's irony, an aporia that she also finds in Cornford. She quotes Buber, for example, as saying that "the character of the contemplation of particular objects . . . [is that] the object of this visual thought is the universal as existence or as a reality higher than existence.

17 Edwards says that Wittgenstein discusses the conception of *showing* twenty-three times in the *Tractatus* (*Ethics Without Philosophy* 14–15).

18 When Wittgenstein wrote the *Tractatus*, he was blinded by the assumption of Western philosophy that human beings can have views or pictures of reality. He also presaged his later theory by contending that "ethical matters lie outside the realm of thought . . . and must be *shown* rather than *said*" (Edwards, *Ethics Without Philosophy* 73).

19 "The world is nothing," according to Edwards's paraphrase of Wittgenstein, "but a collection of contingent states of affairs, altering concatenations of eternally existent simple objects; these contingent configurations are utterly independent of one another; belief in the causal nexus is superstition. In this atomistic world there is no sense of life to be found; there is only what happens. Neither is the sense of life to be found in thought, for thought is always thought about the world" (*Ethics Without Philosophy* 204).

20 As Murdoch commented to Mehta, "Most English philosophers . . . share certain assumptions of Wittgenstein and Austin" (*Fly and the Fly-Bottle* 57).

21 Edwards describes Wittgenstein's perspective in this way.

22 Murdoch borrows the word *attention* from Simone Weil (SG 34).

23 Edwards focuses exclusively on Wittgenstein rather than placing him in the same context in which Murdoch's *Metaphysics as a Guide to Morals* discusses him. Furthermore, Edwards goes further than Murdoch: he infers from the entire body of Wittgenstein's work, and from Wittgenstein's vision of the sound human understanding revealed in *Philosophical Investigations*, the centrality of Wittgenstein's ethical vision and religious sensibility to his oeuvre.

24 Wittgenstein argues that traditional Western scientific philosophy leads to a diseased, narcissistic human understanding when it is dominated by logic alone (Edwards, *Ethics Without Philosophy* 224–29). In *Remarks on the Foundations of*

Notes to Chapter One

Mathematics, Wittgenstein says, "The philosopher is the man who must cure himself of many sicknesses of the understanding before he can arrive at the notion of a sound human understanding" (157).
25 Murdoch's clear examination of nineteenth- and twentieth-century philosophy in the draft of her unpublished chapter of *Sartre* (n. 9, above) helps explain her movement away from both existentialism and scientific realism.
26 Criticism of Murdoch's novels often refers to her examination of "totalitarian man" and "ordinary language man."
27 The dark condition Murdoch calls the void can be the result of suffering, guilt, desperation, bereavement, emptiness, loss of personality, or loss of energy (MGM 500).

CHAPTER TWO   Iris Murdoch's Wittgensteinian Voice

1 "She is both fantasist and realist," Bloom writes in introducing the Chelsea House volume of essays on Murdoch, "each on principle, but her abrupt modulations between the two visions sometimes seem less than fully controlled. Her novels rush by us, each a successful entertainment, but none perhaps fully distinct from the others in our memories" (*Iris Murdoch* 1). If the characters in *The Black Prince* and *The Sea, The Sea* do not distinguish themselves in readers' minds, the reader is probably not concentrating.
2 Yet, as much as Murdoch disagrees with Derrida's view that language is a deterministic sea, readers like Bloom do interpret her novels as dramatizing just such a deterministic trend.
3 Edwards uses the term *lens* throughout *Ethics Without Philosophy* (212, 213, 238). He compares the images in the human mind to lenses: just as one lens gathers some wavelengths of light and others gather different ones, so images gather some knowledge and are unable to absorb and reflect other kinds of knowledge. No lens gathers all the light.
4 Terry Eagleton says in "Wittgenstein and His Friends" that Wittgenstein's work is dialogical, arguing that Socratic irony is dialogical (77). Murdoch has written two Platonic dialogues in *Acastos*. Often theorists refer to the dialogical as dialogism or double-voicedness. Claudine Herrmann is especially good at differentiating among dramatic dialogue, the dialectic, and the dialogic (see chapter 4, n. 3).
5 Wittgenstein argues that an "'alteration of perception/sensibility'" is the "goal of good philosophical practice" (quoted in Edwards, *Ethics Without Philosophy* 135).
6 Wittgensteinian philosophy "is a battle against the bewitchment of our intelli-

gence by means of language" (PI. 2:109). Perhaps her twenty-fifth novel, *The Green Knight*, also achieves this pattern.

7 Nieli provides a concise historical summary: "The 'Vienna Circle'. . . was the name adopted by the group of mathematicians and natural science oriented philosophers organized in the late 1920s by Moritz Schlick, then professor of philosophy at the University of Vienna. Numbered among its members were the mathematicians Hans Hahn, Karl Menger, and Kurt Goedel, the sociologist Otto Neurath, and the philosophers Victor Kraft, Friedrich Waismann, Rudolf Carnap and Herbert Feigl" (Nieli, *Wittgenstein* 3).

8 Mehta writes, "John said he imagined that one-third of his time had been spent doing philosophy and preparing for examinations in logic and moral and classical philosophy" (*Fly and the Fly-Bottle* 15). In her later essays Murdoch makes clear that she would have preferred even more emphasis on the moral and classical philosophy and less on logic.

9 After dabbling a little in the history of different schools, John was asked to read Ludwig Wittgenstein's "Philosophical Investigations," A. J. Ayer's "Language, Truth and Logic" and "The Problem of Knowledge," P. F. Strawson's "Introduction to Logical Theory" and "Individuals: An Essay in Descriptive Metaphysics," issues of the journal *Mind and the Proceedings of the Aristotelian Society*—the richest repositories of Oxford philosophy (Mehta, *Fly and the Fly-Bottle* 16).

10 Before receiving the Sarah Smithson Studentship in Philosophy at Newham College, Cambridge University, in 1947, Murdoch spent four years as a civil servant, during which time she was Assistant Principal in the British Treasury in London (1942).

11 See Byatt, *Degrees of Freedom* 15–16. I discuss the Wittgensteinian metaphor of the net in chapter 3.

12 I appropriate Mikhail Bakhtin's concept here to set the stage for my excavation of such strata in chapter 8. Murdoch acts as an architect-choreographer who creates the strata in which particular characters can act out and define their rituals. "Languages are continually stratifying," Bakhtin writes, "under pressure of the centrifugal force, whose project everywhere is to challenge fixed definitions. Represented characters in a novel exist in order to find, reject, redefine a stratum of their own; formal authors exist to coordinate these stratifying impulses" (DI 433). Bakhtin's habit of personifying and dramatizing these theoretical concepts makes his model appealing, accessible, and exact. Murdoch selects characters from a storehouse in her mind, perhaps a space that itself resembles a Bakhtinian stratum.

13 Clark and Holquist describe Nikolai Bakhtin's conversations with Wittgenstein (*Mikhail Bakhtin*).

Notes to Chapter Two

14 Clark and Holquist's information comes from the Nicholas Bakhtin Archive, University of Birmingham Library, Box 8, Envelope 16; and from Fanya Pascal, Roy Pascal's wife (*Mikhail Bakhtin* 20).
15 Wittgenstein's and Murdoch's statements about "the ordinary" carry on the terminology of philosophical tradition. Russell Nieli characterizes Wittgenstein's attitude here: "Common people, he thought, know the difference between right and wrong, between justice and injustice, even if, in actual decisions, they don't always make the right choices. They are genuinely aware of beauty, of truthfulness, of love, and can be heard all the time talking about these things" (*Wittgenstein* 181).
16 Murdoch identifies with teachers at all levels. The importance of her education to the subject matter of her novels is striking, as is the number of teachers in her novels and the coincidence between a character's goodness and that character's invisibility. Fletcher quotes Leila Eveleigh, a former teacher at Badminton, as describing Murdoch as homesick at first but good at hockey and gifted in painting. He explains that Murdoch painted for Miss Baker, the principal, a picture of Lynmouth Harbor, the school's alternate home during World War II ("Iris Murdoch" 548). Murdoch points out, when asked about her female characters, that being good often means being without power or being marginalized: "They're not self-assertive. I think that a lot of such people who are goodish may *seem*" to lack identity (Heusel, "Dialogue" 12).
17 Guy Openshaw does have many of the characteristics of these four charismatic thinkers.
18 Even though Murdoch insists she has no models for her characters, George Beach Whitman, proprietor of Shakespeare and Co., Paris, claims to be the model for Bledyard.
19 As they find her, and rightfully so, to be more subversive, uneasiness emerges in the critics' readings. Many critics were stupified in 1978 when *The Sea, The Sea* opened with a sea monster; Dipple, on the other hand, believes that that novel initiated Murdoch's "recent expansive style" (*Unresolvable Plot* 185).
20 Nieli bases his analysis on interpretations by Brian F. McGuinness, G. H. von Wright, and Wittgenstein's friend Malcolm Norman.
21 Wittgenstein goes on to declare: "So if it is correct to say that humour was stamped out in Nazi Germany, that does not mean that people were not in good spirits, or anything of that sort, but something much deeper and more important" (quoted in Nieli, *Wittgenstein* 257).
22 See Brian McGuinness, *Young Ludwig*, for the Wittgenstein family's flight from their Jewish heritage, especially pp. 1–2 and 52–53.
23 Wittgenstein dictated "the 'Blue Book' (though he did not call it that) to his class

in Cambridge during the session 1933–34, and he had stencilled copies made. He dictated the 'Brown Book' to two of his pupils (Francis Skinner and Alice Ambrose) during 1934–35. He had only three typed copies made of this" (Wittgenstein, *The Blue and Brown Books* v).

24 Eagleton defines such dialogic discourse: "[Bakhtin's] literary interests are accordingly in those genres—'carnival,' Menippean satire, and indeed for Bakhtin the 'novel' as such—which embody some mighty 'polyphonic' contestation of discourse, genres whose sociality is inscribed in their very form; one language inhering within, relativising and decentring another; one form of discourse invading, subverting, citing, framing, parodying or dismantling another" ("Wittgenstein's Friends" 76–77).

25 Wittgenstein writes in *Philosophical Investigations*, "My aim is: to teach you to pass from a piece of disguised nonsense to something that is patent nonsense" (PI. 1:464).

26 Besides this example that Edwards provides (*Ethics Without Philosophy* 120–21), Wittgenstein cites Lewis Carroll twice in *Philosophical Investigations*.

CHAPTER THREE   Iris Murdoch's Wittgensteinian Voice: *A Word Child*, *Nuns and Soldiers*, and *The Sea, The Sea*

1 Aiken is entirely accurate in asserting that "language, literally, figuratively, and philosophically, dominates *A Word Child*" ("Accidental World" 33). The *Tractatus* was published in German in 1921 under a different title and then in English (in London) in 1922.

2 Murdoch has said that she studies Russian to get beyond her own grammar.

3 She simulates this reality by layering strata made up of different kinds of characters who have family resemblances.

4 Byatt goes on to quote Annandine: "What I speak of is the real decision as we experience it; and here the movement away from theory and generality is the movement towards truth. All theorizing is flight. We must be ruled by the situation itself and this is unutterably particular. Indeed it is something to which we can never get close enough, however hard we may try as it were to creep under the net" (quoted in *Degrees of Freedom* 15).

5 Murdoch is a postmodernist writer in her rejection of at least three elements of High Modernism: its sophisticated formal experimentation, its elitism (such as Pound, Eliot, Woolf, and Joyce displayed), and its tragic sense of alienation, which she calls romantic solipsism. The characteristics Ihab Hassan attributes to postmodern writing in *Paracriticisms: Seven Speculations of Our Time* are obviously characteristics of Murdoch's work, all of the characteristics not being exclusively postmodernist:

Notes to Chapter Three

indeterminancy and contingency, irony, deferral of meaning, and subversion of positivism.
6 Murdoch discusses public and private language in "The Idea of Perfection" (SG 12–15).
7 Plato, according to Murdoch, says, "The sensible world appears as a fallen realm which is a gross irrelevant hindrance to true knowledge, philosophy, and virtue. Hence philosophers 'practice dying' " (FS 48).
8 I appreciate William Rogers's referring me to this text. Henze's note following "Ode II, XX" explains the poet's theme: "Horace prophesies his own immortality. The image of poet-bird has been used by other writers. Both Plato and Euripides use the transformation of poet to swan" (Horace, *Odes* 113). Stanza 3 captures the metamorphosis:

> Already now the roughening skin shrinks down
> Upon my legs; above I become transformed,
> I am a white-winged bird, and through my
> Fingers and shoulders light plumes are sprouting.
>   (*Odes* 112)

9 Murdoch describes such a moral change in a 1987 interview: "The human task is to become unselfish, to unself. . . . It's something that's got to become a way of life. . . . Some people sit in halls of meditation for years, and then perhaps find they haven't really changed themselves. On the other hand, 'invisible' people can be very good" (Heusel, "Dialogue" 6).

CHAPTER FOUR   Radical Otherness: *Sartre, Romantic Rationalist*; *Sovereignty of Good*; and *The Fire and the Sun*

1 In his study of Murdoch, Conradi argues convincingly that her later novels are dark comedies that follow in the great European tradition; they are not philosophical tracts.
2 Terry Eagleton, grounded in the late twentieth-century understanding of the way language works, espouses Jacques Derrida's description of the way all writing, including philosophy, works—that it repeats itself instead of telling the truth: "A text may 'show' us something about the nature of meaning and signification which it is not able to formulate as a proposition" (quoted in *Theory* 134). Derrida rejects the literary/nonliterary opposition: language creates "a continual flickering, spilling and defusing of meaning—what Derrida calls 'dissemination' "; "all language, for

Derrida, displays this 'surplus' over exact meaning, is always threatening to outrun and escape the sense which tries to contain it" (quoted in *Theory* 134).
3 Discourse is language in use; see Paul Bové, "Discourse." Herrmann is especially good at differentiating among dramatic dialogue, the dialectic, and the dialogic: "Dramatic dialogue splits a single discourse into two or more represented voices without threatening the unity of the author's semantic position; the dialogic represents the struggle between two opposing discourses arising out of different contexts, either semantic or sociohistorical. Unlike the dialectic, which seeks to transcend oppositions by means of a synthetic third, the dialogic resists the reconciliation of opposites by insisting on the reciprocity of two or more antagonistic voices. Both the dialectic and the dialogic are based in theories of conflict, but the former attempts to resolve antitheses in a utopian synthesis while the latter seeks to disrupt the assimilation of differences sought by a monologic discourse" (*Dialogic and Difference* 15).
4 Murdoch questions depth models, the decentering of the world and the self, the rejection of elitist aesthetics and experimental formalism.
5 She proclaims in her opening sentences that "to understand Jean-Paul Sartre is to understand something important about the present time. . . . [H]e has the style of the age" (SRR 7).
6 "Good is still somewhere beyond" (SG 93). Conradi explains that "moral terms, for her, are concrete universals, collections of their material instances. The sole exception is the good itself, which acts both as an inexhaustible fund 'elsewhere' from which we draw energy, and also as a quality here which we dimly and always incompletely intuit in good art and good neighbours" (*Saint* 76).
7 Exploring a few questions is useful to any discussion of Murdoch's texts: What are the implications of Murdoch's bigger question about whether language or the worldview came first? How much has our grammar determined our power structure? Could we be subjective before language taught us a dominant subject position and a subordinate object position? Would a patriarchy such as ours have been inconceivable without a language in which dominant individuals are able to subject a person to objectivity? Did the dominant individuals create the grammar and the syntax? Do the ideas of dominant and subordinate determine the creation of the language positions of subject and object—in other words, determine the grammar of most languages? Must there be an object position before there can be a subject position?
8 As storyteller, Murdoch forgoes name-dropping, mentioning neither Wittgenstein's challenge to Saint Augustine that words do not name objects nor A. J. Ayer's

"verification criterion," "the idea that every basic statement must, in order to be meaningful, be verifiable in isolation" (*Oxford Companion to the Mind* 441).

9 See, for example, Hofstadter's discussion of "this 'vortex' of self" vis-à-vis M. C. Escher's lithograph "Print Gallery" (*Gödel, Escher, and Bach* 714).

10 Murdoch comments that Sartre has a different reason to write about language than British linguistic philosophers have: she sums up Sartre's observations as prescriptions for the way he would like to see language used rather than descriptions of its use (SRR 35).

11 Obvious reasons for drawing an analogy between Murdoch's interest in language theory and Bakhtin's are their fascination with Dostoevsky and their celebration of Martin Buber's I-Thou relationship. Clark and Holquist conclude that "the Bakhtinian self is never whole, since it can exist only dialogically. It is not a substance or essence in its own right but exists only in a tensile relationship with all that is other and, most important, with other selves" (*Mikhail Bakhtin* 65). Otherness and dialogue are the ground of our existence; for Murdoch, radical subjectivism is incomprehensible.

12 Lukács's criticisms include a wide range of modernist habits, according to Murdoch: Lukács charges the western writer, who has evidently lost the aspiration to truth (since such an aspiration would require him to come to terms with Marxism), with portraying his characters in a static, monistic manner as denizens of a simple "factual" world or an equally simple emotional world, rather than as active beings who can only be properly characterised by being shown in reciprocal connexion with the society they inhabit. And he picks on the introspective technique of the modern novelist as a symptom of neglect of the complexity of what he takes to be the real nature of human personality (SRR 37–38).

13 She has destroyed the novels she wrote before publishing *Under the Net*, according to A. S. Byatt.

14 Focusing on Plato helps put in perspective Derrida's preference for writing over speech. Focusing on what Murdoch takes from Plato also permits one to bypass the more recent, ultimately derivative Freudian and Lacanian theories of the other. Reiterating her statement in *Fire and Sun*, Murdoch says: "Whitehead scarcely exaggerates in calling it all [philosophy and art] footnotes to Plato" (FS 78).

15 In Murdoch's view, Derrida, who has become well known for introducing the idea that writing preceded speech, has misinterpreted the "Theory of Forms." To the extent that Derrida has, as Murdoch implies, played tricks with the interpretation of the Forms, he fits Plato's description of the sophist. She speaks to this problem in an answer she made to questions at the symposium on her writing held in Amsterdam in 1986 (see Todd, *Encounters with Iris Murdoch* 66). Murdoch apparently did not

foresee Derrida's self-serving use of Plato when she generously labeled Derrida's essay *La Pharmacie de Platon* "brilliant." When she accepted the Medal of Honor for Literature at the National Arts Club in New York on February 21, 1990, Murdoch referred to Derrida as "that brilliant magician" and described his approach as "destructive" and "a menace." The plausibility of poststructuralism, she insisted, "rests upon a number of things which are of themselves comprehensible but which have been joined together in a misleading way. We are faced with a rather chilling picture. Derrida and one or two poets are able to play with language, like seals sporting with a ball at the surface of the water, while the rest of us are down in the dark. This approach is destructive." These remarks come from notes Dennis Moore took at the dinner; see "Dame Iris Receives Medal of Honor in Manhattan."

16 Murdoch's own philosophical writing grew out of the discourse of Simone Weil, whose spiritual search Murdoch experienced through reading *L'Enracinement*. The discourse of love requires disciplining oneself to do "the work of attention" (SG 34), to explain what it means to alter the consciousness by changing vocabulary—composing oneself.

17 See *The Bonds of Love* by Jessica Benjamin. She uses this image of space to represent women's concerns with others and their relational connection with the world. Benjamin says, "Women make use of the space in-between that is created by shared feeling and discovery" (130).

18 "The Good is still somewhere beyond. . . . 'Good is a transcendent reality' means that virtue is the attempt to pierce the veil of selfish consciousness and join the world as it really is" (SG 93).

CHAPTER FIVE Iris Murdoch's Novelistic Discourses: *An Accidental Man*

1 Even though Murdoch was not familiar in mid-1988 with the theories of Bakhtin, her comprehensive knowledge about language theory and her interest in the Russian worldview, Dostoevsky, and Shakespeare make it likely that she and Bakhtin at least absorbed similar knowledge about language and its theories.

2 Influenced by Kant's philosophy of anthropology—studying what it is to have different worldviews in different ages—Bakhtin uses the concept of layered strata to talk about authors and characters in a novel.

3 Holquist and Emerson explain that the novel, for Bakhtin, is a "de-normatizing and therefore centrifugal force"; they say that Bakhtin, comparing centripetal and centrifugal forces in language and culture, finds that "the rulers and the high poetic genres of any era exercise a centripetal—a homogenizing and hierarchicizing—

influence; the centrifugal (decrowning, dispersing) forces of the clown, mimic and rogue create alternative 'degraded' genres down below" (DI 425).

4 Bakhtin's discussion of dialogism provides the means for determining the success of Murdoch's experiments at placing herself on the same plane as her characters. His speech genre theory is helpful for watching the characters working out their destinies in a world of language.

5 Bakhtin says that "each sphere in which language is used develops its own *relatively stable types of . . . speech genres,*" each with its own content, style, and structure ("Speech Genres" 60).

6 Wittgenstein's disciples and Murdoch acknowledge the possibility of an ideal teacher. Caryl Emerson, in an essay arguing that Tolstoy's work is dialogical, says: "Both [Bakhtin and Tolstoy] are fascinated with the image of the ideal teacher" ("The Tolstoy Connection" 69).

7 See Murdoch's *Acastos* for another kind of dialectic in action.

8 Quoting the anonymous interview published in the *Bookman* in November 1958, Conradi reports that "the terms 'open' and 'closed' were reversed in the [Bookman] interview, Nov. 1958; this appears to have been an error" (*Saint* 277 n. 18).

9 See Christine Wick Sizemore's *A Female Vision of the City*, which includes an analysis of Murdoch's use of *labyrinth*, beginning with her first novel, *Under the Net*.

10 Kristeva writes that "literary structure does not simply *exist* but is generated in relation to *another* structure" (WDN 64–65).

11 It is ironic that Darlene D. Mettler finds *An Accidental Man* one of the few Murdoch novels that has no references to music.

12 Bakhtin says the two arose together out of a new self-consciousness in Roman culture: "In this intimate and familiar atmosphere (one that was, of course, semi-conventionalized) a new private sense of self, suited to the drawing room, began to emerge. A whole series of categories involving self-consciousness and the shaping of a life into a biography—success, happiness, merit—began to lose their public and state significance and passed over to the private and personal plane" (DI 143).

13 The traits of what Bakhtin calls "the sideward glance" are "a certain halting quality to the speech, and its interruption by reservations" (PDP 205).

14 Bakhtin explains that this "styliz[ing] another's style in the direction of that style's own particular tasks merely renders those tasks conventional" (PDP 193).

15 Bakhtin says that "the situation is different with parody. Here, as in stylization, the author again speaks in someone else's discourse, but in contrast to stylization parody introduces into the discourse a semantic intention that is directly opposed

to the original one. The second voice, once having made its home in the other's discourse, clashes hostilely with its primordial host and forces him to serve directly opposing aims. Discourse becomes an arena of battle between two voices" (PDP 193).

CHAPTER SIX Polyphonic Novels: *The Philosopher's Pupil* and *The Black Prince*

1 *Carnivalesque* describes the content and form of virtually all of Murdoch's novels—"a spectacle, but without a stage; a game" (78) mirroring the folk game; erotic orgies, mirroring ancient sacred worship; "phantasmagoria" (WDN 82).
2 According to Bakhtin, the carnivalistic is one of the three basic roots of the novel, along with the epic and the rhetorical (PDP 89).
3 Bakhtin argues that the long tradition of the carnivalesque makes its way through Shakespeare. "Certain elements, embryonic rudiments, early buddings of polyphony can indeed be detected in the dramas of Shakespeare" (DI 33): comic doubling, the fools, Falstaff, the Porter in *Macbeth*, and the gravediggers in *Hamlet* are all illustrations of laughter's "association with death . . . food and drink" (DI 220, 79).
4 The question of the distinction between *dialogue* and *dialogic* has been raised profitably by Herrmann. She puts her discussion into a dialogue with herself to show that her responses are not dialogical because they are all going in the same direction, toward the same end—to show that there is a difference. Bakhtin, who considered Dostoevsky the only truly polyphonic writer, explains this difference between drama and the novel:

> Shakespeare, along with Rabelais, Cervantes, Grimmelshausen and others, belongs to that line of development in European literature in which the early buds of polyphony ripened. . . . But to speak of a fully formed and deliberate polyphonic quality in Shakespeare's dramas is in our opinion simply impossible and for the following reasons:
>
> First, drama is by its very nature alien to genuine polyphony; drama may be multi-leveled, but it cannot contain *multiple worlds*; it permits only one, and not several, systems of measurement.
>
> Secondly, if one can speak at all of a plurality of fully valid voices in Shakespeare, then it would only apply to the entire body of his work and not to individual plays. In essence each play contains only one fully valid voice, the

Notes to Chapter Six

voice of the hero, while polyphony presumes a plurality of fully valid voices within the limits of a single work—for only then may polyphonic principles be applied to the construction of the whole.

Thirdly, the voices in Shakespeare are not points of view on the world to the degree they are in Dostoevsky; Shakespearean characters are not ideologies in the full sense of the word (PDP 33–34).

5 Bakhtin uses *carnival* "in the sense of the totality of all the various festivals, rituals and forms of a carnival type" (PDP 100). He says the Socratic dialogue, like the Menippean satire, "grows out of a carnivalistic folk foundation" (PDP 89–90).
6 Dorothy A. Winsor says that "in her study of Plato, Murdoch implies that she shares his idea of eros, or transformed sexual energy, as a prime force, leading one to reach out of the self to the rest of the world, but in her novels, sexual energy more often remains a drive characters seek to satisfy in self-absorbed ways" ("Solipsistic Sexuality" 121).
7 I use a number of Kristeva's words, such as *grafts*, and I have varied her terms *multistylism* and *multitonality* (WDN 83). Kristeva in her introduction to the French translation of *Problems of Dostoevsky's Poetics* coined the term *intertextuality* for "intertextual dialogue."
8 Conradi says *The Philosopher's Pupil* "feeds off Dostoevski's *The Brothers Karamazov*, with three brothers, one of whom—George—carries out a symbolic act of parricide in attacking his teacher Rozanov, the philosopher of the title" (*Saint* 268). See Anna Lisa Crone, *Rozanov and the End of Literature*, who explains that "Vasilij Rozanov (1856–1919) [was a] great critic, religious thinker, and stylist" (11).
9 Scandal, with all its connotations, is the subject of *The Philosopher's Pupil*—this comedy tending, as Kristeva says carnival does, "towards the scandalous" (WDN 82).
10 Even though in the strict sense *roman fleuve* means a novel that is part of a series about generations within a family, Alfred Kazin, undoubtedly thinking of T. S. Eliot's essay, is right to associate *The Adventures of Huckleberry Finn* with the way the French have used the term: "the novel as a river" ("Afterword" 286). In this sense *roman fleuve* describes *The Philosopher's Pupil*, even though the novel contains only thermal baths instead of a great river.
11 Kristeva mentions that pathological states of the soul are an important ingredient in carnival (WDN 83).
12 Elizabeth Dipple wrote early about the voices vying in *The Black Prince* (*Work*).
13 See Altman, *Epistolarity*, particularly 207.

14 Johnson suggests that Murdoch is perhaps self-conscious about the position of the novelist as voyeur.
15 Murdoch has written that although Freud "remains still the greatest scientist in the field which he opened," neither he nor anyone else can be scientific about the mystery of human beings (SG 51).
16 Bakhtin says that an utterance is not over until the speaker gives up the floor.
17 Here Murdoch is arguing issues advanced by Plato and Wittgenstein. Wittgenstein's position is to respect the perpetual obsolescence of utterances, acknowledging that their demise only seems exaggerated. He wanted to destroy his notebooks and his own published writing, which he had outgrown and with which he had come to disagree.
18 Bakhtin explains this phenomenon this way: "The author may also make use of someone else's discourse for his own purposes, by inserting a new semantic intention into a discourse which already had, and which retains, an intention of its own. Such a discourse, in keeping with its task, must be perceived as belonging to someone else" (PDP 189).
19 As editor, Loxias has asked Francis and three others involved in the events if they "wished to make any comments on [the manuscript], these to be published with the book itself" (BP 343). Francis, dabbling in legal jargon to sound like he is addressing himself to a jury, shocks with glittering generalities and threatens with Freudianism. Following this postscript, the editor says of Francis: "'Dr.' Marloe, who told the truth at the trial, pusillanimously fails to repeat it now" (BP 363).

CHAPTER SEVEN Women's Discourse: *Nuns and Soldiers* and *The Message to the Planet*

1 Bakhtin explains that "indirect discourse 'hears' a message differently; it actively receives and brings to bear in transmission different factors, different aspects of the message than do the other patterns. . . . Analysis is the heart and soul of indirect discourse" (PDP 129).
2 Cheryl Bove and I reached this position independently, as have many other readers. Bove expressed a more conservative position than mine in a paper at the MLA convention in 1990, a longer version of which appears in *Critical Essays on Iris Murdoch*.
3 It is intriguing that Franca is Italian, perhaps having some similarity to the Italian girl in the novel by that name.
4 Murdoch says that "only six of the novels have first-person [and male] narration. But

most of the other novels have very important female narrators" (Heusel, "Dialogue" 12–13).

5 Bakhtin says that the loophole "is to one degree or another inherent in all the confessional self-utterances of Dostoevsky's heroes. The loophole makes all the heroes' self-definitions unstable, the word in them has no hard and fast meaning, and at any moment, like a chameleon, it is ready to change its tone and its ultimate meaning. The loophole makes the hero ambiguous and elusive even for himself" (PDP 234).

6 This phenomenon is what Bakhtin calls a "vicious circle" (PDP 229).

7 Do we detect a hidden polemic in this parody? When Murdoch later refers to Franca's "scuttling like a small animal in the house," is she alluding to Gregor—or to Wittgenstein's beetle-in-a-box allegory? Compare Beatrix Potter's "Sometimes a beetle lost its way in the passages" (*Tale of Mrs. Tittlemouse* 14).

8 See Nieli's explanation (*Wittgenstein* 220–22) of Wittgenstein's discussion, in *Philosophical Investigations*, of the beetle in the box (1:258, 293).

9 Emerson paraphrases Bakhtin as saying that "one cannot author oneself—the very fact of expression, aesthetic and otherwise, requires a second consciousness to supply boundaries and impose external integrity. . . . '[O]ne can speak of the absolute aesthetic need of one person for another, for the seeing remembering, gathering, and unifying ability of the other, which alone can create his externally completed personality; the personality will not exist if the other does not create it'" ("The Tolstoy Connection" 70). Emerson cites this phrase from Bakhtin to demonstrate the simplicity of his concepts: "'How the other looks from my position' is the starting point both for aesthetic perception and for an ethical act" (70).

CHAPTER EIGHT Characters Patterning Their Pilgrimages

1 Viewers of the Booker television interview for the BBC see the shock Murdoch felt at discovering suddenly, in a museum in the Czech Republic, a Titian painting previously unknown to her. Murdoch's description of the ecstatic face of Marsyas while his skin is being lovingly stripped away also reveals the many conflicting tensions that she as artist holds in suspension, demonstrating visually what good art elicits in her.

2 The remainder of this quotation is "to combine form with respect for reality with all its odd contingent ways is the highest art of prose" (SBR 186).

3 My conceptualizing a labyrinth of London escalators more than ten years ago was no doubt sparked by reading *A Word Child*, but also perhaps by reading Louis Martz's "The London Novels" (1971).

4 Dipple attributes Murdoch's repetition of patterns to "a single powerful imagina-

Notes to Chapter Eight

tion": "There are innumerable repeated patterns: male role-model played off against adolescent boy, opposition of religious and artistic figures, good versus evil, escapes to India, Australia or America, strong mother-son relationships, men mourning the death of their wives from cancer, identifications with medieval images (questing knight, lady of the fountain). In addition, many of the climactic adventures are comparable and reflect a suffocating (sinking into a bog or mud) or drowning, redolent of the symbolically smothering, death-dealing effect of the reality-denying ego" (*Work for the Spirit* 89).

5 Socrates, in "Art and Eros: A Dialogue about Art," wants to turn the "inside out." Although he asks a binary question—"Isn't it the nature of art to explore the relation between the public and the private?"—Murdoch multiplies connections by turning the inside out, creating novels that mine the unconscious, encouraging a search for the secret to the deeper patterns in the libido.

6 Frank Kermode discusses the "parody of prophetic equivocation, a device as ancient as the Delphic oracle. All plots have something in common with prophecy, for they must appear to educe from the prime matter of the situation the forms of a future. The best of them, thought Aristotle, include a *peripeteia* no less independent than the other parts upon 'our rule of probability or necessity' but arising from that in the original situation to which we have given less attention; *peripeteia* is equivocating plot, and it has been compared, with some justice, to irony" (*Sense of an Ending* 83–84).

7 Françoise Meltzer says that critics have named it thus because "the assumption is that stasis is pleasure and tension displeasure, which must find an outlet (so too, water seeks its own level and will build up pressure if unable to find release). There are times, then, when Freud views the unconscious as a series of involuntary reflexes and an ebbing and flowing of energies. It is as if the unconscious were a throbbing energy center, active and busy, but hidden from the Subject's conscious mind" ("Unconscious" 150–51).

8 See Kristeva's discussion of pre-Oedipal fantasies of violence and destruction in *Powers of Horror*.

9 Murdoch says in *The Sovereignty of Good*: "'Good is a transcendent reality' means that virtue is the attempt to pierce the veil of selfish consciousness and join the world as it really is"; she adds that the "attempt cannot be entirely successful" (SG 93).

10 Such absurd automobile accidents do occur. When Murdoch wrote *An Accidental Man*, a novel about a man or several men whose irresponsibility causes others to suffer, she may have known about the devastating hit-and-run accident that killed Antonia Byatt's son, Stout.

11 Lacan would say the character's Subject is meeting the Other or his Other. Mur-

doch's attitude here is similar to Lacan's notion that the Subject is constituted by something missing, which in turn creates desire.

12 Murdoch makes a Wittgensteinian joke about categorizing and cataloguing in a government bureaucracy: "Mrs. Witcher set herself up . . . as a sort of watchdog over the classifications themselves, not only checking the files but controlling the divisions and sub-divisions into which they were separated" (WC 29).

13 These page numbers are from the Viking edition: week 1, pp. 1–95; week 2, pp. 96–160; week 3, pp. 161–213; week 4, including Sunday, pp. 214–98; week 5, including Sunday, Christmas Eve, and Christmas Day, 299–end.

14 Irigaray asserts that "'woman' can function as place—evanescent beyond, point of discharge—as well as time—eternal return, temporal detour—for the sublimation and, if possible, mastery of the work of death. . . . From that process by which consciousness comes into being and woman remains the place for the inscription of repressions" (*Speculum* 54–55).

15 No doubt, Murdoch's being an only child has contributed to her independence, her willingness to puncture the boundaries of all metaphorical spaces, including generic categories.

16 Through dreams, puns, and slips of the tongue, Murdoch frees her characters to play out all kinds of Freudian dramas.

17 Fineman says that Thucydides "adopts the specifically semiological language and method of the Hippocratic doctor who is concerned to interpret the signs of disease for the sake of diagnosis and prognosis" ("The Anecdote" 54–55).

18 Brother Lawrence (Nicholas Herman, 1611–1691), a "discalced Carmelite lay brother and mystic," learned through his domestic duties as cook at his monastery to live a life of almost constant awareness of God's presence. Being "a humble cook for 30 years" gave him a "reputation for holiness." He wrote *Practice of the Presence of God* (*New Catholic Encyclopedia*).

19 Dipple gives the following information: "Completely intuitive and non-intellectual, Tim was not aware that his painting reflected a compulsive gnostic desire and, even more accurately, illustrated certain French speculations about the form of art that may have roots in Mallarmé, as Murdoch has suggested" (*Work* 338).

20 Dipple suggests that Murdoch sets up Guy and Tim as Apollonian and Dionysian, respectively (*Work* 334–37).

21 Dipple attributes the organic emphasis to the pattern of imagery from the French provinces of Vaucluse and Provence (*Work* 340).

22 The introduction of my dissertation, "Patterned Aimlessness in the Mature Novels of Iris Murdoch," points out the appropriateness of Escher's engraving as a metaphor for Murdoch's world of the novel.

Notes to Chapter Nine

23 Another last-minute, shocking addition which helps contingency pile up at the end of *Nuns and Soldiers* is the suggestion of a lesbian motif—to which no credibility is given. Daisy, because she is unaware of the ways the numerous relationships are shifting, insinuates that Anne must be in love with Gertrude and that Anne must also be sexually interested in her. The reader later overhears an unidentified character in a pub remark that Daisy is said to have taken up with a woman after having been chased by an unfrocked, lesbian nun (Anne). These remarks suggest an absurd Daisy-Anne-Gertrude triangle. Another particularly absurd triangle involves Ned, the tall, handsome young son of Janet Openshaw, who is introduced to Anne at the last cocktail party and falls "totally" in love with her.

24 This juxtaposition of Gertrude and King Lear reveals the distance between the two characters.

25 Murdoch herself came near to drowning in the sea in a similar way.

CHAPTER NINE   Philosophical and Psychological Patterns Underlying the World of Iris Murdoch's Novels

1 Kristeva goes on to say that for writers of Menippean satire the notions of "identity [i.e., fixed referent], substance [i.e., essence], causality and definitions are transgressed so that others may be adopted: analogy, relation, opposition, and therefore, dialogism and Menippean ambivalence" (WDN 86).

2 By *form* I mean shaping patterns, literary form, not metaphysical or ontological form or transcendental essence. Murdoch says: "Form in art is properly the simulation of the self-contained aimlessness of the universe" (86). In my forthcoming study on gender and Murdoch, I demonstrate the ways her form is multiorgasmic rather than emulating the masculine paradigm of moving toward climax.

3 Donna Gerstenberger said in 1975 that Murdoch's method of juggling multiple opinions about issues she dealt with in a novel worked well: "the more varied the expression of opinions, the more truthful the novel tries to be." But, she said, in criticizing *The Red and the Green*, "there are certain emotional responses inherent in the Irish situation which militate against the formula of meaning through objective multiplicity" (*Iris Murdoch* 52–53).

4 The distinction between necessary and contingent statements or truths is less obvious than the difference between necessary and contingent events: "The necessity of events by no means entails that there are necessary truths—statements whose truth is necessary, as opposed to those whose truth is only contingent, that is, those which merely happen to be true. It is also less clear that if a statement is said to be contingently true, it may also be said to be merely possibly true, for there is an

obvious sense in which even a contingent truth must, on occasion, actually hold. It is a contingent truth that flowers bloom in the spring, but it would be wrong to say that it is merely possibly true; it *is* true. . . . Since the latter ['that which *can* be otherwise and is so for the most part, only or sometimes, or as it happens'] corresponds to our notion of contingency, Aristotle apparently would have thought of the contingent in terms of what is possible in an absolute sense. That is to say, the contingent is just what *can* be otherwise in an absolute sense, without reference to anything else" (*Encyclopedia of Philosophy* 198–99).

5 Murdoch points out that the "*Timaeus*, deliberately taking issue with Plato's evolutionary 'materialist' predecessors, offers a carefully modified quasi-teleological cosmogony in the form of a myth, wherein moral imagery and scientific speculation are remarkably blended" (FS 50).

6 In her novel *Possession*, Byatt plays with a fictionalized account of Emily Brontë experiencing orgasm at the ocean (266).

7 I continue to quote from Byatt because she uses the translation *network* instead of *mesh*.

8 Since the 1980s, Peter Conradi has studied Murdoch's interest in the significance to Buddhists of karma. See *Iris Murdoch: The Saint and the Artist* for patterns Conradi attributes to the concept of karma.

9 Conversation with George Steiner in Chapel Hill, N.C., spring 1985. Steiner's commentary on the book jacket of *The Fire and the Sun* reads: "This little monograph is meant to set out Plato's views rather than to rebut them. But discreet as it is, Iris Murdoch's counter-attack is lucid and moving."

10 Murdoch says in "The Sublime and Beautiful Revisited," "to speak of failure here has nothing disgraceful about it. Almost every work of art is a failure" (266).

11 Perhaps he is thinking in neo-Platonic terms. Conradi has inadvertently changed *because* to *when* in his text.

12 Ironically, this is George Russell's (AE's) theory in the "Scylla and Charybdis" chapter of *Ulysses*.

13 According to Frank D'Angelo, readers have known since Lévi-Strauss's work that linear analysis of a text is not sufficient (*Conceptual Theory* 76); therefore, careful readers will examine the "diachronic or temporal which illustrates text progression . . . and the synchronic or spatial which constitutes the underlying paradigm (the vertical plane)" (75).

14 She concludes: "Freud says that the opposite of play is not work but reality. This may be true of fantasy play but not of the playfulness of good art which delightedly seeks and reveals the real" (FS 84).

15 See Dipple, who says that Murdoch "pulls herself out of the subjective socio-

philosophy of our period and hearkens back to certain thought patterns that characterized western comprehension before its cohesiveness spun out of control during the late Renaissance. She cannot be locked glibly into the Great Chain of Being, however, because of her resistance to pattern and insistence on the random and thus holy nature of the particular" (*Work* 95).

16 In "The London Novels" (1971), Louis Martz analyzes the labyrinthine qualities of the London Underground, which contains the Circle Line. Christine Wick Sizemore's *A Female Vision of the City* (1989), which includes a chapter entitled "The City as Labyrinth: Iris Murdoch," argues that Murdoch employs the labyrinth in more positive ways than most modernist and contemporary male novelists do.

17 To chart the varying distances of her characters from the light, I have borrowed Bakhtin's metaphor of the layering of historical strata in the novel and Plato's allegory of the cave and his line diagram. Plato's mathematical construct of the Line and Form diagram in the *Republic* is similar to Bakhtin's history of consciousness.

18 Murdoch's revitalizing of Plato's cave labyrinth is analogous to Bakhtin's revitalizing of Kant's cultural labyrinth.

19 Stephen gives the reader some handle on what Bakhtin labels the *chronotope*, meaning "time-space unit" or "time-space node." This unit is for studying texts according "to the ratio and nature of the temporal and spatial categories represented" (Clark and Holquist, *Bakhtin* 279). Bakhtin says that "our particular totally integrated sense of space and time shapes our sense of reality" (quoted in Clark and Holquist, *Bakhtin* 279). Clark and Holquist explain that "two major variables are fundamental in the evolution of the novel and thus of consciousness as well: attitudes to space and time, and attitudes to language" (*Bakhtin* 277).

20 For background, see West, "Wisdom Literature, Hesiod."

21 David Gordon and I disagree about the ways Murdoch ties these characters into these cosmic patterns. Whereas Gordon finds Murdoch envisioning a deterministic universe, I see her as agreeing more with Plato that there "is only one true artist, God, and only one true work of art, the Cosmos. . . . The rational and good Demiurge creates the cosmos and endows it with a discerning Soul. He works as well as he can, gazing at a perfect model (the Forms), to create a changing sensible copy of an unchanging intelligible original. He cannot, however, create perfectly because he is using pre-existent material which contains irrational elements, the 'wandering causes,' which represent irreducible qualities tending toward some minimal non-rational order of their own. The activity of these causes is called 'necessity' . . . meaning not [a] mechanical system but a semi-random interruption of rational purposes" (FS 50).

22 Bove's *Character Index and Guide* describes the painting: "The figures at the top

Notes to Chapter Nine

of the picture are Time and Truth, who are drawing back a blue veil to reveal the ecstatic kiss which Cupid is giving to his mother. The wailing figure behind Cupid is Jealousy. Beyond the plump figure of the rose-bearing Pleasure, the sinister enamel-faced girl with the scaly tail represents Deceit" (91).

23 "To suggest that God is not omnipotent has always been a prime Christian heresy. The image of a morally perfect but not all-powerful Goodness seems to me better to express some ultimate (inexpressible) truth about our condition. The Jehovah of *Genesis* is totally unlike the artist, human or divine, in that he creates out of nothing and expects perfection. (Perhaps the Demiurge more intelligently realized his limitations at the start, whereas Jehovah realized his later and was correspondingly bad-tempered?)" (FS 52).

24 Speaking of the human position in the universe, she says: "We see what we seem to be, transient mortal creatures subject to necessity and chance. This is to say that there is, in my view, no God in the traditional sense of that term; and the traditional sense is perhaps the only sense" (SG 79).

25 Conradi explains that "Simone Weil believed that extreme affliction is passed on by all but the saintly" (*Saint* 169).

26 Murdoch mentions in the same source that Tallis "hasn't got any voice really," suggesting that the Good stutters (Chevalier, *Rencontres* 76).

27 Eagleton has criticized Murdoch's texts for their upper-middle-class exclusivity.

28 Murdoch adds this description on the verso: "In the centre of the facade a huge pediment supported by 4 pillars rose above the level of the roof. A free dome curved above. The pillars ended at a balustrade at the first floor level" (notebook 1). In one of Murdoch's pieces of correspondence at the University of Iowa Special Collections, she discusses John Bayley's reading of some of her early notebooks. He has written comments on a number of pages of the holograph notebooks of *The Bell*.

29 Todd says that Murdoch explores all forms of sexual expression (*Shakespeare* 76).

30 Bove's *Character Index and Guide* is helpful here.

31 Modern and postmodern thinking, revolutionized by Freudian and then Lacanian perspectives, emphasizes the relationship between sexuality and almost any other human activity.

32 In her interview with Rose, Murdoch said, "'I'm not Freudian. I think Freud discovered a lot of things but I think that this whole business of sexuality and spirituality is very hard to understand,' and to her Russian translator Ivasheva she noted crucially, 'Really I think I am in many ways anti-Freud. (I think love *transcends* sex in a way F. might not recognise)'" (quoted in Conradi, *Saint* 280).

33 See Fineman, "The Anecdote." Comparing the definitions of *anecdote* and *pornography* establishes the similarity in diction of the two. Angela Carter, discussing the

pornography of the Marquis de Sade, says, "Pornography involves an abstraction of human intercourse in which the self is reduced to its formal elements. In its most basic form, these elements are represented by the probe and the fringed hole, the twin signs of male and female in graffiti" (*Sadeian Woman* 4). As Foucault has shown, the language used in medical diagnosis is also similar to that of pornography. Ironically, the Bath Institute in *The Philosopher's Pupil* includes "consulting rooms" (22).

34. Fineman explains that "the orifice—traced out by the anecdote within the totalizing whole of history, is something that is characteristically and ahistorically plugged up by a teleological narration" ("The Anecdote" 61).

35. Dipple calls attention to the passage from Bellamy, describing the importance in Murdoch's thinking of the "paradoxical conjunction of form and formlessness." It "is the basis of the contrast in her work between the would-be artist and the would-be saint, even perhaps in such a novel as A *Fairly Honourable Defeat* between evil and good, as the struggle of Tallis versus Julius will illustrate. In BP Murdoch has constructed a character who, after his education, combines qualities of both and shows through his experience the subtle linking of art and ethics when they perform their proper truth-telling function" (Dipple, *Work* 115).

36. I refer specifically to Bradley Pearson and Charles Arrowby.

37. "Murdoch has compared television with Platonic *eikasia*, the lowest, most irrational kind of awareness, equivalent to a vague image-ridden illusion" (Conradi, *Saint* 65).

38. In "Art as Technique," the Russian formalist Viktor Shklovsky calls this slowing down of the process of perception defamiliarization, or making strange. William Wordsworth was interested in the freshness of vision; Shklovsky and the Formalists use the devices of drawing out and delaying to produce effects of defamiliarization.

39. Modern literature and visual art manifest dozens of modernist artists, Gertrude Stein and Wyndham Lewis, for example, who attempt to translate the visual or the visceral into narrative.

40. Picture the well-known figure that can be perceived as a vase or a pair of faces. Wittgenstein derived the duck-rabbit figure from Jastrow, *Fact and Fable in Psychology*. Wittgenstein explains the switch of gestalt in this way in *Philosophical Investigations*:

> I shall call the following figure, derived from Jastrow, the duck-rabbit. It can be seen as a rabbit's head or as a duck's. And I must distinguish between the "continuous seeing" of an aspect and the "dawning" of an aspect. The picture might have been shewn me, and I never have seen anything but a rabbit in

it. . . . I should simply have described my perception, . . . I should never have thought of superimposing the heads like that. . . . Had I replied "It's a rabbit," the ambiguity would have escaped me, and I should have been reporting my perception.

The change of aspect. "But surely you would say that the picture is altogether different now!"

But what is different: my impression? my point of view? I *describe* the alteration like a perception; quite as if the object had altered before my eyes. (PI. 2:194–95)

41 For a list of the laws of organization and characteristics of Gestalt theory, consult Hochberg, "Gestalt Theory."

42 Without referring to Wittgenstein, Deborah Johnson comments on the connection Murdoch makes in *The Black Prince* between falling in love and the perceptual phenomenon *gestalt*.

43 Joyce uses figure/ground in Stephen's artistic theory as described in *Stephen Hero* partly to carry on his link with Aquinas: "[The] mind to apprehend the object divides the entire universe into two parts, the object, and the void which is not the object. To apprehend it you must lift it away from everything else; and then you perceive that it is one integral thing, that is a thing" (212). Joyce's understanding of poetic process and his concept of epiphany benefited from the Western egoistic tradition (particularly Aquinas) that Harold Bloom discusses in his introduction to *Iris Murdoch*.

44 In *Stephen Hero* Stephen Dedalus means by *epiphany* "a sudden spiritual manifestation whether in the vulgarity of speech or gesture or in a memorable phase of the mind itself" (211).

45 Joyce's strategic overlay of Stephen's idealistic, artistic view and Bloom's realistic, commercial view sets up the possibility that the reader will experience stereoscopic vision (Heusel, "Escher" 144).

46 *The Nice and the Good* is built around the idea of a coded message: the characters have to decode a puzzle. Sophocles valued perceptual knowledge, as did other fifth-century Greek playwrights. In several plays Tiresias makes use of visual patterns that encode knowledge; in *Antigone* he analyzes the behavior of the birds and the burning of the animal fat to discover the answers to Creon's problems. The priests decoded not only oracular messages but visual ones: "At the temple of Apollo in Thebes the priests foretold the future according to patterns they saw in the ashes of the burned flesh of sacrificial victims" (Knox, *Oedipus* 653 n. 4). The result of their observation of the coded messages was narratives suited for the public.

47 Murdoch says, "Most critics who reviewed the book in England didn't appear to realise [that the Black Prince is Apollo], even though there was a picture of Apollo on the front!" (Chevalier, *Rencontres* 78). Conradi says about Apollo: "He is named as Luxius and 'Lycean' in Sophocles' *Oedipus Rex*" (*Saint* 284, n. 6).

48 Norris says in explaining *Finnegans Wake*: "Decentering of the structure, then suggests another, as yet uncategorizable sense of form—which modern poets often call 'open' in contrast to 'closed,' but which is more conveniently defined here as 'freeplay.'" She quotes Derrida as follows: "This field is in fact that of *freeplay*, that is to say, a field of infinite substitutions in the closure of a finite ensemble. This field permits these infinite substitutions only because it is finite, that is to say, because instead of being an inexhaustible field, as in the classical hypothesis, instead of being too large, there is something missing from it: a center which arrests and founds the freeplay of substitutions" (quoted in "Consequence of Deconstruction" 210).

49 In *The Green Knight* (1993), Murdoch again appears to raise a character from the dead.

CONCLUSION

1 A survey of articles and reviews since the mid-1950s shows that critics place Murdoch's novels in categories that range from high culture to pop. Such labels as *theorem, political meditation, learned fable, bitter satire,* and *metaphysical fantasy* cluster at one end, opposite such epithets as *farce, melodrama, soap opera, TV series* (sitcom, presumably), *comic strip, paperback thriller,* and *trash* (see Begnal, *Iris Murdoch*). Many labels such as *game of skill, mating game,* and *black comedy* fit well near either end of the continuum.

2 In attempting to tell it as he sees it, Wittgenstein offers this dilemma in his preface: "My thoughts were soon crippled if I tried to force them on in any single direction against their natural inclination. And this was, of course, connected with the nature of the investigation. For this compels us to travel over a wide field of thought criss-cross in every direction" (PI ix).

 Bibliography

Achen, Sven Tito. *Symbols Around Us*. New York: Van Nostrand Reinhold, 1981.
Adams, Hazard, and Leroy Searle, eds. Introduction to "From *Philosophical Investigations*." In *Critical Theory since 1965*. Tallahassee: Univ. Presses of Florida, 1986. 766–67.
Aiken, Gail Elizabeth. "This Accidental World: The Philosophy and Fiction of Iris Murdoch." Ph.D. diss., Univ. of Tennessee, 1979.
Altman, Janet Gurkin. *Epistolarity: Approaches to a Form*. Columbus: Ohio State Univ. Press, 1982.
Anonymous. [Review.] *Bookman*, November 1958, 26.
Ayer, A. J. *Part of My Life*. New York: Harcourt, 1977.
Ayer, A. J., et al. *The Revolution of Philosophy*. London: Macmillan, 1957.
Bakhtin, Mikhail. *The Dialogic Imagination: Four Essays*. Ed. Michael Holquist. Trans. Caryl Emerson and Michael Holquist. Austin: Univ. of Texas Press, 1981.
———. *Problems of Dostoevsky's Poetics*. Ed. and trans. Caryl Emerson. Theory and History of Literature 8. Minneapolis: Univ. of Minnesota Press, 1984.
———. "The Problems of Speech Genres." In *Speech Genres and Other Late Essays*. Ed. Caryl Emerson and Michael Holquist. Trans. Vern W. McGee. Austin: Univ. of Texas Press, 1986. 60–102.
Baldanza, Frank. *Iris Murdoch*. New York: Twayne, 1974.
———. "The Murdoch Manuscripts at the University of Iowa: An Addendum." *Modern Fiction Studies* 16 (Summer 1970): 201–02.
Bayley, John. *The Characters of Love: A Study in the Literature of Personality*. London: Constable, 1960.
———. *The Uses of Division: Unity and Disharmony in Literature*. London: Chatto and Windus, 1976.
Begnal, Kate. *Iris Murdoch: A Reference Guide*. Boston: G. K. Hall, 1987.
Bellamy, Michael O. "An Interview with Iris Murdoch." *Wisconsin Studies in Contemporary Literature* 18 (1977): 129–40.
Benjamin, Jessica. *The Bonds of Love: Psychoanalysis, Feminism, and the Problem of Domination*. New York: Pantheon Books, 1988.
Biely, Andrey. *St. Petersburg*. London: Weidenfeld and Nicolson, 1960.
Bloom, Harold. *The Anxiety of Influence: A Theory of Poetry*. New York: Oxford Univ. Press, 1973.
———, ed. *Iris Murdoch*. Introduction. New York: Chelsea House, 1986. 1–7.

Bibliography

Boardman, John, Jasper Griffin, and Oswyn Murray, eds. *The Oxford History of the Classical World*. Oxford: Oxford Univ. Press, 1986.

Booth, Wayne C. *The Company We Keep: An Ethics of Fiction*. Berkeley: Univ. of California Press, 1988.

Bove, Cheryl Browning. *A Character Index and Guide to the Fiction of Iris Murdoch*. New York: Garland, 1986.

———. "New Directions: Iris Murdoch's Latest Women." In *Critical Essays on Iris Murdoch*, ed. Lindsay Tucker. New York: G. K. Hall, 1992. 188–98.

Bové, Paul. "Discourse." In *Critical Terms for Literary Study*, ed. Frank Lentricchia and Thomas McLaughlin. Chicago: Univ. of Chicago Press, 1990. 50–65.

Bradbury, Malcolm, ed. *The Novel Today: Contemporary Writers on Modern Fiction*. Manchester, England: Manchester Univ. Press, 1977.

Byatt, A. S. *Degrees of Freedom. The Novels of Iris Murdoch*. New York: Barnes and Noble, 1965.

———. "People in Paper Houses: Attitudes to 'Realism' and 'Experiment' in English Postwar Fiction." In *The Contemporary English Novel*, ed. Malcolm Bradbury and David Palmer. Stratford-upon-Avon Studies 18. London: Edward Arnold, 1979. 19–41.

———. *Possession: A Romance*. New York: Vintage International, 1991.

Carter, Angela. *The Sadeian Woman and the Ideology of Pornography*. New York: Harper Colophon Books, 1980.

Chevalier, Jean-Louis, ed. *Rencontres avec Iris Murdoch*. Caen: Centre des Recherches de Littérature et Linguistique des Pays de Langue Anglaise, 1978.

Chodorow, Nancy. *The Reproduction of Mothering: Psychoanalysis and the Sociology of Mothering*. Berkeley: Univ. of California Press, 1978.

Clark, Katerina, and Michael Holquist. *Mikhail Bakhtin*. Cambridge: Harvard Univ. Press, 1984.

Conrad, Joseph. *The Heart of Darkness: An Authoritative Text, Background and Criticism*. Ed. Robert Kimbrough. New York: Norton, 1971.

Conradi, Peter. *Fyodor Dostoevsky*. Macmillan Modern Novelists. London: Macmillan, 1988.

———. *Iris Murdoch: The Saint and the Artist*. New York: St. Martin's, 1986.

Conroy, Sarah Booth. "The Lasting Powers of Iris Murdoch: Philosophic, Intuitive, Intriguing, Precise—the Novelist at 70." *Washington Post*, March 11, 1990, F1, F6.

Cornford, Francis MacDonald. *The Republic of Plato*. New York: Oxford Univ. Press, 1952.

———. *The Unwritten Philosophy*. Cambridge: Cambridge Univ. Press, 1950.

Crone, Anna Lisa. *Rozanov and the End of Literature: Polyphony and the Dissolution of Genre in Solitaria and Fallen Leaves*. Würzburg: Jal-Verlag, 1978.

D'Angelo, Frank J. *A Conceptual Theory of Rhetoric*. Cambridge: Winthrop Publishers, 1975.

de Man, Paul. *The Resistance to Theory*. Theory and History of Literature 33. Minneapolis: Univ. of Minnesota Press, 1986.

Derrida, Jacques. "Plato's Pharmacy." Trans. Barbara Johnson. In *Dissemination*. Chicago: Univ. of Chicago Press, 1981. 61–172.

———. *Writing and Difference*. Chicago: Univ. of Chicago Press, 1978.

Detweiler, Robert. *Iris Murdoch's* The Unicorn. Intro. Alan Bass. New York: Seabury Press, 1969.

Dipple, Elizabeth. *Iris Murdoch: Work for the Spirit*. Chicago: Univ. of Chicago Press, 1982.

———. *The Unresolvable Plot: Reading Contemporary Fiction*. New York: Routledge, 1988.

Eagleton, Terry. *The Function of Critics: From* The Spectator *to Post-Structuralism*. London: Verso, 1984, 1985.

———. *Literary Criticism: An Introduction*. Minneapolis: Univ. of Minnesota Press, 1983.

———. *Walter Benjamin, or Towards a Revolutionary Criticism*. London: Verso and NLB, 1981.

———. "Wittgenstein's Friends." *New Left Review* 135 (September–October 1982): 64–90.

Edwards, James C. *Ethics Without Philosophy: Wittgenstein and the Moral Life*. Gainesville: Univ. Presses of Florida, 1982.

Eliot, George. *Daniel Deronda*. Ed. Barbara Hardy. Harmondsworth, England: Penguin, 1979.

Emerson, Caryl. "The Tolstoy Connection in Bakhtin." *PMLA* 100 (1985): 68–80.

The Encyclopedia of Philosophy. Ed. Paul Edwards. New York: Macmillan, 1967.

Escher, M. C. "Moebius Strip II." [1963.] In *The World of M. C. Escher*. Ed. J. L. Locher. New York: Harry N. Abrams, 1971. Plate 260.

Faris, Wendy B. *Labyrinths of Language: Symbolic Landscape and Narrative Design in Modern Fiction*. Baltimore: Johns Hopkins Univ. Press, 1988.

Fineman, Joel. "The Anecdote." In *The New Historicism*, ed. Harold Veeser. New York: Routledge, 1989. 49–76.

Fletcher, John. "Iris Murdoch." In *Dictionary of Literary Biography*, vol. 14, ed. Jay L. Halio. Detroit: Gale, 1983. 546–61.

Bibliography

Geertz, Clifford. "Blurred Genres." In *Critical Theory since 1965*. Tallahassee: Univ. Presses of Florida, 1986. 766–67.

German, Howard. "Allusions in the Early Novels of Iris Murdoch." *Modern Fiction Studies* 15 (August 1969): 361–77.

———. "The Range of Allusions in the Novels of Iris Murdoch." *Journal of Modern Literature* 2 (September 1971): 57–85.

Gerstenberger, Donna. *Iris Murdoch*. Lewisburg, Pa.: Bucknell Univ. Press, and London: Associated Univ. Presses, 1975.

Gilligan, Carol, Janie Victoria Ward, and Jill McLean Taylor, eds. *Mapping the Moral Domain: A Contribution of Women's Thinking to Psychological Theory and Education*. Cambridge: Harvard Univ. Press, 1988.

Gindin, James. *Postwar British Fiction: New Accents and Attitudes*. Berkeley: Univ. of California Press, 1962.

Gordon, J. David. "Iris Murdoch's Comedies of Unselfing." *Twentieth Century Literature* 36 (Summer 1990): 115–36.

Greenblatt, Stephen J. *Learning to Curse: Essays in Early Modern Culture*. New York: Routledge, 1990.

Hamilton, Edith. *The Greek Way*. New York: Norton, 1942.

Harmon, William, and C. Hugh Holman, eds. *A Handbook to Literature*. Sixth ed. New York: Macmillan, 1986.

Hassan, Ihab. *Paracriticisms: Seven Speculations of the Times*. Urbana: Univ. of Illinois Press, 1975.

———. *The Postmodern Turn: Essays in Postmodern Theory and Culture*. Columbus: Ohio State Univ. Press, 1987.

Heilbrun, Carolyn. *Reinventing Womanhood*. New York: Norton, 1979.

———. *Toward Androgyny*. London: Victor Gollancz, 1973.

Herrmann, Claudine. *The Dialogic and Difference: "An/Other Woman" in Virginia Woolf and Christa Wolf*. New York: Columbia Univ. Press, 1989.

Heusel, Barbara Stevens. "Can We Tell the Good Art from the Bad? Iris Murdoch's *The Black Prince* and *The Sea, The Sea*." *University of Dayton Review* 19.2 (Summer 1988–89): 99–107.

———. "A Dialogue with Iris Murdoch." *University of Windsor Review* 21.1 (1988): 1–13.

———. "Iris Murdoch's *A Word Child*: Playing Games with Wittgenstein's Perspectives." *Studies in the Humanities* 13.2 (December 1986): 81–92.

———. "Joyce and the Drama of Cognition: Escher as a Visual Analogue." *Twentieth Century Literature* 34.4 (Winter 1988): 395–406.

Hochberg, Julian. "Gestalt Theory." In *Oxford Companion to the Mind*, ed. Richard L. Gregory. New York: Oxford Univ. Press, 1987. 288–93.

Hofstadter, Douglas R. *Gödel, Escher, and Bach: An Eternal Golden Braid*. New York: Vintage, 1980.

Horatius Flaccus, Quintus. "Ode II, XX." In *The Odes of Horace*. Trans. Helen Rowe Henze. Norman: Univ. of Oklahoma Press, 1961.

Howard, Maureen. "Eight Recent Novelists." *Yale Review* 68 (Spring 1979): 432–42.

Irigaray, Luce. *Speculum of the Other Woman*. [1974.] Trans. Gillian C. Gill. Ithaca: Cornell Univ. Press, 1985.

———. *This Sex Which Is Not One*. [1977.] Trans. Catherine Porter with Carolyn Burke. Ithaca: Cornell Univ. Press, 1985.

Johnson, Barbara. *The Critical Difference: Essays in the Contemporary Rhetoric of Reading*. Baltimore: Johns Hopkins Univ. Press, 1980.

———. "Gender Theory and the Yale School." In *Speaking of Gender*, ed. Elaine Showalter. London: Routledge, 1989. 45–55.

———. Translator's Introduction to *Dissemination*, by Jacques Derrida. Chicago: Univ. of Chicago Press, 1981. vii–xxxiii.

———. *A World of Difference*. Baltimore: Johns Hopkins Univ. Press, 1987.

Johnson, Deborah. *Iris Murdoch*. London: Harvester Press, 1987.

Joyce, James. *Stephen Hero*. Norfolk, Conn.: New Directions, 1963.

———. *Ulysses: A Critical and Synoptic Edition*. Ed. Hans Walter Gabler. New York: Garland, 1984.

Kazin, Alfred. Afterword to *In the Adventures of Huckleberry Finn*, by Mark Twain. New York: Bantam, 1981.

Kermode, Frank. *The Sense of an Ending: Studies in the Theory of Fiction*. New York: Oxford Univ. Press, 1967.

Knox, Bernard M. W. Introduction to *Oedipus the King*, by Sophocles. In *The Norton Anthology of World Masterpieces*, ed. Maynard Mack et al. Vol. 1. New York: W. W. Norton, 1985.

Kristeva, Julia. *In the Beginning Was Love: Psychoanalysis and Faith*. Trans. Arthur Goldhammer. New York: Columbia Univ. Press, 1987.

———. *Powers of Horror: An Essay on Abjection*. Trans. Leon Roudiez. New York: Columbia Univ. Press, 1984.

———. "Word, Dialogue, and Novel." In *Desire in Language: A Semiotic Approach to Literature and Art*, ed. Leon S. Roudiez. Trans. Thomas Gora, Alice Jardine, and Leon S. Roudiez. New York: Columbia Univ. Press, 1980. 64–91.

Kuehl, Linda. "Iris Murdoch: The Novelist as Magician/The Magician as Artist." *Modern Fiction Studies* 15.3 (1969): 347–60.

Lacan, Jacques. "The Mirror Stage as Formative of the Function of the I as Revealed in Psychoanalytic Experience." In *Critical Theory since 1965*. Tallahassee: Univ. Presses of Florida, 1986. 734–38.

LaCapra, Dominick. *Rethinking Intellectual History: Texts, Contexts, Language*. Ithaca: Cornell Univ. Press, 1983.

Lentricchia, Frank, and Thomas McLaughlin, eds. *Critical Terms for Literary Study*. Chicago: Univ. of Chicago Press, 1990.

Lévi-Strauss, Claude. *The Savage Mind*. Chicago: Univ. of Chicago Press, 1969.

Levitt, Morton P. *Modernist Survivors: The Contemporary Novel in England, the United States, France, and Latin America*. Columbus: Ohio State Univ. Press, 1987.

Martz, Louis L. "The London Novels." In *Iris Murdoch*, ed. Harold Bloom. New York: Chelsea House, 1986. 39–57.

McGuinness, Brian. *Wittgenstein: A Life, Young Ludwig 1889–1921*. Berkeley: Univ. of California Press, 1988.

Mehta, Ved. *Fly and the Fly-Bottle: Encounters with British Intellectuals*. Boston: Little, Brown, 1961.

Meltzer, Françoise. "Unconscious." In *Critical Terms for Literary Study*, ed. Frank Lentricchia and Thomas McLaughlin. Chicago: Univ. of Chicago Press, 1990. 147–62.

Mettler, Darlene D. *Sound and Sense: Musical Allusion and Imagery in the Novels of Iris Murdoch*. New York: Peter Lang, 1990.

Moore, Dennis. "Dame Iris Receives Medal of Honor in Manhattan." *Iris Murdoch Society Newsletter* 3 (June 1990): 1.

Murdoch, Iris. *Acastos: Two Platonic Dialogues*. New York: Viking, 1987.

———. *An Accidental Man*. London: Chatto and Windus, 1971.

———. "Against Dryness: A Polemical Sketch." *Encounter* 16 (1961): 16–20.

———. *The Bell*. New York: Viking, 1958.

———. *The Black Prince*. New York: Viking, 1973.

———. *The Book and the Brotherhood*. New York: Viking, 1987.

———. *Bruno's Dream*. New York: Viking, 1969.

———. "Discussion." [Following W. Bronzwaer, "Images of Plato in 'The Fire and the Sun' and 'Acastos.'"] In *Encounters with Iris Murdoch*, ed. Richard Todd. Amsterdam: Free Univ. Press, 1988. 64–67.

———. "Existentialists and Mystics." In *Essays and Poems Presented to Lord David Cecil*, ed. W. W. Robson. London: Constable, 1970.

———. *A Fairly Honourable Defeat*. New York: Viking, 1970.

———. *The Fire and the Sun: Why Plato Banished the Artists*. Oxford: Oxford Univ. Press, 1977.

———. *The Flight from the Enchanter*. London: Chatto and Windus, 1956.
———. *The Good Apprentice*. New York: Viking, 1986.
———. *The Green Knight*. New York: Viking, 1994.
———. *Henry and Cato*. New York: Viking, 1977.
———. "A House of Theory." *Partisan Review* 26 (1959): 17–31.
———. *The Italian Girl*. New York: Viking, 1964.
———. "Mass, Might and Myth." *Spectator* 209 (September 7, 1962): 337–38.
———. *The Message to the Planet*. London: Chatto and Windus, 1989.
———. "Metaphysics and Ethics." In *The Nature of Metaphysics*, ed. D. F. Pears. London: Macmillan, 1957. 99–123.
———. *Metaphysics as a Guide to Morals*. London: Chatto and Windus, 1992.
———. *The Nice and the Good*. New York: Viking, 1968.
———. "Nostalgia for the Particular." *Proceedings of the Aristotelian Society* 52 (1952): 243–60.
———. *Nuns and Soldiers*. New York: Viking, 1980.
———. *The Philosopher's Pupil*. New York: Viking, 1983.
———. *The Red and the Green*. New York: Viking, 1965.
———. *The Sacred and Profane Love Machine*. London: Chatto and Windus, 1974.
———. "Salvation by Words." *New York Review of Books*, June 15, 1972, 3–6.
———. *The Sandcastle*. New York: Viking, 1957.
———. *Sartre, Romantic Rationalist*. London: Bowes and Bowes, 1953. Reprint, New Haven: Yale Univ. Press, 1967.
———. *The Sea, The Sea*. New York: Viking, 1978.
———. *A Severed Head*. New York: Viking, 1961.
———. *The Sovereignty of Good*. New York: Schocken Books, 1971.
———. "The Sublime and the Beautiful Revisted." *Yale Review* 49 (December 1959): 247–71.
———. "The Sublime and the Good." *Chicago Review* 13 (Autumn 1959): 42–55.
———. "Thinking and Language." *Proceedings of the Aristotelian Society* 25 (1951): 25–34.
———. *The Time of the Angels*. New York: Viking, 1966.
———. *Under the Net*. New York: Viking, 1954.
———. *The Unicorn*. New York: Viking, 1963.
———. *An Unofficial Rose*. New York: Viking, 1962.
———. "Vision and Choice in Morality." *Aristotelian Society*, suppl. 30 (1956): 32–58.
———. *A Word Child*. New York: Viking, 1975.

Bibliography

New Catholic Encyclopedia. Ed. the Most Reverend William J. McDonald, DD. New York: McGraw-Hill, 1967.

Nieli, Russell. *Wittgenstein: From Mysticism to Ordinary Language: A Study of Viennese Positivism and the Thought of Ludwig Wittgenstein*. Albany: State Univ. of New York Press, 1987.

Norris, Margot C. "The Consequence of Deconstruction: A Technical Perspective of Joyce's *Finnegans Wake*." In *Critical Essays on James Joyce*, ed. Bernard Benstock. Boston: G. K. Hall, 1985. 206–21.

Passmore, John. *Recent Philosophers*. Lasalle, Ill.: Open Court, 1985.

Phillips, Diana. *Agencies of the Good in the Work of Iris Murdoch*. Frankfurt am Main: Peter Lang, 1991.

Potter, Beatrix. *The Tale of Mrs. Tittlemouse*. London: F. Warne and Co., 1910.

"Revelations." Border TV, BBC.

Rose, W. K. "An Interview with Iris Murdoch." *Shenandoah* 19.2 (1968): 3–22.

Rowe, C. J. *Plato: Phaedrus*. Wiltshire: Aris & Phillips, 1986.

Runes, Dagobert D., ed. *The Dictionary of Philosophy*. New York: Philosophical Library, 1942.

Sage, Lorna. "The Pursuit of Imperfection: Henry and Cato." In *Iris Murdoch*, ed. Harold Bloom. New York: Chelsea House, 1986. 111–19.

Scholes, Robert. *Fabulation and Metafiction*. Urbana: Univ. of Illinois Press, 1980.

———. *The Fabulators*. New York: Oxford Univ. Press, 1967.

Schweichart, Patrocinio P. "Reading Ourselves: Toward a Feminist Theory of Reading." In *Speaking of Gender*, ed. Elaine Showalter. London: Routledge, 1989. 17–44.

Seiler-Franklin, Carol. *Boulder-Pushers: Women in the Fiction of Margaret Drabble, Doris Lessing, and Iris Murdoch*. Bern: Peter Lang, 1979.

Shakespeare, William. *Othello, the Moor of Venice*. In *William Shakespeare: The Complete Works*. Ed. Stanley Wells and Gary Taylor. Oxford: Clarendon Press, 1986.

———. *The Tempest*. In *Shakespeare: Complete Works*.

———. *The Tragedy of Hamlet, Prince of Denmark*. In *Shakespeare: Complete Works*.

———. *The Tragedy of King Lear*. In *Shakespeare: Complete Works*.

Shklovsky, Viktor. "Art as Technique." In *Contemporary Literary Criticism: Literary and Cultural Studies*, ed. Robert Con Davis and Ronald Schleifer. New York: Longman, 1989. 54–66.

Showalter, Elaine. *A Literature of Their Own: British Women Novelists from Brontë to Lessing*. Princeton: Princeton Univ. Press, 1977.

———. *The New Feminist Criticism: Essays on Women, Literature, and Theory*. New York: Pantheon, 1985.

Sizemore, Christine Wick. *A Female Vision of the City: London in the Novels of Five British Women.* Knoxville: Univ. of Tennessee Press, 1989.
Sophocles. *Antigone.* Trans. Dudley Fitts and Robert Fitzgerald. In *Literature for Composition,* ed. Sylvan Barnet et al. New York: Harper Collins, 1993.
Spivak, Gayatri Chakravorty, trans. Preface to *Of Grammatology,* by Jacques Derrida. Baltimore: Johns Hopkins Univ. Press, 1974.
Stettler-Imfeld, Barbara. *The Adolescent in the Novels of Iris Murdoch.* Zurich: Juris Druck Verlag, 1970.
Stout, Mira. "What Possessed A. S. Byatt?" *New York Times Magazine* 6 (May 26, 1991): 13–25.
Todd, Richard, ed. *Encounters with Iris Murdoch.* Proceedings of an informal symposium on Iris Murdoch's Work held at the Free University, Amsterdam, on 20 and 21 October 1986. Amsterdam: Free Univ. Press, 1988.
———. *Iris Murdoch.* London: Methuen, 1984.
———. *Iris Murdoch: The Shakespearian Interest.* New York: Barnes and Noble, 1979.
———. "The Presence of Postmodernism in British Fiction: Aspects of Style and Selfhood." In *Approaching Postmodernism,* ed. Douwe Fokkema and Hans Bertens. Philadelphia: John Benjamins, 1986.
Todorov, Tzvetan. *Mikhail Bakhtin: The Dialogical Principle.* [1981.] Trans. Wlad Godzich. Minneapolis: Univ. of Minnesota Press, 1984.
Tominaga, Thomas T., and Wilma Schneidermeyer. *Iris Murdoch and Muriel Spark: A Bibliography.* Metuchen, N.J.: Scarecrow Press, 1976.
Tucker, Lindsey. *Critical Essays on Iris Murdoch.* New York: G. K. Hall, 1992.
Volosinov, V. N. [M. M. Bakhtin.] *Marxism and the Philosophy of Language.* Trans. Ladislav Matejka and I. R. Titunik. Cambridge: Harvard Univ. Press, 1986.
Waismann, Friedrich. *Wittgenstein and the Vienna Circle.* Ed. and trans. Brian McGuinness. New York: Barnes and Noble, 1979.
Waugh, Patricia. *Metafiction: The Theory and Practice of Self-Conscious Fiction.* London: Methuen, 1984.
Weil, Simone. *The Simone Weil Reader.* Ed. George A. Panichas. New York: David McKay, 1977.
West, M. L. "Wisdom Literature, Hesiod." In *Works and Days.* Ed. with Prolegomena and Commentary by M. L. West. Oxford: Clarendon Press, 1978. 3–25.
Winsor, Dorothy A. "Solipsistic Sexuality in Murdoch's Gothic Novels." In *Iris Murdoch,* ed. Harold Bloom. New York: Chelsea House, 1986. 121–30.
Wittgenstein, Ludwig. *The Blue and Brown Books.* Oxford: Basil Blackwell, 1958.
———. *Culture and Value.* 1977. Trans. Peter Winch. Ed. G. H. von Wright. Chicago: Univ. of Chicago Press, 1980.

Bibliography

———. *Letters to Russell, Keynes and Moore.* Ed. G. H. von Wright. Oxford: Basil Blackwell, 1974.

———. *Ludwig Wittgenstein: Zettel.* Ed. G. E. M. Anscombe and G. H. von Wright. Berkeley: Univ. of California Press, 1967.

———. *Notebooks 1914–1916.* Ed. G. H. von Wright and G. E. M. Anscombe. Trans. G. E. M. Anscombe. Oxford: Basil Blackwell, 1969.

———. *Philosophical Investigations.* Trans. G. E. M. Anscombe. Oxford: Basil Blackwell, 1953.

———. *Protractatus.* Ithaca: Cornell Univ. Press, 1971.

———. *Remarks on the Foundations of Mathematics.* Trans. G. E. M. Anscombe. Oxford: Basil Blackwell, 1956.

———. *Tractatus Logico-Philosophicus.* Trans. D. F. Pears and B. F. McGuinness. London: Routledge and Kegan Paul, 1961.

———. "Wittgenstein's Lecture on Ethics." *Philosophical Review* 74.1 (1965): 3–26.

———. "Wittgenstein's Lectures in 1930–33." Recorded by G. E. Moore in *Philosophical Papers.* London: Allen and Unwin, 1959. Reprinted in *Classics of Analytic Philosophy,* ed. R. Ammerman. New York: McGraw-Hill, 1965. 233–84.

Yeats, William Butler. *Sophocles's King Oedipus* (1928). In *The Variorium Edition of the Plays of W. B. Yeats.* Ed. Russell K. Alspach. New York: Macmillan, 1966.

Index

Adorno, Theodor, 91
Alterity, 92, 94, 95, 96, 97, 98, 99, 130, 131, 140–55
Althusser, Louis, 101
Ambrose, Alice, 28
Anscombe, Elizabeth, 4, 27
Antonia and Jane (film), 258
Apollo, 31, 64, 65, 66, 128, 131, 133, 158, 176, 213, 238, 246, 259
Aristotle, 26, 69, 207, 208, 209, 254, 257
Arnold, Matthew, 72, 189; "Dover Beach," 71
Art, 1, 6, 39, 77, 82, 83, 85, 88, 90, 131, 156, 157, 179, 180, 181, 187, 206, 225, 257, 260
Ascesis, 13
Attention, 9, 13, 15, 45, 85, 97, 98, 99, 140, 141, 142, 143, 156, 163, 263
Ayer, A. J., 2, 21, 25–26; *Part of My Life*, 25, 29; *Language, Truth, and Logic*, 26

Bakhtin, Mikhail, 29, 86, 100, 101, 102, 104, 109, 111, 112, 113, 119, 124, 127, 129, 130, 132, 140, 141, 143, 146, 148, 149, 150, 151, 152, 153, 226, 227
Bakhtin, Nikolai, 29
Bayley, John, 28, 215
Begnal, Kate, 119
Bewitchment, 17, 28, 36, 40, 42, 44, 46, 54

Bloom, Harold, 4, 23, 34, 214, 250, 251, 252, 255, 259
Bradbury, Malcolm, 127
Bradley, F. H., 56, 215
Brooks, Peter, 225
Buber, Martin, 5
Buddhism, 31, 59, 68, 240
Byatt, A. S., 24, 47, 48, 107, 209, 210, 234

Cambridge, 2, 26, 27, 29
Carnap, Rudolf, 26, 32
Carnival, 108, 118, 120, 121, 122, 123, 124, 125, 135, 226. *See also* Bakhtin, Mikhail
Carroll, Lewis, 41
Cave, the, 8, 70, 75, 76, 82, 155, 156, 157, 197, 198, 199, 216, 217, 218, 220, 221, 223, 240, 241, 242. *See also* Plato
Centrifugal, 105, 108, 127, 135, 143
Centripetal, 105, 108, 127, 135, 143
Cézanne, Paul, 22
Chodorow, Nancy, 98, 185
Cixous, Hélène, 241
Conrad, Joseph, 87, 217
Conradi, Peter, 24, 28, 85, 104, 127, 135, 163, 214, 215, 225, 255, 257, 259
Consciousness, 1, 9, 16, 18, 20, 21, 24, 50, 54, 73, 82, 93, 94, 95, 96, 98, 102, 127, 143, 146, 154, 161
Contingency, 13, 19, 23, 25, 42, 43, 58, 59, 72, 105, 109, 118, 122, 123, 125,

Index

Unconscious, 54, 124, 125, 155, 191, 198, 199, 201
Unselfing, 13, 15, 98, 99, 249

Waismann, Friedrich, 12
Washington Post, 90, 155
Weil, Simone, 15, 24, 262
Wilder, Thornton, 122
Wisdom, John, 21
Wittgenstein, Ludwig, 1, 2, 5, 7–17, 19, 20, 29–42, 43, 45, 47, 48, 50, 54, 56, 60, 61, 65, 67, 68, 69, 71, 73, 83, 84, 88, 89, 100, 103, 194, 261. Works: *Culture and Value*, 7, 12, 32; *Tractatus Logico-Philosophicus*, 10, 11, 12, 14, 16, 27, 29, 32, 36, 37, 54, 55, 56; *Philosophical Investigations*, 10, 12, 13, 14, 17, 24, 27, 29, 36, 37, 38, 39, 40, 44, 54, 55, 56, 67, 68, 261; "Lecture on Ethics," 11, 16; *Notebooks, 1914–1916*, 15, 17; *Blue and Brown Books*, 25; *Ludwig Wittgenstein: Zettel*, 33
Woolf, Virginia, 90, 91, 94; *Room of One's Own*, 54
Worldview, Murdoch's, 16, 19, 31, 42, 50, 85, 89, 220, 224

Yeats, W. B.: "Leda and the Swan," 63

Index

Adorno, Theodor, 91
Alterity, 92, 94, 95, 96, 97, 98, 99, 130, 131, 140–55
Althusser, Louis, 101
Ambrose, Alice, 28
Anscombe, Elizabeth, 4, 27
Antonia and Jane (film), 258
Apollo, 31, 64, 65, 66, 128, 131, 133, 158, 176, 213, 238, 246, 259
Aristotle, 26, 69, 207, 208, 209, 254, 257
Arnold, Matthew, 72, 189; "Dover Beach," 71
Art, 1, 6, 39, 77, 82, 83, 85, 88, 90, 131, 156, 157, 179, 180, 181, 187, 206, 225, 257, 260
Ascesis, 13
Attention, 9, 13, 15, 45, 85, 97, 98, 99, 140, 141, 142, 143, 156, 163, 263
Ayer, A. J., 2, 21, 25–26; *Part of My Life*, 25, 29; *Language, Truth, and Logic*, 26

Bakhtin, Mikhail, 29, 86, 100, 101, 102, 104, 109, 111, 112, 113, 119, 124, 127, 129, 130, 132, 140, 141, 143, 146, 148, 149, 150, 151, 152, 153, 226, 227
Bakhtin, Nikolai, 29
Bayley, John, 28, 215
Begnal, Kate, 119
Bewitchment, 17, 28, 36, 40, 42, 44, 46, 54

Bloom, Harold, 4, 23, 34, 214, 250, 251, 252, 255, 259
Bradbury, Malcolm, 127
Bradley, F. H., 56, 215
Brooks, Peter, 225
Buber, Martin, 5
Buddhism, 31, 59, 68, 240
Byatt, A. S., 24, 47, 48, 107, 209, 210, 234

Cambridge, 2, 26, 27, 29
Carnap, Rudolf, 26, 32
Carnival, 108, 118, 120, 121, 122, 123, 124, 125, 135, 226. *See also* Bakhtin, Mikhail
Carroll, Lewis, 41
Cave, the, 8, 70, 75, 76, 82, 155, 156, 157, 197, 198, 199, 216, 217, 218, 220, 221, 223, 240, 241, 242. *See also* Plato
Centrifugal, 105, 108, 127, 135, 143
Centripetal, 105, 108, 127, 135, 143
Cézanne, Paul, 22
Chodorow, Nancy, 98, 185
Cixous, Hélène, 241
Conrad, Joseph, 87, 217
Conradi, Peter, 24, 28, 85, 104, 127, 135, 163, 214, 215, 225, 255, 257, 259
Consciousness, 1, 9, 16, 18, 20, 21, 24, 50, 54, 73, 82, 93, 94, 95, 96, 98, 102, 127, 143, 146, 154, 161
Contingency, 13, 19, 23, 25, 42, 43, 58, 59, 72, 105, 109, 118, 122, 123, 125,

301

Index

Contingency (*continued*)
  156, 157, 159, 162, 177, 188, 190,
  198, 205, 226, 227, 255, 261
Cornford, Francis MacDonald, 219, 222

Deconstruction, 1, 2, 4. *See also* Derrida, Jacques
de Man, Paul, 145
Demiurge, the, 32, 202, 211, 212, 214,
  215, 222, 223, 224, 243, 262. *See also*
  Plato
Derrida, Jacques, 2, 3, 5, 6, 13, 23, 43,
  49, 95, 211; *Of Grammatology*, 134
Descartes, René, 1, 5, 7, 13, 23, 26
Determinism, 2, 3, 4, 23, 43
Detweiler, Robert, 258
Dialogic, 35, 55, 67, 71, 85, 86, 105,
  119, 136, 137, 138, 139, 145, 209. *See
  also* Bakhtin, Mikhail
Dionysus, 64, 131, 208, 243, 246
Dipple, Elizabeth, 24, 33, 34, 55, 56,
  119, 129, 202, 210, 260
Dostoevsky, Fyodor, 32, 50, 94, 100,
  107, 113, 118, 119, 128, 146, 147,
  162, 225, 257
Double-voicedness, 41, 105, 122, 123,
  134, 135, 150, 151

Eagleton, Terry, 29, 258, 259
Edwards, James C., 14, 39
Eliot, George, 19, 83; *Daniel Deronda*,
  92; *Middlemarch*, 92
Eliot, T. S., 113, 114–15, 117, 169, 170;
  Waste Land, 112, 114, 116, 149, 171,
  191; *Lovesong of J. Alfred Prufrock*,
  114, 115; *Four Quartets*, 170
Empiricism, linguistic, 9, 13, 18, 20, 21,
  86

Escher, M. C., 203, 262; *Moebius II*,
  158, 203
Existentialism, 2, 18, 19, 26, 27, 94

Fact and value, 2, 3, 4, 11
Ficker, Ludwig, 12
Fiction: relation to philosophy, 23, 24,
  82, 83, 84, 85, 95, 224; relation to
  contingency, 25
Fineman, Joel, 189, 240
Fletcher, John, 260
Foot, Phillippa, 4
Forms, Platonic, 2, 8, 9, 15, 209, 210,
  211
Forster, E. M., 259
Fowles, John, 258
Frazer, James G., 40
Freud, Sigmund, 9, 69, 74, 88, 89, 96,
  134, 136, 137, 158, 163, 185, 186,
  222, 239, 240, 241

Geertz, Clifford, 84
Gilligan, Carol, 98, 185
Good, the, 1, 3, 4, 8, 9, 15, 34, 45, 84,
  89, 98, 99, 217, 239, 250. *See also*
  Plato
Gordon, David J., 214
Grammatical pictures, 35, 36, 37, 38,
  39, 40, 41, 42, 44, 45, 48, 54
Greenaway, Peter, 262
Greenblatt, Stephen, 190

Hampshire, Stuart, 226
Hegel, 21, 93
Heidegger, Martin, 2, 6, 61, 211
Heilbrun, Carolyn, 213
Herrmann, Claudine, 55, 112
Heteroglossia, 101, 102, 104, 105, 109–

302

28 passim, 133, 134, 135, 136, 139, 140–55 passim. *See also* Bakhtin, Mikhail
Homer: *Odyssey*, 63, 204, 238

Influences on Murdoch: Greek, 6, 7, 14, 96, 107, 160, 185, 212, 216–27, 230, 237, 238, 239, 242, 243, 244, 245, 252, 263; Judeo-Christian, 7, 13, 14, 50, 224
Irigaray, Luce, 174, 184, 234, 243; *Speculum of the Other Woman*, 241, 242

James, Henry, 260
James, William, 21
Johnson, Barbara: *Critical Difference*, 239–40
Johnson, Deborah, 129, 234, 241, 242
Jones, Ernest, 135
Jouissance, 55, 57, 65, 113, 125
Joyce, James, 21, 86, 90, 127, 221, 236, 251, 252, 253, 254, 255; *Ulysses*, 221, 251, 252; *Finnegans Wake*, 253, 254

Kant, Immanuel, 4, 5, 6, 8, 9, 10, 11, 14, 15, 17, 18, 25, 34, 56
Kermode, Frank, 259
Kierkegaard, Søren, 26
Kristeva, Julia, 120, 122, 125, 139, 207, 241, 259
Kuehl, Linda, 119, 256

Lacan, Jacques, 5
Language, ordinary, 19, 29, 35
Language games, 36–45, 47, 51, 52, 53, 55, 56, 57, 61–69, 71, 75, 80, 133. *See also* Wittgenstein, Ludwig

Logical positivism, 25, 88
Lukács, 91, 93, 94
Lyons, Nona Plessner, 98

MacKinnon, D. H., 27
Macrocosm, 158, 260
Magic, 31, 32, 118, 122, 133, 189, 191, 199
Mallarmé, Stéphane, 202
Mandela, Nelson, 28
Marsyas, 156, 255, 259
Marvell, Andrew, 130
Masochism, 8, 30
Mehta, Ved, 26, 27, 82
Meltzer, Françoise, 161, 239
Menippean satire, 207
Metaphysics, 1, 2, 3, 6, 8, 10, 18, 19, 36, 87, 88, 92
Microcosm, 45, 158, 260
Mill, John Stuart, 18
Modernism, 85, 86, 87, 89, 90, 91, 93, 94, 119
Monet, Claude, 90, 261
Monologism, 35, 55, 91, 92, 100, 105
Moore, G. E., 2, 19, 21
Morality, 1, 3, 11, 12, 13, 14, 15, 20, 23, 81, 82, 83, 84, 94, 97, 98, 102, 107, 123, 124
Murdoch, Iris: Works:
—of fiction: *Book and the Brotherhood*, 28, 31; *Message to the Planet*, 30, 31, 33, 43, 44, 49, 54, 55, 58, 59, 60, 61, 67, 81, 83, 86, 102, 104, 134, 140, 143, 144, 145, 151, 207, 253, 254; *Nuns and Soldiers*, 30, 31, 41, 43, 49, 53, 54, 55, 57, 58, 60, 140, 156, 197, 200, 201, 205, 210, 218, 219, 223, 238; *Sandcastle*, 30,

Murdoch, Iris: Works (*continued*) 31, 258; *Under the Net*, 30, 44, 47, 48, 49, 83, 190, 226; *Flight from the Enchanter*, 30, 144, 218; *Philosopher's Pupil*, 31, 34, 49, 101, 118, 119, 120, 123, 125, 126, 217, 218, 226, 230, 232, 233, 241, 253; *The Sea, The Sea*, 31, 43, 49, 58, 69, 70, 156, 159, 188, 189, 190, 191, 197, 198, 200, 204, 205, 218, 220, 226, 240, 260; *Black Prince*, 31, 58, 80, 95, 105, 115, 118, 127, 129, 133, 134, 136, 145, 156, 158, 176, 177, 180, 186, 188, 192, 205, 211, 213, 216, 223, 226, 238, 247, 248, 252, 253, 263; *Word Child*, 34, 37, 41, 43, 44, 45, 47, 50, 53, 58, 61, 156, 158, 160, 161, 163, 167, 168, 177, 179, 186, 205, 215, 238, 253, 254; *Good Apprentice*, 34, 243; *Accidental Man*, 41, 49, 55, 58, 104, 105, 106, 114, 116, 118, 119, 120, 127, 260; *Sacred and Profane Love Machine*, 144, 238; *Time of the Angels*, 147, 234; *Nice and the Good*, 169, 218, 220, 223; *Unicorn*, 199, 250, 251, 258; *Fairly Honourable Defeat*, 225; *Henry and Cato*, 227, 228, 229; *Bell*, 234, 235, 241, 242; *Severed Head*, 260
—of philosophy: *Metaphysics as a Guide to Morals*, 1, 3, 4, 5, 6, 7, 9, 10, 11, 18, 21, 23, 25, 34, 35, 76, 81, 82, 87, 90, 102; *Sovereignty of Good*, 4, 13, 16, 45, 82, 85, 88, 96, 97, 98, 101, 105, 134, 142, 157, 174, 196, 211, 260; *Sartre, Romantic Rationalist*, 5, 12, 17, 82, 85, 86, 87, 90, 96, 106, 206; *Fire and the Sun*, 9, 56, 69, 76, 82, 84, 85, 95, 155, 197, 202, 211, 217, 220, 243; "Sublime and the Beautiful Revisited," 18; "Nostalgia for the Particular," 21; "Metaphysics and Ethics," 83; *Acastos: Two Platonic Dialogues*, 160, 220, 247; "Mass, Might and Myth," 209; "Existentialists and Mystics," 249; "Against Dryness," 257

Mystery, 1, 3, 10, 11, 12, 31, 58, 76, 124, 125

Mysticism, 24, 31, 32, 33, 35, 44, 68

Nieli, Russell, 32, 56, 66
Nietzsche, Friedrich, 5, 6, 7, 15, 208, 211
Norris, Margot C., 253

Orwell, George, 102
Oxbridge, 23, 85, 140
Oxford, 2, 25, 26, 29, 104, 107, 110, 111, 145, 165, 219, 257

Pattern, in Murdoch, 40, 42, 45, 54, 100, 113, 118, 119, 156–206 passim, 207–56 passim
Patterned aimlessness, 106, 125, 162, 166, 260, 263
Perspicuous presentation, 37, 38, 42, 45
Peter Pan (play), 170
Philosophers, 1, 3, 4, 12, 14, 21, 23, 24, 26, 46, 54, 95, 96, 98, 102, 238
Philosophy, 1, 2, 3, 5, 6, 7, 8, 9, 10, 17, 22, 23, 25, 35, 38, 55, 69, 82, 83, 95, 124, 209, 257; moral, 1, 2, 3, 4, 26, 82, 85, 86, 88, 89, 98, 99, 248; relation to literature, 1, 15, 83, 119,

156, 157, 197, 224; analytic, 2, 35, 38, 39; linguistic, 14, 26, 35. *See also* Murdoch: Works of philosophy

Plato, 1, 2, 3, 5, 7, 8, 10, 13, 28, 32, 34, 69, 75, 76, 77, 84, 88, 89, 90, 92, 95, 96, 99, 119, 135, 152, 162, 183, 186, 205, 207, 208, 209, 210, 211, 212, 216, 217, 219, 220, 222, 223, 224, 225, 242, 243, 247, 255, 259, 260; *Timaeus*, 6, 222; *Republic*, 84, 96, 212, 219, 220; *Symposium*, 214; *Phaedo*, 224

Polyphony, 81, 104, 105, 108, 109, 110, 111, 114–39 passim, 140–55 passim, 157

Postmodernism, 57, 58, 84, 89, 113, 118

Potter, Beatrix, 148, 149, 153, 154

Proust, Marcel, 86, 87, 88, 90, 93, 251

Psychology, 92, 94, 102; Gestalt, 67, 74, 158, 248, 249, 250, 251, 252; moral, 85, 98, 99, 248

Pupils, in Murdoch, 7, 23, 27, 28, 29, 33, 49, 54, 57, 59, 60, 101, 162, 163, 172, 175, 203

Puritanism, 34, 130, 138

Quantum physics, 1

Recurring cycle, 43, 44, 46, 157–73 passim, 176, 179, 200, 208

Religion, 3, 4, 32, 34, 171, 172, 211

Rencontres, 1, 209, 225, 253, 254, 260

Rilke, Rainer Maria, 21, 22

Roman de Renart, 124

Romanticism, 18, 24, 43, 50, 80, 86, 90, 93, 98, 139, 180, 192, 251

Russell, Bertrand, 2, 26, 28, 31, 32

Ryle, Gilbert, 2, 21, 25

Sage, Lorna, 227

Sartre, Jean-Paul, 5, 19, 24, 26, 86, 88, 89, 90, 91, 92, 93, 94

Saussure, Ferdinand de, 1, 6

Schlick, Moritz, 28, 29

Schopenhauer, Arthur, 4, 15, 32, 41, 56

Shakespeare, William, 106, 107, 108, 109, 111, 113, 118, 121, 136, 175, 212, 217, 259; *Tempest*, 49, 70, 108, 109, 112, 113, 114, 191; *Merchant of Venice*, 62; *Hamlet*, 68, 69, 110, 112, 114, 115, 117, 183, 187, 204; *Midsummer-Night's Dream*, 175; *King Lear*, 199; *Othello*, 205

Showalter, Elaine, 145

Socrates, 6, 24, 28, 55, 107, 160, 207

Sophocles, 160, 162, 251, 252; *Oedipus Rex*, 160, 161, 173, 174, 193

Spenser, Edmund, 117; *Prothalamion*, 65, 116

Spivak, Gayatri Chakravorty, 134

Stichomythic dialogues, 41, 51, 52, 53, 61, 62, 66, 67, 68, 107, 108, 109, 112, 113, 116

Steiner, George, 210, 211

Strategies, narrative, 24, 25, 45, 78, 83, 100–115 passim, 118–39 passim, 154, 155, 157

Structuralism, 1, 2, 3

Teachers, in Murdoch, 7, 23, 27, 28, 29, 33, 49, 54, 57, 59, 60, 101, 162, 163, 172, 175, 203

Todd, Richard, 104, 105, 106, 107

Tolstoy, Leo, 19, 87, 102, 119

Tompkins, Jane, 224

Torgovnick, Marianna, 224

"*Tractatus* Wittgenstein," 10

Index

Unconscious, 54, 124, 125, 155, 191, 198, 199, 201
Unselfing, 13, 15, 98, 99, 249

Waismann, Friedrich, 12
Washington Post, 90, 155
Weil, Simone, 15, 24, 262
Wilder, Thornton, 122
Wisdom, John, 21
Wittgenstein, Ludwig, 1, 2, 5, 7–17, 19, 20, 29–42, 43, 45, 47, 48, 50, 54, 56, 60, 61, 65, 67, 68, 69, 71, 73, 83, 84, 88, 89, 100, 103, 194, 261. Works: *Culture and Value*, 7, 12, 32; *Tractatus Logico-Philosophicus*, 10, 11, 12, 14, 16, 27, 29, 32, 36, 37, 54, 55, 56; *Philosophical Investigations*, 10, 12, 13, 14, 17, 24, 27, 29, 36, 37, 38, 39, 40, 44, 54, 55, 56, 67, 68, 261; "Lecture on Ethics," 11, 16; *Notebooks, 1914–1916*, 15, 17; *Blue and Brown Books*, 25; *Ludwig Wittgenstein: Zettel*, 33
Woolf, Virginia, 90, 91, 94; *Room of One's Own*, 54
Worldview, Murdoch's, 16, 19, 31, 42, 50, 85, 89, 220, 224

Yeats, W. B.: "Leda and the Swan," 63